HANDBOOK OF QUALITATIVE RESEARCH TECHNIQUES AND ANALYSIS IN ENTREPRENEURSHIP

T0327740

Handbook of Qualitative Research Techniques and Analysis in Entrepreneurship

Edited by

Helle Neergaard

Professor of Entrepreneurship, University of Aarhus, Denmark

Claire M. Leitch

Professor of Management Learning and Leadership, Lancaster University Management School, UK

Edward Elgar
PUBLISHING

Cheltenham, UK • Northampton, MA, USA

© Helle Neergaard and Claire M. Leitch 2015

All rights reserved. No part of this publication may be reproduced, stored in a retrieval system or transmitted in any form or by any means, electronic, mechanical or photocopying, recording, or otherwise without the prior permission of the publisher.

Published by
Edward Elgar Publishing Limited
The Lypiatts
15 Lansdown Road
Cheltenham
Glos GL50 2JA
UK

Edward Elgar Publishing, Inc.
William Pratt House
9 Dewey Court
Northampton
Massachusetts 01060
USA

Paperback edition 2017

A catalogue record for this book
is available from the British Library

Library of Congress Control Number: 2015941465

This book is available electronically in the **Elgar**online
Business subject collection
DOI 10.4337/9781849809870

ISBN 978 1 84980 986 3 (cased)
ISBN 978 1 84980 987 0 (eBook)
ISBN 978 1 78811 323 6 (paperback)

Typeset by Servis Filmsetting Ltd, Stockport, Cheshire
Printed and bound in Great Britain by TJ International Ltd, Padstow

Contents

v

Contributors

Alistair R. Anderson is Professor and Director of the Centre for Entrepreneurship at Aberdeen Business School, Robert Gordon University, UK. He also holds a number of honorary and visiting roles including guest professor at SLU (Swedish University of Agricultural Sciences) in Uppsala. He edits the journal *Entrepreneurship and Regional Development*, and serves on a number of editorial boards. His principal research interest lies in understanding entrepreneurship as a socialized phenomenon. He has published several articles on this theme and supervises students with similar interests.

Cecilia Bjursell, PhD, is the Director of Encell at the School of Education and Communication at Jönköping University, Sweden. Her research interests are organization, learning, metaphors, organizational ethnography and narrative perspectives in various empirical contexts. Her earlier studies focused on post-merger integration processes and women's enterprise in family businesses. Current research projects involve stories and older-adult learning, intergenerational learning, knowledge management in technology companies, quality work in adult education, and collaboration as part of an academic portfolio. Bjursell has received several awards for her research. Prior to joining Encell, Bjursell worked at Jönköping International Business School (JIBS) on both research and practical development projects. She also has longstanding experience in teaching and was programme manager for the Business Administration programmes at JIBS. As Director of Encell, networking and collaboration are central to her activities, and Bjursell is involved in several boards, councils and networks.

Anne Bøllingtoft, PhD, is Associate Professor at School of Business and Social Sciences, Aarhus University, Denmark. Anne Bøllingtoft received her PhD from the Aarhus School of Business, Aarhus University in 2005. Her research is within organizational behaviour and theory. Her present research is focused on how leadership behaviour unfolds in different contexts and different organizational forms as well as how leadership strategies affect motivation and performance.

Elizabeth Chell, PhD, retired from full-time academic employment at Southampton University, UK in 2007, but has continued in a part-time capacity through her association with the Small Business Research Centre,

Kingston University, London, where she is a Professor of Entrepreneurial Behaviour. Throughout her career she has published extensively, particularly in specialist areas: the entrepreneurial personality, the critical incident technique and gender. She has published work in notable journals such as *British Journal of Management, Human Relations, R&D Management, International Small Business Journal* and *Entrepreneurship & Regional Development*. She has recently published a chapter on the 'critical incident technique' in her co-edited work, *Handbook of Research in Small Business and Entrepreneurship* published by Edward Elgar (co-editor Mine Karataş-Özkan). She is a Fellow of the British Academy of Management and the Royal Society for the Arts, Manufactures and Commerce (RSA).

Enrique Díaz de León holds a PhD in Management Sciences and Engineering from the University of Waterloo, Ontario, Canada. He currently holds a position as Professor and director of División Innovación y Emprendimiento at Tecnológico de Monterrey, Campus San Luis Potosí, Mexico. His research interests include technological innovation, new technology-based companies, entrepreneurship, venture capital and business strategy. He is a consultant for national and international organizations such as Comisión Federal de Electricidad in Mexico, Master Foods, Geac Software Corporation and Supplier Group, among others. He is also an Associate Researcher at the University of Waterloo, Ontario, Canada and Associate Professor at the Universidad Externado de Colombia.

Carmen Dima holds more than 25 years of combined professional and academic experience acquired around the world (Canada, South Africa, Denmark and Romania). Dr Dima is currently Professor of Business and Management at Niagara College, Ontario, Canada. She holds a Chartered Professional Accountant (CPA) designation, an MBA, an MSc with distinction (strategic focus) and a DBA (Doctor in Business Administration). Her educational credentials were obtained from universities located in Romania, Canada and Scotland. Dr Dima is actively publishing and speaking at national and international conferences on subjects related to managerial behaviour and environmentalism.

Sarah Drakopoulou Dodd is Professor at the Hunter Centre for Entrepreneurship, the University of Strathclyde, UK. Her research focuses on impacts of socio-cultural factors on entrepreneurship, including entrepreneurial networks, alternative entrepreneurship, family business, entrepreneurship education, cross-cultural conceptualizations of entrepreneurs, and relationships between theology, religion and entrepreneurship. Professor Dodd's research has been published in leading entrepreneurship and management journals, including the *Journal of Business Venturing*,

Entrepreneurship Theory and Practice (*ETP*), *Management Decision*, the *Scandinavian Journal of Management, Entrepreneurship & Regional Development* (*ERD*), the *International Small Business Journal* (*ISBJ*), the *Family Business Review*, and the *International Journal of Entrepreneurship and Innovation* (*IJEI*). She is a Board Member of *ETP*, *ERD*, *ISBJ* and *IJEI*. Professor Dodd's previous posts include academic positions at Middlesex University, ALBA Graduate School of Business (Athens, Greece), the American College of Greece, Robert Gordon University (Aberdeen), and the University of Aberdeen.

Paul Guild holds a doctorate from the University of Oxford. He is currently a Professor in the Department of Management Sciences, Faculty of Engineering. He held an industrial research chair in Management of Technological Innovation and Change (1990–2001). Guild is the past Vice-President, University Research (2001–05) for the University of Waterloo, one of Canada's top-ten research-intensive universities. His research interests include: novel approaches for knowledge transfer, open innovation, technology intelligence and planning, and Internet infrastructures to foster commercialization of results of university research; systematic assessment of 'business worthiness' among knowledge-intensive and technology-based new ventures; and ways to reduce the time it takes to formulate ideas for technologically advanced products and services that can be successfully marketed.

Anja Hagedorn studied economics at the University of Leipzig, Germany and afterwards worked as an analyst in the corporate banking sector before she joined HHL Leipzig Graduate School of Management in August 2011. Here she worked for one year as a coach for the founders network 'SMILE' and also did research in the field of crowd-funding. Since 2013 she has been engaged in the project 'Excellence Cluster BioEconomy', which develops chemicals based on wood. In addition, Ms Hagedorn has been Guest Lecturer for Entrepreneurship at Wyższa Szkoła Handlowa we Wrocławiu (WSH) in Poland. She is now working on her PhD, where she discusses the question how founders' coaching influences the development of entrepreneurial competencies.

Richard T. Harrison, BA (Hons), PhD, is Professor of Entrepreneurship and Innovation and Co-Director of the Centre for Strategic Leadership at the University of Edinburgh Business School, UK. He was previously Dean of the Management School at Queen's University Belfast and has held chair positions at a number of universities in the UK, and visiting positions in China and Australia. His research focuses on entrepreneurial finance, with a strong policy focus, and on entrepreneurial strategy, learning and leadership, and he is currently working on research projects in the UK, China, India, Malaysia and Rwanda. He is founding co-editor of *Venture Capital: An International Journal of Entrepreneurial Finance* and author of five books and over 100 academic papers.

Frances M. Hill, BA (Hons), MBA, PhD, was, until her retirement in 2012, Senior Lecturer at Queen's University Management School, Queen's University Belfast, UK, where she was Director of the Executive MBA programme. While her initial research interests were in the areas of organizational change and human relationships, latterly she had become interested in entrepreneurship and published on entrepreneurship education as well as gender and entrepreneurship. Throughout her career she enjoyed working with research students and became a successful and highly regarded supervisor of both part-time and full-time doctoral students.

Sarah L. Jack is Professor of Entrepreneurship at the Institute for Entrepreneurship and Enterprise Development, Lancaster University, UK. Prior to joining academia, Sarah worked in the manufacturing and service industries. Sarah's research has focused on the social aspects of entrepreneurship, especially social networks and social capital. She is also interested in enterprise education.

Rita G. Klapper graduated with a PhD in entrepreneurship from Leeds University Business School (LUBS), UK and has researched and taught entrepreneurship, corporate/international strategy and creativity to undergraduate, postgraduate and executive audiences. She is presently working as Lecturer in Enterprise at the Manchester Enterprise Centre (MEC) at the University of Manchester (UK), teaching and researching entrepreneurship. She previously worked as Senior Lecturer in Enterprise at Manchester Metropolitan University (MMU, UK), as Senior Lecturer in Entrepreneurship and Strategy, in charge of a BSc in Enterprise Development, at the University of Huddersfield (UK) and as Associate Professor for Strategy and Entrepreneurship, in charge of an MSc in International Business Development, at NEOMA (formerly Rouen Business School, France).

Alice de Koning is Associate Professor for Strategy and Entrepreneurship at the Bertolon School of Business, Salem State University, USA. Her research considers how social and institutional contexts affect entrepreneurial cognition and opportunity recognition. Her current projects include metaphors for entrepreneurship in public discourse (with Sarah Drakapoulou Dodd), research scientists as entrepreneurs (with David Deeds), how Champagne World Fairs created entrepreneurial driven growth in twelfth-century Europe, and the business ecology of the

North Shore (MA). Alice graduated from INSEAD, was previously on the faculty at Stockholm School of Economics and J. Mack Robinson College of Business, Georgia State University, and has spent time as a visiting scholar at Boston University and the Wharton School, University of Pennsylvania.

Claire M. Leitch, BA (Hons), MBA, DPhil, is Professor of Management Learning and Leadership at Lancaster University Management School, UK. The main focus of her research is on individual, particularly leader, and organizational development within an entrepreneurial context. Much of her work is at the interface between the fields of entrepreneurship and leadership and through her involvement in the DIANA International network she has become interested in the influence of gender in both these domains. This has led to specific projects exploring the financing of women-owned and women-led businesses and women's networking behaviours. Other areas of research include: identity and identity work in the context of entrepreneurial leadership development and the entrepreneurial learning process. In addition, Claire has a strong interest in research methodology and has extensive experience in working with doctoral students, both national and international.

Edward McKeever is a Researcher and Lecturer at the Institute for Entrepreneurship and Enterprise Development (IEED), Lancaster University Management School (LUMS), UK. After a career in manufacturing, small business and economic development, Ed's PhD and subsequent research focus on the embeddedness of entrepreneurs in the communities and societies from which they emerge and operate. Taking an anthropological perspective, current research interests concern the link between embeddedness, social capital and responsible entrepreneurship.

Susan Moult has been a Director of the company Corners Turned Limited for the past five years. She is also a part-time Lecturer at Aberdeen Business School, Robert Gordon University, UK.

Helle Neergaard, BSc, MSc, PhD, is Professor of Entrepreneurship at Aarhus University, Denmark and currently the President of the European Council of Small Business. The four main pillars of her research are: (1) female entrepreneurs/business owner-managers; (2) the entrepreneurial mindset; (3) forms of entrepreneurial capital; and (4) entrepreneurship education. She has authored close to 100 academic papers and is published in journals such as *Entrepreneurship Theory and Practice* and *International Small Business Journal*. She is internationally recognized as an expert on qualitative methods and she was lead editor of the *Handbook of Qualitative Research Methods in Entrepreneurship* (2007). She organizes doctoral workshops both at home and abroad focusing on qualitative methods and how to write academic articles. She also leads a €7 million international research project within entrepreneurship education.

Rick Newby, PhD, teaches accounting at the University of Western Australia. His primary teaching areas include financial and managerial accounting. He has a broad range of research interests in areas such as: small business and entrepreneurship; performance measurement; behavioural accounting; and behavioural finance. His research has been published in a number of international journals including: *Entrepreneurship Theory and Practice*; *International Small Business Journal*; *Journal of Behavioural Finance*; *International Journal of Gender and Entrepreneurship*; and the *International Journal of Entrepreneurial Behaviour and Research*.

Robert Smith, PhD, is Professor of Enterprise and Innovation at the University of the West of Scotland, UK. His research interests are eclectic but his primary research focus is on study of entrepreneurship in different settings and applications including the socially constructed nature of entrepreneurship and thus entrepreneurial identity, semiotics, narrative and storytelling in organizations including small and family businesses. He has published over 100 journal articles and book chapters to date, many of which have narrative themes. Other areas of research interest include gender and entrepreneurship, entrepreneurial networks, small and family business, criminal entrepreneurship, regional development and rural entrepreneurship.

Susan M. Smith is Assistant Dean for Business Engagement at Teesside University, UK, where she is responsible for developing and delivering the business engagement strategy. Sue has an extensive track record of university business engagement. She is passionate about how people learn to lead and manage, and the real impact this can have on a business. Sue has designed and taught on many leadership development and entrepreneurship programmes for diverse learners in higher education, from undergraduates and postgraduates to post-experience adult learners who do not traditionally engage with universities. Her academic research focuses on two areas. The first is using social theories of learning to look at the impact of small and medium-sized enterprise (SME) peer learning. The second is the relationship between universities, business and government and the impact this can have on the regional economy.

Geoff Soutar, PhD, is Professor at University of Western Australia (UWA). He graduated in economics from the University of Western Australia and undertook doctoral training at Cornell University before returning to teach at UWA. Professor Soutar has been active in research across a wide area, publishing more than 150 research papers in journals and in book chapters, as well as a number of research monographs, across a wide range of management and marketing areas, and presenting more than 300 papers at seminars and conferences. His present research interests include cross-cultural decision-making, new product and service development and the marketing of services, especially educational and tourism services. He has a particular interest in service quality and its impact on organizational success, from which evolved a long-term study of consumption value and its impact on people's willingness to buy, and their subsequent satisfaction or dissatisfaction.

John Watson, PhD, is a Professor in Accounting and Finance at the University of Western Australia. His primary teaching areas include financial accounting, financial statement analysis and business valuation. His research interests lie in the area of performance evaluation and measurement and he has published a number of papers covering topics, such as: the definition of failure; the effect of macro-economic variables on failure rates; the impact of networking on firm performance; and comparing the performances of male- and female-controlled SMEs (adjusting for size and risk). These publications have appeared in a number of leading international journals, such as: *Journal of Business Venturing*; *Entrepreneurship Theory and Practice*; *Journal of Small Business Management*; *Small Business Economics*; and *International Small Business Journal*.

Acknowledgements

This sequel to the *Handbook on Qualitative Research Methods in Entrepreneurship* has, for various reasons, been a long time in coming to fruition from the inception of the idea in 2010. Although that is not unusual for a volume of this kind, we would first like to thank all of our contributors for their patience with the process and for their continuing support. An extra special 'thank you' also needs to be paid to our section anchors without whom this book would not have been possible. The anchors, Claire M. Leitch, Sarah L. Jack, Sarah Drakopolou Dodd, John Watson and Rita G. Klapper, have worked assiduously at identifying researchers who could make interesting and worthwhile contributions, encouraged these individuals to become involved, organized the review process for each chapter in their section and kept the process in motion, which has been no easy task. The anchors have succeeded in engaging contributors from all over the world, both well-established and recognized scholars and relative newcomers to the field. In addition, they have also provided extra input by writing the introductions and postscripts for each section.

We have talked to numerous young scholars about the handbook and have consistently been confirmed in our conviction that there is indeed a need for it and that its publication is awaited with anticipation.

Finally, we would like to thank Francine O'Sullivan from Edward Elgar for her unwavering patience and continuous encouragement.

Helle Neergaard and Claire M. Leitch

Introduction
Helle Neergaard and Claire M. Leitch

INTERVIEWING

This book is a sequel to *Handbook of Qualitative Research Methods in Entrepreneurship*, which provided a reference point for some of the most essential elements and critical choices in qualitative research design, collecting and analysing information. Our aim in this volume is to build on that foundation and to more specifically assist young researchers in particular by providing step-by-step explanations of some of the techniques that have been used by more experienced researchers to explore entrepreneurial phenomena.

Our experience of teaching and working with doctoral students confirms that choosing the most appropriate technique is actually one of the most challenging tasks in the research process. Problems in figuring out precisely the most appropriate data collection and analysis techniques to employ can result from a lack of understanding and knowledge about the origins and subsequent development of many of the methods which have been employed. We believe this has been complicated by two main factors. First, techniques for collecting and analysing data are rarely addressed in detail in published articles, which by default have very short accounts of the methodology adopted and often do not include a philosophical rationale for the choices made. Second, the constant development of new 'tools' and refinement of existing tools employed in qualitative research studies has meant that researchers often face a confusing range from which to choose.

The recent trend in entrepreneurship research, from the dominant positivist tradition, which treats entrepreneurs as fixed entities and being entrepreneurial as an intrinsic property of the individual, to one which emphasizes the role of entrepreneurship within the contemporary business world, also places greater demands on researchers to make the most appropriate data collection and analysis choices. From de-reifying entrepreneurship to exploring the ways in which entrepreneurs involve, engage with and are influenced by the environments in which they operate highlights the importance of context and the social world. Increasingly, researchers acknowledge that entrepreneurial behaviour is better understood within the industrial, geographical, personal, situational, social, cultural, temporal and institutional domains in which it is embedded. As such, entrepreneurship is viewed not as something 'out there' waiting to be discovered but as an enacted, socially situated practice (Bruni et al. 2004). However, while the importance of the constraints and opportunities, which social and institutional contexts have on new ventures and industries was acknowledged almost 30 years ago (see, for example, Aldrich and Zimmer 1986; Low and MacMillan 1988; Aldrich and Fiol 1994), most entrepreneurship research to date has focused on context as just a variable (Welter 2011). Indeed, positivism, with its focus on generalism, universalism and validity irrespective of time and place, is anti-contextual. On the other hand, non-positivist perspectives, which adopt largely qualitative methods, are more appropriate for obtaining nuanced contextual understandings of entrepreneurial phenomena.

While a variety of data collection methods are used in qualitative research (including observations, textual or visual analysis from books or videos), the most common method employed in entrepreneurship is the one-on-one or group interview. While there are three fundamental types of interview – structured, semi-structured and unstructured – most researchers seeking to obtain deep and rich understanding of entrepreneurial processes and practices tend to adopt either of the latter two. However, this broad categorization masks the vast choice of approaches at a researcher's disposal. Given the complexity of entrepreneurial phenomena and the increasing sophistication of qualitative studies, it is important that scholars are able to make the correct choices to ensure the trustworthiness and rigour of their research. Thus, in order to provide a guide, in this handbook we focus on presenting five relatively under-used techniques that have been used to elicit and analyse information from entrepreneurial actors. The studies in which these techniques have been employed have variously emphasized process, dynamism and context, and have led to detailed understandings of the particular social settings in which specific entrepreneurial behaviour has been enacted.

VARIOUS TYPES OF INTERVIEWS

When lay people talk about interviews, they generally refer to those which they hear on television or radio, or are reported in newspapers. These are generally conducted by journalists and, although the techniques employed are actually very similar to those used by researchers, there are also some differences. However, journalists are usually trained in particular questioning techniques, whereas we, as researchers, rarely receive such training, at least if we operate in certain parts of the sciences. Indeed, doctoral students often report that there is a lot of focus on training them in quantitative research methods and techniques, but rather less with regard to qualitative methods and techniques, even though it is just as important to be able to ask the right questions in the right way as it is to know how to construct a Likert scale.

Although one can be critical of journalistic interviewing and particularly the way in which such interviews may be rewritten in order to fit the purpose of the journalist – we guess that many researchers have taken part in interviews where what is written afterwards bears little resemblance to what was actually said – and, although the research interview certainly differs from a journalistic interview, there are things that we can learn from journalism. In journalism it is usual to distinguish between five types of interviews: (1) the experiential interview, (2) the expert interview, (3) the investigative interview, (4) the portrait interview, and (5) the opinion interview (see Table I.1).

The interview may be defined as being either soft or hard. The former is where both the interviewer and the interviewee have similar aims, for example, the portrait interview, the latter when the interviewer's objective is to find out something that the interviewee may not particularly want to divulge, for example, the investigative interview. Journalistic interviews can take place in carefully prepared situations or spontaneously, for example, on the street. The qualitative research interview usually takes

Table I.1   Types of journalistic interviews and their characteristics

The experiential interview	The expert (fact finding) interview	The investigative interview	The portrait interview	The opinion interview
Is used to create a narrative about the interviewee's experiences	Is used to support certain facts to be presented	Is used to investigate a certain area in depth to uncover specific issues that are not immediately accessible. Asks the interviewee to relate to the material already found as well as statements from other interviewees	Is used to provide an understanding of the life of the person interviewed to create a neutral portrait	Is used to create a varied picture of a given situation by involving the opinions of more than one individual

place in a predetermined place, such as at the interviewee's place of business or in the researcher's office. It is easy to imagine that some of these interview forms can be invoked within qualitative research in entrepreneurship because we want to understand in depth the complexity of what is going on. In some way, any research is 'investigative', although this word may not have the same connotation within research as it has within journalism or criminology. Although qualitative researchers do try to find evidence of the particular issue that they are investigating, they tend to be less critically investigative, but usually try to understand the world through the eyes of the interviewee and then interpret this through the lens of theory. Phenomenological interviewing would, for example, attempt to create narratives about the entrepreneur's experiences.

THE QUALITATIVE RESEARCH INTERVIEW

According to Holstein and Gubrium (2003: xx), 'the interview as a procedure for securing knowledge is relatively new historically'. Indeed, there is an increasing literature on the subject, which means that we can probably expect there still to be developments in how we approach interviewing as a research technique.

In general the qualitative research interview is defined as a 'specialized pattern of interaction' (Kahn and Cannell 1957: 16), a two-person face-to-face dialogue, where one person asks the questions and the other answers them to the best of his or her ability. Interviews are used when the objective of the research concern human experience, perceptions and beliefs, and the purpose of the qualitative research interview is to explore in depth these beliefs, experiences and views connected to this experience (see, for example, Kvale 1994). Indeed, we undertake qualitative interviews because we believe that they provide a 'deeper' understanding of social phenomena than those obtained through quantitative interviews such as surveys/questionnaires. Mishler (1991: 10) states that the distinguishing characteristic of the research interview is that it is a 'meaningful speech between interviewer and interviewee as speakers of a shared language'. According to Brinkman and Kvale (2005) the qualitative research interview is a method for gaining knowledge about human existence in detail. The objective of the interview is to obtain the interviewee's own views, feelings, beliefs and motives as clearly as possible but on their own terms, and it is designed to produce knowledge and provides access to a subjective experience of an individual and opportunity for the researcher to describe aspects of that individual's life world. The interaction that takes place influences both the interviewer and the interviewee.

Whichever technique is used there are some prerequisites that are essential to all:

1. Choose your interviewee carefully. Not all interviewees are equally worth listening to. The interviewer therefore has to choose interviewees purposefully in order to gain precisely that information which will help answering the research question/s in the best possible way (Neergaard 2007).
2. If possible, use more than one interviewer: the primary interviewer who asks the primary questions and the secondary who listens carefully, takes notes and can follow up on golden leads that the primary interviewer overlooks because he or she is concentrating on doing the interview and making sure that all the necessary areas are covered.
3. Careful preparation and familiarization with the background of the interviewee is absolutely necessary. This has several purposes: (a) that the interviewee will notice that you have prepared, which will help you ask more relevant questions and make him or her feel more at ease; (b) that you may use this knowledge to help you establish a relationship, which will possibly make the interviewee talk more openly; and (c) from a person's past you learn what questions are likely to trigger a response.
4. An interview is about the interviewer listening, not talking; silence is golden. It is the interviewee who should do most of the talking. The interviewer should ask as few questions as possible, and follow up on replies with probing. Hence, knowing how to probe is essential. This also involves preparing potential probing questions in advance.
5. It is essential to manage your time. Interviewees will usually have set aside a time for you (which needs to be agreed in advance). This ranges typically from about 20 minutes to two hours, depending on whether the interview is completely open ended or very structured. Sometimes the interview will carry on beyond the set time, but do not count on it. So all necessary questions need to be asked within the set time, and then if more time is available it is possible to ask extra questions. Here a related issue crops up. When you turn off the tape recorder, then the interviewee usually feels less restrained and may start to talk more freely. Make sure you take notes if that happens, and ensure that before you leave you obtain permission to use these notes. We also suggest that you make note of the surroundings, even if these are not part of your research. Where the interview takes place can have a huge impact on the information you get. For example, if you interview in a canteen, there might be noise around you, which can affect the quality of the recording. However, it may also tell you something about your

interviewee's relationships with other people at the company if they are comfortable with coming up and interrupting the interview, this might denote that your informant is really approachable and that this is part of the culture of the company.

6. If upon return the tape reveals that it is the researcher who has done most of the talking, the risk is that the information needed to answer the research questions may be lacking. Therefore, in evaluating the quality of the interview there are a number of criteria that the interview has to fulfil: (a) the extent of spontaneous, rich and specific replies; (b) the longer replies the better; (c) did the interviewer remember to follow up and probe; and (d) is there a story that does not require further comment or explanation? If the story is not self-explanatory or there are gaps, then it is necessary to return to the interviewee to fill these gaps.

FORMS OF RESEARCH INTERVIEWS

Generally, in qualitative research we operate with three different forms of research interviews: the structured interview, the semi-structured and unstructured interview, and the open-ended interview. Their characteristics are summarized in Table I.2.

The structured interview should not be confused with the standardized survey/questionnaire (Gillham 2005), nor are they just verbally, face-to-face administered questionnaires as some sources tend to define them (Gill et al. 2008). In the structured closed interview, the interviewees are asked the same questions, in the same way and may be presented with various categories to choose from, but can formulate their own answers, and not just choose from among Likert-like scale replies – for example, 1–5 where 1 is none and 5 is high. In this handbook, we distinguish between the type of questions used by, for example, critical incidence technique (CIT) and the repertory grid, the former being defined as semi-structured and the latter as structured. Although the CIT was originally developed as a positivist methodology, in entrepreneurship it has found its use in both critical realist and social constructivist settings. The repertory grid technique (RGT) is much more structured in that interviewees are asked to choose between predetermined triad groups of elements from which they then have to choose how two are similar and different from the third. Thus, there is more freedom of choice for interviewees in CIT than in RGT.

The semi-structured interview uses key themes and questions derived from theory, which allow the researcher to explore and pursue new avenues of thought based on the response. According to Wengraf (2001: 3), it has

Table I.2   Forms of research interviews

	Unstructured/ conversational interview	Semi-structured interview	Structured interview
Interviewer	Neutral role Asks a beginning question as a start to the conversation: ● Please tell me about . . . ● Think of a time when you . . . and describe it in as much detail as possible Follow-up questions for clarification or elaboration	Interview guide or protocol is used and questions are organized according to themes – or key terms. Interviewer initiates questions and follows up with 'probes' such as: 'I noticed that you mentioned . . . could you tell me a little more about that?' or 'can you describe that in more detail?'	Interviewer follows a predetermined 'standardized' interview guide in a certain sequence
Interviewee	The interviewee answers in own words	The interviewee answers questions and responses are guided by interviewers questions	Interviewee chooses responses from a range of mostly fixed options
Analysis	Data analysed inductively		Data analysed more deductively
Technique	Constant comparative analysis (Part I) Metaphors (Part II)	Critical incident (Part III) Focus groups (Part IV)	Repertory grid (Part V)

to be planned and prepared for like other forms of research activity but what is planned is a deliberate half-scripted interview: its questions are only partially prepared in advance and will therefore be largely improvised by the interviewer. But only largely; the interview as a whole is a joint production, a co-production, meaning-making, sense-making and co-construction of understanding by interviewer and interviewee. Hence, in the general interview guide the researcher prepares a basic checklist prior to the interview based on the a priori conceptual framework. This forms a common set of questions that all interviewees are asked. Hence, this approach assumes that there is common information to be obtained from all persons interviewed (Patton 1990). However, it is flexible in as much as the interview guide is adapted in terms of wording and sequence to the specific interviewees. Thus, the interviewer remains free to build a conversation within a particular subject area but also to ask spontaneous questions, and to develop the conversation into a more conversational style within the boundaries of the interview guide. The researcher is therefore free to follow up on unexpected leads and threads of inquiry in the same way as is possible in an unstructured interview, however, the guide ensures that all questions that are asked help inform the research questions in a way that aims at achieving depth rather than breadth. Some researchers may categorize focus groups as more structured; but this depends on how you use the focus groups. Focus groups should be used to explore opinions and perceptions in a group setting, and not merely to achieve information about questions that a survey would have adequately answered.

The unstructured interview is also called the narrative interview or conversational interview. This type of what we could call phenomenological, ethnographic interview is concerned with lived experience, and forms a mostly uninterrupted narrative. The unstructured interview focuses on eliciting the 'direct description of a particular situation or event as it is lived through without offering causal explanations or interpretive generalizations' (Adams and Van Manen 2008: 618) and is frequently guided by very few open questions, maybe only one or two, with follow-up questions concerned with clarification or elaboration on what is said. Open questions are those that provide broad boundaries within which interviewees can formulate answers in their own words concerning topics of interest for the interviewer. Questions beginning 'Tell me about . . . ' invite interviewees to tell a story, and can generate very detailed descriptions. These descriptions can then be further explored when the interviewer follows up on what has already been said by asking further open-ended follow-up questions, or 'probes', that incorporate the interviewee's own words to elicit further description, such as 'you mentioned that . . . can you describe a specific example of that?', or 'what happened afterwards?'

STRUCTURE OF THE BOOK

The book is divided into five parts that reflect the three forms in Table I.2: constant comparative techniques and metaphor techniques, critical incident techniques and focus group techniques and, finally, repertory grid techniques, each consisting of three chapters illustrating different ways of applying the technique with a focus on 'how to'. The three chapters in each part reflect a range of applications and contexts within entrepreneurship.

Each part commences with an introduction, outlines the origin and provenance of the technique and introduces each of the chapters. Hence, we will not repeat that exercise here in this introduction. Each part is completed with a postscript with considerations about the future of the technique in entrepreneurship research and, in some cases, deliberations concerning quality assessment and the challenges and limitations of this particular method.

Part I: Constant Comparative Technique

Based on the reliance of both techniques on analytic induction, in this part grounded theory is linked with the constant comparative technique. Regarded as a technique, it is purely qualitative and relies on reasoning that allows concepts and relationships between concepts to be modified throughout the research process. With reference to the development of a study on a network for new entrepreneurs, which charted network emergence, change and evolution, in Chapter 1, Jack et al. show how the constant comparative approach can be used to develop theory and understanding about the entrepreneur and the practices in which he or she engages. Through their approach and discussion they demonstrate the usefulness and applicability of the technique and its potential value to entrepreneurship. In Chapter 2, Smith and McKeever offer a practical guide, which they advocate that researchers should adopt when employing constant comparison as a method of analysis. Specifically, they argue that it is the totality of the process of undertaking constant comparison, which contributes to the research journey. Chapter 3 by Bøllingtoft provides a useful and detailed exposition of the process involved in adopting a grounded-theory perspective. In addition to demonstrating its strengths and weaknesses she also shows how the method might be adopted in a way to help overcome criticisms.

Part II: Metaphor Methodologies

Metaphors abound in entrepreneurship research where they are used intentionally or unintentionally, for example, biological metaphors are used prolifically to explain the foundation and growth of entrepreneurial ventures. For instance, we talk about gestation, nascent firms and incubators. This part showcases three different studies which purposefully study this widespread use of metaphors and explain how analysing these can contribute to a better understanding of the field. In Chapter 4 Drakopolou Dodd and de Koning explain the various stages employed when analysing metaphors, and elucidate the benefits and drawbacks of using the methodology, illustrating this with ample evidence from existing research. In Chapter 5, Smith discusses how textbooks on entrepreneurship communicate messages via metaphors in both text and pictures. He explores the more subtle impact that this use may have in the classroom. Chapter 6 by Bjursell investigates the use of metaphors in academic writing and how we as researchers use metaphors to communicate our research.

Part III: Critical Incident Technique

This part outlines the nature and potential contribution of the critical incident technique (CIT) as an approach to entrepreneurship research. All the chapters draw on Flanagan's (1954) original framework but have adopted this to suit the interpretivist tradition. In Chapter 7, Chell revisits and updates earlier work which considered how CIT might be utilized from a phenomenological perspective which enabled her to show the technique could be used to link some critical aspect embedded in a business context to strategies and tactics for handling the situation, and the consequences of doing this (Chell 1988, 2003). In this extension, Chell applies the technique to investigate the entrepreneurial process of opportunity recognition and demonstrates its power in comparison with other qualitative techniques. In Chapter 8, Leitch and Hill reflect on their use of the qualitative variant of the technique, which they employed as a means of gathering data in a research study focusing on women seeking external finance for the development and growth of their businesses. In order to ensure rigour and robustness they developed a guiding framework, rooted in Flanagan's original principles, for the process of operationalizing the research. This, they argue, helps to address the concerns that the method morphs into a generic qualitative interview thus losing its inherent distinctiveness and potency. Chapter 9 by Harrison outlines the nature and potential contribution of the critical incident technique in entrepreneurship. Specifically, he develops Flanagan's original use of the technique within a case study research design. In so doing, he extends the range of methodologies used in CIT studies to include explicative data collection, which draws on the phenomenological tradition.

Part IV: Focus Groups

The part on focus groups exemplifies both traditional and virtual online focus groups. Focus groups constitute a special case of interviews in that they are always conducted in smaller or larger groups. The first example, presented in Chapter 10 by Watson et al., uses focus groups to explore how images of female entrepreneurs visually constructed and represented in television documentaries were perceived and interpreted differently by groups of aspiring and existing female entrepreneurs. In the second example, focus groups were used to explore the findings of two prior studies, which used other methodologies to determine whether those studies provided a sufficiently exhaustive set of influential factors. The two examples discussed in Chapter 11 by Soutar et al. clearly demonstrate the potential benefits of adopting group support system (GSS) technology when undertaking a focus group study with small and medium-sized enterprise (SME) owners. In particular, the results suggest that GSS sessions generate more ideas and, while there are additional costs involved in running these sessions, these additional costs are more than offset by the transcription cost savings. In Chapter 12 the role of computers and information technology in overcoming some of the potential difficulties in conducting traditional focus groups is further examined by Newby and Watson in relation to the use of online focus groups. The two examples discussed clearly demonstrate that useful outcomes can be achieved using technology to facilitate online focus groups (either in real time or asynchronously) with participants whose views and opinions might otherwise be difficult to obtain because they are geographically dispersed.

Part V: Repertory Grid Technique

Chapter 13 by Hagedorn introduces the repertory grid as a data collection technique applicable to entrepreneurial studies. She investigated personal factors that motivate founders to use different business support agents (BSAs) during the venture creation process, concentrating on the personal experience of founders with these different agents. In Chapter 14 Díaz de León and Guild present repertory grids as a useful research method to assist early-stage investors, who are seeking to manage new product portfolios of start-up ventures, in assessing the intangible aspects of new ventures. They present three examples of how the repertory grid technique has been applied in different entrepreneurial settings. In Chapter 15 Dima presents a social constructivist approach to the repertory grid technique which draws on the author's experience conducting studies related to environmental entrepreneurship in Ontario's (Canada) wine industry.

REFERENCES

Adams, C. and M. Van Manen (2008), 'Phenomenology', *The Sage Encyclopedia of Qualitative Research Methods*, **2**, 614–19.

Aldrich, H.E. and C.M. Fiol (1994), 'Fools rush in? The institutional context of industry creation', *Academy of Management Review*, **19** (4), 645–670.

Aldrich, H.E. and C. Zimmer (1986), 'Entrepreneurship through social networks', in D. Sexton and R. Smiler (eds), *The Art and Science of Entrepreneurship*, New York: Ballinger, pp. 3–23.

Brinkman, S and S. Kvale (2005), *Interviews: Learning the Craft of Qualitative Research Interviewing*, London: Sage.

Bruni, A., S. Gherardi and B. Poggio (2004), 'Doing gender, doing entrepreneurship: an ethnographic account of intertwined practices', *Gender, Work and Organization*, **11** (4), 406–29.

Chell, E. (1998), 'The critical incident technique', in C. Cassell and G. Symon (eds), *Qualitative Methods and Analysis in Organisational Research*, London: Sage, ch. 3.

Chell, E (2003), 'The critical incident technique', in M. Lewis-Beck, A. Bryman and T. Futing Liao (eds), *The Encyclopaedia of Research Methods in the Social Sciences*, Thousand Oaks, CA: Sage, pp. 218–19.

Flanagan, J.C. (1954), 'The critical incident technique', *Psychological Bulletin*, **51** (4), 327–58.

Gill, P., K. Stewart, E. Treasure and B. Chadwick (2008), 'Methods of data collection in qualitative research: interviews and focus groups', British Dental Journal, **204** (6), 291–5.

Gillham, B (2005), *Research Interviewing – the Range of Techniques*, Maidenhead: Open University Press.

Holstein, J. and J.F. Gubrium (2003), *Inside Interviewing: New Lenses, New Concerns*, Thousand Oaks, CA: Sage.

Kahn, R.L. and C.F. Cannell (1957), *The Dynamics of Interviewing; Theory, Technique, and Case*, Oxford: Wiley.

Kvale, S. (1994), *InterViews – an Introduction to Qualitative Research Interviewing*, Thousand Oaks, CA: Sage.

Low, M. and I.C. MacMillan (1988), 'Entrepreneurship: past research and future challenges', *Journal of Management*, **14** (2), 139–61.

Mishler, G.E. (1991), *Research Interviewing*, Cambridge, MA: Harvard University Press.

Neergaard, H. (2007), 'Sampling in entrepreneurial settings', in H. Neergaard and J.P. Ulhøi (eds), *Handbook of Qualitative Research Methods in Entrepreneurship*, Cheltenham, UK and Northampton, MA, USA: Edward Elgar, pp. 253–78.

Patton, M.Q. (2004), *Qualitative Evaluation and Research Methods*, Newbury Park, CA: Sage.

Welter, F. (2011), 'Contextualising entrepreneurship: conceptual challenges and ways forward', *Entrepreneurship Theory and Practice*, **35** (1), 165–84.

Wengraf, T. (2001), *Qualitative Research Interviewing*, London: Sage.

PART I

CONSTANT COMPARATIVE TECHNIQUE

An introduction to the constant comparative technique
Alistair R. Anderson and Sarah L. Jack

THE FIELD OF ENTREPRENEURSHIP

Even though entrepreneurship is considered a relatively young field, research in the area has grown impressively in recent decades (Short et al. 2010). Yet, despite this expansion, entrepreneurship methods have been criticized for lacking in systematic approach (Short et al. 2010). In contrast, we argue that a complex domain such as entrepreneurship (Anderson et al. 2012; Drakopoulou Dodd et al. 2013) demands a variety of perspectives and a variety of methodologies and methods that reach beyond any sort of functional determinism, if we are to really understand the phenomenon (Anderson and Starnawska 2008). Regardless of such criticism, the field is becoming known for richness of data, indeed, often a surfeit of rich data, and we need robust techniques to make sense of these data.

Qualitative research allows us to build theory that is thoughtful and robust. Increasingly this is now recognized and the special issue offered by the *Journal of Business Venturing* titled 'Entrepreneurship through a qualitative lens' supports this. It highlights how qualitative research has a long history in entrepreneurship research (Bruton et al. 2015). However, Bruton et al. (2015) also point out that in recent years the use and development of quantitative methods have far outpaced the use and development of qualitative investigations. This is a pity because for entrepreneurship researchers, qualitative work offers opportunities to build good theory. In essence, by making sense of the data we give sense to it, in turn enabling explanation that reflects the richness of our topic. In this part we offer two linked perspectives: grounded theory and the constant comparative technique. We begin with a discussion of each of these perspectives. We then provide an overview of the chapters presented in this part of the book.

GROUNDED THEORY

Grounded theory was first introduced by Glaser and Strauss (1967) who believed that the task of the researcher was to develop theory through comparative method, that is, looking at the same event or process in different settings or situations (Easterby Smith et al. 2008). The discovery of grounded theory (Glaser and Strauss 1967) was seen as a major event for the social sciences because it legitimized methods and research designs that created theory out of data; data that itself reflected the perspective of active participants (Easterby-Smith et al. 2008). Grounded theory has become the most common method researchers claim to use when analysing qualitative data. Versions of grounded theory vary; Glaser (1978, 1992) argued that researchers should start with no presuppositions and allow ideas to emerge from the data; Strauss (1987) and Strauss and Corbin (1998) believe that the researcher should familiarize him or herself with prior research and use structured, mechanistic processes to make sense of the data (Easterby Smith et al. 2008). So, anyone using grounded theory should be aware that these different views exist and articulate his or her position when writing up research (Easterby Smith et al. 2008).

However, while Glaser and Strauss (1967) are credited with founding the term and 'method', the roots of the constant comparative technique can actually be traced back much further, to the ideas originally presented by Florin Znaniecki in 1934 (Katz 2001; Ratcliff 1994) because it rests on the ideas of analytic induction which we return to later in this part introduction.

THE CONSTANT COMPARATIVE TECHNIQUE

An increasing popular way to develop and extend theory is the constant comparative method. Based on direct observation, personal contacts, the use of interviews to identify cases and settings to extend theory, it has been said that this approach follows the principles of grounded theory (Easterby Smith et al. 2008). However, we would argue that the constant comparative technique is aligned more with analytic induction than grounded theory, although it might be seen to borrow ideas from both perspectives. The constant comparative technique has significant differences because it generates and tests theory provisionally, focuses on causation and requires that all data be 'tested against the hypothesis', while grounded theory focuses on generation and constant comparison (http://clinfowiki.org/wiki/index.php/Analytic_Induction, accessed 7 August 2013).

While the constant comparative approach is sometimes referred to as a method, we argue that it is actually a technique which works for analysing data and explaining social situations, links and relationships because it allows for flexibility and adaptability. It is not an easy technique to use because it relies on the ability of the researcher to work the data. It is based on trial and error, it can be very time-consuming, and it is also difficult and a bit messy, especially in the initial stages. Its strengths, however, outweigh the disadvantages because the constant iteration between data and among data, and between data and theory, allows us to 'see' the patterns, themes, continuities and discontinuities in the data. The themes that we detect emerge in context, not isolated from context. While these themes are not in themselves explanations, the patterning of themes, the conditioning of contexts, the very dynamics of entrepreneurship begin to show how the relationships explain events.

The constant comparative technique has been used successfully in entrepreneurship research (see, for example, Jack 2005; Anderson et al. 2007; Jack et al. 2008; Discua Cruz 2009) and is seen as a way to 'undertake empirical research which is informed by prior theoretical understanding, but which is not so determined or constrained by this understanding that the potential for making novel insights is foregone' (Anderson et al. 2010: 24, referring to Finch 2002). In their discussion of the constant comparative technique, Dye et al. (2000) liken the process for data analysis to 'a kaleidoscope of data'. In short, the constant comparative technique, or method if you prefer, makes full use of all the data, by first sifting out the bits that matter, then by relating them to each other to help form an explanation.

Interestingly, both grounded theory and the constant comparative technique rely on analytic induction.

ANALYTIC INDUCTION

Analytic induction is a method of data analysis described by Florian Znaniecki (1934) who named the method, but also systematized many of the associated ideas. However, Znaniecki was careful to note that the essence of analytic induction has been used repeatedly throughout history (1934: 236–7), particularly by scientists in the physical sciences (he cites numerous examples from physics and biology) (Ratcliffe 1994). Seen as a technique rather than a method, 'analytic induction is purely qualitative and relies on reasoning that allows concepts and relationships between concepts to be modified throughout the research process, with the goal of most accurately representing the reality of the situation' (Ratcliffe 1994).

Following Znaniecki's (1934) introduction, the idea of analytic induction became popular. Just some of its uses are demonstrated in work that was undertaken between the 1930s and 1950s. For instance, as Robinson (1951) notes: its use was evident in Angell's (1936) *The Family Encounters Depression*; Sutherland (1939) recommended it be used when studying the causes of crime; Lindesmith (1947) used it when looking at opiate addiction; and so did Cressey (1953) when looking at causes of embezzlement. Robinson (1951) himself revisited it, considering how it was used and the process involved. Znanieciki (1934: 236–7) proposed that analytic induction ought to be the method of the social sciences (Robinson 1951).

The technique of analytic induction sees there as being no methodological value in piling up confirming cases; the strategy is exclusively qualitative, seeking encounters with new varieties of data in order to force revisions that will make the analysis valid when applied to an increasingly diverse range of cases (Katz 2001). The investigation continues until it is no longer practical to pursue negative cases (Katz 2001). Analytic induction is a way to build explanations in qualitative analysis by constructing and testing a set of causal links between events, actions, and so on, in one case and the iterative extension of this to further cases (http://onlineqda.hud.ac.uk/methodologies.php, accessed 5 August 2013). In its application it allows the researcher to collect data, develop analysis and organize the presentation of research findings. Its main objective is causal explanation. So, given the core interest of entrepreneurship researchers, it would seem an appropriate technique to use and one which has obvious links to both grounded theory and the constant comparative technique.

THIS PART

The three chapters presented in this part offer insightful perspectives on the use of grounded theory and the constant comparative technique in entrepreneurship research. In Chapter 1, Jack, Anderson, Drakopoulou Dodd and Moult present data and demonstrate how the constant comparative approach can be used to develop theory and understanding about the entrepreneur and the practices in which he or she engages. This chapter presents an unusual case, the emergence and development of a new network, where the unit of analysis is not the individual or the cluster, but the emergent network itself (Hite and Hesterley 2001; Hite 2003, 2005). Through their approach and discussion they demonstrate the usefulness and applicability of the constant comparative technique, how it operates, applications in practice and its value to the field of entrepreneurship. Chapter 2 presented by Smith and McKeever deals more explicitly with using constant comparison as a method of analysis in entrepreneurship research. Through their discussion, Smith and McKeever offer guidance in the practicalities of methodology and using constant comparison as a way to contribute to the overall quality and rigour of research in the field. Selecting work that has used the method, they show how it has been used from its origins in grounded theory and subsequently as a method to add rigour to the trustworthiness of qualitative data and analysis. Smith and McKeever provide a detailed guide of the steps they advocate should be followed when undertaking the method. They also show how it might be used in the entrepreneurial context. In Chapter 3, Bøllingtoft demonstrates the strengths of grounded theory. In talking the reader through the grounded theory perspective, Bøllingtoft discusses the process involved in detail. She also demonstrates why the method has been criticized and how the method might be adopted in a way which helps overcome such criticisms.

REFERENCES

Anderson, A., J. Park and S. Jack (2007), 'Entrepreneurial social capital: conceptualising social capital in new high-tech firms', *International Small Business Journal*, **25** (3), 243–67.

Anderson, A.R. and M. Starnawska (2008), 'Research practices in entrepreneurship; problems of definition, description and meaning', *International Journal of Entrepreneurship and Innovation*, **9** (4), 221–30.

Anderson, A.R., S. Drakopoulou Dodd and S.L. Jack (2010), 'Network practices and entrepreneurial growth', *Scandinavian Journal of Management*, **26** (2), 121–33.

Anderson, A.R., S.D. Drakopoulou Dodd and S.L. Jack (2012), 'Entrepreneurship as connecting: some implications for theorising and practice', *Management Decision*, **50** (5): 958–71.

Angell, R.C. (1936), *The Family Encounters the Depression*, New York: Scribner.

Bruton, G., R. Suddaby and S. Si (2014), 'Entrepreneurship through a qualitative lens', *Journal of Business Venturing*, **30** (special issue), 1–184.

Cressey, D.R. (1953), *Other People's Money: A Study in the Social Psychology of Embezzlement*, Glencoe, IL: Free Press.

Discua Cruz, A. (2010), 'Collective perspectives in portfolio entrepreneurship: a study of family business groups in Honduras'. *EDAMBA Journal*, **8**, 91–105.

Drakopoulou Dodd, S., S. Jack and A.R. Anderson (2013), 'From admiration to abhorrence; the contentious appeal of entrepreneurship across Europe', *Entrepreneurship and Regional Development*, **25** (1–2), 69–89.

Dye, J., I. Shatz, B. Rosenberg and S. Coleman (2000), 'Constant comparison method: a kaleidoscope of data', *The Qualitative Report*, **4** (1/2), available at: http://www.nova.edu/ssss/QR/QR4-1/dye.html (accessed 5 August 2013).

Easterby Smith, M., R. Thorpe and P.R. Jackson (2008), *Management Research*, 3rd edn, London: Sage.

Finch, J. (2002), 'The role of grounded theory in developing economic theory', *Journal of Economic Methodology*, **9** (2), 213–34.

Glaser, B.G. (1978), *Theoretical Sensitivity*, Mill Valley, CA: Sociology Press.

Glaser, B.G. (1992), *Basics of Grounded Theory Analysis: Emergence v Focusing*, Mill Valley, CA: Sociology Press.

Glaser, B.G. and A.L. Strauss (1967), *The Discovery of Grounded Theory: Strategies for Qualitative Research*, New York: Aldine.

Hite, J.M. (2003), 'Patterns of multidimensionality among embedded network ties: a typology of relational embeddedness in emerging entrepreneurial firms', *Strategic Organization*, **1** (1), 9–49.

Hite, J.M. (2005), 'Evolutionary processes and paths of relationally embedded network ties in emerging entrepreneurial firms', *Entrepreneurship Theory and Practice*, **29** (1), 113–44.

Hite, J.M. and W.S. Hesterly (2001), 'The evolution of firm networks: from emergence to early growth of the firm', *Strategic Management Journal*, **22** (3), 275–86.

Jack, S. (2005), 'The role, use and activation of strong and weak ties: a qualitative analysis', *Journal of Management Studies*, **42** (6), 1233–59.

Jack, S., S. Drakopoulou Dodd and A. Anderson (2008), 'Change and the development of entrepreneurial networks over time: a processual perspective', *Entrepreneurship & Regional Development*, **20** (2), 125–59.

Katz, J. (2001), 'Analytic induction', in N.J. Smelser and P.B. Baltes (eds), *International Encyclopedia of the Social and Behavioral Sciences*, available at: http://www.sscnet.ucla. edu/soc/faculty/katz/pubs/Analytic_Induction.pdf (accessed 5 August 2013).

Lindesmith A.R. (1947), *Opiate Addiction*, Bloominton, IN: Principia Press.

Ratcliffe, D.E. (1994), 'Analytic induction as a qualitative research method of analysis', available at: http://www.scribd.com/doc/129340070/Ratcliff-1994-Analytic-Induction-as-a-Qualitative-Research-Method-of-Analysis (accessed 5 August 2013).

Robinson, W.S. (1951), 'The logical structure of analytic induction', *American Sociological Review*, **16** (6), 812–18.

Short, J., D.J. Ketchen, J. Combs and R.D. Ireland (2010), 'Research methods in entrepreneurship: opportunities and challenges', *Organizational Research Methods*, **13** (1), 6–15.

Strauss, A. (1987), *Qualitative Analysis for Social Scientists*, Cambridge: Cambridge University Press.

Strauss, A.L. and J. Corbin (1998), *The Basics of Quality Research*, 2nd edn, London: Sage Publications.

Sutherland, E. (1939), *Principles of Criminology*, 3rd edn, Philadelphia, PA: Lippincott.

Znaniecki, F. (1934), *The Method of Sociology*, Ann Arbor, MI: University of Michigan.

1 Using the constant comparative technique to consider network change and evolution
Sarah L. Jack, Alistair R. Anderson,
Sarah Drakopoulou Dodd and Susan Moult

INTRODUCTION

Developing greater understanding about if, how and why networks emerge, evolve and support growth has been recognized in the literature as an area for further research (Larson and Starr 1993; Uzzi 1997; Hite and Hesterly 2001). In this chapter[1] we present data and demonstrate how the constant comparative approach can be used to develop theory and understanding about the entrepreneur and the practices in which he/she engages. This Chapter presents an unusual case, the emergence and development of a new network, where the unit of analysis is not the individual or the cluster, but the emergent network itself (Hite and Hesterley 2001; Hite 2003; 2005). In doing so, it demonstrates the usefulness and applicability of the constant comparative technique, how it operates and is used in practice, and its value to the field of entrepreneurship. The case itself draws on longitudinal observation, examination and analysis of network configuration, reconfiguration and change in an entrepreneurial network over a six-year period. Examining rich data about transformation enabled the purpose, content and objectives of entrepreneurial networking to be analysed using the constant comparison technique. From this analysis we propose that networking is fundamentally based on a social enactment of what it means to be enterprising (De Koning 1999; Hill et al. 1999; Singh et al. 1999). Hence, using the constant comparative technique shows that networks are not just about resource acquisition; but are more about softer, socialized issues such as social learning and confidence-building through interdependence and the sharing of experience.

The contribution of this chapter lies in three distinct areas. First, the content of the study, in that the longitudinal case of network change over time demonstrates the evolution and developments from a manufactured grouping of individuals to an interactive organic network. This helps extend recent work, which considers evolutionary perspectives on networks and inter-organizational cooperation (Hite 2005, Neergard and Ulhoi 2006; Jack et al. 2008). Secondly, the lens employed to explore the unit of analysis is different from most previous work. Rather than focusing on the entrepreneur, it considers changes in the actual network and uses this as a mechanism to help enhance understanding about networking. A case study approach combining qualitative and quantitative tools, but with the emphasis on qualitative interpretation using the constant comparative technique, was used. This allowed data about the network and the interactions of the network members to be collected. Analysis of this duality of individual and group used the constant comparative method allowing the dynamics of the relationships and outcomes to be synthesized. Finally, the use of the constant comparative technique allows us to present theoretical observations about the nature of understanding. Our findings illustrate that, through the active formation of network ties, gaps in the entrepreneur's information, asset and social legitimation requirements are bridged. Thus, the network appears to shift and adapt to fit the needs of its participants. Accordingly, this work supports early entrepreneurial social network theory, that networks fluctuate and change over time, but also extends the findings of Mitchell (1969), Aldrich and Zimmer (1986), Birley (1985) and Johannisson (1987, 1988) in that, through action research, it demonstrates that networks are organic structures, responding to the needs of network members.

NETWORKS AND NETWORKING IN THE LITERATURE

Networking is increasingly recognized as a critical factor of the entrepreneurial process and, since the 1990s according to Neergaard et al. (2005), has become a major theme in entrepreneurship research (Hansen 1995; Chell and Baines 2000; Drakopolou Dodd et al. 2002; Jack et al. 2008). Defined as 'a set of actors and some set of relationships that link them' (Hoang and Antoncic 2003: 167), it is acknowledged that network research is not unproblematic (Coviello 2005). One typical problem lies in the unit of analysis; a network can be argued to exist as a *sui generis* entity, something above and different from the members of the network. Networks are constituted from the constellation of dyadic, triadic and multiplex ties between members (Larson 1992; Johannisson 1996; Hite 2005). Hence issues arise about whether we can understand networks best by looking at the ties, which form the structure of networks, or by exploring the interactions between and among these ties. Looking at ties can tell us much about the structural components of the interaction (Johanson and Mattsson 1987; Anderson et al. 1994; Gadde et al. 2003), for example, whether the network link is based on reciprocity and hence calculative or instrumental, or whether the bonds are affective and more about a loose obligation. Using these areas as the focus of enquiry can tell us much about the process of networking, but using this micro examination of ties tells us very little about the network itself. In contrast, if we try to understand the network as an organization, we can count linkages, situate connections and build up a map of the network, but we then know very little about the nature of the process of networking. Such maps of networks are fairly static and difficult to combine with process approaches. It seems that we have a research dilemma; should we study networking or networks?

This is not to say that either research perspective cannot produce interesting results. The networks as organizations literature has made significant advances in our understanding of whether these networks are some sort of intermediate form, located somewhere between markets and hierarchies, or are an entirely new form of organization (Arias 1995). Similarly work on social bonds of trust and commitment between ties (Etzioni 1988; Anderson et al. 2007) has shed considerable light on network interaction. Conceptually these different approaches not only produce different understandings but have very different starting points concerning which variables are dependent or independent. For example, if studying the network, social capital (social capital is often seen as a critical part of network research) can become the explanatory variable (Borgatti and Foster 2003) but if studying alliances, ties become the explanatory variable. Moreover, Fombrum (1982) proposed that we can distinguish two kinds of network: attribute networks, where individuals share a commonality (similarity of attributes, gender and the like), or transactional networks, where the focus is on the exchanges between individuals. Fombrum (1982) notes how, if one begins with transactions, attributes may be seen as explanatory variables. Yet, Anderson and Jack (2002) argued that social capital exists between individuals, is formed on the basis of affinities and that social capital also lubricates the transactions, so these two types of qualities do not serve to distinguish different types of networks. Rather, both elements are likely to exist in a network and have been conceptualized as the structural and relational qualities (Granovetter 1985). Nonetheless, as Neergaard et al. (2005) note, extant research has concentrated on the structural and quantifiable aspects.

In essence, networking research can be seen to be problematic if we are concerned about developing a fuller appreciation and understanding of both network structure and process. By concentrating on the study of one aspect, the other aspect is thrown into shadow. Indeed, this dichotomy is also manifest in the methodologies employed. In addressing questions about structure, how many contacts, how often and with whom, most often a quantitative approach has been employed. This clearly reflects the need for quantifiable data (Birley 1985). In contrast, if we are interested in process, such data is less helpful and we may need a more fine-grained qualitative methodology to address subtle questions (Neergard et al. 2005: 349). However, in practice, many studies of entrepreneurial networking simply avoid the problem of unit of analysis. Nevertheless, Shaw (2006) defended the small firm as the choice and unit of analysis to explore network structure, processes and outcomes.

Borgatti and Foster (2003) argue that the outcome of networking represents the bulk of network research. This, they explain, is a consequence of the need to establish the field as legitimate. Only after it could be shown that networking had important consequences, endorsing networking as a legitimate topic, could work emerge which explored network change over time. This is certainly true of the entrepreneurial literature where networks are seen as a way to extend the potential resource base of the entrepreneur (Johannisson and Peterson 1984; Birley 1985; Aldrich and Zimmer 1986; Carsrud and Johnson 1989; Johannisson et al. 1994; Shaw 2006). Thus networks act as a conduit for information (Steier and Greenwood 1995), improve the possibilities of success (Johannisson and Peterson 1984; Johannisson 1986, 1987; Johannisson and Nilsson 1989; Foss 1994; Ostgaard and Birley 1994; Hansen 1995; Brüderl and Preisendörfer 1998; Jack and Anderson 2002) and, indeed, venture survival (Arocena 1984; Szarka 1990; Brüderl and Preisendörfer 1998; Huggins 2000). However, as Johannisson and Mønsted (1997) point out, this particular strand in the literature emphasizes the resource dependence perspective of networking. While this may address the 'why' questions about new ventures, it actually tells us little about the 'how' questions of entrepreneurial networking. In spite of these studies, recognized gaps in the literature stream remain, most notably in terms of a heightened understanding of the content of network interactions (O'Donnell et al. 2001; Barnir and Smith 2002; Lechner and Dowling 2003), the processes within network relations (O'Donnell et al. 2001) and the dynamic nature of networks over time (O'Donnell et al. 2001; Lechner and Dowling 2003; Shaw 2006). One recent response to this gap in the literature has been a new focus, network change. Network change offers the possibility of charting both structure and process. Larson and Starr (1993) were among the first to argue that entrepreneurial networks change over time. Their evolutionary view saw the shift from fairly simple dyadic relationships into multidimensional relationships, thus illustrating both process and content.

Network Change

The literature on network change (see, for example, Larson and Starr 1993; Schutzens and Stam 2001; Lechner and Dowling 2003; Greve and Salaff 2003; Hite 2005) may well demonstrate that network studies are a legitimate area of study, but they are also a logical development of the resource-based view. Underpinning the temporal dynamics of network change is an assumption about the instrumentality of network resources; network change is seen as a response to changing entrepreneurial requirements. Johannisson (1988), for example, argues that establishing and developing a business requires different contacts and different resources over time. Granovetter (1985) also noted that social network ties are activated according to need, and hence are not fixed. A consequence of this view is that networks, as entities, can perhaps best be seen as a bundle of dynamic relationships, changing and process driven (Chell and Baines 2000; Anderson and Jack 2002). Moreover, what is true at the level of the individual entrepreneur may well be equally true at the level of a network, which comprises many individuals: dynamism, process and change remain key factors. So network change presents an interesting matrix for trying to understand the nature of networks. If the changes are, as the literature seems to suggest, entirely driven by resource acquisition, we may be able to use the matrix of change to develop a fuller understanding of the networks themselves. Typically, the network change literature (Jack et al. 2008) uses and captures transitions, formations and reformations in response to environment and business development needs. But this literature is based on an agglomeration of dyadic relationships; the individual's network changes. Our focus of enquiry is the network itself, thus providing us with a very different perspective, a theoretical platform from which to observe the emergence, development and change within the network as an entity. Moreover, by using the network as the unit of analysis, a medium level rather than purely micro or macro level of analysis is possible.

It is clear that while networks play important roles and change over time, we are less well informed about the dynamics, or indeed the reasons for change, in networking over time. This issue presents our background research problem: in what ways, and for what reasons, do networks change? Dealing with this problem allows very clear research questions to be considered which go some way to help resolve some of the issues discussed earlier. If the unit of analysis is the network itself, we can see at a macro level how network structures change. Accordingly, the research questions address the macro issues. What is the nature of networks? What is the nature of the linkages which form the structure? What makes them work? But since networks are constellations of ties, the micro level of interactions within the network can also be explored. Thus some of the micro issues can be considered, what is the nature of the exchanges within networks and how do they work? As explained earlier, the study presented here is of an emerging and developing network. Borgatti (2002) claims that what was once described as a group, a club or a trade association is now described as a network. But conversely, Fombrum, albeit writing in 1982, claimed that any set of individuals is tied by multiplex bonds. In fact, this study is intended to chart the developments from a group, characterized by very loose ties, into a network, which is tied together by increasingly stronger multiplex bonds.

METHODOLOGY

The research problem identified was to understand network change by examining how and why the network changed over time. Zhang and Lin (2005) comment that although many studies have recognized network dynamic change as an important topic, the literature on change is not extensive. Coviello (2005) suggests that since networks are relationship based and consequently dynamic, network research is also time bound. For her, this suggests that research methodologies should be sensitive to how networks change over time. Moreover, O'Donnell et al. (2001) see it as imperative that networks should be studied over time. Similarly Hoang and Antonic (2003) argue that entrepreneurial studies should be longitudinal and show how network content, governance and structure emerge over time. Birley (1985) argued that the process view was necessary because firm start-up is not a discrete event; rather it is a process which may extend over a considerable time. There are of course some longitudinal studies. For example, Davidsson and Honig (2003) examined human and social capital over 18 months and found bridging and bonding social capital (strong and weak ties) a predictor for nascent entrepreneurs; Schutjens and Stam (2003) used longitudinal questionnaires to study aspects associated with evolution and argued the case for networks to be viewed in a spatial and temporal context. But, as Coviello (2005: 41) notes, the focus of many studies is on counting activities or types of network contacts over time; 'as such, the processes underlying network development are not captured'. Consequently this study addresses a gap in the literature (Shaw 2006).

This study is part of our ongoing interest in networks. Our previous work had concentrated on the social processes within networks, so when we had the opportunity to study this emergent organization, we felt that we could broaden the scope of our understanding. We became aware of the existence of the new 'network' when one of the authors, Susan Moult, joined the group as a student as a way of becoming better acquainted with embryonic entrepreneurship. Her role at that point was participant as observer. Within a few months she was asked to join the committee and eventually took over the role of treasurer. At this point the research group realized it had the opportunity to study the formation and development of a network. Fortunately Susan had kept detailed accounts of her involvement, so that when we decided to make this a formal case study, we had a written record of events as well as her recollections of events. Susan had access to minutes, members' records and correspondence, attendance sheets and key secondary sources detailed below. This review provided qualitative and quantitative data about members' perceptions of the network. Later, when the local enterprise company declared its intention to withdraw financial support, Susan was asked to undertake a formal review of the network to establish whether it was worth continuing. So data were collected, both ethnographically, as participant observer, and also in more 'objective' formats from the surveys and interviews. One task of the others in the research team was to help shape how the later data were collected. But their primary role was in the analysis of the data, discussed in more detail later in the chapter. The team were able, as a team, to compare and contrast the different data, examine its meaning and challenge individual perceptions. Thus, analysis was more soundly based. If analytical errors have been made, they were both joint and several, but overall are more likely to be objective because of the independent data scrutiny and analysis.

As Halinen and Tornroos, (2005) recently noted, research methods and access to data in network studies have gained little attention. The research objective was to try to understand the processes of network formation and development over time. This called for a longitudinal case study approach to allow changes over time to be followed (Easton 1995). Nonetheless, although the unit of analysis was the 'network', the nature of the network could only be understood by studying network members in context. Networks exist as dynamic relationships (Chell and Baines 2000), changing and processual. However, because of the difficulty of studying networks most work does seem to end up taking a 'snapshot' of the network and what is happening within that network but only at a specific point in time. Hence, the changing nature of networks and the processual perspectives are ignored. But networks only exist as a relational artefact; their objectification only becomes real as a product of relational interaction (Anderson and Jack 2002). Consequently to understand a network, we need to know about the members and the interaction of members, since the network, although a *sui generis* thing in itself, is also the sum of interaction of the members. As has been noted elsewhere, networks actually create the environment so that 'networking process is the enactment of the environment' (Jack et al. 2008: 125). To this end, data about both the network and the network members was collected. Case studies are multi-perspectival analyses (Yin 1994). This means that the researcher considers not just the voice and perspective of the actors, but also of the relevant groups of actors and the interaction between them (Halinen and Tornroos 2005). Eisenhardt (1989) also points out that case studies can capture the dynamics. Thus, as Halinen and Tornroos, (2005) argue, it seems obvious that a case strategy is most suitable for the study of business networks.

Within the case approach, researchers need to be clear about techniques. There is broad consensus that when tackling social phenomena such as networks, rich detail is so essential to the research process that qualitative studies are to be preferred (Blackburn et al. 1990; Chell and Haworth 1992; Johannisson and Mønsted 1997; Uzzi 1997; Hill et al. 1999; Zeleny 2001; Hoang and Antoncic 2003; Jack et al. 2008). This is especially so when addressing the process, content, and dynamics of networks, rather than purely structural matters (O'Donnell et al. 2001; Lechner and Dowling 2003). A qualitative approach is also indicated by the relative lack of work in the area (Larson 1992). Additional benefits of qualitative approaches include 'intensive investigation of developmental patterns' (Larson 1992: 79), and 'sensitivity to the details of self-enforcing and trust-building idiosyncratic exchange processes' (Johannisson 1996: 257). A similar case has been made for the use of longitudinal studies, to enhance the knowledge gained by cross-sectional analysis, in the study of dynamic entrepreneurial networks (O'Donnell et al. 2001; Greve and Salaff 2003; Hoang and Antoncic 2003; Jack et al. 2008). O'Donnell et al. (2001) suggest, following Curran and Blackburn (1994), that the interactional aspect of networking calls for a qualitative approach. Aldrich (2001) argues that we need to look at event driven processes. O'Donnell et al. (2001) also note that, within process, the content of network interactions is relatively neglected and suggest that an appreciation of these dimensions would increase our understanding of network processes.

Nonetheless, case study methodology calls for a variety of data collection techniques. This study is probably methodologically unique, in that it adopts a longitudinal, qualitative approach to the study of content, processes and dynamics in entrepreneurial networks, but with some enrichment provided with the use of quantitative data. In this way we try to manage the epistemological divide between the interpretivist and functionalist paradigms (Burrell and Morgan 1979), utilizing methodologies espoused by each paradigm (Gioia and Pitre 1990). Our approach is thus not simply the uncritical methodological 'mix and match' of which much multi-method entrepreneurship research has been justifiably accused (Curran and Blackburn 2001; Grant and Perren 2002) and thus feel that a strength of the research is the multidimensional nature of the research methods employed. This is detailed below.

Desk Research

Access to the network's materials and archival records documenting the history and development of the forum, that is, members' correspondence, marketing material, committee minutes and attendance records, was acquired. Two particularly important secondary sources were used:

1. A members' meeting was held in December 1997 to review the development of the organization to date, membership's aspirations and the way forward. The facilitator's summary was especially informative regarding individual member's perceived aims at that time.
2. A survey administered to members in June 1998, which collected 40 responses relating to background details about membership, types of business activity, business stage, format of meetings and reason for joining the forum. This survey provides a benchmark against which to measure subsequent developments, and is particularly valuable since it summarizes the opinions of the majority of early-stage entrepreneurs within this specific group.

Participant Observation

Previous work has highlighted the relevance of participant observation for network research (Bøllingtoft 2007). During the period December 1997 to April 2003, the lead author regularly participated in the forum's monthly meetings. Additionally, she was an independent observer at a meeting between members' representatives and the local enterprise agency in April 2003, at which the future direction of the organization was determined.

Interviews

Eleven semi-structured interviews were carried out in 2002–03. Respondents included two employees of the enterprise agency and nine members, including the 'chair' and one past, founder member. Table 1.1 provides a detailed overview of respondents.

The majority of the interviewees were selected from the quantitative survey outlined below. Two interviews (1 and 11) were one-hour

Table 1.1   Respondents

	Gender	Age	Age of business	No. of employees, incl. owner	Business activity
RI	Female	56–65	9 months	6 (incl. 3 part-time)	Business support services
R2	Male	36–45	2 years	1	Photographic solutions
R3	Female	56–65	3 months	3	Management consultancy
R4	Female	36–45	6 years	1	Training consultancy
R5	Male	46–55	5 years	2	Cost management
R6	Female	56–65	N/A	N/A	Housewife
R7	Female	56–65	4 years	1	Professional forensic services
R8	Female	46–55	4 years	1	Wine educational consultancy
R9	Male	46–55	In process of start-up	1	Health and safety services
R10	Male	46–55	20 months	10	Manufacturing
R11	Female	46–55	14 months	1	Computer training and PC support
R12	Male	56–65	2 years	1	Motivational coaching
R13	Male	46–55	21 years	2	Architect
R14	Female	46–55	7 years	1	Speciality gifts
R15	Male	26–35	2½ years	1	Corporate leisure activities
R16	Male	46–55	5 years	1	Health and safety consultancy
R17	Female	56–65	2½ years	1	Language training
R18	Male	46–55	2 years	3 + 8 associates	Management consultancy and training
R19	Male	26–35	2 years	1	Internet consultancy and web design
R20	Female	46–55	8 years	1	Consultancy/training
R21	Female	46–55	13 years	2	Team building and coaching
R22	Female	56–65	Considering start-up	N/A	
R23	Male	16–25	N/A	N/A	Student
R24	Male	46–55	In process of start-up	N/A	Life coach
R25	Male	46–55	In process of start-up	N/A	Mobile car services
R26	Male	46–55	9 months	1	Business and IT consultancy
R27	Female	36–45	3½ years	1	Training consultancy
R28	Female	56–65	4 months	1	Project management
R29	Male	36–45	In process of start-up	N/A	Design/manufacturing
R30	Female	46–55	12 years	1	Health promotion
R31	Female	36–45	7 months	1	HR consultancy

face-to-face interviews with key participants; the others were telephone interviews, typically lasting 30 minutes.

Quantitative Enrichment

In December 2002, 39 subscribed members of the club were surveyed and the questionnaire distributed at a monthly meeting with 50 attendees. This resulted in a total of 31 completed questionnaires (29 from members and two from guests). Respondents were asked about benefits, reasons for joining (or considering joining) and how they rated the effectiveness of the network. An important feature of the questionnaire was the open ended nature of many of the questions. Opinions were invited about expectations and experiences as well as the more formal scales.

Data Analysis

An inductive approach to analysing data was employed. Eisenhardt (1989) recommends starting data analysis by first sifting through all the data, discarding whatever is irrelevant and bringing together what seemed most important. The second step consists of a search for patterns (Halinen and Tornroos 2005). This took the form of looking at the data and asking ourselves, 'What is going on here?' Described more formally, this involved the constant comparative method (Glaser and Strauss 1967; Alvesson and Sköldberg 2000; Silverman 2000) of an iterative reviewing of the data with emerging categories and concepts. This has become an accepted approach of dealing with entrepreneurial network analysis (Human and Provan 1996; Hill et al. 1999; Jack 2009).

Wolcott (1990) argued that the objective with qualitative work is not to accumulate all the data you can, but instead identify and then reveal those data with enough context to allow the reader to understand those situations individuals are immersed in. The research process used here generated large amounts of data which, once collected, had to be sorted before it could be analysed. Interviews were taped and transcribed, data from documents, discussions, field notes and observations were collected, written up, merged, synthesized and then organized around the themes which seemed to fit with our interests: networks, networks evolving and network patterns of change. This provided a way of sorting and arranging the rich raw data into useful and explanatory categories.

Data was then examined and explored for detail relating to these themes. This meant comparing and contrasting patterns of activities to determine categories. So, incidents and experiences, observations and responses were continually compared with others within emerging categories. This process helped to improve description, understanding and explanations but it also helped to ensure confidence in our interpretations.

Analysis was not 'full blown' grounded theorizing, with axial and radial coding. Instead, understanding patterns of change was our concern. This constant comparative element of a grounded approach has been used in other studies (see, for example, Anderson et al. 2007; Jack et al. 2008) and provided a way to 'undertake empirical research which is informed by prior theoretical understanding, but which is not so determined or constrained by this understanding that the potential for making novel insights is foregone' (Anderson et al. 2010: 24, referring to the work of Finch 2002).

We can describe our analysis as stages of constant comparative analysis. First, we searched all data for any patterns or themes. Secondly, we refined these themes into descriptive categories, so that an identified theme became a category when we were able to define it descriptively in such a way as to be able to distinguish it clearly. These processes were inductive, but given that they were initially conducted separately by each author, we are confident of the validity and meaningfulness of the categories. Our next stage was to synthesize the descriptive categories into analytical categories. Put differently, how could these categories be combined to help explain processes? Again we first reviewed this material individually, then jointly to try to ensure the reliability of our analysis. In fact this process generated some new insights as ideas and interpretations clashed and fused. Finally, we applied our explanatory categories to the case. The process this entailed is illustrated in Figure 1.1 and in Table 1.2. Phase 1 is used to illustrate in more detail how we moved from descriptive to analytical categories.

Ethical Considerations

The main researcher at the time was a student studying entrepreneurship and she was invited to become involved with the forum. Forum participants became respondents, but at all times were completely aware of her study and agreed to participate. Moreover, it was made clear to respondents that any resources, data and material would be used for academic purposes. Copies of findings were sent to the committee and presented to members for feedback.

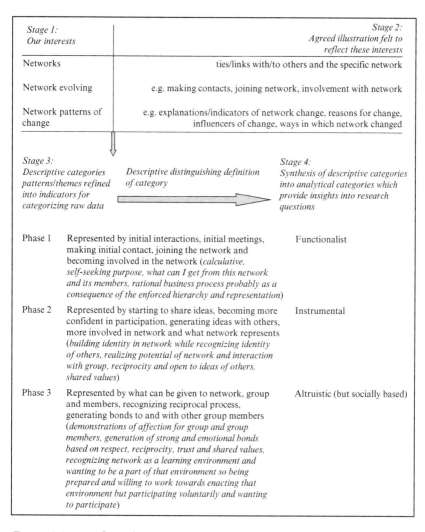

Figure 1.1   Analytical process

THE CASE: CHRONOLOGY OF THE NETWORK EVOLUTION

Phase 1: Formation

The forum for potential entrepreneurs was established in September 1996 by a local enterprise agency in response to the Business Birth Rate Strategy

Table 1.2   Moving from descriptive to analytical categories: the example of Phase 1

Stage 3 Descriptive distinguishing definition of category	Data sources utilized	Examples from these data sources which 'identify the phenomena'	Summary of findings from the data – what's the story?	Stage 4 Synthesis of descriptive categories into analytical categories
Phase 1 (1996–98) Represented by initial interactions, initial meetings, making initial contact, joining the network and becoming involved in the network	Early archival material: flyers, statements of purpose, etc. Facilitator's summary of December 1997 meeting Members' survey June 1998 Participant observation records for 1997–98 Interview transcript material (2002) which reflected back on Phase 1	*Formality* evidenced by rigid organizational structure and process described in archival material *Discontent* with network shown by 37% replying that the network had not helped them (members' survey). Meeting records for early 1998 show high turnover in membership and poor attendance levels (less than 20) Specific and *pre-start up* focus of network: 'the main remit of our organisation is to promote the formation of business ideas' (Ilyer, 1997) *Outcome-driven* expectations of the founding agency, 'connect needs to resources'; 'Business Birth Rate' (agency dialogue) Members expect *concrete outcomes*, and are disappointed by the network's failure to deliver in this area: 'participants seem to offer only marginal interest' (1998 survey) Awareness of the attractiveness of a *more social, supportive side* to the network (facilitator's feedback from 1997 members' meeting)	Calculative, self-seeking purpose 'What can I get from this network and its members?' A rational business process is in place and perceived rather coldly Perhaps this is a consequence of the enforced hierarchy and representation?	Functionalist

(BBRS). This highlighted an enterprise deficit and a disparity between those individuals with an interest in entrepreneurship and those actually going on to launch a business (Scottish Enterprise 1993). The forum's aim was to target pre-start, nascent entrepreneurs and help them develop business ideas and build the momentum for business start-up. The early driver seemed to be to meet the targets of the BBRS and to 'either keep them [clients] in the entrepreneurial loop or encourage them in the development of their business' (Interview 11). The emphasis was on idea generation rather than networking; 'the main remit of our organisation is to promote the formation of business ideas' (club flyer, 1997).

From the beginning, the organization and staging of monthly meetings was managed by the members themselves. The meeting format was to table business ideas, then self-select into syndicates to brainstorm and evaluate the opportunities, which members could then develop in their own time. The aim was to be 'informal', 'approachable' and somewhere to 'kick around' business ideas (club flyer, 1997).

Phase 2: Development and Reconfiguration

By December 1997, there was a growing recognition that improvements could be made. Members highlighted the need to monitor the status of syndicates and the need to 'harvest' more 'members, third parties, business angels and enterprise companies' (facilitator's feedback, December 1997). Other recommendations included improving the meeting format to facilitate 'networking', such as name badges, a members' notice board and a membership directory (facilitator's feedback, December 1997). Following a high turnover in membership and poor attendance levels (less than 20) in the first few months of 1998, an internal survey of members and guests was completed in June. Only four respondents appeared to have been members since inception and, significantly, the characteristics of the membership appeared to have changed. Fully 55 per cent of the respondents were business owners and 18 per cent of the other members already had a business idea. There were numerous suggestions to move away from syndicates and discussion groups and concentrate 'more on the practicalities and problems of getting a business up and running' (survey results, June 1998). There was also a general demand for greater networking opportunities and a wider membership base.

The forum was given a complete makeover, including a new logo and a more professional image. The syndicate structure was initially retained, but a more balanced programme was developed, focused on problems and issues relating to growing businesses, with input from entrepreneurs, business professionals and the support organizations. The perceived improvement was immediate – 'prior to the last two meetings it was going down the tube' (minutes, March 1999) and attendance at meetings gradually rose to between 40 and 60, with one meeting (a motivational speaker) attracting over 100 attendees. Efforts were made to broaden the membership base and our analysis of the marketing literature reveals a changing shift in emphasis. The new flyers highlighted the specific benefits of membership, including 'help', 'support', 'advice', 'contacts', 'ideas' and being 'part of a progressive group of people' (club flyer, 1999). The marketing literature emphasized 'networking' – 'it's not just what you know, but also who you know' (club flyer, 1999) and the forum's role as a 'unique network of entrepreneurs' and 'matchmaking bureau' (chairman's letter 1999/2000). By June, 2000, the new motto was 'Network for Success' (minutes, June 2000).

Phase 3: Survival and Rebirth

The role of the enterprise agency had always been quite 'hands-off'. Apart from the champion within the agency, who sat in an *ex officio* capacity on the committee, support was restricted to providing an individual to handle day-to-day enquiries, undertake mail shots and maintain membership records. Following changes to the organization and strategy of the enterprise agency, it launched a new, different and much larger 'enterprise forum' in April 2002. The new forum was marketed to clients, resulting in membership numbers of the original forum dropping significantly – from an average of 60 to 39 at the survey date. In April 2003, the agency decided to withdraw all further support, including promotion of monthly meetings.

Interestingly, the original forum has survived. The majority of the remaining members decided to 'go it alone' (meeting record, April 2003) and operate without the assistance and support of the agency. Indeed, for some members their 'disillusionment is with the supporting body' (R 20). Currently, the forum is enjoying a rebirth and attendance had considerably increased, from an average of 43 in 2002, to 110 people in January, 2004.

THE EVOLUTION OF THE NETWORK

It is clear from summarizing the major thematic phases over the period of observation that the evolution of the network has been characterized by various stages and crises which resulted in changes to the network's structure, content and process. The forum has developed into a social network which functions independently from its agency-broker. Moreover, the network has developed into its present format in accordance with the underlying network needs and the social context of its members. There is a new ethos to the forum, and the mission now is to 'create a social club where they can really learn' (interviewee 1).

The initial focus by the enterprise agency was the fledgling, pre-start entrepreneur. This suited the agency's own agenda (to improve the business birth rate) and effectively the agency introduced a programme of formal events to encourage idea generation and motivation. The forum's original purpose was as an ideas bank, but by the time of the 2002 survey, seeking a business idea was ranked as the least important reason for joining. Rather, it was the opportunity to network, especially with people in a similar position, which was ranked as the most important reason, and it is the forum's ability to fulfil the social needs and expectations of its members which was central to the transformation process, and ultimately, to the organization's survival.

In explaining the reasons for change, the involvement of the members themselves was a key factor. The agency's stance was 'the group is for you, and should be run by you' (interviewee 11). From the beginning, a members' committee was involved in running the forum and fronting meetings. However, the top-heavy management structure (see Table 1.3) provoked criticism in the 1998 survey, and a more fluid, informal structure emerged, with members rotating the chair and taking turns to host meetings. The members themselves made the decision to continue the forum in 2003 and they used their personal contacts and influence to keep the forum alive and growing. The forum appears to be functioning as a community for a small, but critical, nucleus of members, which enabled it to survive and exist independently from the enterprise agency. A new ethos has evolved which is embedded in the social context of the membership.

Membership Characteristics

To help explain the change in membership we should note the type of member and changes in the membership size and distribution. Although the data available relating to the original members is incomplete, it appears that the early members consisted of both the pre-start 'wannabe' entrepreneur – 'most are in love with an ideal and hope to shed light on their dreams' (welcome letter, 1997) – as well as early stage business owners – 'some of the members do run their own businesses, but want to continue to meet like-minded people' (welcome letter, 1997). By the time of the 1998 survey, the membership profile was much clearer – 74 per cent of respondents either had a business idea or were business owners already.

Table 1.3 Evolution of the network

Phase	Enterprise agency	Dialogue	Members	Structure	Network status
Formation Phase 1: 1996–98	Formed the forum Focus on idea generation and development of business opportunities	A – 'generation of new business', 'support', 'exchange of ideas', 'connect needs to resources', 'meet like-minded people', ideas bank', 'Business Birth Rate'	Mainly 'wannabe' entrepreneurs	Formal hierarchy of Chair, President, Vice President, Secretary, Treasurer and Committee	Loose collection of individuals
Development Phase 2: 1998–2002	Facilitation of network Event focus	A – 'breeding ground for business', 'safe laboratory' New logo, name badges, professional events M – 'network with more members', 'network with the right people', 'benefit from the experience of other', 'contact with others', 'meeting others and learning from them'	New starts and ready to go	Much less formal Treasurer and committee Rotating 'chair'	More tightly knit Like-minded, sharing
Current Phase: Rebirth	Launched new forum Withdrew all support from original forum	A – 'network for success' M – 'contact with kindred spirits', 'peer group support', 'the opportunity to learn', 'chance to feel at home with others'	In business Mature, solo	Unstructured and informal Only a secretary	Close knit

Note: A = agency; M = members.

This profile was confirmed by the 2002 survey, which indicated that 23 of the 31 respondents had their own businesses and a further five were in the process of starting up. More detailed analysis of the 2002 data showed that, with one exception, the businesses were all micro-enterprises, with 18 having no employees. Also, the age distribution of respondents indicated that 75 per cent were over 35 years old. In other words, the forum's appeal has developed for a particular type of entrepreneur – the mature, micro-business owner.

The type of network member is important, as it will naturally influence the shape and content of the network. Johannisson (1996) argues that the need for networking and the structure and degree of networking activity may vary dependent on the stage of the life cycle; therefore the requirements of the person who has already started may be very different from the pre-start hopeful. What starts to emerge is a tension in the network centred round the conflict of needs/interests. When the forum tried to target both interest groups, this was perceived as a weakness. 1998 survey responses stated there was a 'lack of focus' and the forum 'needed to get really clear who the intended members are' (members' survey, June 1998). Moreover, evidence from the members' survey (June 1998) demonstrates that these embryonic entrepreneurs were perceived by some members as adding little value to the network:

'Participants seem to offer only marginal interest';
'With current attendees it is too introspective';
'Most attendees do not have a specific direction or goal and lack the emotional fortitude to push themselves forward'; and, most damning of all,
'It is group therapy for bored housewives'.

Size and Diversity of the Network

The agency and committee used poor attendance at meetings and falling membership numbers as measurements of success for the network. Membership numbers were important for the financial viability of the forum; also, some members appeared disappointed with the quality and diversity of the network contacts and wanted a broader membership base, including larger, more established businesses. However, analysis of the questionnaires revealed that attendance numbers was not a critical point. Although 36 per cent of the 2002 survey respondents admitted to rarely attending meetings, this was largely because of business commitments rather than any dissatisfaction with the forum. Although formal membership was never high (at best 60 members) the 'unofficial' network appeared to be larger, and attendance sheets indicated high numbers of guests and people attending one event only. For example, in 2002, the average monthly attendance was 43, but 197 different individuals attended events. Of these, 69 per cent only attended one event. For some members, this diversity was an attraction – 'I'm meeting lots of different people every meeting – that's the whole purpose' (R7). However, this low-density, weak-tie network was seen as a weakness by others and one response noted the 'high churn rate' and complained that 'insufficient meetings are held to build relationships with fellow members' (R5).

For the remaining nucleus of members, however, the forum seems to have emerged as having a strong tie orientation and the network has developed into a high-density network with most of the members knowing each other (Granovetter 1973). By 2002, approximately a third of the respondents had been members for over three years and responses indicated that they had become 'good friends' (interviewee 1 and R14) and had developed strong tie relationships. Even at the early stages, there is evidence that strong ties were being formed and new members complained that 'the established members are too cliquey'. Indeed, the syndicate system itself promoted the development of a strong tie network. In fact, what emerges is that the small size of the organization actually suits some members and is within their comfort zones – 'we don't want it to get too huge – if it got too huge it would lose the familiarity. Obviously, we need about 40 or 50 – that's quite nice. It's just attracting a few more people regularly to give a more consistent number of people' (R7).

Perceived Benefits of the Network

The membership of the network changed over time, but because the members were not homogeneous, they had different expectations and needs. What emerges through the different stages are the multifaceted, multidimensional needs of the network members, which is illustrated in Table 1.3. There is a shift, from needing and wanting more than motivation and business ideas, to improving communication skills, building confidence and creating an emotional support network. The divergent needs can be seen as early as December 1997. Analysis of the vocabulary used by members at the first annual review indicates a growing awareness of the forum as a social network – as somewhere to 'meet interesting, enthusiastic people' and 'kindred spirits'. There was much more focus by members on being connected – 'sharing', 'exchange', 'tapping into nuggets', 'access to other skills', 'connect needs to resources' and 'support'. It appears that the members' expectations and needs were beginning to change and influence the development of the network (facilitator's feedback, December 1997).

By the time of the 1998 survey, the tension is clearer. Some members listed benefits such as 'hearing about business ideas', 'identified a business opportunity', 'idea generation and interpersonal skills' and 'business patents and copyright' (members' survey, June 1998). However, only 52 per cent of respondents felt that the forum had helped them with their business in some way, 37 per cent replying that it had not. For some more established members, the forum was perceived as seeming to 'meet the needs of those not already in business than those who have started up' and there were demands 'to allow people who already have ideas to go away into a corner of the room to network with like-minded people' (members' survey, June 1998). Yet there is also evidence that the forum was changing and starting to meet the members' social needs. Typical benefits were listed as 'mutual support', 'meeting people with similar interests', 'speaking to like-minded people', 'help sustain motivation in an otherwise lonely environment', 'like-minded co-members', 'meeting others and learning from them'; and 'meeting similar people has given me confidence and a morale boost' (members' survey, June 1998).

By the time of the final survey, the members' satisfaction levels are high, despite the fall in membership number (see Figure 1.2).

The detailed responses describing the types of benefits gained reflected a broad range of benefits, including 'confidence' (R8, R24, R29), 'motivation' (R17), 'personal development' (R13, R17, R29), 'customers' (R14), 'contacts and suppliers' (R1, R11, R15, R21) and 'ideas' (R7, R15, R17, R30). Overall, however, the respondents appeared to indicate more personal benefits than tangible business benefits. It was the social

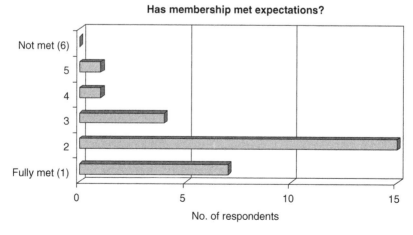

Figure 1.2   Satisfaction levels – 2002 survey

interaction between members which was valued, and the opportunity to network and interact with peers which was critical. The mature business owner appeared to seek a social network, 'peer group support' (R30), 'like-minded business people' (R5) and 'contact with kindred spirits' (R16). This is evidenced by the interview and survey responses:

> 'I'm looking for people with maturity and intelligence. They are a personal network as opposed to an opportunity to make money out of' (R28);
> 'The main benefits have been social in that as a self-employed, one-man-band it is nice to meet people in the same situation' (interviewee 1);
> 'I'd rather exchange notes with fellow entrepreneurs and pool our own expertise' (R17); and
> 'Time is quite precious but the people I've got to know – sometimes I just go for the networking even though the subject is not that exciting' (R21).

The forum had changed to allow its small business owner members to share learning experiences and to interact in a favourable environment. The entrepreneurial learning process has become embedded in the relationships themselves, which is consistent with the literature on experiential learning. The development of a personalized exchange network with peers has been shown to help entrepreneurs learn and overcome the liability of newness and help diminish feelings of isolation and loneliness. The forum appears to have met this need and the emphasis as it moves forward will be on 'buddying, or mentoring or banging heads together' (interviewee 1).

The 'network' was created by a local enterprise company as a forum for individuals who were considering business start-up to share business ideas. The forum complied with the strategic objectives of the enterprise agency in that it would serve as a catalyst for new business start-ups and was a much formalized, top-down approach to networking, simply creating an arena where like-minded people could receive and exchange ideas and information. This very instrumental approach appeared to be premised on the assumption that a network was based on transactions, albeit with potential for reciprocity and mutualized self-interest.

Although originally highly 'artificial', in the sense that the network was manufactured, a top-down creation, the data demonstrates that the network quickly took on a meaning and purpose of its own. The nature of ties changed from purely calculative; ownership and organization of the network was wrested from the enterprise company and invested in network members. Eventually the network had changed completely, in structure, members, purpose and the bonds between members. Self-interest had given way to joint interest, network membership benefits were described in terms of mutual support and transactional benefits were almost entirely replaced by deferred reciprocity. Network links became affective ties, built upon social relationships.

The analysis (Table 1.4) indicates that the network evolved into its current format reflecting changes in the underlying network need and reflecting the social context of the network members. There was an evolution from generating ideas to a mutual support mechanism, and as the network passed through its different phases, it matured, and the strength of the ties became more crucial (Figure 1.3).

CONCLUSIONS

Neergard and Ulhoi (2006) found that government agency may destroy existing cooperative arrangements. From the study reported here it can be argued that, at least initially, the agency performed an important broker role (Aldrich, 1989), providing an extensive network of contacts which was key in marketing the forum, organizing speakers, providing added value for members and facilitating networking opportunities. However, latterly, the agency perceived 'networking' to entail name badges, membership directories, notice boards and 'a networking event on a big scale . . . with gingham table cloths, candles, wines and cheeses' (minutes, August 2000). These are simply mechanisms which might facilitate the act of networking. They could also, of course, be read as a collection of symbolic artefacts redolent of the public sector origins of the agency, and as such, unlikely to promote a positive response in entrepreneurs. It seems then that the enterprise agency was either not aware of the significance of interaction, or that they simply did what they could in the ways that matched their strategic objectives. What is evident is that it may not be possible to 'create' a real entrepreneurial network in this way. Networks seem to be about the people within them and are operated by the networking process; itself a relational dimension. These characteristics and processes cannot be imposed or created artificially; they emerge. Yet, over time, the network did evolve into something the members found very useful. In many ways the evolved network matches what the literature describes as a social network. Indeed, the outcomes – identity, social learning and enactable environments – are the characteristics of a viable social network.

The findings demonstrate that networking is a social process. When this network was only about opportunity driven ties, many of the members became involved in transforming it from a resource-based view. If what we have noted is actually evolution, it could be argued that natural selection

Table 1.4   *Analysis of network evolution*

	Nature of network	Purpose and content	Type of network tie	Characteristics	Governance
Phase 1	Functionalist	Own interest and about tapping resources	Calculative	Purposeful	Hierarchy
Phase 2	Instrumental	Realization of shared benefits, confidence and identity building	Instrumental and normative	Reciprocity, learning from others	Shared values
Phase 3	Altruistic? But certainly socially based	Learning and enactment	Affective	Emergence of deferred reciprocity, emotional bonds and attraction	Trust? But voluntaristic

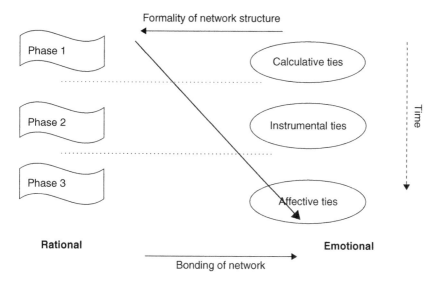

Figure 1.3   Strength of ties during network evolution

favours social networks! This is arguable because although the social context changed, this was also related to the underlying change in the members' needs. From a Lamarckian evolutionary perspective the species changed as well as the environment. Nonetheless, change is reflected in the network content and structure, which constantly shifted to fit its members' needs. The network will not satisfy all of its members all of the time; certainly, the forum's present development into a small, strong-tie network will not suit those seeking a larger network of indirect ties to substantially increase their access to information. However, it is argued that 'networking involves expanding one's circle of trust' (Aldrich 1989: 108) and this involves nurturing casual, weak ties into strong ties. This appears to be the process that we observed. While similar findings have been made for dyadic ties moving from weak and instrumental to strong and multiplex (Larson 1992; Johannisson et al. 1994; Jack et al. 2004), this is the first time that a similar dynamic has been identified at the level of the network itself.

While previous work within the entrepreneurship, economic and industrial marketing literature has recognized the need to examine exchange relationships (Mitchell 1969; Grannovetter 1985; Casson 1990; Easton and Håkansson 1996; Denrell et al. 2003; Ford et al. 2003; Biggart and Delbridge 2004; Casson and Guista 2007), in this chapter a detailed discussion is provided which demonstrates what happens within exchange relations and also considers the development of a network. The findings, therefore, have a number of implications for network research. The key implication from this study is that theory, which prioritizes networks as primarily based on resources, is much too narrow. Resource dependency is a key aspect and undoubtedly a motivation to network, however, what seems to make the 'net' work is the interactions and these are based on social factors: affinity, shared attitudes and trust. Theory, which tries to explain from purely a functional perspective, cannot encompass what it means to network. Attempts to chart this network, with all the caveats that must accrue to a single study, suggest that networking may have a calculative instrumental purpose which provides a guide to how structures evolve. However, the process of networking is profoundly social. It is based on knowledge of the other and derived through interaction that satisfies human rather than material needs. Thus the network process is emotional. In consequence it can be argued that while networks may emerge from a rational instrumental concern to extend resources, the bonding process that characterizes how networks work is less about reciprocity of resources but more about social exchange and mutuality.

With this study, we have arrived at understanding by using the constant comparative technique. Glaser and Strauss described the constant comparison method as following four distinct stages. These are (1) comparing incidents applicable to each category, (2) integrating categories and their properties, (3) delimiting the theory, and (4) writing the theory. According to Goetz and Le Compte (1981: 58) this method 'combines inductive category coding with a simultaneous comparison of all social incidents observed'. As social phenomena are recorded and classified, they are also compared across categories. Thus, hypothesis generation (relationship discovery) begins with the analysis of initial observations (Goetz and Le Compte 1981: 58). This process undergoes continuous refinement throughout the data collection and analysis process, continuously feeding back into the process of category coding; as events are constantly compared with previous events, new topological dimensions, as well as new relationships, may be discovered (Goetz and Le Compte 1981: 58).

It has been said that the constant comparative technique follows the principles of grounded theory (Easterby Smith et al. 2008). Given it is a technique that is based on direct observation and personal contact and tends to involve the use of interviews and looks to identify new cases and settings which will stretch theory (Easterby Smith et al. 2008), this seems an appropriate view. However, we would argue that the constant comparative technique is aligned more with analytic induction than grounded theory, although it might be seen to borrow ideas from both perspectives. It has significant differences because it generates and tests theory provisionally, focuses on causation and requires that all data be tested against the hypothesis while grounded theory focuses on generation and constant comparison (http://clinfowiki.org/wiki/index.php/Analytic_Induction, accessed 7 August 2013).

Furthermore while the constant comparative technique is often referred to as a method, we would argue that it is actually a technique, which works for analysing data and explaining social situations, links and relationships because it allows for flexibility and adaptability. It is not an easy task technique to use because it relies on the ability of the researcher to work the data. It is based on trial and error, can be very time-consuming, and it is hard and a bit messy, especially in the initial stages. It is useful if researchers are theoretically sensitized and so have the skills, ability and awareness required for carrying out qualitative research (Glaser and Strauss 1967; Strauss and Corbin 1998). This can impact on the interviews and extent of information generated, but it is important to remain neutral and non-judgemental and report things in an unbiased and balanced way (Hoepfl 1997).

What we have shown in this chapter is that the constant comparative technique is not easy to do. It relies on the ability of the researcher to really 'work' the data. It is based on trial and error and can be very time-consuming. It is also very messy, especially in the initial stages and, when attempting it for the first time, the messiness can be difficult to deal with. However, we have also shown that when used appropriately it is an extremely effective technique for developing understanding about the entrepreneur and the processes in which he or she is immersed.

NOTE

1. This chapter was previously published in the *International Small Business Journal*, **28** (4), 315–37, as an article titled 'An entrepreneurial network evolving: patterns of change'. Reprinted with permission.

REFERENCES

Aldrich, H.E. (1989), 'Networking among women entrepreneurs', in O. Hagan, C. Rivchun and D. Sexton (eds), *Women-owned Businesses*, New York: Praeger, pp. 103–32.
Aldrich, H.E. (2001), 'Who wants to be an evolutionary theorist; remarks on the occasion of the year 2000', *Journal of Management Enquiry*, **10** (2), 115–27.
Aldrich, H.E. and C. Zimmer (1986), 'Entrepreneurship through social networks', in D. Sexton and R. Smilor (eds), *Art and Science of Entrepreneurship*, Cambridge, MA: Ballinger, pp. 3–23.
Alvesson, M. and K. Sköldberg (2000), *Reflexive Methodology: New Vistas for Qualitative Research*, London: Sage Publications.

Anderson, A.R. and S.L. Jack (2002), 'The articulation of entrepreneurial social capital: content and process', *Entrepreneurship and Regional Development*, **14** (3), 193–210.

Anderson, A.R., J. Park and S.L. Jack (2007), 'Entrepreneurial social capital; conceptualizing social capital in new high-tech firms', *International Small Business Journal*, **25** (3), 243–67.

Anderson, A.R., S. Drakopoulou Dodd and S.L. Jack (2010), 'Network practices and entrepreneurial growth', *Scandinavian Journal of Management*, **26** (2), 121–33.

Anderson, J.C., H. Håkansson and J. Johanson (1994), 'Dyadic business relationships within a business network context', *Journal of Marketing*, **58** (4), 1–15.

Arias, J.T.G. (1995), 'Do networks foster innovation', *Management Decision*, **33** (9), 52–6.

Arocena, J. (1984), 'Le Genie et le Carnet D'Adresses' ('The genie and the address book'), *Autrement*, 59 (April), 182–7.

Barnir, A. and K. Smith (2002), 'Interfirm alliances in the small business: the role of social networks', *Journal of Small Business Management*, **40** (3), 219–32.

Biggart, N. and R. Delbridge (2004), 'Systems of exchange', *Academy of Management Review*, **29** (1), 28–49.

Birley, S. (1985), 'The role of networks in the entrepreneurial process', *Journal of Business Venturing*, **1** (1), 107–17.

Blackburn, R.A., J. Curran and A. Woods (1990), *Exploring Enterprise Cultures: Small Service Sector Owners and Their Views*, Kingston upon Thames: Small Business Research Centre, Kingston University.

Bøllingtoft, A. (2007), 'A critical realist approach to quality in observational studies', in H. Neergaard and J.P. Ulhoi (eds), *Handbook of Qualitative Research Methods in Entrepreneurship*, Cheltenham, UK and Northampton, MA, USA: Edward Elgar, pp. 406–33.

Borgatti, S.P. (2002), 'The state of organizational social network research today', available at: www.analytictech.com/mb874/Borgatti%2020The%20state%20of%20organizational%20network%20research%202.doc (accessed 23 February 2006).

Borgatti, S.P. and P.C. Foster (2003), 'The network paradigm in organization research', *Journal of Management*, **29** (5), 991–1013.

Brüderl, J. and P. Preisendörfer (1998), 'Network support and the success of newly founded businesses', *Small Business Economics*, **10** (3), 213–25.

Burrell, G. and G. Morgan (1979), *Sociological Paradigms and Organizational Analysis*, London: Heinemann Educational Books.

Carsrud, A.L. and R.W. Johnson (1989), 'Entrepreneurship: a social psychological perspective', *Entrepreneurship & Regional Development*, **1** (1), 21–31.

Casson, M. (1990), *Enterprise and Competitiveness*, Oxford: Clarendon.

Casson, M. and M. Guista (2007), 'Entrepreneurship and social capital: analysing the impact of social networks on entrepreneurial activity from a rational action perspective', *International Small Business Journal*, **25** (3), 220–44.

Chell, E. and Baines, S. (2000), 'Networking, entrepreneurship and micro business behaviour', *Entrepreneurship & Regional Development*, **12** (3), 195–215.

Chell, E. and J.M. Haworth (1992), 'The development of a research paradigm for the investigation of entrepreneurship: some methodological issues', *Proceedings of UIC/AMA Research Symposium on Marketing and Entrepreneurship*, INSEAD, France, June, pp. 1–15.

Coviello, N.E. (2005), 'Integrating qualitative and quantitative techniques in network analysis', *Qualitative Marketing Research: An International Journal*, **8** (1), 39–60.

Curran, J. and R. Blackburn (1994), *Small Firms and Local Economic Networks: The Death of the Local Economy*, London: Paul Chapman.

Curran, J. and R. Blackburn (2001), *Researching the Small Enterprise*, London: Sage.

Davidsson, P. and B. Honig (2003), 'The role of human and social capital among nascent entrepreneurs', *Journal of Business Venturing*, 18 (3), 301–31.

De Koning, A.J. (1999), 'Opportunity formation from a socio-cognitive perspective', paper presented at Babson College/Kauffman Foundation Entrepreneurship Research Conference, Columbia, SC, May.

Denrell, J., C. Fang and S. Winter (2003), 'The economics of strategic opportunity', *Strategic Management Journal*, **24** (10), 977–90.

Drakopolou Dodd, S., S.L. Jack and A.R. Anderson (2002), 'Scottish entrepreneurial networks in an international context', *International Small Business Journal*, **20** (2), 213–19.

Easterby Smith, M., R. Thorpe and P.R. Jackson (2008), *Management Research*, 3rd edn, London: Sage.

Easton, G. (1995), 'Methodology and industrial networks', in K. Möller and D.T. Wilson (eds), *Business Marketing: An Interaction and Network Perspective*, Norwell, MA: Kluwer Academic, pp. 411–91.

Easton, G. and H. Håkansson (1996), 'Markets as networks: editorial introduction', *International Journal of Research in Marketing*, **13** (5), 407–13.

Eisenhardt, K.M. (1989), 'Building theories from case study research', *Academy of Management Review*, **14** (4), 532–50.

Etzioni, A. (1988), *The Moral Dimension, Towards a New Economics*, New York: Free Press.

Finch, J. (2002), 'The role of grounded theory in developing economic theory', *Journal of Economic Methodology*, **9** (2), 213–34.

Fombrun, C.J. (1982), 'Strategies for network research in organizations', *Academy of Management Review*, **7** (2), 280–91.

Ford, D., L.-E. Gadde, H. Håkansson and I. Snehota (2003), *Managing Business Relationships*, Chichester: John Wiley.

Foss, L. (1994), 'Entrepreneurship: the impact of human capital, a social network and business resources on start-up', unpublished PhD thesis, Norwegian School of Economics and Business Administration, Bergen.

Gadde, L.E., L. Huemer and H. Håkansson (2003), 'Strategizing in industrial networks', *Industrial Marketing Management*, **32** (5), 357–65.

Gioia, D. and E. Pitre (1990), 'Multiple perspectives on theory building', *Academy of Management Review*, **15** (4), 584–602.

Glaser, B. and A. Strauss (1967), *The Discovery of Grounded Theory: Strategies for Qualitative Research*, New York: Aldine.

Goertz, J.P. and M.D. Le Compte (1981), 'Ethnographic research and the problem of data reduction', *Anthropology and Education Quarterly*, **12** (1), 51–70.

Granovetter, M. (1973), 'The strength of weak ties', *American Journal of Sociology*, **78** (6), 1360–80.

Granovetter, M. (1985), 'Economic action and social structure: the problem of embeddedness', *American Journal of Sociology*, **91** (3), 481–510.

Grant, P. and L. Perren (2002), 'Small business and entrepreneurial research: meta-theories, paradigms and prejudices', *International Small Business Journal*, **20** (2), 185–211.

Greve, A. and J.W. Salaff (2003), 'Social networks and entrepreneurship', *Entrepreneurship Theory and Practice*, **28** (1), 1–22.

Halinen, A. and J. A. Tornroos (2005), 'Using case study methods in the study of contemporary business networks', *Journal of Business Research*, **58** (9), 1285–97.

Hansen, E.L. (1995), 'Entrepreneurial networks and new organisation growth', *Entrepreneurship Theory and Practice*, **19** (4), 7–19.

Hill, J., P. McGowan and P. Drummond (1999), 'The development and application of a qualitative approach to researching the marketing networks of small firm entrepreneurs', *Qualitative Market Research*, **2** (2), 71–81.

Hite, J.M. (2005), 'Evolutionary processes and paths of relationally embedded network ties in emerging entrepreneurial firms', *Entrepreneurship: Theory and Practice*, **29** (1), 113–44.

Hite, J.M. and W.S. Hesterly (2001), 'The evolution of firm networks: from emergence to early growth of the firm', *Strategic Management Journal*, **22** (3), 275–86.

Hoang, H. and B. Antoncic (2003), 'Network-based research in entrepreneurship: a critical review', *Journal of Business Venturing*, **18** (2), 165–87.

Hoepfl, M.C. (1997), 'Choosing qualitative research: a primer for technology education researchers', *Journal of Technology Education*, **9** (1), 47–63.

Huggins, R. (2000), 'The success and failure of policy-implanted inter-firm network initiatives: motivations, processes and structure', *Entrepreneurship & Regional Development*, **12** (2), 11–135.

Human, S. and K. Provan (1996), 'External resource exchange and perceptions of competitiveness within organizational networks: an organizational learning perspective', *Frontiers of Entrepreneurship Research*, Wellesley, MA: Babson College, available at: www.babson.edu/entrep/fer/papers96/human/ (accessed 15 June 2015).

Jack, S. (2009), 'Approaches to studying networks: implications and outcomes', *Journal of Business Venturing*, **25** (1), 120–37.

Jack, S., S. Drakopoulou Dodd and A. Anderson (2008), 'Change and the development of entrepreneurial networks over time: a processual perspective', *Entrepreneurship & Regional Development*, **20** (2), 125–59.

Jack, S.L. and A.R. Anderson (2002), 'The effects of embeddedness on the entrepreneurial process', *Journal of Business Venturing*, **17** (5), 467–87.

Jack, S.L., S.D. Dodd and A.R. Anderson (2004), 'Social structures and entrepreneurial networks: the strength of strong ties', *International Journal of Entrepreneurship and Innovation*, **5** (2), 107–20.

Johannisson, B. (1986), 'Network strategies: management technology for entrepreneurship and change', *International Small Business Journal*, **5** (1), 19–30.

Johannisson, B. (1987), 'Beyond process and structure: social exchange networks', *International Studies of Management and Organisation*, **17** (1), 3–23.

Johannisson, B. (1988), 'Business formation: a network approach', *Scandinavian Journal of Management*, **49** (3/4), 83–99.

Johannisson, B. (1996), 'The dynamics of entrepreneurial networks', *Frontiers of Entrepreneurship Research*, Wellesley, MA: Babson College, available at: www.babson.edu/entrep/fer/papers96/johannis/ (accessed 5 August 2013).

Johannisson, B., O. Alexanderson, K. Nowicki and K. Senneseth (1994), 'Beyond anarchy and organization: entrepreneurs in contextual networks', *Entrepreneurship & Regional Development*, **6** (3), 329–56.

Johannisson, B. and M. Mønsted (1997), 'Contextualizing entrepreneurial networking', *International Journal of Management and Organization*, **27** (3), 109–37.

Johannisson, B. and A. Nilsson (1989), 'Community entrepreneurs: networking for local development', *Entrepreneurship & Regional Development*, **1** (1), 3–19.

Johannisson, B. and R. Peterson (1984), 'The personal networks of entrepreneurs', paper presented at the ICSB Conference, Ryerson Polytechnical Institute, Toronto.

Johanson, J. and L. Mattsson (1987), 'Interorganisational relations in industrial systems: a network approach compared with a transaction cost approach', *International Studies of Management and Organisation*, **17** (1), 34–48.

Larson, A. (1992), 'Network dyads in entrepreneurial settings: a study of the governance of exchange relationships', *American Science Quarterly*, **37** (1), 76–104.

Larson, A. and J. Starr (1993), 'A network model of organization formation', *Entrepreneurship Theory and Practice*, (Winter), 5–15.

Lechner, C. and M. Dowling (2003), 'Firm networks: external relationships as sources for the growth and competitiveness of entrepreneurial firms', *Entrepreneurship & Regional Development*, **15** (1), 1–26.

Mitchell, J.C. (1969), 'The concept and use of social networks', in J.C. Mitchell (ed.), *Social Networks in Urban Situations*, Manchester: Manchester University Press, pp. 1–50.

Neergaard, H. and J. Ulhoi (2006), 'Transformation of interorganizational entrepreneurial networks', *Entrepreneurship Theory and Practice*, **30** (4), 519–39.

Neergaard, H., E. Shaw and S. Carter (2005), 'The impact of gender, social capital and networks on business ownership: a research agenda', *International Journal of Entrepreneurial Behaviour and Research*, **11** (5), 338–57.

O'Donnell, A., A. Gilmore, D. Cummins and D. Carson (2001), 'The network construct in entrepreneurship research: a review and critique', *Management Decision*, **39** (9), 749–60.

Ostgaard, T.A. and S. Birley (1994), 'Personal networks and firm competitive strategy – a strategic or coincidental match?', *Journal of Business Venturing*, **9** (4), 281–305.

Schutjens, V. and E. Stam (2003), 'The evolution and nature of young firm networks: a longitudinal perspective', *Small Business Economics*, **21** (2), 115–34.

Scottish Enterprise (1993), *Improving the Business Birth Rate: A Strategy for Scotland*, Glasgow: Scottish Enterprise.

Shaw, E. (2006), 'Small firm networking. An insight into contents and motivating factors', *International Small Business Journal*, **24** (1), 5–29.

Silverman, D. (2000), *Doing Qualitative Research*, London: Sage.

Singh, R.P., G.E. Hills, G.T. Lumpkin and R.C. Hybels (1999), 'The entrepreneurial opportunity recognition process: examining the role of self-perceived alertness and social networks', paper presented at the 1999 Academy of Management Meeting, Chicago, IL.

Steier, L. and R. Greenwood (1995), 'Venture capital relationships in the deal structure and post-investment stages of new firm creation', *Journal of Management Studies*, **32** (3), 337–58.

Strauss, A.L. and J. Corbin (1998), *The Basics of Quality Research*, 2nd edn, London: Sage Publications.

Szarka, J. (1990), 'Networking and small firms', *International Small Business Journal*, **8** (2), 10–22.

Uzzi, B. (1997), 'Social structure and competition in interfirm networks: the paradox of embeddedness', *American Science Quarterly*, **42** (1), 35–67.

Wolcott, H.F. (1990), 'Writing up qualitative research', *Qualitative Research Methods Series 20*, Thousand Oaks, CA: Sage Publications.

Yin, R.K. (1994), *Case Study Research: Design and Methods*, 2nd edn, Thousand Oaks, CA: Sage.

Zeleny, M. (2001), 'Autopoiesis (self-production) in SME networks', *Human Systems Management*, **20** (3), 201–7.

Zhang, J. and C. Lin (2005), 'Changing structures of SME networks: lessons from the publishing industry in Taiwan', *Long Range Planning*, **38** (2), 145–62.

2 Using constant comparison as a method of analysis in entrepreneurship research
Susan M. Smith and Edward McKeever

INTRODUCTION

Until the mid-1990s, research in the area of entrepreneurship was often described as a mono-method field, heavily reliant on surveys and questionnaires (Aldrich 1992). This focus on 'numbers' and the dominance of a positivist paradigm has been explained by the existence of a more or less dominant set of philosophical assumptions and associated methodological procedures (Silverman 2001; Bryman and Bell 2003). In terms of distinctiveness, positivist or natural scientific inquiry is best understood in terms of a desire to deduce and measure the nature of reality and represent it in quantifiable terms (Zaner 1970; Bryman 1988). Since the turn of the millennium however, entrepreneurship and small business journals have started to reflect a growing openness to new philosophies and methods of inquiry (Gartner and Birley 2002). This increased maturity and tolerance of previously unorthodox approaches has been explained in part as a reflection of the philosophical and methodological sophistication of a growing body of interpretive business research (Anderson 2000; Cope 2005a; Jack 2005). It also reflects a shift in the types of questions being asked by researchers with roots in the more established social sciences relating to the 'how', 'why', 'when' and 'where' surrounding entrepreneurship and the contexts in which it takes place (Chell and Pittaway 1998; Kodithuwakku and Rosa 2002). Gartner and Birley (2002) have commented that this represents the progression of qualitative research from being a 'special case' to being recognized as a useful and coherent method of exploring the rich and complex phenomenon of entrepreneurship.

Cope (2005b) argued that the increased acceptance of research adopting interpretivist methodologies represents the growing tendency and ability of researchers to plausibly demonstrate the progression from research philosophy, to methodology, to findings in their work. In spite of this progress, even advocates of an interpretive perspective with an emphasis on qualitative methods have recognized some of the weaknesses in the approach (Huberman and Miles 2002). The most common criticisms are that qualitative research: (1) is often an assemblage of anecdotal evidence and personal impressions, (2) is strongly subject to researcher bias, (3) is difficult to reproduce, and (4) is lacking in terms of generalizability (Hycner 1985). It is also a common view that qualitative methods tend to generate detailed understanding of a small number of settings (Hycner 1985; Cope 2005b). Mays and Pope (1995) contend that these criticisms are often compounded when researchers neglect to give adequate descriptions in their reports of their assumptions and methods, particularly with regard to data analysis. While these types of concerns are not new, their persistence reflects a general desire among the qualitative research community to rigorously demonstrate how their philosophical commitments to rich and honest interpretation can be translated into a commonly recognized methodological approach (Bygrave 1989). Among sociologists, social anthropologists and management scholars in particular, the constant comparison method has emerged as a potentially unifying principle for dealing consistently with what Dye et al. (2000) have called the kaleidoscopic messiness of qualitative data. Despite being well received by a paradigmatic core, Cope (2005a) argued that more work needs to be done to make the approach a better understood part of the entrepreneurship researcher's methodological arsenal.

Glaser (1965) originally saw the constant comparison method as a set of procedures guiding (but not necessarily determining) the qualitative analysis of behaviour and experience as well as context, allowing behaviour and experience to be made meaningful to the outsider (Geertz 1973). In this sense the core aim of the constant comparison method is to provide what Holstein and Gubrium (1994) call an honest and uncompromised interpretation of both actions and their meanings from the perspective of participants. Despite being rooted in the work of the pioneers of grounded theory (Glaser 1965; Glaser and Strauss 1967), supporters and critics have highlighted the need for the current generation of scholars to remain cognizant of their philosophical and methodological responsibilities and the importance of rigour in their work (Baxter and Eyles 1997; Silverman 2005). Aware that philosophical and methodological inattention may represent the Achilles heel of interpretivist entrepreneurship research, we feel that the time is now right for work which offers researchers some practical guidance in the practicalities of methodology, and which can only contribute to the overall quality and rigour of research within the field.

QUALITATIVE RESEARCH IN ENTREPRENEURSHIP

Cope (2005) has argued that while a well-established interpretive tradition exists within the wider social sciences, it is only in recent years that interpretive research in entrepreneurship and small business has emerged. For example, Bouchikhi (1993) used an interpretive perspective and qualitative techniques to explore how entrepreneurs understood and experienced the pursuit of performance. Chell and Pittaway (1998) employed a similar approach to understand the role of critical incidents in the way restaurateurs developed their businesses, while Costello (1996) used in-depth case studies to explore 'learning and routines' in high-technology small and medium-sized enterprises (SMEs). More recently, Jack (2005) used a qualitative approach to explore in depth the role, use and activation of strong and weak ties (Granovetter 1973). Within these studies, the complex nature of the topics under investigation required the use of a range of qualitative techniques for data gathering and analysis. As Curran and Blackburn (2001) suggest, qualitative methods are best suited to exploring subject areas where limited previous knowledge exists. Stewart (1990: 148) predicted that this should not surprise the emerging field of entrepreneurship, where the term itself seems to be emerging 'less a concept than a prize in a definitional free-for-all'. These examples demonstrate a collective commitment to exploring the rich complexity of how entrepreneurs experience and give meaning to their venturing activities. The ground-breaking nature of this work has led to the development of a growing paradigmatic community of interpretivist research as the approach becomes applied to a growing range of phenomena including entrepreneurial learning (Rae 2000), new venture creation (Steyaert 1998), entrepreneurial failure (Cope 2003), networks and social capital (Jack 2005), female entrepreneurship (DeBruin et al. 2007) and social enterprise (Haugh 2005). Table 2.1 provides a selection of research, which has been conducted to date using the constant comparison method.

Based on the views and concerns outlined above, the purpose of this chapter is to provide a practical guide for entrepreneurship scholars interested in adopting the constant comparison method in their work. To do this the rest of the chapter is structured as follows. First we provide an overview of the principles underpinning the constant comparison approach, and its emergence as a social scientific method. This is followed by a section outlining in some detail the steps involved in applying the constant comparison method in qualitative investigation. In the final section the stages of constant comparison are brought to life by drawing reflectively on a piece of qualitative research within a peer learning community of entrepreneurs. In keeping with the tradition of Glaser (1965),

Table 2.1   *Research using constant comparison in management and entrepreneurship*

Author	Subject	Findings
Crozier (1964)	The bureaucratic phenomenon	The necessity for members of different internal groups to live together. Differential power allows the bureaucracy to function rather than destroy itself
Kanter (1977)	Androcentric management practices	While a management career is presented as gender neutral – in reality it is based on male life–work patterns
Stewart (1989)	Team entrepreneurship	A team atmosphere firms can stretch their innovation ambitions and stretch the efficiency with which they employ resources
Chell and Pittaway (1998)	Critical incidents in business development	Operational considerations and incidents regarding business development were the most dominant topics discussed by business owners
Shaw (1999)	Networks and small firm development	Information, advice, bartering-exchanges and normative expressions were contained within each firm's social network
Rae (2000)	Entrepreneurial learning	Findings indicate benefits from designing development programmes for current and aspirant business owners with a greater emphasis on personal development
Anderson and Jack (2002)	Entrepreneurial social capital	Social capital is not a thing but a process. Creating a mutual condition for the effective exchange of information and resources
Haugh (2005)	Social enterprise	Unclear understanding of the value contribution, management practices, and business models of social enterprise
Cope (2011)	Learning from failure	Failure provides powerful learning outcomes that are future oriented, and which increase the entrepreneur's preparedness for further activity

Hycner (1985), Thompson et al. (1989) and Cope (2003), we feel that that this chapter should be read as a set of guidelines and not as a series of rules on the way research should be conducted. It is therefore not our intention to advocate one method of analysis, but instead to offer a guide to one way of working with and making sense of qualitative data relating to the behaviour and activities of entrepreneurs.

THE PRINCIPLE OF CONSTANT COMPARISON IN QUALITATIVE RESEARCH

A key aim of qualitative inquiry is to generate an interpreted understanding of the subjective nature of lived experience from the perspective of those experiencing it (Corbin and Strauss 1990). This is achieved by exploring the meanings and explanations that individuals attribute to their experiences and actions (Denzin and Lincoln 2003). At a general level, commentators have argued that meanings are socially constructed and that the central goal of the qualitative researcher is to uncover and interpret these meanings (Merriam and Associates 2002). From an analytical perspective, Geertz (1983: 9) argued that what qualitative researchers call data are really constructions or 'thick descriptions' of other people's constructions of what they and those around them are up to. Geertz (1973) felt that these rich contextual descriptions should be understood as the descriptive interpretation of contextually grounded behaviour. This purposeful interpretation has been described as an exciting and at times daunting exercise, often producing large amounts of spoken and observed data codified through the written word (Denzin and Lincoln 1998). According to Guba and Lincoln (1989) the challenge facing qualitative researchers is to provide a trustworthy interpretation of phenomena, and to convince the reader of the plausibility of the theory offered. Cronbach (1982) insisted that the plausibility of the conclusion is what counts, and that this lies metaphorically in the ear of the beholder.

According to Glaser and Strauss (1967), constant comparison provides a structured basis for generating theory, which is 'true-to' or 'grounded' in the data. In the words of Tesch (1990: 96): 'The main intellectual tool is comparison. The method of comparing and contrasting is used for practically all intellectual tasks during analysis ... The goal is to discern conceptual similarities, to refine the discriminative power of categories, and to discover patterns.' Corbin and Strauss (1990) have argued that theory which is grounded in the patterns and exceptions of the context should be capable of explaining as well as describing behavioural phenomena. It should also seek to determine 'how' and 'why' actors respond to changing conditions and to the consequences of their actions. An early example of this is Glaser and Strauss's (1965) exploration of how individuals experience death. Corbin and Strauss (1990) go so far as to argue that it is the researcher's responsibility to capture this context specificity as authentically as possible. It is within the reality of those being studied (whether they are dying or behaving entrepreneurially) that constant comparison has been described as a process of 'double fitting', where conceptual images are generated, and then shaped and reshaped according to ongoing observations (Glaser and Strauss 1967; Ambert et al. 1995). In his original work, Glaser (1965: 483) was explicit about what constant comparison was and was not:

> The constant comparison method is *not* designed (as methods of quantitative analysis are) to guarantee that two analysts working independently with the same data will achieve the same results; it *is* designed to allow, with discipline, for some of the vagueness and flexibility which aid the creative generation of theory.

The procedures and principles of constant comparison have subsequently been described as a means of assisting, systematizing and supplementing the abilities of analysts in generating theory which is integrated, consistent and plausible (Guba and Lincoln 1989).

By focusing on comparison, the researcher is led to tasks appropriate to developing a theory more or less inductively, categorizing, coding, defining and delineating categories and connecting them. According to Boeije (2002), this implies that constant comparison goes hand in hand with theoretical sampling where the researcher decides which data will be gathered next and where to locate them on the basis of developing theoretical ideas. In this evolutionary sense it is possible to unearth and answer additional questions during data collection and analysis. Boeije (2002: 393) explained that such questions: 'concern interpretations of phenomena as well as boundaries of categories, assigning segments or finding relations between categories. The data in hand are then analysed again and compared with the new data'. This cycle of comparison and reflection can happen as many times as is necessary until new cases do not add anything new to the analysis, and where categories can be considered saturated. While the literature outlined above describes the logic and ambitions of those advocating the constant comparison method, they provide little guidance on how one should go about its practice.

DOING CONSTANT COMPARISON

At the most extreme some authors advise researchers to compare each piece of data with every other piece of relevant data (Morse and Field 1998). Boeije (2002) sees this type of blanket guidance as impractical and even unhelpful, since the question of what are 'relevant' data remains unaddressed. In this sense the majority of work to date on constant comparison has been limited to describing its function, with little work focusing on the actual procedures involved. Boeije (2002: 394), one of only a few contributions on this topic, has argued that 'There is more to this

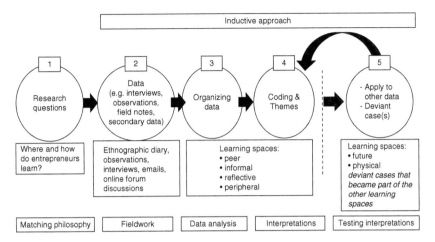

Figure 2.1   The process of constant comparison in qualitative research

process than just comparing everything that crosses the researcher's path. The lack of clear cut questions and a prior coding system means that data have to be produced by the researcher in the course of the study'. This is supported by the views of Eisenhardt (1989) and Baxter and Eyles (1997) who argue that scholars, whether in the geosciences, sociology or entrepreneurship require additional guidance in how to produce theory. They see this happening predominantly in the data analysis stage, and a critical way of demonstrating both the rigour and quality of qualitative work. It is this understanding which now leads us to outline our stepwise framework. The main steps involved are portrayed in Figure 2.1.

A Stepwise Approach

Figure 2.1 provides a flow diagram illustrating the inductive logic and developmental processes typical of most qualitative research. According to Bryman (2007) this process represents a theory-building journey aimed at reconstructing the perspectives of those under investigation. For the purposes of this chapter, the theory building and journey metaphors provide an opportunity to situate the constant comparison method of analysis in the context of an actual qualitative research project. In the sections which follow we discuss each stage of Figure 2.1 in more detail.

Matching questions, philosophies and appropriate methods

According to Silverman (2005) the starting point of any qualitative research is an explicit statement of what the focus of exploration will be.

This notion of exploration, Schwandt (1994) and Hycner (1985) feel, locates interpretivist, constructivist and phenomenological modes of inquiry firmly in the context of discovery rather than justification. This manifests itself in the types of questions asked. For example, Anderson and Jack (2002) asked first how, and if, entrepreneurs form or create social capital and, second, questioned the nature of the social condition created. Similarly, Shaw (1999a: 60) set out to broadly question 'the impact that the social networks in which small service firms are embedded have upon their development'. In a third example, Cope (2005a) asked: how do entrepreneurs perceive, think about and give meaning to the process of their learning over time? This provided the basis for then questioning the dynamic relationship between organizational growth and entrepreneurial learning. These examples demonstrate researchers identifying topics and areas with little previous research attention. Ambert et al. (1995) feel that identifying a distinctive topic, captured in a broad question, provides an opportunity for researchers to then state the philosophical considerations underpinning and directing their research. However this is often neglected. Cope (2005b) feels that it is often impossible to be certain about an author's ontological or paradigmatic position. In justifying her philosophical and paradigmatic position, Shaw (1999b) argued that the nature of her research question dictated an approach capable of dealing holistically with the whole phenomenon, exploring network processes; the qualitative paradigm provided the opportunity to observe behaviour in the mundane of everyday life (Schutz 1967). Likewise, Anderson and Jack (2002) argued that, 'a qualitative approach was used because soft issues were being dealt with which are not amenable to quantification; meanings which lie behind actions, and the objectives of the research were related to understanding rather than measuring'. By matching questions with the appropriate paradigmatic perspective, researchers are able to effectively tell the reader 'why' they are going about their endeavour in a particular fashion. Penrose (1971) and Piore (1979) used this approach to justify becoming involved in the research context and connecting with the experiences and perceptions of strategy makers. Crotty (1998) felt that this early focus on matching clear research intentions with appropriate philosophies, reassures the reader, and is the first basis on which the plausibility of finding are constructed. This statement of intent and clarity of philosophical stance then provides the basis for justifying an appropriate methodology for collecting and organizing data. This provides the basis for introducing the sampling methods used to recruit participants and the techniques used to elicit meaningful data from them.

Theoretical sampling and qualitative interviewing

According to Boeije (2002) theoretical sampling goes hand in hand with the constant comparison method. The logic behind being purposeful in the pursuit of theoretically relevant and variant cases lies in seeking out a full range of information rich sources for study in-depth. According to Patton (1990) this technique enhances internal validity and works best by identifying a research context rich in interesting and informative individuals, who can expand on their experiences in the most illuminating detail. Focusing on comparison within the widest variety of exemplar cases provides the opportunity to focus on identifying similarities and differences in behaviour, motivation, experience and perception across the full spectrum of the phenomena (Cope 2005a).

Constant comparison

As the research progresses, fieldwork will produce data in various formats. By employing philosophically appropriate techniques, an array of data can emerge including interview transcripts, observational notes, field notes and secondary data. The types of data produced will depend on the choices of philosophy, epistemology and methodology derived from step 1. According to Hallberg (2006), making explicit the linkages between the research question, the philosophical stance and the data collection methods provides an added source of confidence and a trustworthy platform from which analysis can be conducted and findings presented. This leads to the next step, which is how to analyse data and how to go about using constant comparison as a method of analysis. (See all the analytical steps in Table 2.2.)

Qualitative research can produce an overwhelming amount of data. A qualitative interview of 40 minutes can easily translate into 30 pages of a written transcript. As with any research project, the researcher needs to think about what data they want to and can use and how to organize it into a suitable format amenable to the type of analysis being carried out. Using constant comparative methods is no different in this respect but it is helpful to think about presenting the data in a way which lends itself to being able to undergo a constant comparison approach. Mason (2002) writes about integrating data from different methods and sources, although equally you have data which comes from the same method (for example, interview) or source. What is important is getting the data into some form of order that makes it easier to analyse. We strongly agree with Mason's ontological integration considerations in doing this as 'you will need to ask whether your data are ontologically consistent. In other words, are they based on similar, complementary or comparable assumptions about the nature of social entities and phenomena?'

Table 2.2   *Analytical steps in the process*

Type of comparison	Analysis undertaken	Aim	Activities	Outcome
Comparison within a single interview	Open coding; summarizing the core issues raised; finding a consistent story among data fragments; getting to know and understand each participant in depth	To develop categories	Asking what is the core message of the interview? Is the interview consistent? Checking for inconsistencies or contradictions?	Interview summary Descriptive case profiles Narrative synopsis Detailed memos Data reduction
Comparison between accumulating interviews	Axial coding; developing criteria for comparing interviews; identifying conceptual patterns in the growing body of data	To conceptualize the subject To produce an emergent typology	Asking are respondents talking about the same thing? Exploring patterns of concepts and experiences? What criteria underlie this	An expansion of code words Conceptual descriptions Criteria for comparing interviews Clusters of interviews
Comparison of interviews from emerging categories	Triangulating data sources	To more clearly define categories Complete the picture Enrich the information	Cross-case 'detective work' identifying distinguishing and differentiating themes? Matching and merging explanatory themes and patterns	Verification of categories and thematic relationships Clarification of the emerging conceptual categories Richer concept level memos
Detailed comparisons made to look at the full range of experiences	Selecting themes from open coding that concern the relationship; seeking consensus on the interpretation	Conceptualization of main issues Deeper understanding of these	What are the central issues	Deeper understanding of inter-category relationships
Comparison between similar cases of the same experience	Identifying core patterns within each category Hypothesize about patterns in each category	Find criteria for comparison Produce a final typology	What are the differences between categories? What might cause these? On what criteria can experiences be compared?	Criteria for comparing categories Clusters of relationships – final typology

61

(Mason 2002: 35). When you are happy that your data is amenable both in ontological terms and in a suitable format you can begin the analysis.

You may be close to your data but simply knowing it in such a general sense is not substantial enough. As a researcher you should strive to achieve reliable and rigorous analysis, and therefore you need to find a way of looking across all the data in as neutral a way as possible. Cope (2005a) argues for a degree of naivety when approaching the data in relation to his study of how managers learn. Cope draws upon Eisenhardt (1989) who recognizes that it is impossible for researchers to start with a 'clean theoretical slate'. Constant comparison is a way of managing the analysis and working with the data in an inductive way to find meaning from the data.

Strauss and Corbin (1990) note that many qualitative researchers collect data prior to the beginning of systematic analysis. They argue that in grounded theory the analysis using constant comparison needs to be undertaken from the start because the analysis is used to direct the next process of data collection. It depends then what kind of methodology you use. To be true to grounded theory, gathering the data and then analysing it would, according to Strauss and Corbin (1990), violate the method.[1] However, constant comparison can be used outside of grounded theory and you will need to decide how it fits with your methodology and whether you are using constant comparison as analysis which informs further data collection or whether you are using it to analyse data already collected.

Data analysis is a process of what Cousin (2007) argues involves thinking with the data. Cousin (2007: 3) notes: 'This would mean refusing the claim that truths derive from thinking from the data, as if an inert pile of interview data, field notes or statistics had the agency to yield truth independently of human intervention.' Constant comparison is a method which can enable this to happen, although the researcher still needs to interpret the meanings from what the data is showing (this links to trustworthiness, which is addressed below). When you approach your data it is advisable to read through the data and ask questions of it. Do not be in a rush to conceptualize the data; descriptions will suffice. A useful way of going about this is to give each piece of data (for example, each interview transcript) a cover sheet specifying the main issues that are coming from it. This is sometimes referred to as a crib sheet. Coding is a way of enabling you to see patterns within and across the data. Chell and Pittaway (1998) argue that coding data is dependent on the aims and objectives of the research. Coding the data gives you a way of helping to interpret the data and explore meanings. Charmaz (2003: 94–5) offers a useful set of questions when working with your data and trying to find themes which can be coded:

- What is going on?
- What are people doing?
- What is the person saying?
- What do these actions and statements take for granted?
- How do structure and context serve to support, maintain, impede or change these actions and statements?

Coding

The constant comparison method needs to be carried out by analysing the data through a process of coding. It is a way of examining the qualitative data and applying codes (or labels) to them. As mentioned above, although lots of qualitative research results in text, such as interviews, you may have other data too, such as visual images or audio/video recordings. These can be coded too and will need to be consistent with how you code all of your data (within any given piece of research). The grounded theorists advocate that you need to be open minded when you approach your data and how you code them (see Glaser and Strauss 1967 and Strauss and Corbin 1990). Within grounded theory there are three types of coding:

- Open coding is the first approach of organizing the data to make some sense of it. It is an interpretive process used to break the data down analytically and categorize it. Corbin and Strauss (1990: 12) note that conceptual labels are given to similar events, actions and so on which are grouped together to form categories. By means of systematic comparisons, data are arranged in appropriate classifications (see also Wicker 1985).
- Axial coding is a way of interconnecting the categories which are coming from open coding. Strauss and Corbin (1990: 96) describe it as a set of procedures 'whereby data are put back together in new ways after open coding, by making connections between categories'.
- Selective coding is a systematic way of relating the codes to other categories in order to refine the codes, validate or refute them. It can be seen as a way of developing a story between the categories.

You can also use hierarchical coding or flat or non-hierarchical coding. Hierarchical coding involves codes with sub-codes and is sometimes referred to as tree coding with branches of sub-codes, which relate to the parent codes. Flat or non-hierarchical coding, on the other hand, arranges the codes with no sub-codes (see Strauss and Corbin 1990). Either way, the codes need to be more than just descriptive (although they may start off being so) and they need to analytical.

You may wish to use computer-aided qualitative analysis (CAQDAS) using NUD*IST, Ethnograph, ATLAS or Hypersoft, for example, as a way of indexing and managing your data. Computer-aided qualitative analysis has its place and, although it is often time-consuming, it can be a useful approach to data management. If you do decide to use such software, you need to ensure that it fits with your approach to epistemology. You need to keep in mind that the process of using constant comparison is fundamentally to help the researcher develop some theories from the data; computer packages will not develop theories, they will only manage and organize the data.

There are other ways you can code your data also that might not strictly adhere to the grounded-theory approach. Chell and Pittaway (1998) even show how coding qualitative data can lead to quantifiable data. Codes may be conceptual or they can be descriptive, perhaps they are literature or research-question led or maybe they are data led, coming from the data. Ryan and Bernard (2003) look at different ways in which coding interview data can help to find new themes in other data. However you approach coding your data, it is useful to keep a master list of all the codes that are developed which can be useful when you start looking for similar themes or testing the reliability of your interpretations across your data. Mason (2002: 155) argues there is no point in indexing just for the sake of it. The same is true when applying codes or finding themes. How you interpret your data needs to make analytic sense.

Testing interpretations, trustworthiness and crystallization

The constant comparison process is iterative and incidents, which are coded, should be compared against other incident for similarities and difference (see Corbin and Strauss 1990: 9). The constant comparative method is a process in which any newly collected data is compared with previous data that was collected in one or more earlier studies. This is a continuous ongoing procedure because theories are formed, enhanced, confirmed or even discounted as a result of any new data that emerges from the study. You want to get to a point where your data begin to stop producing new interpretations or anything new about the social process you are exploring. The process of constant comparison entails looking for irregularities, sometimes known as deviant cases or variation. Silverman (2005) argues that comprehensive data treatment involves actively seeking out and addressing anomalies or deviant cases. According to Corbin and Strauss (1990: 10) the data must be examined for regularity and for an understanding of where that regularity is not apparent.

If you are gathering new data alongside your analysis, you need to make sure that the two are working together. Knight (2002) argues that industrious data collection does not lead to good research, what is needed is purposefulness. Knight notes: 'the emphasis must be on intelligent action rather than following research recipes' (2002: 17). Such intelligent action also pertains to the reliability and validity of the research and findings. Research reliability often refers to the extent to which the findings could be reproduced if conducted on different samples (Alvesson and Deetz 2000: 68). Oakley (1999) suggests that there is a tendency among qualitative researchers who use small samples to generate insights and hypotheses to act as though their findings are applicable to populations outside the range of the research. The important point is that it is not the typicality or the representativeness of the case itself that allows us to generalize from it, but the clarity of the theoretical reasoning. Constant comparison is a good way of helping to add rigour to the trustworthiness of the data. Strauss and Corbin (1990) argue constant comparison can assist the researcher in guarding against bias. Much has been written about research bias in qualitative research (see Fetterman 1998; Coffey 1999, 2002; Krenske 2002). Writing about ethnography in qualitative research, Atkinson and Hammersley (1994: 251) note: 'Much thinking . . . in recent years has been based on a rejection of "positivism," broadly conceived as the view that social research should adopt scientific method . . . and that it consists of the rigorous testing of hypotheses by means of data that take the form of quantitative measurements.'

A better approach might be to consider the concept of trustworthiness or credibility of the research, the methods and the data analysis. The terms credibility and dependability are often used rather than validity and reliability for judgement of the quality of the research (see Kvale 1995). Adler and Adler (1994: 381) argue that observers rely on their own perception and are susceptible to bias from their own interpretation. Terms such as validity are rooted in a positivist approach to research and we argue that such labels are not necessarily the right labels for qualitative research and constant comparison to be considered rigorous. This also connects with the need for triangulation. One different way of thinking about triangulation is presented by Richardson and Adams St. Pierre (1994: 522) who argue that in postmodern research: 'we do not triangulate; we *crystallize*. We recognize that there are far more than three sides from which to approach the world' (emphasis in the original). We propose that the term 'crystallization' is better suited to qualitative research in general. Ellingson (2009: 11) states: 'crystallization depends upon including, interweaving, blending, or otherwise drawing upon more than one genre of expressing data'. Constant comparison is part of this process particularly when you are testing your interpretations and refining the labels you have given to certain themes and the number of codes you have used.

AN ILLUSTRATION OF THE STEP-BY-STEP APPROACH

This section takes the reader through a real example of how the constant comparison method was used in a study of a peer learning community of entrepreneurs. This group was made up of 25 entrepreneurs who ran micro businesses (defined as less than 20 employees). The learning community was together for 10 months on a programme specifically designed for entrepreneurs. Accordingly, they engaged in different learning interventions including master classes, one-to-one coaching, experiential events, learning and reflection sessions, and carried out a series of shadowing activities and business exchanges with one another. The programme was supported by an online discussion forum. Ethnographic research was conducted throughout the duration this learning community was together and included a virtual ethnography of the online discussion forum. Figure 2.2 depicts the research journey, which encompasses constant comparison as a method of analysis. Like Figure 2.1 above, Figure 2.2 takes the reader through the figure using the entrepreneurial context of a peer learning community.

Part A

Research questions and fieldwork

The overarching research inquiry was to explore learning within a group of entrepreneurs. The example presented draws from a research project which sought to understand the learning processes within a network of entrepreneurs, all of whom were owner-managers of small businesses across a diverse range of sectors. Research shows that networks and networking can be extremely beneficial to SMEs (see Jack 2005) and the

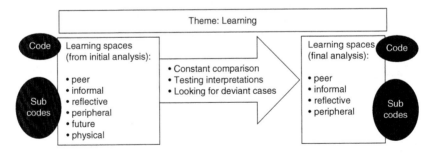

Figure 2.2   The research journey using constant comparison in the entrepreneurial context

study set out to understand the meanings and nuances associated with the learning experiences which, we argue, are socially constructed.

The research journey in this example starts with the research questions: 'where and how do entrepreneurs learn?' The questions were explored through a qualitative methodology using ethnography. The methods included participant observation and interviews supported by other data such as the researcher's own diary and reflections plus emails from the research subjects. Other forms of data included materials produced by the entrepreneurs such as visual depictions of their learning, presentations of their experiences in the learning community and written stories on the impact of the learning on their companies.

Working with the data

The analysis of the data was approached inductively which meant the analysis was concerned with theory generation rather than theory testing. Accordingly, the data analysis was underpinned by systematic process similar to grounded theory's 'methodological package'. Generally an inductive stance advocates that theory is the outcome of research. Bryman and Bell (2003: 14) argue: 'the process of induction involves drawing generalizable inferences out of observations'. The process of analysing and interpreting the data was an iterative one that involved moving between the fieldwork and literature on different theoretical perspectives. Each informed the other. This process was not straightforward and many blind alleys were explored. This is an inevitable part of any research. Coding the data enabled the data to be managed at the same time as exploring and interpreting meaning from the data.

Coding

As discussed coding is the process of identifying themes in accounts and attaching labels or codes to index them. The process of coding in this research made use of a template as a way of managing the data and grouping the themes together. Template analysis refers to a particular way of thematically analysing qualitative data. The process involves a coding 'template' which summarizes themes identified as important in the data and organizes them in a meaningful and useful manner. Themes are features which were seen as relevant to the research question. Given the analysis was inductive the process of finding themes and coding them went through iterations of modifying and applying the template, inserting new themes and deleting unwanted ones. This involved a process of prioritization while trying to maintain openness towards the data and themes. King (1998: 127) recognizes the problems of when to stop the process of development, arguing that this decision is always going to be unique to a particular project and a particular researcher. A pragmatic decision was made in that an acceptable version of the template was reached when it was felt there were no relevant parts of the data that were uncoded. It is important to note that template analysis may not be the right approach for you but you will need to think about how you are going to manage the data and how you can easily compare what is coming from the data.

The example concentrates on one of the codes, which led to sub-codes in an approach using hierarchical coding. The code under investigation was that of 'learning spaces', which hypothesized that the entrepreneurs were learning in different conceptual spaces. The idea of learning spaces emerged intuitively from a group of themes which centred around space, learning, network effects and process. The learning spaces presented here provide a different way of conceptualizing spaces and entrepreneurial learning generally. The sub-codes showed that initially there were six spaces in which learning was taking place. These were peer, social, reflective, peripheral, future and physical. These learning spaces were theorized as ways of looking at the taken for granted practices of the community and represent the social and cultural ways of being in the peer learning community of entrepreneurs. The identified learning spaces were constantly compared across the data which involved a process of data reduction and refinement and deviant cases were explored, which leads on to part B.

Part B

Testing interpretations, trustworthiness and crystallization
The next part of using constant comparison as a method of analysis involved two activities in order to crystallize the data and analysis and to test the emergent theory that entrepreneurs were learning in conceptual learning spaces. Figure 2.3 shows how this process of constant comparison, looking for deviant cases and testing the interpretations led to a refinement of the number of learning spaces. Since the template and coding were aids to the interpretation and not an end in themselves, the interpretation evolved through the process of constant comparison within the data and applied to other data to test the hypothesis. First, the concept of learning spaces was constantly compared across the data in order to look for deviant cases and refine the codes. This is shown in the arrow above the final circle leading back to the box in the first half of part B in Figure 2.2. Through iterations of working with the data and comparing the codes across, it led to the initial six conceptual learning spaces being reduced to four as the future and physical learning spaces were not deemed strong enough to stand on their own and were subsumed into the other learning spaces. Looking for deviant cases and testing the hypothesis on

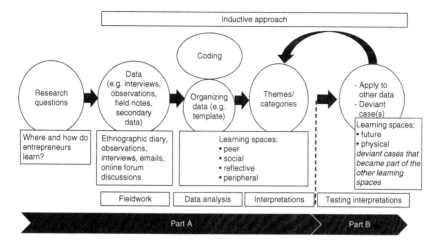

Figure 2.3   Reduction of themes through constant comparison

other data was the second part of this process, which involved an iterative process between themes and testing the interpretations on other data outside of the study. This involved looking at the online forums from two previous learning communities which had completed the programme and two that were nearing the end at the time this analysis was conducted. The online discussions were explored to see how many of the conceptual learning spaces applied to the experiences of the other learning communities. This was deemed to be a useful process in testing the assumptions and interpretations. This process led to a refinement of the number of identified learning spaces through comparison with this other data and looking for deviant cases. This was part of the process of crystallizing that data and analysis and it was felt necessary to look for learning spaces across other data to lend more rigour to the process. This comparison method did not show any further deviant cases that could negate the importance of one of the learning spaces or bring another into the framework. Thus the final analysis rested with four conceptual learning spaces (instead of six). These learning spaces have been used to theorize how and where entrepreneurs learn within learning communities (see Peters 2010).

The intention of this analysis in the entrepreneurial context is to show the reader how the process of constant comparison was carried out in practice. A detailed understanding of the actual context of the conceptual learning spaces is not needed; it is more about showing the reader how constant comparison can be used in qualitative research in the entrepreneurial context.

SUMMARY

In this chapter we have presented a practical guide for qualitative researchers to use the constant comparison method, which is applicable to the field of entrepreneurship. We rooted the method in its historical context and have shown how it has been used from its origins in grounded theory and subsequently as a method, which, we argue, adds rigour to the trustworthiness of qualitative data and analysis. We have provided a detailed guide of the steps we advocate need to be taken when undertaking the method and have shown how it can be used in the entrepreneurial context. It is the totality of the process of undertaking constant comparison that we see as contributing to the research journey. Accordingly, we feel that that this chapter should be read as a set of guidelines and not as a series of rules on the way research should be done. In doing so we have offered a guide to one way of working with and making sense of qualitative data relating to the behaviour and activities of entrepreneurs.

NOTE

1. There is a difference in how Glaser and Strauss use the meaning of theory generation in their subsequent work after their 1967 collaboration. Hallberg (2006) gives a detailed overview of the separation of Glaser and Strauss in relation to grounded theory.

REFERENCES

Adler, P.A. and P. Adler (1994), 'Observational techniques', in N.K. Denzin and Y.S. Lincoln (eds), *Handbook of Qualitative Research*, Thousand Oaks, CA: Sage, pp. 377–92.
Aldrich, H. (1992), 'Methods in our madness? Trends in entrepreneurship research', in D.C. Sexton and J.D. Kasarda (eds), *The State of the Art of Entrepreneurship*, Boston, MA: Kent, pp. 191–213.
Alvesson, M. and S. Deetz (2000), *Doing Critical Management Research*, London: Sage.
Ambert, A., P. Adler, P. Adler and D. Dertzner (1995), 'Understanding and evaluating qualitative research', *Journal of Marriage and Family*, **57** (4), 879–93.
Anderson, A.R. (2000), 'Paradox in the periphery: an entrepreneurial reconstruction', *Entrepreneurship & Regional Development*, **12** (2), 91–109.
Anderson, A.R. and S.L. Jack (2002), 'The articulation of social capital in entrepreneurial networks: a glue or a lubricant?', *Entrepreneurship & Regional Development*, **14** (3), 193–210.
Atkinson, P. and M. Hammersley (1994), 'Ethnography and participant observation', in N.K. Denzin and Y.S. Lincoln (eds), *Handbook of Qualitative Research*, Thousand Oaks, CA: Sage.
Baxter, J. and J. Eyles (1997), 'Evaluating qualitative research in social geography: establishing "rigour" in interview analysis', *Transactions of the Institute of British Geographers*, New Series, **22**, 505–25.

Boeije, H. (2002), 'A purposeful approach to the constant comparative method in the analysis of qualitative interviews', *Quality and Quantity*, **36** (4), 391–409.

Bouchikhi, H. (1993), 'A constructivist framework for understanding entrepreneurial performance', *Organisational Studies*, **14** (4), 551–69.

Bryman, A. (1988), *Quantity and Quality in Social Research*, London: Unwin Hyman.

Bryman, A. (2007), 'The research question in social research: what is its role?', *International Journal of Social Research Methodology*, **10** (1), 5–20.

Bryman, A. and E. Bell (2003), *Business Research Methods*, Oxford, Oxford University Press.

Bygrave, W. (1989), 'The entrepreneurship paradigm (I): a philosophical look at its research methodologies', *Entrepreneurship Theory and Practice*, **14** (1), 7–26.

Charmaz, K. (2003), 'Grounded theory: objectivist and constructivist methods', in N.K. Denzin and Y.S. Lincoln (eds), *Strategies for Qualitative Inquiry*, 2nd edn, Thousand Oaks, CA: Sage Publications, pp. 249–91.

Chell, E. and L. Pittaway (1998), 'A study of entrepreneurship in the restaurant and café industry: explanatory work using the critical incident technique as a methodology – grounded theory procedures and techniques', *International Journal of Hospitality Management*, **17** (1), 23–32.

Coffey, A. (1999), *The Ethnographic Self: Fieldwork and the Representation of Identity*, London: Sage.

Coffey, A. (2002), 'Ethnography and self: reflections and representations', in T. May (ed.), *Qualitative Research in Action*, London: Sage, pp. 313–31.

Cope, J. (2003), 'Entrepreneurial learning and critical reflection: discontinuous events as triggers for higher-level learning', *Management Learning*, **34** (4), 429–50.

Cope, J. (2005a), 'Researching entrepreneurship through phenomenological inquiry: philosophical and methodological issues', *International Small Business Journal*, **23** (2), 163–89.

Cope, J. (2005b), 'Toward a dynamic learning perspective of entrepreneurship', *Entrepreneurship Theory and Practice*, **29** (4), 373–98.

Cope, J. (2011), 'Entrepreneurial learning from failure: an interpretative phenomenological analysis', *Journal of Business Venturing*, **26** (6), 604–23.

Corbin, J. and A. Strauss (1990), 'Grounded theory research: procedures, cannons, and evaluative criteria', *Qualitative Sociology*, **13** (1), 3–21.

Costello, N. (1996), 'Learning and routines in high tech SME's: analysing rich, case study material', *Journal of Economic Issues*, **30** (2), 591–7.

Cronbach, C. (1982), *Designing Evaluations of Educational and Social Programs*, San Francisco, CA: Jossey-Bass.

Crotty, M. (1998), *The Foundations of Social Research: Meaning and Perspective in the Research Process*, London: Sage.

Cousin, G. (2007), 'Thinking with data', *Educational Developments*, March, available at: http://www.seda.ac.uk/resources/files/publications_16_eddev8_1.pdf (accessed 12 October 2013).

Crozier, M. (1964), *The Bureaucratic Phenomenon*, London: Tavistock.

Curran, J. and R.A. Blackburn (2001), *Researching the Small Enterprise*, London: Sage.

De Bruin, A., C. Brush and F. Welter (2007), 'Advancing a framework for coherent research on Women's entrepreneurship', *Entrepreneurship Theory and Practice*, **31** (3), 323–39.

Denzin, N.K. and Lincoln, Y.S. (1998), *The Landscape of Qualitative Research: Theories and Issues*, Thousand Oaks, CA: Sage Publications.

Denzin, N.K. and S. Lincoln (eds), (2003), *Collecting and Interpreting Qualitative Materials*, London: Sage.

Dye, J.F., I.M. Schatz, B.A. Rosenberg and S.T. Coleman (2000), 'Constant comparison method: a kaleidoscope of data', *The Qualitative Report*, **4** (1/2). Available at: http://www.nova.edu/ssss/QR/QR3-4/dye.html (accessed 15 June 2015).

Ellingson L. (2009), *Engaging Crystallization in Qualitative Research: An Introduction*. Thousand Oaks, CA: Sage.

Eisenhardt, K.M. (1989), 'Building theories from case study research', *The Academy of Management Review*, **14** (4), 532–50.

Fetterman, D.M. (1998), *Ethnography Step by Step*, Thousand Oaks, CA, Sage.

Gartner, W.B. and S. Birley (2002), 'Introduction to the special issue on qualitative methods in entrepreneurship', *Journal of Business Venturing*, **17**, (5), 387–95.

Geertz, (1973), *The Interpretation of Cultures*, New York: Basic Books.

Geertz, C. (1983), *Local Knowledge: Further Essays in Interpretive Anthropology*, New York: Basic Books.

Glaser, B.G. (1965), 'The constant comparative method of qualitative analysis', *Social Problems*, **12** (4), 436–45.

Glaser, B. and A. Strauss (1965), *Awareness of Dying*, Chicago, IL: Aldine.

Glaser, B.G. and A.L. Strauss (1967), *The Discovery of Grounded Theory: Strategies for Qualitative Research*, New York: Aldine De Gruyter.

Granovetter, M. (1973), 'The strength of weak ties', *American Journal of Sociology*, **78** (6), 1360–80.

Guba, E. and Y. Lincoln (1989), *Fourth Generation Evaluation*, Newbury Park, CA: Sage.

Hallberg, L. (2006), 'The core category of grounded theory: making constant comparisons', *International Journal of Qualitative Studies on Health and Wellbeing*, **1** (3), 141–8.

Haugh, H. (2005), 'A research agenda for social entrepreneurship', *Social Enterprise Journal*, **1** (1), 1–12.

Holstein, J. and J. Gubrium (1994), 'Phenomenology, ethnomethodology, and interpretive practice', in N.K. Denzin and Y.S. Lincoln (eds), *Handbook of Qualitative Research*, Thousand Oaks, CA: Sage, pp. 262–72.

Huberman, A. and M. Miles (2002), *The Qualitative Researchers Companion*, London: Sage.

Hycner, R. (1985), 'Some guidelines for the phenomenological analysis of interview data', *Human Studies*, **8** (3), 279–303.

Jack, S.L. (2005), 'The role, use and activation of strong and weak network ties: a qualitative analysis', *Journal of Management Studies*, **42** (6), 1233–59.

Kanter, R.M. (1977), *Men and Women of the Corporation*, New York: Basic Books.

King, N. (1998), 'Template analysis', in G. Symon and C. Cassell (eds), *Qualitative Methods and Analysis in Organizational Research: A Practical Guide*, London: Sage, pp. 118–34.

Knight, P.T. (2002), *Small Scale Research*, London: Sage.

Kodithuwakku, S. and P. Rosa (2002), 'The entrepreneurial process and economic success in a constrained environment', *Journal of Business Venturing*, **17** (5), 431–65.

Krenske, L. (2002), 'You're researching what? The importance of self in ethnographic research', in S.B. Merriam and Associates (eds), *Qualitative Research in Practice*, San Francisco, CA: Jossey-Bass, pp. 283–5.

Kvale, S. (1995), 'The social construction of validity', *Qualitative Inquiry*, **1** (March), 19–40.

Mason, J. (2002), *Qualitative Researching*, 2nd edn, London: Sage.

Mays, N. and C. Pope (1995), 'Qualitative research: rigour and qualitative research', *British Management Journal*, **311** (6997), 109–12.

Merriam, S.B. and Associates (2002), *Qualitative Research in Practice: Examples for Discussion and Analysis*, San Francisco, CA: Jossey-Bass.

Morse, J. and P. Field (1998), *Nursing Research of Qualitative Approaches*, Cheltenham: Stanley Thornes.

Oakley, A (1999), 'Paradigm wars: some thoughts on a person and public trajectory', *International Journal of Social Research Methodology: Theory and Practice*, **2** (3), 247–55.

Patton, M. (1990), *Qualitative Evaluation and Research Methods*, Thousand Oaks, CA: Sage.

Penrose, E.T. (1971), *The Growth of Firms, Middle East Oil, and Other Essays*, London: Cass.

Peters, S. (2010), 'Where does the learning take place? Learning spaces and the situated curriculum within networked learning', paper presented at the Seventh International Conference on Networked Learning, 3–4 May, Aalborg, Denmark.

Piore, M. (1979), *Birds of Passage: Migrant Labour and industrial Societies*, Cambridge: Cambridge University Press.

Rae, D. (2000), 'Understanding entrepreneurial learning: a question of how?', *International Journal of Entrepreneurial Behaviour and Research*, **6** (3), 145–59.

Richardson, L. and E. Adams St. Pierre (1994), 'Writing: a method of inquiry', in

N.K. Denzin and Y.S. Lincoln (eds), *Handbook of Qualitative Research*, Thousand Oaks, CA: Sage, pp. 516–29.

Ryan, G.W. and H.R. Bernard (2003), 'Techniques to identify themes', *Field Methods*, **15** (1), 85–109.

Schutz, A. (1967), *The Phenomenology of the Social World*, trans G. Walsh and F. Lehnert, Evanston, IL: North Western University Press. (Original German work published 1932.)

Schwandt, T.A. (1994), 'Constructivist, interpretivist approaches to human inquiry', in N.K. Denzin and Y.S. Lincoln (eds), *Handbook of Qualitative Research*, Thousand Oaks, CA: Sage, pp. 118–37.

Shaw, E. (1999a), 'A guide to the qualitative research process: evidence from a small firm Study', *Qualitative Market Research: An International Journal*, **2** (2), 59–70.

Shaw, E. (1999b), 'Networks and their relevance to the entrepreneurial/marketing interface: a review of the evidence', *Journal of Research in Marketing and Entrepreneurship*, **1** (1), 24–40.

Silverman, D. (2001), *Interpreting Qualitative Data, Methods for Analysing Talk, Text, and Interaction*, 2nd edn, London and Thousand Oaks, CA: Sage Publications.

Silverman, D. (2005), *Doing Qualitative Research*, 2nd edn, London: Sage.

Stewart, A. (1989), *Team Entrepreneurship*, Newbury Park, CA: Sage.

Stewart, A. (1990), 'The Bigman metaphor for entrepreneurship: a "library tale" with morals on alternatives for further research', *Organization Science*, **1** (2), 143–59.

Steyaert, C. (1998), 'A qualitative methodology for process studies in entrepreneurship', *International Studies of Management and Organisation*, **27** (3), 13–33.

Strauss, A. and J. Corbin (1990), *Basics of Qualitative Research: Grounded Theory Procedures and Techniques*, Newbury Park, CA: Sage.

Tesch, R. (1990), *Qualitative Research: Analysis Types and Software Tools*, Bristol, PA: Falmer.

Thompson, C., W. Locander and H. Pollio (1989), 'Putting consumer experience back in consumer research: the philosophy and method of consumer research', *Journal of Consumer Research*, **16** (2), 33–146.

Wicker, A.W. (1985), 'Substantive theorizing', *American Journal of Community Psychology*, **17** (5), 531–47.

Zaner, R. (1970), *The Way of Phenomenology*, New York: Pegasus.

3 Grounded theory analysis in entrepreneurship research

Anne Bøllingtoft

INTRODUCTION

> New discoveries are always the result of high-risk expeditions into unknown territory. Darwin, Columbus, and Freud, each in different ways, were conducting qualitative inquiries.

These were the words from Suddaby (2006: 633), commenting on an *American Management Journal* survey (Bartunek et al. 2006) revealing that articles identified as 'interesting research' were the product of qualitative methods. One member of the family of qualitative methods is grounded theory, initially presented by Glaser and Strauss in their book *The Discovery of Grounded Theory*, published in 1967. Grounded theory is a qualitative methodology for developing theory that is grounded in data, which are systematically gathered and analysed. The theory evolves during the research process itself and is a product of a continuous interplay between analysis and data collection (Glaser and Strauss 1967; Strauss and Corbin 1990, 1998). The label 'grounded theory' reflects the source of the developed theory, which is ultimately grounded in the behaviour, words and actions of those under study (Glaser and Strauss 1967). Of central importance is thus that the researcher should be part of or work in the actual environments in which the actions take place, in natural situations, in order to analytically relate informants' perspectives to the environments through which they emerge. The methodology is most commonly used to generate theory where little is already known, or to provide new perspectives on existing knowledge. The strength of grounded theory is by many considered to be its ability to develop theory through the use of prescribed, yet flexible, tools for analysis (Charmaz 2001, 2005), hence making it relevant for a broad number of research areas.

Although much of the original research using grounded theory was undertaken by sociologists, the use of the methodology has never been restricted to this group (Strauss and Corbin 1994). Because grounded theory is a general methodology (Strauss and Corbin 1999), a way of thinking about and conceptualizing data, it was easily adapted by its originators and their students to studies of diverse phenomena (Strauss and

Corbin 1994; Locke 2001). Thus the grounded theory style of qualitative research has travelled to, for example, psychology, anthropology, information science, social work, education, to many communities of practice within health care (especially nursing) as well as to marketing, management and organization studies (see, for example, Strauss and Corbin 1994; Locke 2001; Goulding 2002; O'Reilly et al. 2012). All these fields have, some increasingly, used grounded theory procedures alone or in conjunction with other methodologies.

The grounded theory style of qualitative research has also travelled to entrepreneurship. It would be an overstatement to suggest that the field of entrepreneurship research has a strong and widespread tradition with respect to applying grounded theory, but examples of studies either inspired by or applying a grounded theory approach are present in the literature, in particular in more recent years. For instance, Gemmell et al. (2012) investigating how entrepreneurs obtain the creative ideas they need to develop innovative new products; Lopes et al. (2009) explained how entrepreneurs attract critical resources to venture creation and development; Khavul et al. (2009) employed grounded theory using comparative cases involving informal micro-financed businesses in East Africa in order to build a theoretical foundation for studying the establishment and evolution of family firms in emerging markets; Petkova et al. (2008) explored the processes and mechanisms of reputation-building by new ventures; Bouwen and Steyaert (1990) followed the perspective of grounded theory in describing and conceptualizing the process of creating an entrepreneurial firm through the early years of its existence and Frederick and Monsen (2011) applied a grounded theory approach to explain why New Zealand exhibits only a moderate level of economic development despite its high level of entrepreneurship. What unites these studies is the fundamental idea within grounded theory that theory should emerge directly out of the data and is returned to the data for verification.

The field of entrepreneurship as a well-established academic discipline is still considered relatively young (Shane and Venkataraman 2000), and the field is still benefiting from contributions from more established research areas (Bygrave 1989; Zahra 2007; Wincent and Örtqvist 2009). Grounded theory therefore offers the opportunity to develop theories grounded in the field under study, thus being able to take into consideration that entrepreneurship often begins with a disjointed, discontinuous, non-linear event, which is highly unlikely to be studied successfully with methods developed for examining smooth, continuous and linear processes (for example, Bygrave 1989). Grounded theory hence offers the opportunity to develop insightful grounded empirical models and theories that describe and explain observed phenomena as accurately as possible in the actual environments in which the actions take place.

It is also important to highlight common misconceptions in grounded theory. Grounded theory is not a loose collection of tools for handling and analysing data or simply a means by which to code data. Nor is grounded theory a 'synonymous descriptor for any emergent qualitative design' (O'Reilly et al. 2012: 248). The grounded theory procedures are designed to systematically build theory, and researchers who use grounded theory only as a way of coding data are neglecting the main purpose of the method, that is, if their intention is to apply grounded theory. Much confusion, though, seems to be apparent when authors claim to be using grounded theory (Suddaby 2006), and some authors apply what O'Reilly (2012) refers to as an 'a la carte approach' to grounded theory, meaning that the methodology is not used as a holistic approach to research and theory-building but rather as a piecemeal approach to data analysis.

However, looking more closely at the studies applying grounded theory (not limited to the studies within entrepreneurship research mentioned above), a variation and flexibility within a grounded theory style of qualitative research is revealed. All of the above-mentioned studies within entrepreneurship research claim to apply a grounded theory approach. However, while some authors are very explicit regarding the grounded theory procedures followed, others are less so. Consequently, it can be challenging for the reader to follow exactly how grounded theory has been applied in the studies, and it can be difficult to recognize the grounded theory elements. The reasons for this may be many. Some journals, for example, do not have a tradition for devoting lengthy space to elaborate on methodology issues in detail, or some authors choose not to devote much space to elaborate on methodological issues. The purpose of this chapter is not to be the judge of when 'true' grounded theory is applied, or when it is the 'a la carte approach to grounded theory' (O'Reilly et al. 2012). In fact, it is highly questionable if there is one 'true' version of grounded theory, just one simple formula for doing grounded theory. The important point is that it can be difficult to get a comprehensive overview of how to apply the methodology in practice by reading articles where it has been used. Worth quoting here, however, is also Denzin, one of the editors of the widely read and cited *Handbook of Qualitative Research* (1994). He highlighted the status of the grounded theory approach to qualitative research with the statement that 'the grounded theory perspective is the most widely used qualitative interpretive framework in the social sciences today' (Denzin 1994: 513). Taking this point even further, he notes that 'when one peels back the layers of discourse embedded in any of the numerous qualitative guides to interpretation and theory construction, the core features of the

Strauss approach are present, even when Strauss and associates are not directly named' (ibid.: 513).

As also illustrated in Chapter 2 in this volume, part of what is considered as grounded theory procedures can be applied outside of grounded theory. This can partly explain Denzin's observation. However, authors not familiar with grounded theory, who are using parts of grounded theory procedures, risk being accused of applying an à la carte approach to grounded theory or using an unreflective methodological approach. The aim of this chapter is therefore to provide the reader with a better understanding of grounded theory and to provide an overview of the methodology as a primer for those who may consider using it in their work. With this aim in mind, the rest of the chapter will be structured as follows: first, grounded theory is introduced in a historical perspective. Following this the chapter provides an overview of the central ideas and principles underpinning grounded theory, and the steps involved in applying grounded theory are outlined and illustrated with an example. The chapter ends with a discussion of some of the risks and problems associated with grounded theory. It is important to emphasize that this chapter can by no means be considered as doing more than highlight some of the most essential features of grounded theory. It is a good starting point, but the reader must bear in mind that books on the methodology are recommended to be read before actually using grounded theory (for example, Glaser and Strauss 1967; Strauss and Corbin 1990; Glaser 1992).

GROUNDED THEORY IN A HISTORICAL PERSPECTIVE

Grounded theory was initially developed by Glaser and Strauss as a reaction against the quantitative research paradigm, which at the time dominated much of the social sciences (Strauss and Corbin 1994; Charmaz 2001; Suddaby 2006). Rather than as viable endeavours in their own right, qualitative studies were generally viewed as a preliminary exercise through which researchers could refine their quantitative instrument before the real research began. Glaser and Strauss challenged this view, and disputed that the social and natural sciences dealt with the same type of subject matter. The work of Glaser and Strauss has been labelled revolutionary because it challenged:

1. arbitrary divisions between theory and research;
2. views of qualitative research as primarily a precursor to more 'rigorous' quantitative methods;

3. claims that the quest for rigour made qualitative research illegitimate;
4. beliefs that qualitative methods are impressionistic and unsystematic;
5. separation of data collection and analysis; and
6. assumptions that qualitative research could produce only descriptive cases rather than theory development (Charmaz 2001: 511).

The professional background of the founders of grounded theory adds to the understanding of grounded theory (Locke 2001; Goulding 2002; Suddaby 2006; O'Reilly et al. 2012). Glaser was trained at Columbia University, which had a strong tradition of formal theorizing, verification and quantitative methods. He applied his rigorous positivistic methodological training in quantitative research to the development of qualitative analysis. The methods of grounded theory were thus founded upon his epistemological assumptions, methodological terms, inductive logic and systematic approach. In contrast, Strauss was trained at the University of Chicago, which had a reputation for critical and qualitative approaches (observation and intensive interviewing). He brought the Chicago school field research and symbolic interactionism to grounded theory, thus contributing the pragmatist philosophical study of process, action and meaning into empirical inquiry through grounded theory.

Despite their different professional backgrounds, Glaser and Strauss shared a strong belief in (1) the need to get out in the field if one wants to understand what is going on, (2) the importance of theory grounded in reality, (3) the nature of experience in the field for the subjects and researcher as continually evolving, (4) the active role of persons in shaping the worlds they live in through the process of symbolic interaction, (5) an emphasis on change and process and the variability and complexity of life, and (6) the interrelationship between meaning in the perception of subjects and their action (Glaser 1992: 16). Together, they (Glaser and Strauss 1967) proposed grounded theory as a practical method for conducting research that focused on the interpretive process by analysing the actual production of meanings and concepts used by social actors in real settings (Gephart 2004). Their argument was that new theory could be developed by paying careful attention to the contrast between 'the daily realities (what is actually going on) of substantive areas'[1] (Glaser and Strauss, 1967: 239) and the interpretations of those daily realities made by those who participate in them (the 'actors'). With grounded theory, Glaser and Strauss (1967) offered an organic process of theory emergence based on (1) how well data fit conceptual categories identified by an observer (researcher), (2) how well the categories explain or predict ongoing interpretations, and (3) how relevant the categories are to the core issues being observed. Emphasis is on theory-building and the ultimate goal is to develop theory which goes beyond 'thick description'. Accordingly, Glaser and Strauss laid out very clear guidelines regarding the criteria that the developed theory should meet. The theory should (Glaser and Strauss 1967: 3):

- enable prediction and explanation of behaviour;
- be useful in theoretical advances in sociology;
- be applicable in practice;
- provide a perspective on behaviour;
- guide and provide a style for research on particular areas of behaviour; and
- provide clear enough categories and hypotheses so that crucial ones can be verified in present and future research (Glaser and Strauss 1967: 3).

Further, two key concepts play a prominent role in grounded theory (Glaser and Strauss 1967; Suddaby 2006): constant comparison and theoretical sampling. Constant comparison involves comparing like with like, to look for emerging patterns and themes as data are collected and analysed simultaneously. In order to compare 'like with like', theoretical sampling is needed. This involves the purposeful selection of a sample according to the developing categories and emerging theory. Thus, decisions about which data should be collected next are determined by the theory that is being constructed. Both of these concepts violate positivist assumptions about how a research process should work (Suddaby 2006). Constant comparison contradicts the ideal of a clean separation between data collection and analysis, and theoretical sampling violates the ideal of hypothesis testing as the direction of new data collection is determined by the ongoing interpretation of data and emerging categories contrary to a priori hypotheses. Consequently, grounded theory is a methodology that is more appropriate for some questions than others (Charmaz 2001; Sousa and Hendriks 2006; O'Reilly et al. 2012). Grounded theory is generally appropriate and suited when the purpose is to make knowledge claims about how individuals interpret reality and when the aim is to understand the process by which actors construct meaning out of inter-subjective experience. Furthermore, Sousa and Hendriks (2006) argue that exploratory qualitative methods such as grounded theory are well suited for work when (1) there is insufficient theoretical guidance to support the research inquiry, (2) the researcher's experience and viewpoints are vital to the inquiry and (3) the meanings and relationships of concepts are fragile. Similarly, grounded theory is less appropriate when the purpose is to make knowledge claims about an objective reality, and for research inquiries that are (1) well covered in the literature, (2) used to test previously established hypotheses or (3) an attempt to replicate other studies.

The Splintering of Grounded Theory: Theory Forcing versus Theory Emergence

Glaser and Strauss's personal differences changed over the years since their joint publication in 1967, and it is important to be aware that there are now two distinct versions of grounded theory. One version is mainly associated with Barney Glaser, while the other is mainly associated with Anselm Strauss. The differences between the two versions have been elaborated on in detail in the literature (see, for example, Glaser 1992; Charmaz 2001; Heath and Cowley 2004), but essentially the two differ on the grounds of theory forcing versus theory emergence. While Glaser emphasizes and favours creativity and openness, Strauss together with Corbin (Strauss and Corbin 1990) advocate a much more linear method, a highly complex system of coding, designed to take the researcher through every stage of the research, thus favouring a more structured design for analysing data. Glaser regards the approach suggested by Strauss and Corbin as forcing, rather than allowing, the emergence of theory (Glaser 1992; Douglas 2003). For Glaser (1992: 43), the use of systematic comparison is enough: 'Categories emerge upon comparisons and properties emerge upon more comparison. And that is all there is to it.' Both versions, however, have their potential problems and it is important not to be blind to this (Goulding 2001, 2002). Glaser's approach may be seen as highly risky and unfocused by those who are reluctant to give themselves up to the data and 'wallow' in the creative process. Strauss and Corbin's approach, on the other hand, can potentially stifle creativity by making the methodology overly mechanistic, highly formulistic and inflexible as a result of their many analytic questions and recommended methodological techniques. Consequently, for a researcher not familiar with grounded theory, it is important to recognize the differences so as to avoid confusion over terminology and procedures.

GROUNDED THEORY: GETTING STARTED ON THE PROCESS

With the main point of departure in Glaser and Strauss's book from 1967, the overall process of grounded theory can be illustrated as in Figure 3.1.

When applying grounded theory, concepts and theories are developed from the data rather than using existing frameworks or extant theory to

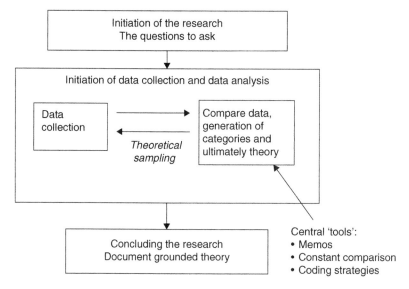

Figure 3.1   Illustration of the overall process of grounded theory

guide the research in the early stages. While perceived by critics as an over-emphasis on induction, Glaser (1978) emphasizes that entering a research field with as few predetermined ideas as possible increases the theoretical sensitivity[2] of the researcher. It is acknowledged that hardly anybody starts a research project with a 'totally blank sheet'. All researchers have a disciplinary background including knowledge previously learned, which will provide a perspective from which to investigate a problem or phenomenon. Thus, when undertaking grounded theory, theories and knowledge previously learned are perceived as providing the investigator with sensitivity and focus, both of which aid the interpretation of the data collected during the research process (Glaser and Strauss 1967). Grounded theory research is not a-theoretical and reading is not forsaken during the initial stages (Goulding 2002), but using grounded theory does call for an open mind and a willingness to have faith in the data. In more practical terms, the recommendation is that a detailed literature review comes after (parts of) the data have been collected and when tentative theories or concepts have started to emerge. This is proposed in order to avoid bringing into the field preconceptions and explanations borrowed from the work of others (Becker 1993; Goulding 2002). Difficulties in applying grounded theory emerge if the studied area has a long and credible as well as empirically based literature. The researcher may thus enter the field with a prior disposition, conscious of it or not, and a challenge emerges in developing unbiased insights (Backman and Kyngäs 1999). It is generally recommended that the researcher enter the field at a very early stage in order to avoid this.

BOX 3.1   INTRODUCTION TO EXAMPLE

The empirical context of my PhD project was a phenomenon with many of the same characteristics as business incubators, so it is here referred to as such. The term 'business incubator' is an umbrella term for any organization that provides access to affordable office space and shared administrative services (Allen and McCluskey 1990). The entrepreneurs studied were in a similar way all located in the same building and were offered access to shared office services such as, for example, Internet, printers and meeting rooms. Although there was – on the surface – a great resemblance to traditional business incubators, this was not the case on all points. The empirical context of my PhD project did not provide any 'specialist' advice services, such as assistance in developing business and marketing plans, obtaining capital and building management teams. Furthermore, there was no professional manager, and the building was rented jointly by the companies. The entrepreneurs perceived and referred to themselves as a 'network of companies', which was also presented to be the fundamental idea behind the incubator. The entrepreneurs thus had a positive attitude towards cooperation as well as sharing of knowledge with each other. In short, the studied business incubator was based on:

- The prospect of economies of scale;
- Cooperation between the companies, and
- Social and professional gathering.

This kind of setting had not been studied systematically before, and it was the first of its kind in Denmark of this size (12 companies when I started my PhD project, but almost 60 companies a few years later). Furthermore, the business incubator seemed to be very successful as regards the survival of the companies.

My PhD project had the aim to provide an account of the networking and cooperation activities going on between the companies. From the perspective of the entrepreneurs, the purpose was to shed light on why the entrepreneurs chose to place their company within such a setting, what kind of cooperation and networking took place between the companies within such a setting and how the entrepreneurs benefited from it in their own understanding and perception. Furthermore, the purpose of my PhD project was to identify and explain the mechanisms facilitating and/or enabling inter-organizational networking and cooperation between the companies within the investigated setting.

My aim was thus to understand the setting from the perspective of the entrepreneurs (the actors). Furthermore, I was facing an empirical setting where there was no long and credible or empirically based literature. I chose initially to carry out an observation study in order to gain an initial understanding of the phenomenon, and thus I started to collect data within the first month of my PhD project.

INITIATION OF DATA COLLECTION AND DATA ANALYSIS

Initially, the researcher will go to the most obvious places and the most likely informants in search of information (also referred to as the concentration site, that is, a unit where the area of interest goes on in concentration – Glaser 2001). As to what data to include, grounded theory allows for a wide range of data, including company reports, secondary data, interviews, observations and, even, statistics providing the information has relevance to the study (Glaser and Strauss 1967; Corbin and Strauss 1990). Glaser and Strauss describe this as gathering 'slices of data' (1967: 65) as different data sources provide different vantage points from which to understand a potential conceptual category. Essentially, Glaser and Strauss advocate what is now common referred to as 'triangulation' (Locke 2001). The following elements are central to the process.

Theoretical Sampling

Grounded theory is about the simultaneous collection and analysis of data. As concepts are initially identified based on the first data (and the theory starts to develop), further individuals, situations or places needed to be included in the study are identified. This is known as theoretical sampling, and it is defined by Glaser (1978: 36) as:

> the process of data collection for generating theory whereby the analyst jointly collects, codes and analyses the data and decides what data to collect next and where to find it, in order to develop the theory as it emerges. This process of data collection is 'controlled' by the emerging theory.

Thus, data collection and data analysis are parallel and iterative processes. In grounded theory, representativeness of concepts, not of persons, is crucial. Thus, informants are selected for their relevance for furthering the development of emerging categories and concepts (Glaser 1978). The nature of theoretical sampling means that samples cannot be identified prior to the research. Consequently, this has implications for the timescale of the research, which cannot be foreseen.

Memos

A central part of grounded theory is the use of memos throughout the research process. Memos can be used with any form of data, and are essentially the ideas which have been noted during the data collection process. They describe the scene, events and behaviours under study. Memos can be just a few lines or several pages. According to Glaser (1978), the researcher should write freely, write down as ideas strike and take chances with ideas. Thus, memos are vital as they provide a bank of ideas, they help map out the emerging theory and are used to identify concepts. Glaser recommends that memos and data should be kept separate, that is, interpretation of data should be separate from the actual data. The exception can be in cases where data can be used to illustrate a particular case, or where it is appropriate to refer to specific field notes. Each memo should be introduced by a title or a caption, which is sometimes a category or a concept. Any concepts which appear in the memos should be highlighted and their relationship discussed. Memos help the researcher to generate relationships as well as more general problems. Memos provide an excellent source of direction for future theoretical sampling.

Constant Comparison

A fundamental feature of grounded theory is the application of the constant comparative method. As implied by the name, constant comparison involves comparing like with like, to look for emerging patterns and themes. The constant comparative method involves the simultaneous coding and analysis of data (Glaser and Strauss 1967). All new data are compared to earlier data iteratively to enable adjustment of theoretical categories based on the ongoing analysis surrounding participant issues, problems and concerns (Glaser and Strauss 1967). Thus, 'analysis explicitly compares each incident in the data with other incidents appearing to belong to the same category, exploring their similarities and differences' (Spiggle 1994: 493–4). This process facilitates the identification of concepts, which is a progression from merely describing what is happening in the data, to explaining the relationship between and across incidents. These incidents in the data need to be checked against each other in order to validate interpretation. Constant comparison is typically experienced as a continuous cycling back and forth from the first bits of data through the last. Glaser and Strauss (1967) describe the four stages of the constant comparative method as follows:

Stage 1: Comparing incidents applicable to each category.
Stage 2: Integrating categories and their properties.
Stage 3: Delimiting the theory.
Stage 4: Writing the theory.

This method of generating theory is a continuously growing process. Each stage is transformed into the next, although earlier stages do remain in operation simultaneously throughout the analysis, and each stage provides continuous development to its successive stage until the analysis is terminated (Glaser and Strauss 1967).

Coding Strategies/Theoretical Coding

Theoretical coding is a systematic process used to make sense of research data by categorizing and grouping similar examples from the data. The coding process is used to identify the properties, dimensions and boundaries of each category in an effort to expose the theoretical underpinnings of the phenomenon (Isabella 1990). This is happening throughout an iterative process of naming and comparing events in the data and examining each for similarities and differences until the consistencies and constancies can be identified in the data (Locke 2001; Goulding 2002).

During the coding process, each relevant event in the data is coded into as many subcategories of analysis as possible, as categories emerge or as data emerge to fit an existing category (Glaser and Strauss 1967). Each piece of data is 'systematically and thoroughly examined for evidence of data fitting into categories' (Isabella 1990: 13), which consequently results in subcategories that are continuously challenged and restructured as the data collection and analysis progresses.

The coding process in grounded theory is vital for generating theoretical properties of the subcategories and ultimately enables discovery of the 'core category', the term Glaser and Strauss use to designate the key indicator or explanation of behaviour that occurs in a specific situation. The quality of grounded theory ultimately rests on the goodness of fit between the empirical observations and the conceptual categories they purport to indicate (Locke 2001).

Inspired by Strauss (for example, Corbin and Strauss 1990; Strauss and Corbin 1998), Goulding (2001, 2002) describes the above process with slightly more structure, which might be perceived more helpful for a novice researcher. Initially, interviews, observations and other forms of data are broken down into distinct units of meaning, which are labelled to generate (emerging) concepts. The starting point is 'open coding'. In the beginning, the analysis will naturally be very broad and lack focus. As data are collected they are analysed simultaneously by looking for all possible interpretations. The open coding usually starts with a full transcription of an interview, thereby making a 'line by line' analysis possible. All keywords or phrases, which provide insight, are highlighted in order to identify what is happening in the data. In this way hundreds of codes can be generated – codes which are 'open' and unrelated. The next stage is to continue transcribing interviews and repeat the process of line-by-line analysis, using the constant comparison method to search for similarities or patterns. It is in this process initial categories are formed, but most likely they will be revised later. Throughout this process (and the following), the researcher should try to lift the analysis to a more abstract level, away from description and towards theory development. This is done through a process of abstraction, where the researcher collapses more empirically grounded categories into higher order conceptual constructs. In order to do this, it is necessary to move beyond open coding, which basically describes what is happening in the data, to more sophisticated conceptual forms of analysis known as axial coding. In axial coding, relationships are specified between a category and its subcategories. 'Axial coding is the appreciation of concepts in terms of their dynamic interrelationships which should form the basis for the construction of the theory' (Goulding 2001: 27). Having identified a concept, the attributes or properties may be explored in greater depth. The final stage is the construction of a core category. This pulls together all the strands in order to offer an explanation of the behaviour under study. This is usually when the theory is written up and integrated with existing theories to show relevance and new perspectives. It is important to remember that development of the core category should be traceable back through the data (Glaser and Strauss 1967), and the criteria that a core category must meet include the following:

- It must be central and account for a large proportion of behaviour.
- It must be based on reoccurrence in the data.
- A core category takes longer to saturate than other categories.
- It must relate meaningfully to other categories.
- The theoretical analysis should be based on the core category.
- It should be highly variable and modifiable.

CONCLUDING THE RESEARCH

The point of theoretical saturation is reached when no new subsequent data incidents that are examined provide new information, either in terms of refining the category or its properties, or its relationships to other categories (Locke 2001). Thus, saturation means that no additional data are being found whereby the researcher can develop properties of the category (Glaser and Strauss, 1967: 61). Category saturation is vital to verification in grounded theory and, as explained by Goulding (2002: 44), 'Grounded theory has a built-in mandate to strive towards verification through the process of category saturation. This involves staying in the field until no further evidence emerges. Verification is done throughout

BOX 3.2   EXAMPLE OF DATA COLLECTION AND ANALYSIS

During my PhD study I collected a wide range of data, including data about the incubator as well as the companies it was housing. Data were from websites, I did observation studies, and I conducted unstructured, semi-structured as well as structured interviews with the entrepreneurs. I also conducted a few focus groups. I produced notes from my observation studies, and all interviews were transcribed.

From the beginning I had a logbook,[3] which essentially contained my memos. My collected data were in separate files, but all my ideas, thoughts, reflections and unanswered questions were in my logbook. These thoughts, reflections, ideas and questions were, together with the analysis of the data collected, guiding me in which data to collect next (theoretical sampling), whom to talk to next and what questions to ask.

Although it was not the intention from the outset of the PhD project to apply a grounded theory approach, the fact that my data collection and analysis was (without any doubt) part of the same process inspired me to read about grounded theory. Furthermore, I desperately needed a 'tool' to help me get a hold on my data, so I sought inspiration from the theory-building principles proposed by Glaser and Strauss (1967). Although in the beginning I had doubts as to whether I was doing 'real' grounded theory or not, I found good support in reading about how to analyse data within grounded theory.

Arguing that concepts should emerge from data through relatively unbiased coding reveals a tendency to regard established theories as an impediment rather than a resource (Danermark et al. 2002). The viewpoint I applied was that the research process is most productive when a fairly open attitude towards the data is combined with the use of established concepts as a resource. Thus, I reviewed the literature directly related to the field of study, for example, theory on business incubators as well as theory in general on networking and cooperation between entrepreneurs. This, however, was not undertaken before I entered the field, but rather, simultaneously with collecting and analysing my data. In practical terms, I regularly reflected upon and analysed my notes on different aspects about the setting I studied and compared them to existing theory.

A highly useful aspect from grounded theory is the comparative analysis. Somehow I had to 'organize' and analyse my notes according to the principles of comparative analysis, which involves comparing like with like and looking for emerging patterns and themes (Glaser and Strauss 1967; Goulding 2002; Locke 2001; Strauss and Corbin 1990). I read my notes and interview transcriptions carefully, and I made notes in the margin of the text (line-by-line analysis). These margin notes could consist of basically every thought that came to my mind in regard to the material. These margin notes were used to categorize the observation notes as well as interview transcriptions, and thus a re-ordering of my notes took place several times. I physically split the text and re-organized it according to the dominant categories emerging from the margin notes. These dominant categories were found and revised by re-reading the margin notes and identify the more frequent categories and themes within the categories.

In my PhD project I identified a core category that could explain the mechanisms facilitating and/or enabling inter-organizational networking and cooperation between the companies within the investigated setting. This core category was made up of four dominant categories, which together could explain and predict the behaviour observed. As the purpose of this chapter is merely to illustrate the process applied in grounded theory, I only illustrate the identification of one of the dominant categories.

One dominant category that emerged I labelled 'personal relations'. 'Relations before transactions', the entrepreneurs told me again and again. Without exception all the entrepreneurs that I interviewed strongly emphasized that personal relations between the entrepreneurs were in fact the condition for the evolvement of network activities. The meaning of the expression 'personal relations' was described in different ways by the entrepreneurs, though, which is also reflected in the indicators in Figure 3.2. The indicators identified in the table are based on numerous quotes from the entrepreneurs as well as observations of incidents.

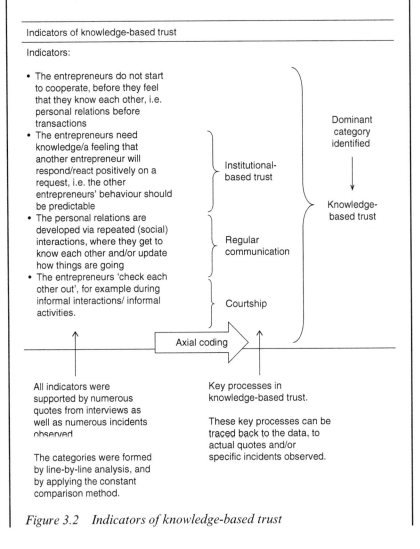

Figure 3.2   Indicators of knowledge-based trust

Each indicator is to be considered as a subcategory to the category 'personal relations'.

In lifting the analysis to a more abstract level, away from description and towards theory development, axial coding was applied. My data told me that 'trust' was of great importance, but I also realized (both from analysing my notes and reading the literature on trust) that trust is a complex concept and has many nuances. This process of abstraction – the move from the concrete level (the empirically-grounded categories) to higher-order conceptual constructs – was extremely time-consuming, both in terms of analysing my data applying constant comparison and in terms of lifting my data and categories to an abstract level. There is no easy way to do this. It is a matter of hard work and a lot of data analysis and reading – and all the time you must not forget what your data tell you.

My data told me that initiatives to network activities would typically take place if an entrepreneur were able to 'predict' that another entrepreneur would respond/react positively to a request. The entrepreneurs' emphasis on the importance of personal relations with each other, of knowledge about each other and of knowledge (or as a minimum a feeling) about the other entrepreneur's attitude towards internal network activities is in the literature also referred to as knowledge-based trust (Child and Faulkner 1998; Lewicki and Bunker 1996; Shapiro et al. 1992). I will not go into detail with this literature here, but merely emphasize that there are several key processes in knowledge-based trust, which are also reflected in Figure 3.2. These key processes all have different properties, which were expressed in different implications for my findings. For example, the overall implication of knowledge-based trust was that the entrepreneurs needed to make an active effort to get to know each other. They needed to make an 'investment' where some of the primary costs were paid in the form of time invested in social activities and 'small-talk' with the other entrepreneurs. Just to move into the investigated setting and passively wait for the network activities to take place would not lead to network activities or cooperation. In consequence, the importance of knowledge-based trust also meant that even if there were rather obvious potentials for cooperation between two companies, this would not take place unless the entrepreneurs had developed knowledge-based trust with each other. More nuanced implications could however also be identified from the key processes in knowledge-based trust.

the course of the research project, rather than assuming that verification is only possible through follow-up quantitative data.'

Locke (2001) points out that as Glaser and Strauss describe these processes in their first book, their writing of 'discovering' categories and theories and categories 'emerging' from the data can pose problems to novice researchers during this delimiting phase of the analytic work. Their language can invite researchers to believe and expect that there is a theoretical reality out there in the social situation, which will more or less reveal itself. This is not always the case. As Locke (2001: 55) emphasizes:

The practical reality is that as researchers we will have to decide on and articulate the story our data makes it possible to tell. My own experience is that after a time, analysts find that the conceptual categories we have in process are developed to the point where they are able to account pretty much for our data, and we become clear about the story. In terms of the former, this usually means that we do not exhaust every fragment and every potential category in our data. Accordingly, our theory will not be a complete account of the phenomenon we have been studying. For although our in-process framework with its constituent conceptual categories does stabilize, it cannot be considered finished. Given the understanding that theory development is emergent and processual, the theoretical framework can always be developed further. Nevertheless, a point does come in the research process where the theoretical framework is sufficiently worked out for analysts to have something substantive to say about the phenomenon they studied. We have to actively decide, though, that we have reached the point where we need to bring closure to our analysis.

Goulding (2001) also warns that it is wrong to assume that a theory will automatically emerge. Sometimes there may not be a theory to be found. In that sense, grounded theory is risky. Moving beyond open coding to seeing meaningful patterns in the data can take a long time, and it can be a period when researchers experience panic and the thought of giving up is present. Glaser refers to this as the 'drugless trip' (Glaser 1978).

There is no strict formula for how to present the theory, when it is fully developed (Goulding 2002). The form in which theory is presented may be independent of the process by which it was generated. It may take the form of a well-codified set of propositions, or it may consist of a running theoretical discussion using conceptual categories and their properties (Glaser and Strauss 1967). Thus, the presentation stage usually entails dilemmas over the structure the presentation should take, how many methodological details to include and the amount of data to present in order to provide evidence and support for the identified core categories. Preferably, the researcher should illustrate how concepts have emerged and developed from the data, how the researcher had moved from description through the process of abstraction and how the core categories were generated. There should be evidence to support the validity of the theory, i.e. interpretations must include the perspectives and voices of those studied.

CONCLUDING RECOMMENDATIONS

Grounded theory is a qualitative methodology that is enjoying increasing popularity within the social sciences. The main appeal lies in the promise of theory generation as a result of following the principles for data collection and interpretation. The fundamental procedures of grounded theory do offer a systematic method for handling and analysing data, and if applied with creativity it may lead to insightful and innovative new perspectives.

Nonetheless, it is important to bear in mind that grounded theory does not necessarily suit everyone and every question. Also, especially when attempting it for the first time, it can be messy, time-consuming and difficult to deal with. But for those who enjoy challenges, the end results can be extremely rewarding.

Young scholars considering attempting grounded theory for the first time should bear in mind six important points identified by Suddaby (2006). He notes that when reviewing manuscripts for the *Academy of Management Journal*, he sees grounded theory often used as 'rhetorical sleight of hand by authors who are unfamiliar with qualitative research and who wish to avoid close description or illumination of their methods' (Suddaby 2006: 633). In short, scholars must bear in mind:

1. Grounded theory is not an excuse to ignore the literature. This misassumption is based on the myth that grounded theory requires that the researcher enters the field without any knowledge of prior research. As pointed out by Suddaby (2006), there are several variants of this myth, but they all seem to be based on the false premise that a researcher is a blank sheet devoid of experience or knowledge.
2. Grounded theory is not presentation of raw data. This misassumption sometimes arises from the epistemological problem of confusing grounded theory with phenomenology or because the author has failed to 'lift' data to a conceptual level, meaning that the researcher has failed to completely analyse the data (the process of abstraction).
3. Grounded theory is not theory testing, content analysis or word counts. This misconception is sometimes found in manuscripts where authors have used interpretive methods to analyse 'realist' assumptions. The manuscript may begin with clear positivist assumptions, including hypotheses, and then proceed to report 'tests' of the hypotheses with sets of interviews or counts of words.
4. Grounded theory is not simply routine application of formulaic technique to data. This myth has several manifestations, where one is to present grounded theory as a series of rigid rules, for example, 'saturation is achieved when one has conducted between 25 and 30 interviews'. Another common characteristic is a neurotic overemphasis on coding, but making no interpretive effort at any stage of the coding. Consequently, conceptual categories can become divorced from both the data and the original research question.
5. Grounded theory is not perfect. Grounded theory research was founded as a practical approach to help researchers understand complex social processes. It was also designed as a method that might occupy a pragmatic middle ground between some slippery

epistemological boundaries. Following this genealogy, grounded theory techniques are inherently 'messy'.

6.   Grounded theory is not easy. A well-executed grounded theory study is the product of considerable experience, hard work, creativity and, occasionally, a healthy dose of good luck. Many of the techniques of grounded theory research are developmental, and the quality of application improves with experience.

NOTES

1.   In *The Discovery of Grounded Theory*, Glaser and Strauss make much of the difference between substantive and formal theory (1967: 32). Formal theory is the sociologist's goal, but to be valid it must be developed from a substantive grounding in concrete social situations.
2.   Theoretical sensitivity is basically an abstract term that refers to the researcher's ability to give meaning to data and to recognize data that are important and add meaning to the emerging theory versus data that do not.
3.   The logbook can also be described as field notes. As described by Van Maanen (1988), field notes are an ongoing stream-of-consciousness commentary about what is happening in the research, involving both observation and analysis – and preferably separated from one another.

REFERENCES

Allen, D.N. and R. McCluskey (1990), 'Structure, Policy, services and performance in the business incubator industry', *Entrepreneurship Theory and Practice*, **15** (2), 61–77.
Backman, K. and H.A. Kyngäs (1999), 'Challenges of the grounded theory approach to a novice researcher', *Nursing and Health Sciences*, **1** (3), 147–53.
Bartunek, J.M., S.L. Rynes and R.D. Ireland (2006), 'What makes management research interesting, and why does it matter?', *Academy of Management Journal*, **49** (1), 9–15.
Becker, P.H. (1993), 'Common pitfalls in published grounded theory research', *Qualitative Health Research*, **3** (2), 254–60.
Bouwen, R. and C. Steyaert (1990), 'Construing organizational texture in young entrepreneurial firms', *Journal of Management Studies*, **27** (6), 637–49.
Bygrave, W.D. (1989), 'The entrepreneurship paradigm (I): a philosophical look at its research methodologies', *Entrepreneurship Theory and Practice*, **14** (1), 7–26.
Charmaz, K. (2001), 'Grounded theory. objectivist and constructivist methods', in N.K. Denzin and Y.S. Lincoln (eds), *Handbook of Qualitative Research*, 2nd edn, Thousand Oaks, CA: Sage, pp. 509–35.
Charmaz, K. (2005), 'Grounded theory in the 21st century. Applications for advancing social justice studies', in N.K. Denzin and Y.S. Lincoln (eds), *The Sage Handbook of Qualitative Research*, 3rd edn, Thousand Oaks, CA: Sage Publications, pp. 507–35.
Child, J. and D. Faulkner (1998), *Strategies of Co-operation. Managing Alliances, Networks, and Joint Ventures*, Oxford: Oxford University Press.
Corbin, J. and A. Strauss (1990), 'Grounded theory research: procedures, canons, and evaluative criteria', *Qualitative Sociology*, **13** (1), 3–21.
Danermark, B., M. Ekström, L. Jakobsen and J.C. Karlsson (2002), *Explaining Society. Critical Realism in the Social Sciences*, London and New York: Routledge.

Denzin, N. (1994), 'The art and politics of interpretation', in N.K. Denzin and Y. Lincoln (eds), *Handbook of Qualitative Research*, Thousand Oaks, CA: Sage, pp. 500–515.

Douglas, D. (2003), 'Grounded Theories of management: a methodological review', *Management Research News*, **26** (5), 44–52.

Frederick, H. and E. Monsen (2011), 'New Zealand's perfect storm of entrepreneurship and economic development', *Small Business Economics*, **37** (2), 187–204.

Gemmell, R.M., R.J. Boland and D.A. Kolb (2012), 'The socio-cognitive dynamics of entrepreneurial ideation', *Entrepreneurship Theory and Practice*, **36** (5), 1053–73.

Gephart, R. (2004), 'Qualitative research and the Academy of Management Journal', *Academy of Management Journal*, **47** (4), 454–62.

Glaser, B. (1978), *Theoretical Sensitivity: Advances in the Methodology of Grounded Theory*, Mill Valley, CA: Sociology Press.

Glaser, B. (1992), *Basics of Grounded Theory Analysis: Emergence v Forcing*, Mill Valley, CA: Sociology Press.

Glaser, B.G. (2001), *The Grounded Theory Perspective. Conceptualization Contrasted with Description*, Mill Valley, CA: Sociology Press.

Glaser, B.G. and A. Strauss (1967), *The Discovery of Grounded Theory. Strategies for Qualitative Research*, Chicago, IL: Aldine.

Goulding, C. (2001), 'Grounded theory: a magical formula or a potential nightmare', *The Marketing Review*, **2** (1), 21–33.

Goulding, C. (2002), *Grounded Theory. A Practical Guide for Management, Business and Market Researchers*, London, Thousand Oaks, CA and New Delhi: Sage Publications.

Heath, H. and S. Cowley (2004), 'Developing a grounded theory approach: a comparison of Glaser and Strauss', *International Journal of Nursing Studies*, **41** (2), 141–50.

Isabella, L.A. (1990), 'Evolving interpretations as a change unfolds: how managers construe key organizational events', *Academy of Management Journal*, **33** (1), 7–41.

Khavul, S., G.D. Bruton and E. Wood (2009), 'Informal family business in Africa', *Entrepreneurship Theory and Practice*, **33** (6), 1219–38.

Lewicki, R.J. and B.B. Bunker (1996), 'Developing and maintaining trust in work relationships', in R.M. Kramer and T.R. Tyler (eds), *Trust in Organizations: Frontiers of Theory and Research*, Thousand Oaks, CA, London and New Delhi: Sage Publications, pp. 114–39.

Locke, K. (2001), *Grounded Theory in Management Research*, London, Thousand Oaks, CA and New Delhi: Sage Publications.

Lopes, M.P., M.P.E. Cunha and P.J.D. Palma (2009), 'Case studies on what entrepreneurs actually do to attract resources: a two-route framework', *Journal of Enterprising Culture*, **17** (3), 323–49.

O'Reilly, K., D. Paper and S. Marx (2012), 'Demystifying grounded theory for business research', *Organizational Research Methods*, **15** (2), 247–62.

Petkova, A.P., V.P. Rindova and A.K. Gupta (2008), 'How can new ventures build reputation? An Exploratory study', *Corporate Reputation Review*, **11** (4), 320–34.

Shane, S. and S. Venkataraman (2000), 'The promise of entrepreneurship as a field of research', *Academy of Management Review*, **25** (1), 217–26.

Shapiro, D.L., B.M. Sheppard and L. Cheraskin (1992), 'Business on a handshake', *Negotiation Journal*, **8** (4), 365–77.

Sousa, C.A.A. and P.H.J. Hendriks (2006), 'The diving bell and the butterfly: the need for grounded theory in developing a knowledge-based view of organizations', *Organizational Research Methods*, **9** (3), 315–38.

Spiggle, S. (1994), 'Analysis and interpretation of qualitative data in consumer research', *Journal of Consumer Research*, **21** (3), 491–503.

Strauss, A. and J. Corbin (1990), *Basics of Qualitative Research. Grounded Theory Procedures and Techniques*, Newbury Park, CA, London and New Delhi: Sage Publications.

Strauss, A. and J. Corbin (1994), 'Grounded theory methodology. An overview', in N.K. Denzin and Y.S. Lincoln (eds), *Handbook of Qualitative Research*, Thousand Oaks, CA: Sage Publications, pp. 273–85.

Strauss, A. and J. Corbin (1998), *Basics of Qualitative Research. Techniques and Procedures for Developing Grounded Theory*, 2nd edn, Thousand Oaks, CA, London and New Delhi: Sage Publications.

Strauss, A. and J. Corbin (1999), 'Grounded theory methodology: an overview', in A. Bryman and R. Burgess (eds), *Qualitative Research*, vol. 3, London: Sage, pp. 72–93.

Suddaby, R. (2006), 'From the editors: what grounded theory is not', *Academy of Management Journal*, **49** (4), 633–42.

Van Maanen, J. (1988), *Tales of the Field*, Chicago, IL and London: University of Chicago Press.

Wincent, J. and D. Örtqvist (2009), 'Role stress and entrepreneurship research', *International Entrepreneurship and Management Journal*, **5** (1), 1–22.

Zahra, S.A. (2007), 'Contextualizing theory building in entrepreneurship research', *Journal of Business Venturing*, **22** (3), 443–52.

The future for the constant comparative technique

Alistair R. Anderson and Sarah L. Jack

A good study can help anticipate the future, not because it predicts but because it provides a road map or guide (Hoepfl 1997: 57). It has been said that 'researchers should use tools and techniques that will really bring out a deeper understanding and appreciation about entrepreneurial work as it is enacted in practice and in thought' (Short et al. 2010: 10). While entrepreneurship provides opportunities for researchers, it has also been confronted by challenges and criticism. Short et al. (2010: 9) argue that increased reliance on prominent guides to qualitative research such as Lincoln and Guba (1985), Yin (2003), Gephart (2004) and Miles and Huberman (1994) could remedy the mixed impressions entrepreneurship research has received.

We are fortunate in entrepreneurship research because we may have more control in selecting contexts that are theoretically grounded. We can often also select purposeful samples, those that reflect the phenomenon, or aspect of the phenomenon, we want to understand. We contrast this favourably to approaches which have to begin with a representative sample; we have the luxury of theoretical choice. Yet in spite of this advantage, too much poor quality work is labelled as grounded theorizing. It is unsurprising then that grounded theory has been criticized on several grounds: it is rarely done properly, there seem to be several different grounded theories, in the sense it is meant to be used, it is actually very difficult to do and in reality often does not work very well. This is because grounded theory relies on, or seems to rely on, the 'theory' emerging from the data. But does it? In reality, it is the links and relationships between the bits in the data that have the potential to provide explanation (theory). But, these links have to be recognized. The data will not tell the researcher they are there. Instead, the researcher has to be able to spot and be alert to the themes and patterns that emerge (or do not emerge) from the data. Yet this too is the strength of constant comparison.

By its very nature, qualitative research can be intellectually and even emotionally taxing. It is time-consuming but offers rich analysis not obtainable through statistical techniques (Hoepfl 1997: 61). However, it requires skill and a solid understanding of the research paradigm and use of qualitative observation and analysis techniques (Hoepfl 1997: 61). By accepting the complex and dynamic nature of the social world, qualitative researchers seek 'illumination, understanding and extrapolation to similar situation' (Hoepfl 1997: 48). However, our work has to be publishable. To achieve this it has to be robust and reviewers will look for three key qualities: (1) coherency, (2) consensus and (3) instrumental utility. Our hope is that the three chapters offered in Part I will help support researchers in their endeavours.

The three chapters in Part I have each provided a detailed exposition of how researchers have employed either grounded theory (Bøllingtoft, Chapter 3 in this volume; Smith and McKeever, Chapter 2 in this volume) or the constant comparison technique (Jack et al., Chapter 1 in this volume) that should help support other scholars in their own research endeavours. The very comprehensive accounts provided illustrate the challenges of adopting such research methods, in particular the importance of researchers to have the skills, ability, sensitivity, resilience and patience to conduct both data collection and analysis. Throughout Part I the close origins and similarities as well as the differences between the two techniques have been highlighted. In deciding which technique to choose, researchers perhaps should bear in mind that as the constant comparison technique is aligned more closely with analytic induction than grounded theory is, this potentially permits greater scope. In essence, grounded theory focuses on the generation of theory and constant comparison, while the constant comparative technique is more comprehensive as it generates and tests theory provisionally, focuses on causation and requires that all data be tested against the hypothesis (Jack et al., Chapter 1 in this volume). Accordingly, this adds rigour to the trustworthiness of qualitative data and analysis. Despite the challenges inherent in both techniques, they are both extremely effective in situations where there is some prior understanding of the research context and where flexibility and adaptability of research approach are required. Further, both have the potential for making additional insights and increasing knowledge about the behaviours and activities of entrepreneurs and the entrepreneurial process.

REFERENCES

Gephart, R.P. (2004), 'Qualitative research and the *Academy of Management Journal*', *Academy of Management Journal*, **47** (4), 454–58.

Hoepfl, M.C. (1997), 'Choosing qualitative research: a primer for technology education researchers', *Journal of Technology Education*, **9** (1), 47–63.

Lincoln, Y.S and E.G. Guba (1985), *Naturalistic Inquiry*, Beverley Hills, CA: Sage.

Miles, M.B. and A.M. Huberman (1984), *Qualitative Data Analysis: A Source Book of New Methods*, Beverly Hills, CA: Sage.

Short, J., D.J. Ketchen, J. Combs and R.D. Ireland (2010), 'Research methods in entrepreneurship: opportunities and challenges', *Organizational Research Methods*, **13** (1), 6–15.

Yin, R.K. (2003), *Case Study Research: Designs and Methods*, 3rd edn, Thousand Oaks, CA: Sage Publications.

PART II

METAPHOR METHODOLOGIES

Metaphor methodologies: exploring entrepreneurship research, pedagogy and researchers
Sarah Drakopoulou Dodd and Alice de Koning

This part presents research projects which use metaphors to study entrepreneurship, and tries to evaluate the relative advantages and disadvantages of the different methods used. This part introduction touches on the theoretical background to using metaphor methodologies and reviews the entrepreneurship metaphor literature. The three chapters in this part consider the process of metaphor methodologies, and address the methodological challenges faced by researchers in the real world.

Understanding how entrepreneurs are perceived contributes to our appreciation of the context for enterprise, generates insights into related topics such as entrepreneurial identities and roles, and may also show how entrepreneurial meaning is made and shared. There has been a noticeable, if rather restrained, trend over the past few years towards the use of metaphors as a source of perceptions and conceptualizations of the entrepreneur.

THE EPISTEMOLOGY OF METAPHORS

At some level, all science is metaphorical in nature. Scientific models are abstractions from reality, they assert that it is 'as if' things were like this. To this degree, all entrepreneurship scholarship is metaphorical. At the level of individual theory-building, metaphors are also utilized. Examples of metaphors used in theory-building within the entrepreneurship literature include population ecology theories, which abduct theoretical material from biology, as well as the more colourful parenting metaphor abducted by Cardon et al. (2003) and, as Johannisson (1995) has noted, the myriad metaphors contained in network theory.

The epistemological uses of metaphors indicate what an important tool they are for making sense and giving sense. This is as true for entrepreneurs, policy-makers, venture capitalists, societies and so forth as it is for scholars. Because metaphors represent tentative mental models, by which people create meanings, and communicate those meanings to others, they offer 'raw material' to social scientists wishing to study the sense-making and sense-giving processes. How groups of people perceive entrepreneurs, and the entrepreneurial process, has long been argued to be of fundamental importance in driving entrepreneurial motivation and legitimation. Metaphors give access to these perceptions, and it is this type of metaphor which we are especially interested in within the current section.

METAPHORICAL FORAYS IN ENTREPRENEURSHIP RESEARCH

Metaphor methodology has been extensively employed in sister-disciplines such as organizational studies, marketing and strategy. However, entrepreneurship scholars have tended to rely on other methodologies in their work, and our literature search revealed 14 studies which use metaphor as their main tool in exploring entrepreneurs and entrepreneurship. (One or both of us are the guilty parties in six of the 14 cases.) A variety of methods were used by these scholars, as the next section, presented in chronological order, shows, and as illustrated by Table II.1.

Hill and Levenhagen (1995) developed a framework to explain how entrepreneurs develop mental models to make sense of their experiences, perceptions and plans, as well as to communicate this sense to others. Koiranen (1995) used a questionnaire-based survey, with more than 300 respondents, to generate and then compare perceptions of the entrepreneur, asking people to share their dominant metaphors for the entrepreneur. Martyn Pitt (1998) developed quasi-narratives inter-subjectively from longitudinal case studies, and studied the metaphors used by the two case entrepreneurs to make sense of the different roles they had adopted over the years in question. Perren and Atkin (1997) use metaphor analysis to examine entrepreneurial decision-making, and determinants/ constraints of growth. Cosgel (1996) explained the inability of neoclassical economics to accommodate the entrepreneur as being due to rhetorical methods of economics, especially mechanistic metaphors. Mahlamäki-Kultanen and Hakala (n.d.) examine the educational implications of rural entrepreneurs' beliefs in Finland, studying the metaphors in a huge sample of interview transcripts. Hrysky (1999) followed Koiranen's approach, using a large-scale questionnaire-based survey, comparing perceptions of the entrepreneur across countries, genders, and occupation.

Drakopoulou Dodd (2002) developed a grounded model of US entrepreneurship, using metaphor analysis of Internet sources. De Koning and Drakopoulou Dodd (2002) set out initial findings from a six-country study of newspaper articles about the entrepreneur. Cardon et al. (2005)

Table II.1 Studies of entrepreneurial metaphors

Authors	Research objective	Data source	Main metaphor themes
Hill and Levenhagen (1995)	Paradigm of how mental models are developed and implemented	Entrepreneurial stories and examples, mainly from the IT sector (USA)	Last Force for Freedom (Apple); Revolution (Apple/NEXT); Knowledge Navigator (Apple)
Pitt (1998)	Theories of action – entrepreneurial roles	2 semi-structured conversational narratives (UK)	Experimenter; shoe-stringer; commando; poacher; team captain; servant; gambler; boxer; predator; visionary guru; team coach; mountain climber
Perren and Atkin (1997)	Growth & perceptions of the environment	16 autobiographic interview transcripts (UK)	Adversity; victim; combat; journey; burden
Mahlamäki-Kultanen and Hakala	Educational implications of rural entrepreneurs' beliefs	136 thematic qualitative interviews (Finland)	Hard worker on an endless stony path; mother of the family
Koiranen (1995)	Perceptions of the entrepreneur	Questionnaire, international (EU) sample, 316 respondents	Creative, industrial actor; special characteristics; machine; nature; sportsman; adventurer
Hrysky (1999)	Perceptions of the entrepreneur	Questionnaire, international (EU) sample (751 respondents)	Machinery; adventurer; sportsman; innovative, industrious actor; nature; disease; food item; special characteristics
Drakopoulou Dodd (2002)	Grounded model of (US) entrepreneurship	Popular business press articles, online	Journey; race; war; iconoclasm; passion; building
De Koning and Drakopoulou Dodd (2002)	The entrepreneur in national public discourse of six countries	150 newspaper articles from six (global) countries	The fight is on; It's alive; what a character; The show must go on; Homely arts; Myths and classics; Road travelled; Things of the spirit

Table II.1 (continued)

Authors	Research objective	Data source	Main metaphor themes
Nicolson and Anderson (2005)	Changes in UK (enterprise) culture	Articles, from a single (UK) newspaper, compared over time	(2000) Alchemy; ability; gentle giants; fall of the hero; myth; theatre; online kings; polite rebels; dodgy geezers
Cardon et al. (2005)	Applicability of parenting metaphors as a frame for entrepreneurial theory	Reflection and extension of the parenting metaphor (in scholarly and practitioner discourse)	Parent; baby; conception; gestation; birth; infancy; toddlerhood; childhood; adolescence; guardians; miscarriage; infant mortality
De Koning and Drakopoulou Dodd (2008)	Cross-cultural constructions of warrior entrepreneurs	150 newspaper articles from six (global) countries	The fight is on (studied in detail)
Anderson et al. (2009)	Perceptions of entrepreneurs in European schools	Questionnaire, international (EU) sample (374 respondents)	Aggressor, outsider, winner and victim
De Koning and Drakopoulou Dodd (2010)	Using metaphorical gambits to link stories to other stories and make shared sense	*The Republic of Tea* (US book)	The republic; tea; business as a person; the journey; poetry, film production and art; the game mother's little helper
Drakopoulou Dodd et al. (2012)	Admiration and repugnance for the entrepreneur in European schools	Questionnaire, international (EU) sample (374 respondents)	Positive and negative metaphors of the entrepreneur

Source: This table is a (very slight) adaptation of table 1 from Drakopoulou Dodd et al. (2013), which started life as a much shorter, less detailed table 1 in De Koning and Drakopoulou Dodd (2004).

explore the richness of the parenthood metaphor for explaining key aspects of entrepreneurship. Nicholson and Anderson (2005) compare metaphors about the entrepreneur from the same newspaper, over a long time frame, to capture changing cultural perceptions. Anderson et al. (2009) present the social construction of the entrepreneur as encountered within European senior/high schools. Drakopoulou Dodd et al. (2013) extend this study, examining negative and positive metaphors of the entrepreneur within the same group. De Koning and Drakopoulou Dodd (2010), honoured to be included in the first issue of Bill Gartner's *ENTER*, examined the early communication exchanges within an entrepreneurial team, as (re-)presented in their book, *The Republic of Tea*, through the lens of metaphorical gambits. These 14 studies into entrepreneurship, each using a variant of metaphor methodology, allow us to present illustrative examples of some of the choices available to scholars at various stages in the research process.[1]

PRACTICAL METHODOLOGIES TO FULFIL THE THEORETICAL PROMISE OF ANALYSING METAPHORS

As a field we have yet to fully embrace this promising methodological tool kit. One reason for this may be anxiety about the practicalities of metaphor-driven research. Our aim is to address this anxiety, by reviewing methods used, and evaluating alternative choices open to researchers at differing stages in the research process. Our Chapter 4 on metaphors for entrepreneurs and entrepreneurship breaks down the methodology of metaphor into discrete stages, presents options available at each stage, illustrates these choices with examples from extant scholarship, or our own experimentation, and reviews the advantages and disadvantages of each of these options. The chapter thereby provides a menu of metaphorical methodologies, with the aim of making these valuable methods more accessible to a wider audience, as well as of indicating how researchers can achieve the requisite methodological rigour. Chapter 5 by Robert Smith on visual metaphors discusses a study of entrepreneurship textbooks and the incongruity of the metaphors in visual images and the textual discussions. This chapter challenges academics to pay attention to both the explicit and more subtle messages communicated in the classroom. Chapter 6 by Cecilia Bjursell on metaphors in scientific writing by academics turns our attention to ourselves, encouraging greater self-consciousness as researchers in how we communicate our theories and findings. This kind of attentiveness by academics is essential not just to the discussion of entrepreneurship among researchers, as discussed by Bjursell, or with students, as discussed by Smith, but also to the actual analysis of metaphors using a hermeneutical approach, as discussed in the chapter on metaphors for entrepreneurs and entrepreneurship.

We will combine consideration of the work of our entrepreneurship colleagues in making use of metaphor methodologies with a more detailed examination of what we have learnt from a series of controlled studies in own research programme. Read, pay attention, and enjoy!

NOTE

1. A recent, innovative and very strong contribution to the field has subsequently been made by Cornelissen et al. (2012) who explore metaphors in the speech and gestures of two entrepreneurs who are 'giving sense' in an attempt to win support for their novel, early stage ventures.

REFERENCES

Anderson, A., S. Drakopoulou Dodd and S. Jack, S. (2009), 'Aggressors; winners; victims and outsiders: European schools' social construction of the entrepreneur', *International Small Business Journal*, **27** (1), 126–33.

Cardon, M., C. Zietsma, P. Saparito, B.P. Matherne, and C. Davis (2005), 'A tale of passion: new insights into entrepreneurship from a parenthood metaphor', *Journal of Business Venturing*, **20** (1), 23–45.

Cornelissen, J., J. Clarke and A. Cienki (2012), 'Sensegiving in entrepreneurial contexts: the use of metaphors in speech and gesture to gain and sustain support for novel business ventures', *International Small Business Journal*, **30** (3), 213–41.

Cosgel, M. (1996), 'Metaphors, stories and the entrepreneur in economics', *History of Political Economy*, **28** (1), 57–76.

De Koning, A. and S. Drakopoulou Dodd (2002), 'Raising babies, fighting battles, winning races: entrepreneurial metaphors in the media of 5 English speaking nations', paper presented at the 2002 Babson Kauffman Entrepreneurship Conference, 6–8 June, Boulder, CO.

De Koning, A. and S. Drakopoulou Dodd (2008), 'Metaphors of entrepreneurship across cultures', *Journal of Asia Entrepreneurship and Sustainability*, **4** (2), 87–101.

De Koning, A. and S. Drakopoulou Dodd (2010), 'Tea and understanding: metaphors in the entrepreneurial narrative of tea republic', *ENTER*, **1** (1), 33–50.

Drakopoulou Dodd, S. (2002), 'Metaphors and meaning: a grounded cultural model of US entrepreneurship', *Journal of Business Venturing*, **17** (5), 519.

Drakopoulou Dodd, S. and A. de Koning (2004), 'Methodology and metaphors', presented at the Babson Kauffman Entrepreneurship Conference, 3–5 June, Strathclyde University, Glasgow.

Drakopoulou Dodd, S., S. Jack and A. Anderson (2013), 'From admiration to abhorrence: the contentious appeal of entrepreneurship across Europe', *Entrepreneurship & Regional Development*, **25** (1–2), 69–89.

Hill, R.C. and M. Levenhagen (1995), 'Metaphors and mental models: sense making and sense giving in innovative and entrepreneurial activities', *Journal of Management*, **21** (6), 1057–75.

Hyrsky, K. (1999), 'Entrepreneurial metaphors and concepts: an exploratory study', *International Small Business Journal*, **18** (1), 13–34.

Johannisson, B. (1995), 'Paradigms and entrepreneurial networks–some methodological challenges', *Entrepreneurship & Regional Development*, **7** (3), 215–32.

Koiranen, M. (1995), 'North-European metaphors of "entrepreneurship" and "an entrepreneur"', in W.D. Bygraves, S. Birley and N.C. Churchill (eds), *Frontiers of Entrepreneurship Research*, Waltham, MA: P & R Publications, pp. 203–16.

Mahlamäki-Kultanen, S. and R. Hakala (n.d.), 'Educational implications of rural entrepreneurs' beliefs and metaphors', unpublished working paper, available at: http://citeseerx.ist.psu.edu/viewdoc/download?doi=10.1.1.200.1807&rep=rep1&type=pdf (accessed 27 May 2015).

Nicolson, L. and A. Anderson (2005), 'News and nuances of the entrepreneurial myth and metaphor: linguistic games in entrepreneurial sensemaking and sensegiving', *Entrepreneurship Theory and Practice*, **29** (2), 153–72.

Perren, L. and R. Atkin (1997), 'Women-manager's discourse: the metaphors-in-use', *Journal of Applied Management Studies*, **6** (1), 47–61.

Pitt, M. (1998), 'A tale of two gladiators: "reading" entrepreneurs as texts', *Organization Studies*, **19** (3), 387–414.

4 Enacting, experimenting and exploring metaphor methodologies in entrepreneurship

Sarah Drakopoulou Dodd and Alice de Koning

INTRODUCTION

This chapter follows a staged model of metaphor-driven methodology. We review our own work using analysis of metaphors to study the context of entrepreneurship as well as that of other people. (See the part introduction for a summary of the papers referenced in this chapter.) The detailed description and discussion of methodological issues is grounded in almost a decade of shared endeavour between the two co-authors trying to figure out rigorous techniques for studying metaphors of the entrepreneur, through reading, experimentation, and debate.

The chapter is organized in seven sections, following the logic of metaphor methodology, which can be modelled as comprising seven main processes:

1. Setting the research objective.
2. Generating and/or selecting source material.
3. Identifying metaphors within source material.
4. Developing metaphor codes and categories.
5. Applying coding schemes to the metaphors.
6. Analyzing coded metaphors.
7. Presenting results.

An extensive literature review was carried out to identify and study the variety of methods adopted by entrepreneurship scholars using metaphors as their primary source data. This was supplemented by a wider foray into the metaphor literature, particularly that of organizational studies. Having carried out this bibliographic work, we then incorporated a variety of the methods and techniques identified in the literature into an ongoing international study of entrepreneurial conceptualization. This permitted a research design including careful and controlled testing, and comparison, of the techniques utilized, within the framework of a specific piece of research. Findings as to the ease of use, advantages, disadvantages and special characteristics of each method tested were harvested using contemporaneous notes by the research team. Our first review of metaphor methodologies was presented at the 2004 Babson Conference (Drakopoulou Dodd and de Koning 2004), and this chapter brings the ongoing story up to date. In parallel, we have also engaged in other experimental work using metaphor methodologies, both with each other, and with other colleagues. All of these sources provide the raw material from which this chapter is constructed.

THE SEVEN PROCESSES IN METAPHOR METHODOLOGY

Stage One: Setting the Research Objective

Hill and Levenhagen (1995) consider metaphor as a tool used by the entrepreneur for creating meaning, and Cardon et al. (2005) use the metaphor of parenthood as a springboard for scholarly reflection. However, Table 4.1 shows that the research objectives of almost all studies have focused on perceptions, or conceptions, held about the entrepreneur, the entrepreneurial process, and entrepreneurship.

In some cases, the perceptions have been ascribed to a specific national culture, as with Nicolson and Anderson's (2005) study, as well as Drakopoulou Dodd (2002). In other cases, the perceptions of specific groups have been contrasted with each other, such as successfully growing entrepreneurs with non-growers and failed growers (Perren and Atkin 1997), as well as comparisons between industrial sectors (Mahlamäki-Kultanen and Hakala n.d.), nations (Koiranen 1995; Hrysky 1999; De Koning and Drakopoulou 2002, 2008; Anderson et al. 2009; Drakopoulou Dodd et al. 2013), genders (Hrysky 1999) and, even, between two specific entrepreneurs (Pitt 1998). While the subject and level of analysis may vary, however, the constant object of study – perceptions/conceptualizations of entrepreneurship – remains. Making and sharing meanings of the entrepreneur is what metaphors are all about, so it should not come as a big surprise to find such commonality of purpose among scholars.

Stage Two: Generating and/or Selecting Source Material

There have been, to date, three main sources of metaphorical material in entrepreneurship research, as column two of Table 4.1 highlights. Semi-structured interviews with entrepreneurs, typically aiming at generating autobiographical narratives, although sometimes focused on a theme of

Table 4.1   Perceptions of entrepreneurship questionnaire

Please list five metaphors which describe for you the characteristics of an entrepreneur. Follow your first instincts. There are no wrong answers
Metaphor 1: Entrepreneurs are like: Metaphor 2: Entrepreneurs are like: Metaphor 3: Entrepreneurs are like: Metaphor 4: Entrepreneurs are like: Metaphor 5: Entrepreneurs are like:

special interest, have provided original source material for metaphorical analysis. Several scholars have utilized questionnaires which ask respondents to create metaphors illustrating their perception of the entrepreneur. Newspaper, Internet and magazine articles about, or by, entrepreneurs have provided researchers with access to metaphors used in cultural constructions of entrepreneurship.

Each of these has provided useful, relevant and interesting data. In general terms, we may conclude that surveys have worked well when the views of specific populations are sought, and quantitative methods anticipated, especially for comparative purposes. Interview data provide insights into the life of the entrepreneur, and allow for detailed and rich interaction with the subjects of the study. Newspapers and magazines allow access to public discourse, to the social constructs specific societies have created about the entrepreneur.

Surveys

First deployed by Matti Koiranen, and then by Hyrsky, the survey method asks respondents 'to form metaphorical expressions describing entrepreneurs and entrepreneurship. Informants were instructed to come up with five metaphors in both categories' (Hrysky 1999: 17). Anderson et al. (2009) drew on the field work of the EUROPE project, which used the template questionnaire in Table 4.1 to elicit metaphors from its sample of school stakeholders, following Koiranen's approach closely.

EUROPE Project Leader Professor Joseph Hassid from the University of Pireaus and the other participating universities around the continent administered questionnaires, which included this metaphor section, mostly face to face. This meant that members of the research team were able to explain in more detail to respondents what we meant by metaphors, which did indeed prove necessary on several occasions.

Care was taken to avoid using example metaphors for the entrepreneur, since anecdotal empirical evidence suggested that this could become strongly suggestive to respondents. Another related problem with this approach is that it inevitably harvests literal expressions, as well as metaphors; in spite of explanations, some respondents simply are unwilling, or unable, to provide metaphors.

Nevertheless, in terms of generating a large, manageable data-set of metaphors for analysis, the survey method is efficient and timely. It also permits access to respondent groups whose perceptions of the entrepreneur may not have been expressed metaphorically in any other way, so that other textual sources for analysis are not available to scholars.

Interview data

Martin Pitt provides the most detailed description of this approach to gathering interview data in a fashion which facilitates generating narrative transcripts rich enough to permit metaphor analysis in Appendix One of his 1998 *Organization Studies* paper. As well as analysis of metaphors of identity, Pitt's wider model of entrepreneurs' personal theory of action incorporated context statements, action templates and dilemmas, so extensive longitudinal multi-method data collection was required. However, at the heart of his field work remained the qualitative interview, which he describes superbly as follows:

> Simple questions prompted narratives about context, perceptions of key events, personal goals, problems and opportunities, roles and styles of operating, etc. Informants had the scope to declare facts, express currently held opinions and tell more elaborate stories. The salient issues were rarely covered fully in one session, justifying the request for a follow up. Subsequent sessions covered outstanding issues and explored new topics prompted by previous interviews. Greater use was made of 'devil's advocacy' to explore seeming inconsistencies and more controversial themes. Ideas and opinions were often reflected back to the subject for clarification, elaboration or rebuttal. Allegedly significant historical events were also discretely checked for consistency in later interviews with the informant and with others. Interviewing required patience, listening skills and alertness to ensure that the conversation stayed on a broadly appropriate track without foreclosing on potentially valuable, if seemingly tangential anecdotes. (Pitt 1998: 408)

A similar approach was also used by Perren and Atkin, who solicited 'a taped autobiographic account' from their respondents, 'with the researcher taking as passive a role as possible' (Perren and Atkin 1997: 48). Essentially, interview methods aim to generate rich narratives which are reflective enough to contain metaphors. This is likely to require a focus on the meaning of events, on conceptualization of respondents' own identity, on informants' wider perceptions of their entrepreneurial stories.

Having once or twice, mostly out of curiosity, examined interview transcripts gathered for other research aims to try and identify possible metaphors, we found that, although always present to some degree – and with one or two absolute little treasures hidden away in the transcripts – there was not really enough metaphorical material present to justify using this analytic approach. While some respondents naturally reached for metaphors as a routine part of their sense-making, even in conversation with researchers, others preferred a much more focused form of interview interaction. It thus seems likely that special effort and skill is needed to elicit rich, allusive stories from entrepreneurs, and qualitative material gathered for other purposes may not be amenable to this approach. However, when such material is forthcoming, the depth of analysis which can emerge from these quasi-narratives is impressive, critical and engaging, as the papers surveyed here illustrate.

Metaphors in the media
Sociologists argue that newspapers can represent public discourse because publishers must create products that appeal to a broad base of readers. Analysis of conventional and novel metaphors may capture entrepreneurial narratives of public discourse. A growing body of work uses newspaper analysis to study values, ideas and ideologies (for example, Lacey and Longman 1993; Mann and Roseneils 1994; Alasuutari 1995). Newspaper analysis is increasingly included in the methodological toolbox to examine shared meanings (Soothill and Grover, 1997). As Nicholson and Anderson point out: 'Semiological processes, or the creating and transmission of meaning, are the reason newspapers exist. As with culture and communication, the role newspapers play in mirroring or manipulating reality seem to converge' (2005: 157–8).

Beyond these strong theoretical arguments for using newspapers as a source material for metaphors, there are more practical arguments, as Nicholson and Anderson (2005) also point out, such as convenience, regular daily provision and being in written form. Nicholson and Anderson chose the British newspaper, the *Independent*, because it is considered a high-quality, politically neutral paper. Wanting to explore changes over time, these colleagues selected the years 1989 and 2000, and then searched a CD-ROM of the *Independent*'s archives for these years, using the term entrepreneur(s). Having quickly checked the resulting articles (more than 1200 in total) the first and last ten articles of each month were retained for the study, with some further culling taking place to exclude, for example, listings, birthdays, and very short articles.

Our own joint fieldwork using this approach was reported in De Koning and Drakopoulou Dodd (2008), where we explain that our chosen time horizon was a ten-week period between December 2001 and February 2002. Because we wanted to examine cross-cultural perceptions of the entrepreneur, and avoid ethnocentric bias, we selected six countries from four continents which offered both cultural similarities and differences: Australia, Canada, Ireland, India, the United Kingdom and the United States of America. The countries were required to have an extensive (if not exclusive) anglophone press, so that we could avoid complicating matters further still by the need for translation. For the larger countries, we selected two nationally distributed newspapers; for the smaller countries, one nationally distributed newspaper was selected, resulting in the selection of nine newspapers. For Canada and India, given the language restriction we imposed on the study, our study is biased to the Anglophile elements of those countries. It is also worth noting that one of our practical criteria, a decade ago, that newspaper archives be digitally searchable, restricted our options then rather more than it would do now. The search term which we used to pinpoint articles within these digital archives was 'entrepreneur*' – thus including entrepreneurship, entrepreneurs, entrepreneurial, and so on. This meant our search included, but was not limited to, feature articles about individual entrepreneurs, thus avoiding an *a priori* bias towards heroic narratives that focusing only on biographical articles might have created. This collection of 150 articles became the source material within which we then began the hunt for metaphors.

Stage Three: Identifying Metaphors within the Source Material

Where the source material has been questionnaire driven, as in the work of Hyrsky (1999) and Koiranen, (1995), the metaphors are presented directly to the researcher, removing the need for detailed study to identify metaphors. This method therefore has efficiency benefits over alternatives, by effectively removing one of the most complex and time-consuming stages from the overall process. However, it is important to check for literal metaphors, which respondents may mistakenly include in their answers.

Table 4.2 shows an excerpt from a typical spreadsheet showing results from such a metaphor survey, in this case UK data from the EUROPE study, gathered by the University of Hertfordshire's Julie Gregory. The spreadsheet contains codes for key variables which the research team wanted to explore – occupation, country, and gender – as well as a code for the respondent, and a reference for each metaphor. Column six contains

Table 4.2   Excerpt from EUROPE Study data, for UK pupils

Occupation	Country	Gender	Code	Reference	Metaphor
Pupil	5	2	UK1001	UK10011	Inventors
Pupil	5	2	UK1001	UK10012	Trees rising above the rest
Pupil	5	2	UK1001	UK10013	A huge business brain
Pupil	5	2	UK1001	UK10014	birds
Pupil	5	2	UK1001	UK10015	children
Pupil	5	1	UK1002	UK10021	You will have to be very hardworking
Pupil	5	1	UK1002	UK10022	You will have to have a bit of trust in your employees
Pupil	5	1	UK1002	UK10023	You will have to be sure your business will be a success
Pupil	5	1	UK1002	UK10024	You will have to have enough money to carry it out
Pupil	5	1	UK1002	UK10025	You will have to have confidence in yourself
Pupil	5	2	UK1003	UK10031	Baby turtles leaving the nest there are a lot of threats from predators but if you try your hardest you would make it to the sea
Pupil	5	2	UK1003	UK10032	logs on a fire only certain logs will help make the flame grow and burn bright
Pupil	5	2	UK1003	UK10033	the throw of a bowling ball a good throw will pick up speed and knock down all the pins
Pupil	5	2	UK1003	UK10034	a song you need to reach all the right notes for the song to be popular
Pupil	5	2	UK1003	UK10035	a sports team you're only as good as the people you play with just as entrepreneurs are only as good as their suppliers

the data, the five metaphors provided by each of these three English schoolchildren. This sample data illustrates well that some respondents will be quite brief, and thin, as with the first respondent (code UK1001) who provides some very basic metaphors like 'birds', or 'children'. The second respondent has provided a list of behavioural prescriptions for becoming an entrepreneur, and their answers, such as 'you will have to be sure your business will be a success', were therefore excluded from this study, being classified as literal text. The final respondent, however, illustrates the potential gloriousness of this method, with the provision of rich, powerful metaphors like 'logs on a fire only certain logs will help make the flame grow and burn bright'.

Where textual, or semi-textual, data is used the identification of metaphors is much harder. As the other studies show, individuals or groups need to read the text several times, in detail, to pick put each metaphor. Our experience coincides with that of Perren and Atkin (1997), who noted that this is actually a very hard task, since it is easy to overlook metaphors when reading articles or transcripts.

This is not an insignificant methodological anxiety. In later stages of the process, such as analysis, the divergent views and insight generated by the differing subjective readings of each scholar are an integral and essential part of hermeneutics. Indeed, it is to be welcomed if a research team brings different insights, perceived themes and interpretations to the table during the analysis stage. However, identifying metaphors is of a rather different nature, and any scholar reviewing a text for metaphors should be able to come up with a list which, if complete, is functionally identical to that of any other. It is a discrete and finite task, providing that a clear description of what counts as a metaphor is agreed. It is also critical to subsequent analysis that this task is carried out as thoroughly as possible, otherwise researchers are not working from a full and representative data-set.

One of the goals we both set for our cross-national study was therefore to test several different approaches to metaphor identification. This was in part due to sustained feedback from colleagues when we presented our initial findings, asking how we could demonstrate that all metaphors had been picked out of the articles we were working from. Indeed, this feedback was often couched in quite firm terms, suggesting that unless we could demonstrably solve this puzzle, there was no point in submitting to a top journal. Cognitively, it is indeed likely that routine metaphors might be skimmed over, for example, or disagreeable ones ignored. We were familiar enough with the literature in the area to realize that it would not provide us with any additional help in these areas, so that we were forced to address the issues of identification (and classification) empirically. Indeed, we felt that such a laboratory experiment might prove valuable to other scholars also. In order to investigate identification techniques, we implemented and compared four methods, and reported our findings at the 2004 Babson Conference.

Each of us read, in detail and repeatedly, all of the articles in the study, and extracted every metaphor we found to a spreadsheet. This allowed

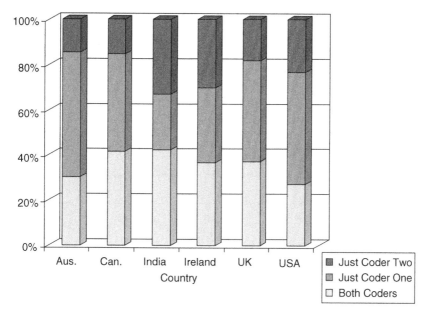

Figure 4.1   Two expert coders – metaphor identification

us to compare our performance as individual 'expert' coders. Next, we created a combined list of metaphors identified by us both, giving us a basis for examining the performance of a dyad of expert coders. As Figure 4.1 shows, a relatively small proportion of metaphors were identified by both expert coders. Indeed, the overall percentage of metaphors identified by both coders was only around 37 per cent. Of the total (1447) metaphors which the two expert coders identified between them, coder 1 (Alice) successfully identified 76 per cent, and coder 2 (Sarah) 60 per cent. If a single coder had been used, then between 40 per cent and 20 per cent of the metaphors in the sample text would have been overlooked. The task was rendered more difficult because of the sheer volume of articles studied – much higher than is normal for qualitative work. However, these findings raise questions about the reliability of studies based on single coder metaphor identification. And Sarah still owes Alice several large beers.

A relevant question at this point is to wonder whether there is any pattern to the drop error. It might have been anticipated that each coder would score better when dealing with material from their own country. However, Figure 4.1 shows that Canadian Alice – Coder One – had the best individual performance when working with the Australian material,

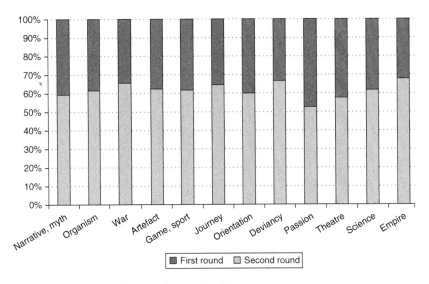

Figure 4.2   First and second round coding

and British Sarah – Coder Two – when working with the Indian data-set. Country of origin does not seem to play a role in improving metaphor identification.

A second possibility is that the coders noticed metaphors of special interest to them, or those which reinforce their preconceptions about the meaning of entrepreneurship. If this were so, then we should see a substantial variance, after second-round coding (see below), where all identified metaphors are incorporated into the classification system. We investigated this by comparing the classifications of Coder Two using (1) only those metaphors she had identified (first round coding), and (2) all metaphors, including those identified just by Coder One (second round coding). Figure 4.2 shows that there is not a dramatic difference in the proportions for first and second round codings across thematic groups. Coder Two (Sarah) was slightly less likely to have individually noticed science and nature, as well as deviancy, metaphors, and slightly more likely to have noticed passion metaphors. A more dramatic divergence in the proportions across groups would have been anticipated if this was a major causal factor in metaphor identification.

A closer reading of the dataset suggests a more mundane reason behind the drop error. Table 4.3 shows an extract from the master spreadsheet, for a *Financial Times* article. The article begins with seven lines of literal text, but lines 8 and 9 are dense in terms of metaphor usage. This provides a clear signal to both coders, who each identify all but one of the

Table 4.3   Identifying metaphors

Line		Coder One	Coder Two
8	the Valley's pioneering company, Fairchild, had spun off the first of the famous 'Fairchildren',	1	1
8	venture capitalists were flocking	1	1
8	semiconductor revolution was (in full swing)	1	0
8	Spurred by the invention of the integrated circuit	1	1
8	semiconductor (revolution) was in full swing	1	1
9	Of the six 'clones' that Rosenberg examines	0	1
14	the route followed by Nokia in Finland and Ericsson in Sweden	1	0
14	to attack one of the few segments of the market that are not dominated by US incumbents	1	0
17	governments should not try to jump-start clusters by direct intervention,	0	1
17	nor they should they engage in protectionism or 'infant industry' policies.	0	1
19	clusters are more likely to flourish	1	0
20	British entrepreneurs shy away from	1	0

metaphors in these two lines. Then, after line 9, the article switches again to more literal language, and the coders begin to hunt for the next metaphor. Coder One spots the two metaphors in line 14, but Coder Two misses these, and jumps straight to line 17. She then fails to notice the two metaphors at the end of the article. Coder One, by contrast, jumps from line 14 to line 18, missing the two metaphors in line 17. The dataset shows many similar patterns, where a run of joint identification is followed by several lines where only one coder has noticed any metaphors. In the light of our only too extensive experience of playing hunt-the-metaphor, our conclusion is that sustained and detailed concentration is very hard to maintain. Typically, after a dense piece of text has signalled a switch to metaphorical language, the coder increases concentration until the end of the section. Thereafter, there is a tendency to relax, until another strong signal is noticed. Our experience was that we tended to miss some of these signals completely, and hence all metaphors in the subsequent section.

This finding confirmed our suspicions that metaphors in public discourse must be studied using hermeneutic methods. To confirm this conclusion, we recruited three undergraduate students who specialized in rhetoric, but not entrepreneurship. A rigorous protocol was created, and piloted, the students were trained as coders, and the data divided so that each article was coded by two students (in addition to the co-authors). Each student list was also double-checked, to ensure that no literal expressions had been included in their dataset, which proved to be a necessary step. Interestingly, a similar low inter-rater reliability was found, if we just measure how many coders identified similar metaphors. No individual identifier achieved more than 30 per cent success. (A more statistically accurate measure, which compares agreement on which words and phrases were not metaphors and which ones were, would improve this measure. The majority of words were definitely not metaphors, and thus the more accurate statistic would be a high percentage and significant, but would also be significantly misleading regarding the challenge of identifying metaphors.) We were also hopeful that using such identifiers would allow us to delegate this task in future, and thereby avoid spending a large proportion of our future careers with a highlighter pen in hand. This was intended to be an efficient and effective method, conserving researcher time, but unfortunately it proved slow, difficult to manage, and time-intensive.

When the metaphors identified by all five coders, in both stages of the process, were combined into a single, combined and re-checked dataset, the final count at this stage reached around 4638 items. That is, we two original 'experts' had apparently only managed to identify around 25 per cent of the overall metaphors within these articles. (Later analysis showed the undergraduates' lack of life experience led them to identify lots of work-related terminology as metaphors, so the final count was lower, and our performance closer to 35 per cent.) It should perhaps be noted that both of us have first degrees from the humanities, with considerable training and experience in textual analysis, and, in spite of this and our own passion for perfection, we did not spot 65–75 per cent of the metaphors within the sample articles. This is indeed a difficult task, and we conclude that (1) identification of metaphors in public discourse must be an iterative, multi-rater task, and (2) newspapers are a rich source of metaphors in the public discourse of entrepreneurship, considering how many metaphors these articles were eventually found to contain. When this stage of the empirical study was completed, however, we had a master-list of about 4638 phrases which, we felt confident, contained a high enough proportion of the articles' metaphors to be reliable. Reaching this final list of metaphors, to reiterate, required about four years of work, and four types of identification methods:

1.   individual 'expert' coders;
2.   dyad of expert coders;

3.   individual non-expert coders; and
4.   team of non-expert coders.

Stage Four: Developing Metaphor Codes and Categories

At this stage, with a dataset of metaphors ready and waiting for action, coding can finally begin. To analyse metaphor data, it is very helpful to reduce the richness of the distinct metaphors by categorizing. We have found this to be a more manageable process if the data is presented to coders in spreadsheet format, as illustrated in Figure 4.2 and Table 4.1, although complete source material should also be kept close to hand so that context and narrative are not lost. Coding metaphors has sometimes used pre-established frames, some of which have been derived from the literature (Pitt 1998) and others of which were determined by the nature of the study (Mahlamäki-Kultanen and Hakala n.d.; Drakopoulou Dodd et al. 2013). For example, in Drakopoulou Dodd et al. (2013), co-author Alistair Anderson decided it would be instructive to re-code the entire dataset according to whether metaphors were negative, positive or neutral about the topic of entrepreneurship. Combined with earlier, grounded coding of metaphor themes, this pre-established frame permitted focused analysis of a specific area of interest. An alternative, and more popular, approach has been to classify metaphors, based on their semantic group-ings, into clusters derived from groups of root metaphors (Koiranen 1995; Hrysky 1999, Drakopoulou Dodd 2002, de Koning and Drakopoulou Dodd 2002; Nicholson and Anderson 2005; de Koning and Drakopoulou Dodd 2008). Perren and Atkin (1997) describe their approach to this stage in the process thus:

> Each metaphor in the first 250 lines of owner-manager transcript which had a double underline from a rater was extracted in its entirety and coded to allow traceability back to its original source. This allowed a flexible approach to data analysis and categorisation, with metaphors being iteratively grouped together until patterns emerged (Riley, 1990). The data was fully reported and coded according to its original source. This addressed the risk of a gap developing between the actual data set and the conclusions which were distilled. (Miles and Huberman, 1984)

Both approaches are well-supported methodologically (see Table 4.4 for a summary of the approaches used in the various papers under review). Using pre-established frames allows for more structured coding of data, and thereby facilitates the subsequent use of quantitative analytic tools. It also permits a tighter connection to be made between specific theoretical motivations and the data, so may be useful in testing precise researcher propositions. A grounded approach, which tries to allow the data to drive the group classifications, is perhaps more appropriate for exploratory studies, or where it is intended to analyse the data using only qualitative methods. Large data-sets are difficult and time-intensive to classify in a grounded fashion.

Inductive theming

Returning now to a discussion of our own ongoing work, as well as carrying out a controlled study into the fraught issue of identifying metaphors in textual material, we also wanted to use our cross-cultural study to explore empirically possible approaches to the coding phase in the process of metaphor methodology. Here, subjective scholarly interpretation is an asset, rather than a drawback, but we still felt there should be some way to measure and explain our subjectivity, and to mention other possible interpretations. So, in this stage we trialled three main categorization techniques, so that we could better ascertain the merits of each, but also to be as sure as possible as to the merits of the final classification scheme which we agreed. The first approach which we tried was a 'classic' inductive, grounded emergence of themes. We also applied a Q Sort method, using a structured sub-sample of metaphors, and some brave volunteers. Additionally, we returned to the literature to see if there were

Table 4.4   Methods of coding metaphors

Entrepreneurship studies using metaphors	Coding approach
Pitt (1998)	Four-fold frame, then grouped by theme
Perren and Atkin (1997)	Iteratively grouped until patterns emerged
Mahlamäki-Kultanen and Hakala (n.d.)	Seven-fold frame, coded using software
Koiranen (1995)	Qualitative classification of metaphor groups
Hrysky (1999)	Themed clusters based on semantic properties of metaphor
Drakopoulou Dodd (2002)	Coded by vehicle, object and root metaphor
Nicolson and Anderson (2005); de Koning and Drakopoulou Dodd (2002); De Koning and Drakopoulou Dodd (2008)	Themed clusters based on semantic properties of metaphor
Drakopoulou Dodd et al. (2013)	Three-fold frame, negative, positive and neutral metaphors

common themes which we might also expect to find within our own new dataset. Each of these approaches will now be presented and assessed in turn.

We again went through the process of coding separately, and then comparing our findings, as part of the iterative process of qualitative textual analysis. Both authors separately used inductive methods to work slowly through the textual sample material, 'emerging' themes as they immersed themselves in the articles. This detailed engagement with the textual material also familiarized the authors with the extensive dataset in all its richness. Expert-coder classification took place in several rounds. First, each of the two coders worked on the dataset of metaphors which they had identified individually. Then, they added the metaphors found by the other coder to the dataset, revising and revisiting earlier work in the process. Only when the second phase classification was complete were results compared, and a first draft coding scheme agreed.

Coder One (Alice) utilized a broad strategy to categorize metaphors. She generated more than 100 metaphor classifications, and then worked to group these into a smaller number of themed groups. Coder One's approach was thus highly grounded in nature. Coder Two (Sarah) adopted the opposite strategy, beginning with a tight set of very few categories, based on initial readings of the metaphors, and on the extant literature. The list included, for example, journey, war, game and organisms. This more structured approach necessitated expanding the set of themed groups when the list of unclassified metaphors indicated that a new group had been revealed. For example, a large number of metaphors using words such as 'behind the scenes', 'blockbuster', and 'new act in this exciting drama' led to the creation of a theatre-themed group. A list of 15 themed groups emerged. In contrast to the narrowing-down approach of her co-author, in this case the theming strategy involved increasingly opening out of themes, and we were curious to see if we would eventually arrive at more or less the same place. We then took a break from this approach, while we experimented with Q Sorting and revisited themes from the literature.

Q Sort

The second technique which was implemented to develop theme categories was a formal Q-Sort process. Q Sort methods are designed to capture the subjective responses of participants to, among other things, sets of representative statements. We developed a framework for selecting 80 metaphor statements from the larger dataset, which used the six countries studied as one axis of the frame, and the object of metaphors (what they are about) as the other. The object axis included success, failure, opportunities, the entrepreneurial environment and the entrepreneur in action. The process was twice piloted to test the clarity of instructions, and provide an early indication of usefulness. After reviewing the results of the first two coders, the protocol was improved. We then recruited four more coders, all quite expert in entrepreneurship and/or organizational studies. Our sorters represented several of the countries in the study, too, although we would have very much liked to include representatives of all six countries.

Sorters were presented with a computerized list of these 80 statements, and requested to sort them into up to 11 groups. This computerized Q Sort, which encouraged sorters to use 11 radio buttons next to each sample metaphor to group metaphors into cognate clusters, allowed them to name these clusters, and to update and edit their groups continuously until they were content with their clustering. In practice, the maximum number of groups which our Q Sorters came up with was ten. To be very specific, we asked these four coders to Q Sort the sample metaphors into groups, based on congruence between the semantic meanings of the metaphorical terms. They were also requested to name and briefly explain their groups. Table 4.5 shows that the four coders show considerable similarities with each other (categories have been re-ordered in Table 4.5 to facilitate comparison).

It is, however, also possible to carry out a lower-technology Q Sort, as the Anderson, Jack and Drakopoulou Dodd team did with the EUROPE data.

Table 4.5   Q Sort of entrepreneurial metaphors into groups

	Q Sorter 3	Q Sorter 4	Q Sorter 5	Q Sorter 6
Group 1	Mythological	Myth & magic	Magic & mystics	Mystery/magic
Group 2	Gambling	Sport & gambling	Gambling	Gamble/risk
Group 3	Adventure/ military	Warfare & hunting	War/fighting	War/conquest
Group 4	Journey	Planning & learning	Driving/ machines	Racing
Group 5	Comparison to an object	Expanding	Theatre/ magicians	Personification
Group 6	Life cycle	Failure	Birth & death	Biological/life cycle
Group 7	Games	Targeting	Sports/games	Play/fun/game
Group 8	Energy	Passions	Romance	Climb/ambition
Group 9		Envisaging	Illness/medicine	Artistic/vision
Group 10		Kingdoms & control	Good & evil	Building

Sarah (Drakopoulou Dodd) had carried out an inductive categorization of the data as part of the wider EUROPE project methodology. In order to provide some diversity in the methods used to generate themes, the two other members of the team used a structured sub-sample card sort approach. A sub-sample of the metaphor dataset was derived, comprising slightly over our target of 10 per cent of the total. The random sub-sample was generated using a proportional matrix based on respondent occupation and nationality, corrected only to ensure that at least one metaphor was drawn from each cell in the matrix. This resulted in a sub-sample of 97 metaphors. Sets of sort cards were then produced, one for each of these 97 metaphors, and the two co-authors independently carried out an iterative clustering of metaphor themes manually. Their themes were found to be very close to Drakopoulou Dodd's, and a final agreed categorization was produced.

Themes in the literature
The third and final technique utilized was driven by the extant – if rather scant – entrepreneurship literature which has carried out empirical studies working with metaphors (from a variety of sources). At the time we carried out this exercise (2004), seven such studies were available to us. Four of these articles, which used metaphor methodology to study perceptions of enterprise/entrepreneurship, presented clear lists of metaphor groups in their findings. For three of these, the number of coding groups used was fairly small, while the fourth study (Nicholson and Anderson 2005) presented a larger list. We therefore collapsed some of Nicholson and Anderson's themes (myth, for example, appears in several of their groups). We also used Pitt's (1998) entrepreneurial role metaphors as a source for this process. We prepared a consolidated list from this literature by selecting each cluster-theme which had appeared in more than one study. This provided us with the following list of eight cluster-themes, and the similarities with the Q Sort themes above is immediately apparent:

- Sportsman, gameplayer, race athlete
- Machinery, buildings and other physical objects
- War, warriors and battlers
- Pioneer, adventurer, explorer
- Special characteristics and features
- Creative, innovative and industrious actors
- Alchemy and magic, visionary guru
- Nature.

This list is derived from empirical literature using data from the USA, UK, Finland, the Baltic States and Sweden. It thus has some claims on generalizability, but will probably not include idiosyncratic country-specific perceptions of the entrepreneur, nor are perceptions from countries outside the Anglo-Saxon and Nordic cultures likely to be well represented. Nevertheless, it is instructive that so many metaphor themes of the entrepreneur repeat across studies and cultures. It is also fascinating to note the inherent complexities and contradictions within this list, where the entrepreneur can be seen as a pioneering adventurer, a child at play, or a wizard 'magicking' the future into being.

At this point, we had a remarkable resource upon which to draw when developing the coding schema of metaphor themes for the current study. The resource included the two grounded lists of metaphor themes, one from each author, arrived at in different ways ('narrowing down' versus 'opening out'), and the deeper understanding of the article narratives and metaphor data generated via engagement with this process.

In addition, the eight categories found more than once in the wider literature, and the results of the four Q Sorts on the specific dataset, provided further inspiration, insight, and perspective. Reflection on these resources, extensive discussion, and iterative hermeneutical analysis of the text by the authors lead to refining the inductive categories. For example, on a single table we compared and analysed the various approaches: literature driven, grounded themes (Coder 1: broad category to narrow; Coder 2: narrow category to broad); and Q Sorted categories (for Q Sorters 3–6). Table 4.6 shows the top half of that table, to illustrate the kinds of overlaps, commonalities, and divergence which influenced our final coding frame decisions.

The ultimate coding schema for our cross-cultural study included 18 metaphor vehicle themes, and a null code for phrases or words which were found to be ultimately literal rather than metaphorical (Table 4.7). This is potentially problematic from the point of view of writing for journal publication, of course, since with even a single page devoted to each theme, word limits become an immediate issue.

A protocol document was then prepared for each of these themes which detailed theme scope, presented examples from the dataset, highlighted areas of potential overlap, and indicated how such dilemmas might be resolved. This document was continually updated and extended as application of the scheme to the data continued.

Stage Five: Applying Coding Schemes to the Metaphors

Having developed the coding scheme, the next task was to apply this to the dataset of 4638 metaphors. A key part of that process was testing and piloting the protocol together, so as to ensure its effectiveness. We also wanted to be sure that our categorization process was carried out in

Table 4.6 Comparison of multiple sorting schemes

	Literature driven	Alice	Sarah	Q Sorter 3	Q Sorter 4	Q Sorter 5	Q Sorter 6
There is a complex set of overlapping groupings here that present the entrepreneur in terms of mythical hero, magician, shaman, visionary, showman, artist, spiritual being	Alchemy and magic, visionary guru		Narrative, myth, religion, magic	Mythological	Myth and magic	Magic and mystics	Mystery/magic
	Creative, innovative and industrious actors	Things of the spirit			Envisaging		Artistic/vision
	Special characteristics and features	The show must go on	Theatre/media/Hollywood				
Animals, people, lifecycles, illness, birth and death	Nature	It's alive	Organism: animals, plants life cycle	Life cycle	Expanding	Birth and death	Biological/life cycle
		The family				Illness/medicine	Personification
Games, gambling, sport, racing (overlap with journey)	Sportsman, game player, race athlete	Gambling and risk taking	Game	Gambling	Sports and gambling	Gambling	Gamble/risk
Journeys of differing kinds	Pioneer, adventurer, explorer	Let's party/let's play	Sport, toy	Games		Sport, games	Play/fun/games
		Road travelled	Journey	Journey			Racing

127

Table 4.7 Protocol themes

Code	Theme title and illustrative example	Theme scope synopsis
0	Literal language 'new product development'	A word for which *no* more concrete, neutral, specific term exists. Includes some technical management terms
1	Myths, mystics and magic 'He was Icarus in red suspenders'	Narratives – especially legends and myths – and which may portray individuals, or firms, as story-book heroes, villains, or monsters. Metaphors with religious, shamanist, visionary and spiritual overtones
2	The show must go on 'to grab more of the limelight'	Theatre, cinema, and other forms of dramatic show or public performance, like art exhibitions, the circus, and so on
3	It's alive 'to budding small scale industrialists'	Images of living organisms, and their life cycles: animals and plants, as well as anthropomorphic metaphors of a general nature. Life-cycle references include those to birth, growth and death
4	A throw of the dice 'placing a multi-billion dollar bet'	Betting and gambling
5	Let's play 'looking forward to playing around in the sandbox'	Play, games, sports, and amusement
6	Road travelled 'Their journey wasn't always easy'	Journeying and travelling images; allusions to difficulties and barriers on the road, getting started on the journey, completing journeys, travelling through new terrain, moving quickly forward, driving towards a given destination; starting a journey through launching (a rocket or a boat?), floating or so on; other movement up and forwards metaphors, like soaring, the route of the journey, such as 'landmarks', or 'view ahead'

7	*Conquest and control* 'the flagship of Sir Terrence's retail empire.'	Political, royal or imperial dominance, and the process of conquest, which lead to the acquisition of this controlling power. Social and political hierarchy metaphors. Pushing references may also be about power, especially if the context suggests revolution, new markets, eras, or other forms of 'kingdom'
8	*The fight is on* 'Smelter is retrenching'	War, aggression, fighting and the military: sports that emphasize aggressive competition between two players or teams
9	*Ready, aim, fire* 'turned him into a target. He had to be shot down.'	Targeting, taking aim, focusing, and other purposeful and careful – but also aggressive – similar actions. Hunting, fishing and predation, as well as capturing
10	*Machine* 'Ryanair's well-oiled publicity machine'	Machines, engines, their components and processes for 'running' something (like a business) if this can be seen as mechanistic in nature
11	*Buildings* 'Even more importantly, it opens the door for Toll to move'	Generic building references, but also staking a claim, breaking ground, the laying of foundations, the pouring (of concrete), the building of walls, and so forth. It includes noun-based metaphors relating to buildings in general, and specific types of building, as well as to parts foundings and foundations
12	*The theory is* 'to prove their business model'	Conceptual metaphors; models, frameworks and theories; the planning and design of artefacts or structures; things which are normally found on charts (such as downturns); metaphors which imply theory-testing (such as 'trial and error')
13	*Force of nature* 'the waters are becoming thick with mud'	The natural world: such as water, mountains, the rules and energy forces of physics, or weather events. Processes most commonly occurring in the natural world, such as lightning strikes, disruption, inflation (sometimes), shake ups (quakes), also are coded here

Table 4.7 (continued)

Code	Theme title and illustrative example	Theme scope synopsis
14	*Woe is me* 'fell victim to another fad of the late 1990s'	Spiritual and physical misery: victims, suffering, disease and its treatment.
15	*Exclusion* 'Scratch Conran's elegantly besuited surface and there's a posh barrow boy.'	Images of social exclusion. The theme thus encompasses criminal metaphors, and those which depict other shady characters and their activities. Exclusion metaphors which are social in nature, alluding to individuals who are in some way beyond the social pale, or outcast
16	*Homely arts and crafts* 'This is their bread and butter'	House-making, cooking, husbandry, crafts and other related arts, such as painting or playing music for private pleasure
17	*Passion* 'Our passion about the business, it rubs off.'	Passion and romance: love, kissing, hugging, sex, courting and marriage
18	*Bits, biz and buzz* 'We call it "Brailling" the culture'	This 'other', or miscellaneous category contains all metaphors which cannot be classified elsewhere. It is also home to some smaller metaphor groups such as: legal issues, and signing/signalling

similar ways by both coders. This is a different knot than that encountered in metaphor identification, since our discussion and debate at this stage was a very productive and essential form of shared analysis.

To begin with, we randomly selected 5 per cent of the overall sample, to perform further coding experiments and tests upon. Taking 100 of these metaphors, the two authors coded them separately, using the detailed and agreed theme protocols. Analysis of this coding task revealed a quite respectable 61 per cent inter-rater reliability level but, more importantly, also highlighted areas where further fine-tuning of the protocols was required. When, for example, would 'creation' be coded as a divine or mythic act, and when is it essentially dramatic, or crafted? A total of 20 additional refinements and additions to the coding protocol were agreed upon at this stage. Next, a further 100 metaphors from the randomized list were coded by the two authors separately. As well as the 18 code themes set out in the revised protocol, we also created a theme code for language we judged to be literal rather than metaphorical (code 0). A column was added to the spreadsheet for flagging metaphors which were quite straightforward (0), which could be construed as belonging in more than one themed group (1), or that required discussion and reflection (2). In this round, inter-rater reliability was raised to 67 per cent.

One final check was performed, as each author coded another 100 random metaphors. We agreed a further six clarifications and/or adjustments to the theme protocol in the light of this round of discussion. After these three iterative rounds of review and discussion in this phase of the coding process, our inter-coder reliability had risen to around 90 per cent, and we had strong mechanisms for identifying and analysing the remaining 10 per cent. We therefore felt confident that the protocol was now robust enough, taken together with the example of 400 metaphors, to allow us to tackle the remaining dataset with speed and accuracy. Our protocol document was quite formally written up and formatted, eventually running to nearly 13 000 words, which is even longer than this chapter, for example. Table 4.7 shows the 18 themes in synopsis, and a full copy of the protocol is available from the authors. Essentially, the guidance which the protocol attempts to provide requires detailed reading of the context and extension of the metaphors within the text, to try and figure out what the main thrust of the ambiguous metaphor is. So, for example, a regular issue we encountered was whether metaphors of warlike heroes should be themes for 'the fight is on', or 'myth, mystics and magic'. The excerpt below shows how we deal with this topic:

- Metaphors depicting martial heroes, and their narratives, are examined to ascertain if emphasis is placed on the warlike element of the metaphor (Theme 8, The fight is on), or its heroic and narrative content. A TITAN may be invoked mostly to emphasize its mythical proportions (Theme 1) or, for example, its aggression (Theme 8).

This is a fairly straightforward dilemma, relatively speaking. We encountered far more complicated problems with many other words, such as metaphors constructed around the verb to fall, as the following section from our protocol indicates:

- Falling metaphors require careful consideration to figure out what their primary (and possibly subsidiary) metaphorical allusions are. A fall from grace, suggestive of Lucifer, or Icarus, (from the sky, into the sea and so on) seems most likely to fit within Theme 1 (Myths, mystics and magic). Falling by the wayside has strong connotations of Road travelled (Theme 6). 'Fall and climb' ups and downs suggest some combination of Road travelled (Theme 6) with The theory is (Theme 12). However, there may be some Force of nature intimations, such as tides rising and falling in a fashion which is beyond agent control (Theme 13). These may be reminiscent of other natural phenomena such as temperature falling. But where some sense of modelling/graphing is also picked up, then The theory is (Theme 12) should probably be used as one of two (or more!) themes selected. Falling into trouble of various types may have Woe is me as a primary, secondary or even tertiary meaning (Theme 14). 'Falling over themselves' is redolent of small creatures, and hence organisms (It's alive; Theme 3). There are also lots of expressions where fall is used to convey a very specific meaning, and which can only be 'decoded' from the surrounding context. For example, to 'fall back on' is often military (Fight is on, Theme 8), 'falling short' may be Theme 9, Ready aim fire. 'Falling from favour' might contain a Passion reference (Theme 17), while falling prey is hunting and thus Ready, aim, fire (Theme 9).

We reiterate that after many years spent engaging with this dataset, and experimenting with techniques and methods that we felt delivered adequate rigour, the need for a very detailed and specific coding protocol became evident. Such precision is required if the full richness of the metaphors encountered is to be exploited, and their meanings classified reliably.

Once our detailed protocol was very well developed, and we were satisfied with our inter-rater reliability in coding the metaphors according to our well-established frame, we next separately coded our remaining individual allocation of the sample (about 50 per cent of the remainder each). Table 4.8 shows an illustrative sample of the spreadsheet we used to carry out this

Table 4.8 Coding sample

ID	doc	pg	line	Metaphor	Metaphor phrase	query	cat1	cat2	cat3
87	4	2	58	It is a lunge at the heart	'It is a lunge at the heart of the profession. If there can be no editorial independence, there can be no integrity.'	0	ready, aim, fire		
90	4	2	62	razor guy	'He's a real razor guy,' he said.	1	exclusion	the fight is on	
91	4	3	63	breed	'He's come from monopoly markets, and monopoly markets breed monopoly thinking.'	0	homely arts and crafts		

task. Columns 1–4 contain identification codes for the metaphor, allowing us also to quickly check back to the original article to review context. We have also found it very important to include larger sections of text surrounding the metaphor in the spreadsheet, for the same purpose: coding without (narrative) context is neither feasible nor desirable. It is enormously helpful to have a printed code sheet in hard copy close by at all times during the process, as well as keeping a copy of the protocol open on the computer. It is perhaps also worth noting that while Alice was very accurate in directly and immediately coding in theme numbers, Sarah's performance when she tried to do this was simply woeful, and she coded by typing in theme names, and replacing these afterwards with numbers automatically.

As mentioned above, the 'query' column allowed us to flag up metaphors where we felt some ambiguity, coded (1) for 'multiple themes', and (2) for 'requires discussion' (or, 'what the hell do you think?'). The '1' code shown in Table 4.8 indicates that we feel both a primary and secondary meaning are intended, and hence two categories are coded for. One of the reasons that writers use a metaphor is that it can combine a number of complex meanings into a single image, as the 'razor guy' example here shows, and we felt it important that our coding systems could cope with this. (Indeed, since entrepreneurship is a complex, contested and ambiguous concept, it seems likely that dual-meaning metaphors are especially interesting and appropriate.) A tertiary meaning is also possible, although we encountered relatively few such examples.

One additional task which took place at this stage was a final consideration as to how many different metaphors a specific phrase contains, and whether some items needed to be split out further, or recombined. These problematic metaphor phrases were highlighted, and resolved by a team discussion. Each coder then reviewed the other's work, focusing especially on flagged metaphors. It is perhaps also worth noting, on a very practical note, that the depth, accuracy, speed and enjoyment of these last coding tasks were dramatically enhanced by us both sharing an office for a week, and chatting our way through the dataset. Towards the end of the week, we found increasing supplies of alcohol invaluable to sustaining researcher focus and morale. By this means, we painstakingly produced a fully themed dataset of 4132 metaphors, having agreed that 506 phrases should be removed from the study as being literal.

Stage Six: Analysing Coded Metaphors – Developing Meaning from Results

Having reached the point of having coded, themed, or otherwise prepared metaphor data for analysis, the next stage is to begin working out what the data means. Analysis of coded metaphor material within entrepreneurship has been both quantitative and qualitative in nature. Quantitative approaches have included cross-tabulations and factor analysis (Koiranen 1995), as well as mapping clusters and trends using Excel (Nicolson and Anderson 2005). Software has also been used to assist in the qualitative analysis of one very large textual dataset (Mahlamäki-Kultanen and Hakala, n.d.). In general, though, scholars have used the time-honoured qualitative tool of deep, considered and informed reflection to interpret their findings, usually considering them in the light of their contextual setting, whether this occurs at national or individual level. Since this reflection is centred on textual material, it can be classified as hermeneutics.

The usual advantages and disadvantages of quantitative and qualitative methods apply in this case also. In exploratory work, where depth, detail, subtlety and context are deemed relevant, qualitative techniques are strongly recommended. For large datasets some basic descriptive data at a minimum is required to efficiently summarize results. When the study is aiming to test specific hypotheses, and measuring differences is called for, then quantitative techniques, especially cluster analysis, have much to offer.

However, a word of caution is called for here: the relevance of metaphors is in their meaning, and this can be obscured by an over-reliance on statistics. For example, our study shows many uses of gambling metaphors, but counting their frequency, and comparing this to the frequency

---

BOX 4.1   COMPARATIVE ANALYSIS OF AMERICAN AND
BRITISH METAPHORS

The UK emphasis on entrepreneurial personality and attitude can be seen in the use of metaphors which describe entrepreneurs as pugnacious, and **fighting hard and dirty**, as having **battled hard** and expended a lot of **blood, sweat and tears**. Competitors are seen by entrepreneurs as the **enemy**, disputed takeovers as **ferocious battles**, entrepreneurs' offices as **battle headquarters**, from where **tanks are put on the competitors' lawn**. Nevertheless, although the UK material portrays the entrepreneur as an over-ambitious, aggressive, individualistic **outsider** – for whom just **punishment is surely waiting** – they also do not hesitate to complain about the paucity of support for entrepreneurs from banks and the state, and about the lack of an enterprise culture in the UK. This is, at the very least, a confused and contradictory view of enterprise.

In the US material, several of the **warlike** metaphors are used to depict the entrepreneur engaged in **struggle** with various forms of large-scale organizations, **battling tirelessly against regulators**, holding the inner city as the **last bastion** of the small entrepreneur. Takeovers are again seen in aggressive terms, as, for example, a **strategic coup**. Overall, the entrepreneurial story is re-told as one of glamour, excitement and heroism. This is especially so for the **little guy** who stands up with integrity and honour, against large-scale firms.

---

of other groups, would obscure the fact that for some countries we studied the metaphors were used very positively to celebrate entrepreneurial risk-taking, while in others quite the opposite was true. We have chosen to present frequency data numerically, but also place much emphasis on expounding the meaning held within the metaphor groups through literary analysis. In Box 4.1, we present short extracts from our comparative analysis of American and British metaphors, as an example of such textual analysis; the material in bold indicates the use of metaphors from the dataset (De Koning and Drakopoulou Dodd, 2008).

Stage Seven: Presenting Results

Presentations of metaphor findings have often used tables and lists to show themed groupings, with plenty of illustrative metaphor examples adding richness (see Table 4.9). A more expansive textual presentation is also sometimes employed, but the larger the dataset, the harder this becomes to manage in terms of space restrictions. Indeed, this is a major problem for those who wish to adopt metaphor analysis. Because the methodology is fairly unusual, a long section justifying and explaining the approach is needed in the front-end of a paper. This uses a disproportionate amount of space, which could be better used for presenting findings. The strength

Table 4.9   Presentation of metaphor results

Pitt (1998)	Text and table, by entrepreneurial role
Perren and Atkin (1997)	Text and table, by type of entrepreneur
Mahlamäki-Kultanen and Hakala	Textual description
Koiranen (1995)	Text, and lists in text
Hrysky (1999)	Text, and lists in text
Drakopoulou Dodd (2002)	Text, and a summary model
Nicolson and Anderson (2005)	Charts, tables and text
De Koning and Drakopoulou Dodd (2004)	Tables, by country and theme, and text
De Koning and Drakopoulou Dodd (2008)	Tables, by country and theme, and text
Anderson et al. (2009)	Tables, text, and a summary model
De Koning and Drakopoulou Dodd (2010)	Textual description

of metaphor analysis is in the richness of the results, and this can only be conveyed by re-presenting for readers as many examples as possible of metaphors. It is also the only mechanism for laying bare the hermeneutics used to generate results, allowing readers – and reviewers – to assess the competence and validity of conclusions.

One of the weaknesses of many of the papers we have reviewed is that, once lengthy methodology and results sections have been written, very little space is left for serious and rigorous discussion of the findings. This is a problem that we continue to wrestle with, with some drafts of our study passing the 15 000-word mark. A serious issue here is that many journals are not receptive to very long articles, so the larger and more comprehensive the metaphor study, the harder it is to get it published. We hope that one of the contributions of this chapter is that it will provide a detailed reference point for work in the area, including our own, which may obviate the need for such lengthy methodological justifications within article manuscripts.

We also note that reviewers and readers have found it helpful to see some sort of framework, or model, illustrating how themes might combine to create a holistic social construction of the entrepreneur (for example). Our experience is that for some datasets (Drakopoulou Dodd 2002; Anderson et al. 2009) such models emerge quite naturally through the wider coding and analysis stages. For other datasets, we have not been able to summarize and connect findings in diagrammatic form. We judge this to be a combination of researcher inspiration, as well as being data-driven; some stories just cannot be re-told in images.

CONCLUSION

We believe that these 14 studies provide a good basis for an analysis of metaphor methodologies, particularly given the inclusion of our own detailed experiments. We conclude that we now have enough information to justify using this approach, given the compelling nature of the findings which these studies have shared with us. Furthermore, we have confirmed that single scholar identification of metaphors has a very high drop error, which appears to be due to 'metaphor indigestion'. We note that all three coding approaches deliver similar results, and that the Q Sort appears so far to offer the best mix of data-specificity, richness and efficiency. We note that many of the 18 themes represented in our protocol have also appeared in other studies of the entrepreneurial metaphors, and we hope that our protocol may offer colleagues a thorough coding template for entrepreneurial metaphors. Some numbers are probably needed to describe results, and coherent findings are susceptible to graphic illustration. However, the words really need to shine through, to bring the results to life. Metaphor methodology remains, in our experience very, very time-costly; it has taken us almost ten years to get ourselves into a position where we can base this chapter upon our own data.

Nevertheless, it is hoped that this chapter will encourage more scholars to adopt this fruitful and growing approach to the study of entrepreneurs, and, in particular, provide them with a straightforward toolbox for examining the meaning of entrepreneurship in a variety of contexts, using a diversity of approaches. By understanding what entrepreneurship means to societies, sub-cultures, support agencies, scholars and entrepreneurs, we will be better placed to facilitate communication between these groups, so as to improve entrepreneurship development and education activities. We may also be able to draw sound conclusions as to the relationship between entrepreneurial motivation and societal perceptions of the entrepreneur, as well as to compare and contrast the entrepreneurial heritage of societies, sectors and cultures.

REFERENCES

Alasuutari, P. (1995), *Researching Culture: Qualitative Method and Cultural Studies*, London: Sage.

Anderson, A., S. Drakopoulou Dodd and S. Jack, S. (2009), 'Aggressors; winners; victims and outsiders: European schools' social construction of the entrepreneur', *International Small Business Journal*, **27** (1), 126–33.

Cardon, M., C. Zietsma, P. Saparito, B.P. Matherne, and C. Davis (2005), 'A tale of passion:

new insights into entrepreneurship from a parenthood metaphor', *Journal of Business Venturing*, **20** (1), 23–45.

Cornelissen, J., J. Clarke and A. Cienki (2012), 'Sensegiving in entrepreneurial contexts: the use of metaphors in speech and gesture to gain and sustain support for novel business ventures', *International Small Business Journal*, **30** (3), 213–41.

Cosgel, M. (1996), 'Metaphors, stories and the entrepreneur in economics', *History of Political Economy*, **28** (1), 57–76.

De Koning, A. and S. Drakopoulou Dodd (2002), 'Raising babies, fighting battles, winning races: entrepreneurial metaphors in the media of 5 English speaking nations', paper presented at the 2002 Babson Kauffman Entrepreneurship Conference, 6–8 June, Boulder, CO.

De Koning, A. and S. Drakopoulou Dodd (2008), 'Metaphors of entrepreneurship across cultures', *Journal of Asia Entrepreneurship and Sustainability*, **4** (2), 87–101.

De Koning, A. and S. Drakopoulou Dodd (2010), 'Tea and understanding: metaphors in the entrepreneurial narrative of tea republic', *ENTER*, **1** (1), 33–50.

Drakopoulou Dodd, S. (2002), 'Metaphors and meaning: a grounded cultural model of US entrepreneurship', *Journal of Business Venturing*, **17** (5), 519.

Drakopoulou Dodd, S. and A. de Koning (2004), 'Methodology and metaphors', presented at the Babson Kauffman Entrepreneurship Conference, 3–5 June, Strathclyde University, Glasgow.

Drakopoulou Dodd, S., S. Jack and A. Anderson (2013), 'From admiration to abhorrence; the contentious appeal of entrepreneurship across Europe', *Entrepreneurship & Regional Development*, **25** (1–2), 69–89.

Hill, R.C. and M. Levenhagen (1995), 'Metaphors and mental models: sense making and sense giving in innovative and entrepreneurial activities', *Journal of Management*, **21** (6), 1057–75.

Hyrsky, K. (1999), 'Entrepreneurial metaphors and concepts: an exploratory study', *International Small Business Journal*, **18** (1), 13–34.

Koiranen, M. (1995), 'North-European metaphors of "entrepreneurship" and "an entrepreneur"', in W.D. Bygraves, S. Birley and N.C. Churchill (eds), *Frontiers of Entrepreneurship Research*, Waltham, MA: P & R Publications, pp. 203–16.

Lacey, C. and D. Longman (1993), 'The press and public-access to the environment and development debate', *Sociological Review*, **141** (2), 207–43.

Mahlamäki-Kultanen, S. and R. Hakala (n.d.), 'Educational implications of rural entrepreneurs' beliefs and metaphors', unpublished working paper, available at: http://citeserx.ist.psu.edu/viewdoc/download?doi=10.1.1.200.1807&rep=rep1&type=pdf (accessed 27 May 2015).

Mann, K. and S. Roseneils (1994), '"Some Mothers Do 'Ave 'Em": backlash and the gender politics of the underclass debate', *Journal of Gender Studies*, **3** (3), 317–31.

Miles, M.B. and A.M. Huberman (1984), *Qualitative Data Analysis: A Sourcebook of New Methods*, Beverly Hills, CA: Sage Publications.

Nicolson, L. and A. Anderson (2005), 'News and nuances of the entrepreneurial myth and metaphor: linguistic games in entrepreneurial sensemaking and sensegiving', *Entrepreneurship Theory and Practice*, **29** (2), 153–72.

Perren, L. and R. Atkin (1997), 'Women-manager's discourse: the metaphors-in-use', *Journal of Applied Management Studies*, **6** (1), 47–61.

Pitt, M. (1998), 'A tale of two gladiators: "reading" entrepreneurs as texts', *Organization Studies*, **19** (3), 387–414.

Riley, J. (1990), *Getting the Most Out of Your Data*, London: Technical and Educational Services Ltd.

Soothill, K. and C. Grover (1997), 'A note on computer searches of newspapers', *Sociology*, **31** (3), 591–6.

5 Con'text'ualizing images of enterprise: an examination of 'visual metaphors' used to represent entrepreneurship in textbooks
Robert Smith

VISUALIZING ENTREPRENEURSHIP: AN INTRODUCTION

It is widely accepted that despite a considerable research effort no generic definition of entrepreneurship exists. This was ably articulated by Bill Gartner over 20 years ago (see Gartner 1988). Indeed, Gartner further argues that there is a problem with obtaining conceptual clarity (Gartner 1989). This led him to argue that it is especially important in entrepreneurship that we examine and articulate our logic of discovery, and most especially, the 'assumptions we make about this phenomenon' (Gartner 2001: 27). Given that it is so difficult to define the phenomenon, how easy is it to visualize it? The famous phrase 'You will know it when you see it' springs to mind. In this chapter, we will therefore concern ourselves with contextualizing what entrepreneurship looks like.

In researching the visual (as advocated by Emmison and Smith 2002), this chapter explores the linkages between images, imagination and imagining the complex social phenomenon that is entrepreneurship. In particular, the chapter concentrates on visual images associated with entrepreneurship in its myriad forms and delves into the messy world of semiotics and visual metaphors. To illustrate this methodological approach, I carry out a worked example, using images from entrepreneurship textbooks, and consolidate this via learning exercises. This approach is important because for many of us, especially undergraduates and postgraduate students, entrepreneurship is a social context we first encounter in textbooks. Upon perusing a textbook the first thing we as a reader usually encounter is a photographic image printed on a dust jacket – placed there to gain our attention. Older books are usually bereft of this anchoring concept, the dust jacket having been removed because of wear and tear. In this respect, first impressions are often important and can influence how we react when presented with social stimuli. To read or not to read, is a question we often ask ourselves. Such images act as visual metaphors triggering our interest to read further. However, as will be articulated, textbooks are an under-researched phenomenon in entrepreneurship research circles. This is important because increasingly academic scholarship and reputation are driven by publication in top-tier journals.

Metaphor research is an established area of research activity (for example, see Hyrsky 1998a, 1998b; Drakopoulou Dodd 2002; Nicholson and Anderson 2005). This chapter makes a contribution to metaphor research in entrepreneurship by extending it to consider sociocultural images and objects associated with entrepreneurship as a genre. Images, objects, contexts and interactions play an important part in achieving *verstehen* (working towards understanding) (Emmison and Smith 2002). Moreover, in western societies, entrepreneurship and thus enterprise is presented, and represented, as a heroic activity enacted and performed by masculine elites and increasingly this image is emphasized in a business school environment. Moreover, the heroic nature of entrepreneurship is well recorded (Burns 2007; Drakopoulou Dodd and Anderson 2007).

Visual images of enterprise act as exemplars of entrepreneurship (Mitchell and Dino 2011). My interest in images of entrepreneurship, and enterprise, began at an early stage of my doctoral research in the early noughties (*circa* 2002) when I obtained a copy of the book *Images of Entrepreneurship and Small Business* written by Bengt Johannisson and Hans Landström (Johannisson and Landström 1999). Being interested in media imagery associated with the social construction of entrepreneurship and taking a literal reading from the title, my eyes were drawn to the surreal image on the dust jacket of the book. It did not represent any image of enterprise as understood by me. From a cultural perspective, confusion reigned. Thus began a personal obsession or quest with collecting images of entrepreneurship and enterprise.[1] This approach influenced the direction of my doctoral study (Smith 2006). From the said study emerged the notion that visual metaphors associated with entrepreneurship are often associated with archetypes and archetypal imagery. Indeed, the two most common metaphors I encountered were of the entrepreneur as 'Hero' and 'Villain' (Smith 2006). At a storied level entrepreneurship and entrepreneurial identity are socially constructed by heroic stereotyping, cliché, narrative, archetype, storytelling, myth and metaphor. Indeed, I (Smith 2006) conducted a semiotic textual analysis of the entrepreneurship literature in order to identify dominant rhetorical tropes such as myth and metaphor. Accordingly, metaphors play a significant role in this chapter too.

Using semiotic analysis, in this chapter, I conduct an analysis of 'visual metaphors' commonly used to portray enterprise on the covers of over 50 entrepreneurship textbooks. A visual typology emerges depicting a range of metaphors associated with enterprise including biological metaphors, fairy-tale images and 'sexed' up images of enterprise but the norm is an abstracted amorphous image devoid of the excitement and imagination we have come to associate with the entrepreneurial construct. By doing this I illustrate the process by providing a worked example to lead readers through the methodology. This chapter discusses implications for us as entrepreneurship scholars in relation to how we approach unusual research methodologies, as well as for publishers and readers of such textbooks. This study is important because it challenges the hegemony of accepted metaphorical stereotypes commonly used to portray entrepreneurship. In this study, paradoxically, it was found that pictorial images of enterprise, or photographs, used to represent entrepreneurship on the covers of textbooks (as a general rule) do not mirror such heroic imagery. In later sections we shall discuss why and what this tells us as scholars.

This chapter is organized as follows. The following section presents a literature review of research in relation to metaphor and entrepreneurship. This is followed by a methodology section. Thereafter, by a section which presents the results of the metaphorical analysis. The concluding section serves to recontextualize our knowledge of metaphors associated with entrepreneurship.

IN SEARCH OF IMAGES OF ENTREPRENEURSHIP AND ENTERPRISE: A REVIEW

Given that entrepreneurship is so difficult to define it is obviously necessary to use heuristic devices to better understand it. Metaphor is one such device. As stated above, metaphor research in entrepreneurship and management studies is already widespread – see endnote 2 for examples.[2] This lengthy citation tail demonstrates that metaphor is (and continues to be) an important strand in entrepreneurship research. See Table 5.1 for a brief overview of metaphor research already conducted in entrepreneurship and management studies.

From a reading of the material contained in Table 5.1 it is apparent that the current tranche of metaphor research is concentrated upon the 'textual' and 'the written word' as opposed to the wider semiotic and less appreciated aesthetic elements of the entrepreneurial construct. This is in alignment with the views of Pink (2009, 2010, 2011), who conducts visual ethnographic research, that much semiotic research concentrates on the written word and text. This absence of the visual is telling because ultimately, metaphor research belongs to a wider research effort relating to an examination of literary tropes such as semiotics, archetype, myth and metaphor. Tropes are figures of speech that influence and shape our lived experience as powerful rhetorical devices which help us explain entrepreneurship

Table 5.1   An overview of extant research relating to metaphor in entrepreneurship and management studies

Author	Contribution
Easton and Aroujo (1981)	An early conference paper on language, metaphors and networks.
Greenfield and Strickon (1981)	A study relating to new paradigms for the study of entrepreneurship.
Student (1989)	A doctoral study of the use of metaphors in studying uncertainty in entrepreneurs.
Hill and Levenhaugh (1995)	A seminal study of entrepreneurial metaphor and mental modelling.
Koiranen (1995)	Another seminal study of entrepreneurial metaphor, demonstrating its socially constructed nature.
Cosgel (1996)	A study detailing the importance of metaphor and story and also on the exclusion of the entrepreneur from economic rhetoric.
Perren and Atkin (1997)	An exploration of the masculine nature of entrepreneurial metaphors.
Pitt (1998)	Advocated reading entrepreneurs as texts and discussed the uses of metaphor by entrepreneurs.
Hyrsky (1998a, 1998b)	A further robust study/exploration of entrepreneurial metaphor highlighting negative as well as positive aspects of entrepreneurial metaphor.
Busenitz et al. (2000)	This study examined cultural differences across entrepreneurial metaphors.
Ogbor (2000)	Explored the links between entrepreneurship and mythology and in particular discussed the invisibility metaphor.
Ljunggren and Alsos (2001)	An exploration/semiotic analysis of media presentation of the entrepreneur in Swedish media.
Nicolson (2001)	An MSc thesis conducting an exploration of social construction and metaphor usage in British media.
Drakopoulou Dodd (2002)	A study which developed a tentative grounded cultural model of US entrepreneurship.
De Koning and Drakopoulou Dodd (2002)	A further study of entrepreneurial metaphors again highlighting negativity.
Pitt (2004)	An article which discusses entrepreneurial identity and metaphor.
Anderson (2005)	An article which introduces the concept of 'enacted metaphor' and metaphors of theatricality that pertain to entrepreneurship.

Table 5.1   (continued)

Author	Contribution
De Koning and Drakopoulou Dodd (2008)	A study based on a sample of 150 newspaper articles about entrepreneurs and entrepreneurship, over a ten week period (Dec. 2001–Feb. 2002) from nine national newspapers. These were analysed for common metaphors.
Drakopoulou Dodd et al. (2009)	An examination of metaphor across seven European countries.
Cannice and Bell (2010)	This article developed a 'catalogue of metaphor families' that Silicon Valley venture capitalists use in their public communications.
Drakopoulou Dodd and de Koning (2010)	An examination of metaphor in the book *The Republic of Tea*.

Source: Author generated.

to those (such as students) who have not encountered, nor experienced it at first hand. Indeed, we cannot know or understand something that we do not recognize. Moreover, archetype, myth and metaphoric tropes generate connotative imagery that can transcend literal meaning as part of a larger system of associations that predates each of us and moreover is beyond our control. Such underlying figurative tropes contain hidden semiotic thematic frameworks, which guide our actions and communications and thus our understanding. In the following sections we will examine the metaphorical and mythical building blocks to the entrepreneurial construct.

Examining Metaphor and Metaphorical Building Blocks

A metaphor is a figure of speech used to compare something that it resembles, not literally and fundamentally, but in certain marked characteristics. According to Bellert (1980: 25) metaphorical text is not supposed to be interpreted literally. Instead we are meant to read meaning out of it. For Lakoff and Johnson (1980: 5) 'the essence of metaphor is understanding, and experiencing, one kind of thing in terms of another'. Metaphors thus express a concept in more familiar terms, allowing us to make imaginative leaps of recognition, acting as conduits into different worlds (Reddy 1979). Alternatively metaphor can act as a window into a different universe or paradigm, inducing images of other possible worlds (Suvin 2002).

Metaphors thus induce variation and encompass other transformative figures of speech such as rhetorical tropes, analogy, simile, euphemism, cliché, irony and humour. Culler (2001: 201) refers to tropes of fantasy as a cultural reality maintenance system governing how things are represented. Repeated exposure develops and sustains tacit agreement with others of shared societal assumptions. Lakoff and Johnson (1980) developed a helpful framework, mapping the constructionist element of metaphoric types, namely: orientational metaphors; ontological metaphors associating activities, emotions and ideas with entities and substances (metaphors involving personification); structural metaphors; and overarching metaphors (building on the other two types) which allow us to structure one concept in terms of another. Such metaphors are culturally specific and are derived from our physical, social and cultural experience. These form metaphorical clusters of meaning which as will be demonstrated are often extended into myths. Indeed, Leland (1998: 76) argues that metaphor can be explained as a form of socio-typing providing guidance in understanding cultural mindsets.

Thus metaphors are heuristic action orientated labels, which aid our understanding and assembling of complex constructs. For Culler (2001: 43) their value lies in innovating and inaugurating, and for Barthes (1988: 138) it is the language of invention. This makes metaphor a valuable tool in terms of creativity and innovation. Metaphors enrich language and are units of analysis in larger meaning systems (Suvin 2002). Indeed, the meaning systems, ideology and morality which underpin the entrepreneurial construct are all expressed using language and semiotic communication. As a consequence, Suvin (2002) argues that metaphors are imbued with the sum of our cultural topoi, including presupposed values attributable to a text, and Leland (1998: 69) highlights the 'dense, highly metaphoric' nature of language. For Suvin (2002) metaphor provides unitary meaning between 'disparate conceptual units from different universes of discourse'. Metaphor thus presents a complex cognition by sudden confrontation, resulting in the perception of a possible relationship establishing a new norm of its own. In metaphor, we draw and redraw our own conclusions.

Metaphor, as imaginative micro-storia, allow action to become embedded within it, leading to a sequential change of state, overcoming impossibilities using flashes of insight, subjecting complex phenomena to a detailed scrutiny that can only be satisfied in a story. From a philosophical perspective, Dibben (2000: 6) argues that, 'Literal metaphors, do not describe our experiences ... they merely allude to them'. As society changes, new ways of describing change have to be developed because metaphors become tired and oxidized (Dibben 2000: 10). This suggests that metaphors are essential to social constructionism because Gergen (2001: 64–5) argues that metaphor and narrative influence our definitions of ourselves thereby assisting in the processes of renewal and reconstitution. For Lakoff and Johnson (1980: 4–5), dominant metaphors reflect and influence cultural values and language reflects the conceptual system of its speaker providing 'the foundation not only for our language but for our entire conceptual system. Since the latter plays an important role in determining our thought and deeds, metaphors have a fundamental influence on our thoughts and actions'. Metaphor therefore plays a role in entrepreneurship as a legitimizer and signifier into accepted worlds. As discussed below, attempts to understand metaphor have played a significant part in contemporary entrepreneurship research.

Metaphor in Entrepreneurship Research

As elucidated above, using metaphors as a way of understanding entrepreneurship is increasing as evidenced by the list of entrepreneurship and management scholars whose work considers metaphor (see Table 5.1). This makes it acceptable to refer to entrepreneurial metaphor as a collective (and growing) body of knowledge. However, according to Drakopoulou Dodd (2002: 521–4) metaphor can be invoked innocently, or deliberately. Nevertheless, metaphor allows one to research the life-stories of entrepreneurs in their 'own words'.

Hyrsky (1998b: 1x) describes the functions of entrepreneurial metaphor as being (1) compacting and representing a subject including salient and perceptual features; (2) enabling us to talk about experiences, which cannot literally be described; (3) portraying complex concepts more concisely than literal descriptors; (4) enhancing understanding by rendering abstract ideas and concepts more concrete and more easily remembered; (5) portraying imagery providing a vivid, memorable emotive representation of perceived experience; and (6) exploring stereotypical images. Items 5 and 6 are of particular interest in this study. Moreover, images may help us to compact and represent the nuances of entrepreneurship and enable us to picture experiences which we find difficult to talk about and describe. Images are concise yet complex. An image is more easily remembered.

The use of metaphor to explain entrepreneurship was pioneered by the work of Koiranen and Hyrsky (1995) (1988). For Hyrsky (1998b: 408) metaphors highlight 'various priceless qualities associated with entrepreneurs'. Both examined the explanatory role of metaphor. Central to their work is the utility of metaphors as descriptors of sets of behaviours and traits through which lived experience is constructed (Koiranen 1995: 2). Both uncovered examples of action orientated metaphors, such as sportsmen, game player, adventurer, warrior, battler, all of which help construct mythical heroic status. Koiranen explored metaphorical analysis of figurative language uncovering the usage of the metaphors such as 'self-made man'; 'Jack of all trades'; 'Outlaw'; 'Gambler' and 'Cheat'.

BOX 5.1   COMMONLY FOUND WESTERN METAPHORS FOR ENTREPRENEURS

Mechanistic metaphors: Jack of all trades; a supporting pillar of society; a melting pot; a tabula rasa.

Concerning adventurers, warriors, battlers: the captain of a ship; outlaw, maverick.

Concerning games players: a rip-off merchant; gambler; bookie.

Concerning innovative and industrious actors: a self-made man/woman; an artist; an innovator; a mover and shaker; wheeler/dealer; a go getter.

Concerning nature: God; chameleon; sly fox; lone wolf; snake in the grass; ugly duckling; black sheep; slippery eel; rough diamond.

Concerning disease: ego maniac; sociopath; misfit; an eyesore to a tax inspector; parasite.

Concerning special characteristics and failures: priest; Icarus; trusty as a two bob watch; a prisoner of society; mainstay of society; a village idiot; crook; scavenger; unemployed in disguise; capitalist; risk seeker; a dream accomplisher; maker of the future; blowing your own trumpet; a Holy Grail; a monopoly game with real money; putting oneself about; blazing new trials; breaking the mould; free spiritedness; criminality within the law.

Source: Adapted from Hyrsky (1998b: 406).

Hyrsky conducted research, using a sample of men and women from three different countries whom were asked to describe entrepreneurs using metaphors of their own choice. A selection of these as listed by Hyrsky (1998b: 406) are provided in Box 5.1.

Many of the metaphors listed above are pejorative, portraying a dichotomous perception of the entrepreneur.

Wade and Jones (2003: 2) argue that entrepreneurship scholars have metaphorically created a monstrous creature – the heroic, charismatic entrepreneur. Also, established myths and legends can be transferred from one person to another, by virtue of shared names or word association. Golding and Middleton (1982: 136) refer to mythologies sharpened by authority or popular credibility. The substantive study by Cannice and Bell (2010) developed a 'catalogue of metaphor families' that Silicon Valley venture capitalists use in their public communications by coding and categorizing more than 10 000 words of direct venture capitalists' (VC) communications. They found that VC communications fall into 14 dominant metaphor families (including Darwinism, physics and religion). This catalogue approach is useful.

As can be seen there is also a considerable degree of overlap between the different types of metaphor. There is a negative side of metaphor. Indeed, Kirby (2003: 149) argues metaphors and analogies 'construct falsification to liberate the imagination'. McQuail (1994: 222) went as far as to suggest that irony, fantasy and allegory are devices for evading direct responsibility and accountability for a story. For Lakoff and Johnson (1980) they highlight part of the concept and hide others, and the social constructionist Gergen (2001: 73) argues that metaphor and analogy can be associated with 'pretty talk' and deception.

In my readings, I found further evidence of entrepreneurial metaphor. See Table 5.2 for details of this typology.

It is of note that many of these metaphors were located in texts outside the entrepreneurship literature. There is a gender element to entrepreneurial metaphor too. Indeed, Hyrsky (1998b: 407) found that male respondents viewed entrepreneurship in a more favourable light and that male imagery glorified entrepreneurs, 'holding that every man had to fend for himself and make due sacrifices in order to succeed surface time and time again'. Heroic metaphors feed masculine imagery associated with the entrepreneur perpetuating ideal type myth. Hyrsky suggested that metaphors used by female respondents contained more controversial and negative imagery than men's; and most metaphors referring to food items and diseases were female in origin. Warren (2003: 15) argues that for women organic metaphors of entrepreneurship emphasizing family and community are preferable to masculine warlike-economic metaphors. Hyrsky (1998b) concluded that people perceive entrepreneurs in two opposite ways. The majority being positive and idealistic, conjuring up a modern hero, while more cynical, disparaging metaphorical statements convey an alternative image.

From a perusal of the material presented in Box 5.1 and Table 5.2, it can be seen that entrepreneurial metaphor is powerful because it contains elements of romanticism, emotion and even visual imagery which can embody value judgements. The entrepreneur is thus presented as a romantic figure, invoking an emotive response projected in semiotic format as visual imagery. Appropriate metaphors are important as entrepreneurship covers such a wide gamut of socio-economic behaviour. However, the visual aspects of metaphor often remain implicit and back-grounded.

Unleashing the Power of Mythic-metaphor

In the section above, we encountered the powerful concept of mythic-metaphor. As this is a chapter on visual metaphor we must restrict our consideration of myth to that which relates to the visual. According to Edelman (1977: 16–17) mythology is linked to metaphors, which evoke 'mythic structures'. Metaphor analysis is useful because it identifies heuristic devices which help explain the collective and metaphysical natures

Table 5.2   Metaphors commonly invoked in entrepreneur stories

Common analogies used to describe entrepreneurs	Robber barons (Josephson 1934); the Gold Rush analogy (O'Conner 2002a, 2002b); a commando raid (Wansell 1998); being out of step; a rebel; a maverick; a conjurer; a magician; an alchemist; a financial wizard; treading one's own path; striking out on one's own. Often such analogies are clichéd – e.g. sailing close to the wind, a finger in every pie, a nice little earner, nobody's fool; mould breaking (Beaumont 2002: 1). Thus we know we are encountering an entrepreneur story when we read specific clichéd words or phrases which are regularly invoked in telling entrepreneur stories. The game-player metaphor is regularly invoked in relation to entrepreneurs and business angels (Jansson 1994). Barthes (1988: 140) introduces the heroic journey metaphor encompassing travelling, arriving, remaining. Stewart (1990) posited the big man metaphor for entrepreneurship, as a 'library tale replete with morals'.
Trait-based descriptors acting as metaphor	Trait-based descriptors can also be used as clichéd, micro-metaphoric connections to wider social narratives. For example, Beaumont (2002: 2) in discussing the entrepreneur George Hudson invoked such clichés – hard-working, poorly educated, self-indulgent, roughly spoken, visionary, quick witted, unbearably arrogant, strangely humble.
Masculine and military metaphor	Masculine and military metaphors predominate (Ljunggren and Alsos, 2001: 9). It is common to encounter references to male entrepreneurs in collocation with words such as 'attacked' and references to 'bringing home victories in all battles'. Moreover, Sinclair (1994) makes reference to heroic, militaristic images pervading the masculine construct. Nevertheless, the heroic content of entrepreneurial narrative perhaps has more to do with the social construction of metaphoric language, laden with mythological masculine imagery than the entrepreneurial act. Indeed, Chinen (1996) in *Beyond the Hero* identified a need to develop a more mature masculine imagery. On a similar note, Golding and Middleton (1982: 66) in analysing images of social welfare noted that a prominent and recurrent theme is the coverage of armies, fighting and battles. It is important rhetoric in establishing the image of the outsider or enemy and whipping up hysteria. The striking rhetoric and vocabulary of warfare undermine those who flout the ethics and values of the hard-working, for instance, invasion, clamp-downs, crack-downs, swoops, ferreting out, battles, and the vocabulary of dramatic conflict (Golding and Middleton, 1982: 83–4). This is powerful evidence of social constructionism and constructed masculine identity.

The metaphor of the self-made man	The metaphor 'self-made man' is a common euphemism in entrepreneurial narrative. Wyllie (1966) discussed the self-made man in America in relation to the myth of rags to riches; McCabe (1970) explored the struggles and triumphs of the self-made in relation to their great fortunes; Cawelti (1988) researched a new generation of self-made in America likening them to apostles; while Cleveland (1997) examined the self-made man in American life. Catano (2000) examined the rhetoric of self-made men in America and the prevalence of it as a theme in literature. It is not confined solely to the entrepreneur for Pasley (2004) uses it as a descriptor for the infamous American gangster Al Capone.
Historical	Invoking comparison with famous historical figures legitimizes the status of the individual entrepreneur, e.g. MacIntyre (1997) contrasts the Victorian 'Master Criminal' Adam Worth to the tycoon J.P. Morgan, referring to Worth as the Napoleon of crime and Morgan as the Napoleon of Wall Street. Similarly, Beaumont (2002: 125) makes reference to an article in *The Times* newspaper referring to George Hudson as 'the William the conqueror of railways'. Entrepreneurs are seldom accorded the status of king.
Biblical	MacIntyre (1997: 246) refers to J.P. Morgan as the 'Goliath of American finance'. David and Goliath comparisons are common. Also Haines (1998: 158) refers to the Solomon complex, or need to be seen as a problem solver, in relation to Robert Maxwell.
Mythic	These are common, for example Fallon and Srodes (1983: 198) make reference to entrepreneur John DeLorean's 'Olympian attitude' and Beaumont (2002: 135) invoked Herculean mythology stressing that George Hudson must have had the constitution and nervous system of Hercules to withstand the stress of his downfall. Beaumont (2002: 69) narrates that Hudson was blessed with a Midas touch and (2002: x) and refers to the 'Icarian Tale'. Wansell (1998: 358) invokes the myth of Croesus, likening James Goldsmith to being as rich as Croesus and Kochan and Whittington (1991: 24) refer to an Arab entrepreneur Sheik Zahid as a 'Croesus' (wealthy person). Another mythical creature associated with the entrepreneurial narrative is the phoenix rising out of the ashes.
Heroic metaphor	These are common in entrepreneur stories. Beaumont (2002: 77) refers to an image of the entrepreneur George Hudson as 'The conquering hero' returning. Aidis (2002: 6) likens independent thinking entrepreneurs to 'Warriors of Justice' against a corrupt legal system. Fallon and Srodes (1983: 35) refer to an entrepreneur as a 'Wall Street Gunfighter', while Wansell (1998: 308) refers to the 'Bloody battle' metaphor. Wansell (1998: 245) invokes the 'fighting alone' metaphor when referring to Goldsmith's struggle against the establishment.

Table 5.2 (continued)

Power/success	Entrepreneurs are on occasion described as being kings, emperors or historical figures/status types such as Mongol chieftain Attila the Hun are also invoked.
The entrepreneur as a God-like figure.	It is common to elevate individual entrepreneurs to a god-like status by personalizing their traits to create new words. For example, Beaumont (2002: 6) invokes the epitaph of Hudsonian in respect of George Hudson (also consider Maxwellian or Bransonian).
Metaphors associated with place	Entrepreneurial metaphors can be used to designate place as well as person as in Puritan rhetoric saturated with biblical and life metaphors. Thus the milk and honey metaphor describes New England. Indeed, Puritan rhetoric is rich in entrepreneurial ideology. Morgan (1980) identified the relationship between metaphor and milieu, thus we draw our metaphors from our own eclectic experience. An entrepreneur from a building background may invoke occupation specific metaphors, whereas a criminal would invoke a different lexicon. Both examples are aids to understanding.
Personalized metaphor	McAdams (1993) refers to the concept of personalized myths and metaphors. Thus if an entrepreneur is named Arthur the legendary King Arthur epitaph inevitably follows as will Arthurian metaphor. For example, Wilson (1998) referring to the legendary Arthur Guinness alludes to such Arthurian legends.
Metaphors used to disparage individuals	MacIntyre (1997: 259) refers to the popular Victorian perception of J.P. Morgan as a barbarian, while Beaumont (2002: x) uses the 'destroyer' descriptor in relation to George Hudson and Fallon and Srodes (1983: 1) invoke the Maverick label for John DeLorean.

of entrepreneurship. Sahlins (1976: 166–204) observed that the Western mindset constructs intricate mythologies, akin to those of primitive societies. In western society the entrepreneur is such a mythological creature (Rehn and Taalas 2002: 1). Indeed, consideration of the entrepreneur as a mythic character (Mitchell 1997) and mythic hero grows (De Koning and Drakopoulou Dodd 2002; Drakopoulou Dodd 2002). Drakopoulou Dodd (2002) identified recurring themes in American entrepreneurship literature including entrepreneurship as a journey; as war; and as passion. Cardon et al. (2005) also identified the metaphoric themes of passion and parenthood in entrepreneurship texts.

According to Barthes (1984) mythology reinforces capitalist ideology by fabricating reality in accordance with the bourgeois view of the world, covertly propagating bourgeois values as self-evident. Indeed, Barthes (1993: 141) makes reference to the norm as dreamed, whereby the display and consumption of wealth is idealized in the press, media and in literature.[3] Nevertheless, entrepreneurial mythology draws on traditional mythology for inspiration because entrepreneurial myth acts as a visual and symbolic allegorical tale as envisaged by Fontana (1993: 26). In such circumstances it may even become – mythaphor. This enables it to be used as an identity and stylized model for human behaviour. Moreover, myths (including the pictorial) evolve and are constantly generated in contemporary society.

Mythic-metaphors as established storylines are inserted into contemporary entrepreneur stories thus imbuing them with the legitimacy of mythic status. Entrepreneur stories are primarily based on actions–exploits, resulting in success or failure documenting the traits (often exaggerated) of the hero of the story, turning them into stories with a purpose. From a reading of heroic entrepreneurial narrative, I encountered several commonly used mythic-metaphors in entrepreneur stories, drawn from classical mythology. See Table 5.3 for details.

What is ironic about the myths discussed above is that they are invariably invoked in entrepreneurial narrative as tragic tales (Leech 1969). Nevertheless, these mythic-metaphors legitimize individual action and act as heroic templates, providing mythic role models for entrepreneurs to follow in the construction of their personal stories. Mythical heroes embody destructive human traits thus Icarus is invoked to remind us of hubris, Midas and Croesus of greed, Pandora of over inquisitiveness and meddling, and Prometheus of overstretching. They are perhaps traits personified and clothed in narrative. An appreciation of the power of myth as an explanatory tool in entrepreneurial studies is growing (Robertson 1980; Ogbor 2000; De Koning and Drakopoulou Dodd 2002). However, J.R.R. Tolkien (1982: 142) warns that myth leans towards the un-analysable.

Table 5.3   Mythic-metaphors encountered in entrepreneurial narrative

The Icarian tale	Based on the classical Grecian story of Icarus who ignoring advice flew to close to the sun, melted his wings and plunged to the ground. In entrepreneurial mythology it symbolizes the fall from grace of those driven too hard by ambition signifying the expected meteoric descent (Beaumont 2002, Fontana 1993: 86)
The Midas touch	King Midas turned all that he touched into gold. Kets de Vries (1985: 166) narrates the story of an entrepreneur who likened himself to Midas
The Promethean myth	Anderson (1995: 10) citing Landes (1969) likens the entrepreneur to 'Prometheus unbound'. De Koning and Drakopoulou Dodd (2002) in 'The entrepreneur as a mythic hero: a Prometheus of our time' make the same analogy. Prometheus, the wisest Titan in Greek mythology, gave fire to man and could predict the future. For Leech (1969: 13) he was a great rebel. Promethean means 'pertaining to or resembling Prometheus who made a man of clay and put life into him by fire stolen from heaven' (*Chambers Dictionary*). For Nicolson (2001), entrepreneurs have feet of clay
The myth of Croesus	The myth of Croesus (King of Lydia *c.* 563–546) is frequently invoked (as in as rich as Croesus). A biblical myth used as a prophetic warning against hubris
The Pandorian myth	Robinson (2002) invokes this using the descriptor *Pandora's Daughters* for achieving, enterprising women. In the original Greek myth Pandora was endowed with a box by the god Zeus and in opening it, against his express instructions, unleashed evil upon the world. In remodelling the myth, Hesiod reshaped the tale to describe it as the lovely curse of the wicked women. Once again mythology is used to demonize and influence our perception of entrepreneurs

Examining Mythological Aspects of Metaphor

In the above two sections we encountered many examples of mytho-logical and archetypal influences in the entrepreneurial construct. Indeed, Fontana (1993: 21–3) suggests archetypal symbols have power and form recurring motifs embodying 'energies projected onto the outside world' and are imbued with enigmatic, metaphoric qualities (ibid.: 12). In my doctoral study (Smith 2006), I also examined the mythological elements which influence metaphors of entrepreneurship and thus our understanding.[4] To better understand the power of myth in shaping metaphor it is necessary to briefly consider some of the nuances of myth, mythology and myth making.

For a general discussion of myth as a type of speech see Lévi-Strauss (1974); Morgan (1980); Barthes (1984). For Barthes a myth cannot be an object (but myths can be objectified in image and objects can achieve mythical status by transference). Furthermore, Lewis (1961: 186) argues that mythologies transport one into other worlds – as do metaphors and images. Importantly, for Catano (2001: 34) myths are active engagements and visible enactments of cultural doxa. Note the emphasis on the visible. Moreover, Catano (2001: 76) stresses that the whole purpose of entrepreneurial myth is to present an 'engaging portrait' of oneself'. Furthermore, for Hess (1998: 172–92) myths illuminate and gild and there is a circular reciprocity between myth and reality accentuated by portrayal in the media, novels, films, television and discourse. I also established that themes of 'heroic masculinity' and 'heroism' pervaded mythology and also narratives and stories about entrepreneurs – particularly male entrepreneurs. The problem with mythology is that it is embedded in and narrated in stories. Thus although it is easy to convey mythology and the mythological in written textual form – it is more difficult to portray it via visual imagery. We now turn to examine how visual metaphors can act as an aid to understanding entrepreneurial iconology.

Using Visual Metaphors as an Aid to Understanding Entrepreneurial Iconology

Metaphors can involve symbolism and possess iconic modality. In semiotic terms, a metaphor involves using one signified as a signifier referring to a different signified. Visual metaphor is at its most potent when created by comparing two separate generic images, but works as a single image. Metaphorical images are powerful tools allowing the transference of qualities between signs. They enlighten and illuminate. Hess (1998: 80) refers to visual similes, and Kress and van Leeuwen (1996: 168) to our cultural affinity with the visual preference. What we see becomes the measure for what is real and true. Images can broadcast powerful, iconic symbolism that can metaphorically represent entrepreneurship and relate to possessions and artefacts associated with power and wealth. Thus a single photograph of the iconic Sir Richard Branson signifies the personification of entrepreneurship as an image of an expensive car can signify wealth and success. An example of visual metaphor can be found on the cover of the book *Entrepreneurship* by Kirby (2003) portraying a picture of an acorn because entrepreneurship is about new creation and growth.

The discussion of metaphor and mythic-metaphor above illustrates the socially constructed nature of entrepreneur stories, which are constructed as serious semi-tragic narratives, or explained by virtue of culturally accepted myth, metaphor. Metaphor builds upon myth and merges with other linguistic mechanisms and micro-storia such as parables, proverbs, fable, fairy tales and fantasy which help construct entrepreneur stories. We now turn to consider issues of methodology.

METHODOLOGY, METAPHOR, SEMIOTICS AND VISUALIZATION

It is necessary to consider briefly issues in relation to methodology and being methodological when analysing visual metaphor because being methodological is problematic when you make metaphor the central focus as you are in effect making metaphor both the method and the methodology. Moreover, it is also significant that only a few of the published articles on metaphor actually have a robust methodology section. Instead, the pioneering authors appear to concentrate on telling readers what they did and why. This observation is relevant because metaphor and method can indeed merge into 'Methaphor'. This is not merely authorial playfulness with words.

The basic methodology used in this chapter is that of semiotic analysis (Chandler 2007). Semiotic analysis involves commonsensical ideological analysis because ideological sign systems are not neutral and because signs persuade and refer, helping to naturalize and reinforce particular frames of reality. This is important because those who control the sign systems control the construction of reality. It is worth noting that semiotic analysis forces us to focus upon synchronic analysis (the study of a phenomenon frozen at one moment in time) rather than diachronic analysis (changing over time) and underplays the dynamic nature of media conventions (Chandler 1994). Conversely, visual analysis is used to deconstruct visual images. In performing metaphorical analysis one must adopt various metaphors and try them on for fit. These can be solicited from respondents or occur as spontaneous metaphors (Smith 1981).

For Heywood and Sandywell (1999) semiotics permits one to interpret and appreciate how visual metaphors and tropes organize and structure our understanding of the world and to explore the creative interplay between 'sight' and 'insight'. Interest in visual ethnography and other visual research methods is increasing (Harper 1984, 1987, 2002; Schwartz 1989; Banks 1995; Emmison and Smith 2002; Rose 2007; Pink 2007, 2009, 2011; Mannay 2010). Photographs act as 'visual ethnographic narratives' (Harper 2002: 13) invoking deeper elements of human consciousness and appear to present an authentic reality (Tagg 1988). According to Twine (2006) photographs are a collaborative methodological tool as well as being a source of primary data. Rigg (2005) argues that photograph can be read as a visual ethnography or visual language. According to Gleason (2009) image metaphors link one concrete object to another and thereby promote visualization in the mind of the reader. They thus act in a reverse process to textual metaphors and instead of promoting a visual image give rise to textual visualization.

I analysed over 50 textbooks – see the Appendix to this chapter for the list. As the focus of the book is on 'how to do' it is prudent to provide further details of how I conducted the research which forms the basis of this chapter. In the staged list provided below I will talk you through the process of:

- how I picked the sample;
- why I made the choices I did;
- how I arrived at decisions and in particular coding decisions;
- how I classified my themes from the codes.

Stage 1: First I perused publishers' catalogues to identify key texts and then physically collected the images by conducting a trawl of the Internet using keywords as well as visiting publishers' websites.[5] I made my choices and selected my sample based on the availability, or non-availability of an image. I downloaded these into a file in the order encountered taking care not to pre judge or analyse them.

Stage 2: I then analysed the photographic images individually, listing points of interest or observation. This entailed writing down observations on Post-it notes. It is important to make the analysis 'stand-alone' based solely on what one sees in the photographs rather than on other innate knowledge. This is contrary to what is encouraged in other forms of traditional ethnography. First, I wrote down what saw and then expanded it to include word and image association.

Stage 3: These observations were then coded and collapsed into the themes discussed below.

Stage 4: These observations and themes were then written up as a research vignette (Finch 1987). Vignettes are compact stories or literary sketches and photographs can be visual vignettes, particularly when presented with a caption.

From a process of constant comparative analysis, I arrived at the following list of classifications:

- Biological/Growth;
- Scientific/Technical;

- Adventure/Movement;
- Masculinity/Gender;
- Craft based/Craftsman;
- Strategic/Directional;
- Miscellaneous/Surrealist;
- Hybrid;
- Other.

In each of the categories it was possible to arrive at other sub-categories or codes. For example in the biological or growth-orientated category, sub-categories were plant versus human anatomy as well as innate objects. In the scientific category the sub classifications were scientific artefacts such as computers particularly in juxtaposition with human figures. For example, in the Adventure/Movement section sub-themes were danger and risk. The process continued down the categories. See the next section for fuller details of the analysis. This process was necessary to build up a robust methodological framework and because there is an inherent artificiality about the process, once it becomes so very reflexive between method and methodology.

REVISUALIZING ENTREPRENEURSHIP AND METAPHORS OF ENTREPRENEURSHIP

As discussed in the methodology section above, this research entailed examining the covers of over 50 entrepreneurship textbooks to identify the types of visual images and metaphors encountered. See Table 5.4 for details of the visual metaphors encountered.

It is noticeable that the notion of individualism is absent from the images. From an examination of the covers the following metaphors were evident. Images associated with green issues are common, such as the socially responsible entrepreneur as protector of the universe (Choi and Gray 2010). This is a long way from the image of the entrepreneur as 'exploiter and Master of the Universe'. Another common metaphor is the 'Dragons den metaphor' (Nwankwo and Gbadamosi 2010). It is also pertinent that visual images are much less mythic than textual ones because they have different special and sequential qualities. Visual metaphors have a different mythological aura because they allude to the scientific and the genius of the inventions of men. Thus it is possible to collapse the imagery into image types as opposed to word types.

However, not all the metaphors encountered were of a visual nature. For instance, Bjerke and Ramo (2011) in examining the subject of

Table 5.4 Visual metaphors commonly encountered in entrepreneurship texts

Visual metaphor	Descriptive narrative	Authors/text
Biological/ Growth	These are generally plant orientated as in acorns, trees with roots, or shoots signifying growth. Another variant is animal related as in eggs; goldfish; or a swarm of bees; while another is stones; images of the earth	Kirby (2003); Hindle and Klyver (2011); Fayolle and Matlay (2010); Smith and Sutherland (2011); Alsos et al. (2001); Shane (2003); Fayolle (2010); Alexander et al. (2008)
Scientific/ Technological	Such covers are illustrated with images resonating with science such as light bulbs, windmills, gears, keyboards, computers and laptops; a laser beam; a key and a magnifying glass; complexity and change	Teng (2008); Coulter (2000); Wüstenhagen and Wuebker (2010); Olson and Kerharwani (2009); Handscombe and Patterson (2004); Fayolle (2010); Shockley et al. (2008); Rickards et al. (2011); Casson and Buckley (2010); Davidsson (2005, 2008)
Strategic/ Directional	Such metaphors are common in strategic entrepreneurship texts illustrated with arrows and other symbols of direction. Walking a tightrope	Wickam (2006)
Adventure/ Movement	Covers relating to adventurous activity such as mountaineering are common. Another theme is movement and climbing – as signified by ladders or by hot air balloons. The movements series – introduced the elements of water, shifting sands. A road ahead; an open door; surfing is another example	Mitchell and Dino (2011); Davisson (2005, 2008); Steyaert and Hjorth (2003); Barringer and Ireland (2009); Hisrich et al. (2009)
Craft based/ Craftsman	A hand working with a chisel; a hand working with pottery. The proverbial garden shed – beloved of entrepreneur stories.	Read et al. (2010); Barringer and Ireland (2009)

Table 5.4 (continued)

Visual metaphor	Descriptive narrative	Authors/text
Masculinity/Gender	A picture of a gentleman smoking a cigar. A man carrying a bag	Fielden and Davidson (2010); Halkias et al. (2011); Ucbasaran (2006)
Miscellaneous/Surrealist	Such covers relate to action-orientated and surreal topics, such as exploding fireworks, a white-suited man walking on a white runway; an exploding head; open scissors; floating bubbles; a target; a Grecian pillar; a pram laden with miscellaneous objects	Keisner (2009); Bjerke and Ramo (2011); Parker (2011); Nwankwo and Gbadamosi (2010); Choi and Gray (2010); Litan (2011); Kariv (2009); Casson (1990); Butler et al. (2006)
Hybrid	Often there is a crossover between themes such as goldfish or a brain inside a lightbulb, or a lightbulb within a man-made framework	Vedin (2010); Rosenberg (2009); Mitra (2011)
Other/People orientated	Human heads thus linking with thought and cognition; linked hands; mythical rings; gaming dice; reading glasses and a pen; brown carrier bags	Salama (2011); Sommer (2006); Nyssens (2006)
Traditional	Such titles have no anchoring image	Casson (1990); Alvarez (2005); Cuervo et al. (2007)

entrepreneurial imagination look at schedules and places of production, working times and working places and generally examine the subjects of time and space to arrive at a phenomenological understanding of entrepreneurial action and business ventures. This brings the topics of space and place into play. Scherdin et al. (2011) explore the creative and entrepreneurial processes as played out in the field of art. Art is in itself an interesting metaphor for entrepreneurial endeavour.

Upon considering to what degree the findings reflect the source of the images (that is, the textbooks), rather than the form (image versus text) of the metaphor per se, it is apparent that images provide a reader with a richer more visual form of metaphorical access that highlights and reinforces important themes and arguments which would otherwise remain mostly literal in textual terms. Thus Biological/Life-bearing imagery conveys and reinforces the metaphorical connotations between the inevitability of change and new growth – presenting entrepreneurship visually as an inevitable part of a Darwinian natural order. In sharp contrast, the Scientific/Technological iconology provides us with a wonderful array of man-made artefacts of entrepreneurial ingenuity. Similarly, the Strategic iconology offers an insight into how humankind through the mediums of enterprise and entrepreneurship control and dominate their natural environment whilst reinforcing notions of ingenuity and change. In the Craft/Activity-based iconology we see a continuation of human creativity and ingenuity. A parallel theme of creating value is evident. However, these themes of controlling and changing the natural order are continued in the iconology of Adventure/ Movement where individuals risk life and limb to conquer their natural environment. The dominant visual metaphor is that of risk taking and courage. In the Miscellaneous/Surreal we see a contextual reflection of the sociocultural and historical imagery associated with entrepreneurial endeavour. Finally, the iconology associated with Masculinity/Gender serves to illustrate the documented divide between the sexes in terms of the visibility/invisibility debate.

Critics of semiotics and of visual methodologies may say that I am merely making observations which fit perceived knowledge on how entrepreneurship is perceived and depicted. For this reason it is important that you as readers experience visual methodologies at first hand. It is an active methodology which requires practice. One does visual ethnography or semiotic analysis. In order to allow readers to experience the joy and frustration of such analysis, I have set a series of short exercises in Box 5.2. These would also make sound tutorial activities for students.[6] If you do not like exercise(s) please feel free to skip this section.

What you will learn from this iterative process is to have fun and lose

---

BOX 5.2   EXERCISE

Exercise 1 – Try replicating this study by conducting your own search for images. Download them and analyse them yourself. Use your intuition and ask yourself if you agree with the analysis presented or try and expand upon the analysis. It does not matter if your interpretation differs from mine – that is the nature of qualitative research. You may want to narrow your search to a particular genre, for example gender, or widen it to include other aspects of entrepreneurial identity.

Exercise 2 – Make a similar search for textbook images associated with other cognate disciplines such as leadership and/or strategic management. You will find that textbooks on those subjects often share similar images, particularly in relation to mountaineering and engaging in outdoor activities.

Exercise 3 – Alternatively, you may want to use visual images from newspapers, magazines or other databases to analyse. Using the same techniques you could compare and contrast images associated with entrepreneurship with the images on the textbook covers. This is helpful because to conduct semiotic analysis one has to compare and contrast images and associated text. In comparing and contrasting you can discuss the themes which emerge and for the more developed students consider issues such as how images are socially constructed.

---

yourself in the doing and the fun of it.[7] However for best results adopt a coding system using Post-it notes to help formalize the analysis. Also, in conducting the above exercises use your emotional intelligence and get in touch with emotive and aesthetic dimensions.

RECON(TEXT)UALIZING ENTREPRENEURIAL METAPHORS

In the written word we can engage playfully with myth and metaphor. It has been said that 'a picture paints a thousand words' and this is used to justify the arts and the use of semiotics. Yet there are more words than there are colours and shades. It is significant that although Anderson (2005) has articulated that the romantic and convenient myth of the entrepreneur as a heroic individual still holds sway, in the visual images associated with entrepreneurship encountered in this study we do not find much evidence of the entrepreneur being represented as a mythic hero. Nor do the images appear to perpetuate the metaphorically generated gendered biases found in written texts. This is interesting because it suggests that in the written word there is perhaps greater scope for using abstract and often culturally bounded concepts such as metaphor and analogy than in communicating via visual imagery. In the latter case, you may be restricted to making analogy by resorting to the presentation of familiar objects. Note that as we move from the textual towards the pictorial we move subtly from the metaphysical world towards the more tangible and scientific objectification of reality. This is important because it restricts the human imagination and thus entrepreneurial creativity. Moreover, as well as being notoriously difficult to define, as this study has demonstrated, entrepreneurship is also notoriously difficult to illustrate and objectify. The textbook images of enterprise examined for this study illustrate a fascinating variety of available imagery and visual metaphor but the critical point is that entrepreneurship seems to elude a complete iconography per se. The concept reflects the definitional problematic in that it is simply too broad to fit a single image. So what we see are illustrated dimensions.

NOTES

1. Such images included photographic images from books, newspapers and magazines as well as cartoons and other visual media associated with entrepreneurs.
2. As evidenced by the works of Easton and Aroujo (1981), Greenfield and Strickon (1981), Student (1989), Johanisson (1990), Hill and Levenhaugh (1995), Koiranen (1995), Cosgel (1996), Perren and Atkin (1997), Hyrsky (1998a), Pitt (1998), Busenitz et al. (2000), Ogbor (2000), Ljunggren and Alsos (2001), Koiranen and Hyrsky (2001), Nicolson (2001), De Koning and Drakopoulou Dodd (2002), Drakopoulou Dodd (2002), Pitt (2004), Anderson (2005), Drakopoulou Dodd et al. (2007), Drakopoulou Dodd and Anderson (2007), Drakopoulou Dodd et al. (2009) and Cannice and Bell (2010).
3. As a consequence entrepreneurs are presented in the media as being successful and wealthy and photographic images encountered portray capitalist imagery with expensive suits and cars being very much on display.
4. During this research into the social construction of entrepreneurship, I conducted extensive readings – including journal articles, textbooks, and magazine and newspaper articles. In many of these it was apparent that reference was being made to ancient myth. Myths are ancient narratives fixed by tradition but transcend cultural boundaries by relating an aspect of everyday life to mythical-ideological elements underpinning an accepted worldview of the subject.
5. This is relevant because without the internet it would not be possible to access or amass the amount of images of enterprise that float free in the Cybernet. The metaphor of Cybernet is sound because a net is not discriminatory as it catches everything that cannot pass safely through the mesh.
6. I use visual metaphors exercises with undergraduate students in tutorials to allow them to explore trait research/theory in a more palatable manner. I present the students with images associated with particular entrepreneurial traits and in groups encourage them to discuss and explore the trait in more detail and to find other images which may depict the traits. I find this a better approach than lecturing students on trait approaches. Using stock photographs avoids copyright issues. Also the images can be printed off as cards and laminated or distributed to students via a pdf/ppt document.
7. One could argue that there are only a limited number of stock photographs that publishers can work with, that publishing houses have a brand image across disciplines or that many management subjects share similar social constructions.

REFERENCES

Aidis, R. (2002), 'Officially despised yet tolerated: open air markets and entrepreneurship in post-socialist countries', paper presented at the Babson Kauffman Entrepreneurship Conference 2002, Boulder, CO, 5–9 June.

Alvarez, S.A. (2005), *Theories of Entrepreneurship*, Boston, MA: Now.

Anderson, A.R. (1995), 'The Arcadian enterprise: an enquiry into the nature and conditions of rural small business', PhD thesis, University of Stirling.

Anderson, A.R., (2005), 'Enacted metaphor: the theatricality of the entrepreneurial process', *International Small Business Journal*, **23** (6), 587–603.

Banks, M. (1995), 'Visual research methods', *Social Research Update*, **11**, Winter, University of Surrey.

Barthes, R. (1984), *Mythologies*, trans. A. Lavers, New York: Hill & Wang.

Barthes, R. (1988), *The Semiotic Challenge*, trans. R. Howard, London: University of California Press.

Barthes, R.M. (1993), *Œuvres complètes (Complete Works)*, Paris: Editions du Seuil.

Beaumont, R. (2002), *The Railway King: A Biography of George Hudson Railway Pioneer and Fraudster*, London: Headline.

Bellert, I. (1980), 'Sherlock Holmes' interpretation of metaphorical texts', *Poetics Today*, **2** (1), 25–44.

Bjerke, B. and H. Ramo (2011), *Entrepreneurial Imagination: Time, Timing, Space and Place in Business Action*, Cheltenham, UK and Northampton, MA, USA: Edward Elgar.

Burns, P. (2007), *Entrepreneurship and Small Business*, Basingstoke: Palgrave Macmillan.

Busenitz, L., C. Gomez and J.W. Spencer (2000), 'Country institutional profiles: unlocking entrepreneurial phenomena', *Academy of Management Journal*, **43** (5), 994–1003.

Cannice, M.V. and A.H. Bell (2010), 'Metaphors used by venture capitalists: Darwinism, architecture and myth', *Venture Capital: An International Journal of Entrepreneurial Finance*, **12** (1), 1–20.

Cardon, M., C. Zietsma, P. Saparito, B.P. Matherne and C. Davis (2005), 'A tale of passion: new insights into entrepreneurship from a parenthood metaphor', *Journal of Business Venturing*, **20** (1), 23–45.

Catano, J.V. (2001), *Ragged Dicks: Masculinity, Steel, and the Rhetoric of the Self-Made Man*, Carbondale, IL: Southern Illinois University Press.

Cawelti, J.G. (1988), *Apostles of the Self-made-man: Changing Concepts of Success in America*, Chicago, IL: University of Chicago Press.

Chandler, D. (1994), 'Semiotics for beginners', available at: http://www.aber.ac.uk/media/Documents/S4B/ (accessed 21 September 2011).

Chandler, D. (2007), *Semiotics: The Basics*, 2nd edn, London: Routledge.

Chinen, A.B. (1996), *Beyond the Hero: Classic Stories of Men in Search of Soul*, London: Warner Books.

Choi, D.Y. and E. Gray (2010), *Values Centered Entrepreneurs and Their Companies*, London: Routledge.

Cleveland, G.C. (1997), *The Self-Made Man in American Life*, New York: Best Books.

Cosgel, M. (1996), 'Metaphors, stories and the entrepreneur in economics', *History of Political Economy*, **28** (1), 57–76.

Culler, J. (2001), *The Pursuit of Signs*, London: Routledge.

De Koning, A. and S. Drakopoulou Dodd (2002), 'Raising babies, fighting battles, winning races: entrepreneurial metaphors in the media of 6 English speaking nations', paper presented at the Babson Kauffman Entrepreneurship Research Conference, Boulder, CO, June.

De Koning, A. and S. Drakopoulou Dodd (2008), 'Metaphors of entrepreneurship', *Journal of Asia Entrepreneurship Sustainability*, **5** (2), 87–101.

Dibben, M. (2000), *Exploring Interpersonal Trust in the Entrepreneurial Venture*, Basingstoke: Palgrave Macmillan.

Drakopoulou Dodd, S. (2002), 'Metaphors and meaning: a grounded cultural model of US entrepreneurship', *Journal of Business Venturing*, **17** (5), 519–35.

Drakopoulou Dodd, S. and A.R. Anderson (2007), 'Mumpsimus and the mything of the individualistic entrepreneur', *International Small Business Journal*, **25** (4), 341–60.

Drakopoulou Dodd, S. and A. de Koning (2008), 'Metaphors of entrepreneurship across cultures', *Journal of Asia Entrepreneurship and Sustainability*, **4** (2), 87–101.

Drakopoulou Dodd, S. and A. de Koning (2010), 'Tea and understanding: metaphors in the entrepreneurial narrative of Tea Republic', *ENTER*, **1** (1), 33–50.

Drakopoulou Dodd, S., A.R. Anderson and S. Jack (2009), 'Aggressors, winners, victims and outsiders – European schools social construction of the entrepreneur', *International Small Business Journal*, **27** (1) 126–36.

Drakopoulou Dodd, S., S. Jack, A.R. Anderson and S.A. Drakopoulos (2007), 'Entrepreneurship in prospect: using metaphors to identify cultural perceptions amongst young Europeans', *Frontiers of Entrepreneurship Research*, **27** (19): art. 1.

Easton, G. and L. Araujo (1991), 'Language, metaphors and networks', Seventh I.M.P. Conference, Uppsala University, Uppsala, Sweden, 6–8 September.

Edelman, M. (1977), *Political Language*, New York: Academic Press.

Emmison, M. and P. Smith (2002), *Researching the Visual*, London: Sage.

Fallon, I. and J. Srodes (1983), *Delorean: The Rise and Fall of A Dream Maker*, London: Hamish Hamilton.

Fielden, S.L. and M.J. Davidson (eds) (2010), *International Research Handbook on Successful Women Entrepreneurs*, Cheltenham, UK and Northampton, MA, USA: Edward Elgar.

Finch, J. (1987), 'The vignette technique in survey research', *Sociology*, **21** (1), 105–14.

Fontana, D. (1993), *The Secret Language of Symbols: A Visual Key to Symbols and their meanings*, London: Piatikus.

Gartner, W.B. (1988), 'Who is an entrepreneur? is the wrong question', *Entrepreneurship Theory and Practice*, **13** (4), 47–68.

Gartner, W.B. (1989), 'Some suggestions for research on entrepreneurial traits and entrepreneurship', *Entrepreneurship Theory and Practice*, **14** (1), 27–38.

Gergen, K.J. (1991), *From Self to Relationship: The Saturated Self: Dilemmas of Identity in Contemporary Life*, New York: Basic Books.

Gergen, K.J. (2001), Social Construction in Context, London: Sage.

Gleason, D.W., (2009), 'The visual experience of image metaphor: cognitive insights into imagist figures', *Poetics Today*, **30** (3), 423–70.

Golding, P. and S. Middleton (1982), *Images of Welfare: Press and Public Attitudes to Poverty*, Oxford: Martin Robertson.

Greenfield, S. and A. Strickon (1981), 'A new paradigm for the study of entrepreneurship and social change', *Economic Development and Cultural Change*, **29** (3), 467–99.

Haines, J. (1998), *Maxwell*, London: Futura.

Halkias, D., P. Thurman, N. Harkiolakis and S.M. Caracatsanis (2011), *Female Immigrant Entrepreneurs: The Economic and Social Impact of a Global Phenomenon*, Abingdon: Gower.

Harper, D. (1984), 'Meaning and work: a study in photo elicitation', *International Journal of Visual Sociology*, **2** (1), 20–43.

Harper, D. (1987), 'The visual ethnographic narrative', *Visual Anthropology*, **1** (1), 1–19.

Harper, D. (2002), 'Talking about pictures: a case for photo-elicitation', *Visual Studies*, **17** (1), 13–26., available at: http://www.nyu.edu/classes/bkg/methods/harper.pdf (accessed 21 June 2014).

Heywood, I. and B. Sandywell (eds) (1999), *Interpreting Visual Culture: Exploring the Hermeneutics of the Visual*, London: Routledge.

Hess, H. (1998), *Mafia and Mafiosi: Origin, Power and Myth*, trans. E. Osers, London: C. Hurst.

Hill, R. and M. Levenhaugh (1995), 'Metaphors and mental models: sense making and sense giving in innovative and entrepreneurial activities', *Journal of Management*, **21** (6), 1057–74.

Hyrsky, K. (1998a), 'Persistent fighters and ruthless speculators: entrepreneurs as expressed in collocations', paper presented at the Babson College Entrepreneurship Research Conference, Arthur M. Blank Center for Entrepreneurship, Wellesley, MA.

Hyrsky, K. (1998b), 'Entrepreneurship: metaphors and related concepts', *Journal of Enterprising Culture*, **6** (4), 391–410.

Jansson, D. (1994), 'The use of techniques for investment appraisal: the game metaphor', research paper, Ekonomiska Forskningsinsttet vid Handelshogskolen I Stockholm.

Johannisson, B. (1990), 'Economics of overview – guiding the external growth of small firms', *International Small Business Journal*, **9** (1), 32–44.

Johannisson, B. and H. Landström (eds) (1999), *Images of Entrepreneurship and Small Business*, Lund: Studentlitteratur.

Josephson, M. (1934), *The Robber Barons: The Great American Capitalists 1861–1901*, New York: Harcourt-Brace.

Kets de Vries, M.F.R. (1985), 'The dark side of entrepreneurship', *Harvard Business Review*, **85** (6), 160–67.

Kirby, D.A. (2003), *Entrepreneurship*, London: McGraw-Hill Education.

Kochan, N. and B. Whittington (1991), *Bankrupt: The BCCI Fraud*, London: Victor Gollancz.

Koiranen, M. (1995), 'North-European Metaphors of "Entrepreneurship" and Entrepreneur', *Frontiers of Entrepreneurship Research*, Wellesley, MA: Babson College.

Koiranen, M. and K. Hyrsky (1995), 'Entrepreneurs as expressed in collocations. An exploratory study', available at: www.alliedacademies.org/archive/aej/aej2- (accessed 2 January 2015).

Koiranen, M. and K. Hyrsky (2001), 'Entrepreneurs as expressed in collocations: An exploratory study', available at: http://www.alliedacademies.org. (accessed 23 July 2011).

Kress, G. and T. van Leeuwen (1996), *Reading Images: The Grammar of Visual Design*, London: Routledge.

Lakoff, G. and M. Johnson (1980), *Metaphors We Live By*, Chicago, IL: Chicago University Press.

Landes, D.S. (1969), *The Unbounded Prometheus: Technical Change and Industrial Development in Western Europe from 1750 to the present*, New York: Cambridge University Press.

Leech, C. (1969), *Tragedy: The Critical Idiom*, London: Methuen.

Leland, C.T. (1998), *The Art of Compelling Fiction*, Cincinnati, OH: Story Press.

Lévi-Strauss, C. (1974), *The Savage Mind*, London: Weidenfeld & Nicolson.

Lewis, C.S. (1961), *An Experiment in Criticism*, Cambridge: Cambridge University Press.

Ljunggren, E. And G.A. Alsos (2001), 'Media expressions of entrepreneurs: frequency, content and appearance of male and female entrepreneurs', paper presented at the Babson-Kauffman Entrepreneurship Research Conference, Jonkoping, Sweden, June.

MacIntyre, B. (1997), *The Napoleon of Crime: The Life and Times of Adam Worth – the Real Moriarity*, London: HarperCollins.

McAdams, P.D (1993), *The Stories we Live by: Personal Myths and the Making of the Self*, New York: Guilford Press.

McCabe, J.D. (1970), *Great Fortunes and How They Were Made: Or the Struggles and Triumphs of the Self-made-man*, North Stratford, NH: Ayer Co Publishers.

McQuail, D. (1994), *Mass Communication Theory: An Introduction*, London: Sage.

Mannay, D., (2010), 'Making the familiar strange: can visual research methods render the familiar setting more perceptible?', *Qualitative Research*, **10** (1), 91–111.

Mitchell, R.K. (1997), 'Oral history and expert scripts: demystifying the entrepreneurial experience', *International Journal of Entrepreneurial Behaviour & Research*, **3** (2), 122–39.

Morgan, G. (1980), 'Paradigms, metaphors, and puzzle solving in organization theory', *Administrative Science Quarterly*, **25** (4), 606–22.

Nicolson, L. (2001), 'Modelling the evolution of entrepreneurial mythology', unpublished dissertation MSc Entrepreneurship, University of Aberdeen, September.

Nicolson, L. and A.R. Anderson (2005), 'News and nuances of the entrepreneurial myth and metaphor: linguistic games in entrepreneurial sense-making and sense-giving', *Entrepreneurship: Theory and Practice*, **29** (2), 153–72.

Nwankwo, S. and T. Gbadamosi (eds) (2010), *Entrepreneurship Marketing: Principles and Practice of SME Marketing*, London: Taylor & Francis.

Ogbor, J.O. (2000), 'Mythicising and reification in entrepreneurial discourse: ideology-critique of entrepreneurial studies', *Journal of Management Studies*, **37** (5), 605–35.

Pasley, F.D. (2004), *Al Capone: The Biography of a Self-Made Man*, Milton Keynes: Lightning Source UK, Ltd.

Perren, L. and S. Atkin (1997), 'Women-manager's discourse: the metaphors-in-use', *Journal of Applied Management Studies*, **6** (1), 45–62.

Pink, S. (2007), *Doing Visual Ethnography: Images, Media and Representation in Research*, 2nd edn, London: Sage Publications.

Pink, S. (2009), *Doing Sensory Ethnography*, London: Sage.

Pink, S. (2011), 'Multi-modality and multi-sensoriality and ethnographic knowing: or can social semiotics be reconciled with the phenomenology of perception and knowing in practice', *Qualitative Research*, **11** (1), 261–76.

Pitt, M. (1998), 'A tale of two gladiators – reading entrepreneurs as texts', *Organization Studies*, **19** (3), 387–414.

Pitt, M. (2004), 'External influences on the enterprising identity – the case of small owner-managed engineering firms', *International Journal of Entrepreneurship and Innovation*, **5** (1), 37–51.

Reddy, M.J. (1979), 'The conduit metaphor – a case of frame conflict in our language about language', in A. Ortony (ed.), *Metaphor and Thought*, Cambridge: Cambridge University Press, pp. 284–97.

Rehn, A. and S. Taalas (2002), Cosa Nostra – this thing of ours: on moralist tendencies and systems of disequilibria, paper presented at the ESBRI New Practices of Entrepreneurship Workshop. Stockholm, 23–26 May.

Rigg, C. (2005), 'It's in the way they talk: a discourse analysis of managing in two small businesses', *International Journal of Entrepreneurial Behaviour and Research*, **11** (1), 58–75.

Robertson, J.O. (1980), *American Myth, American Reality*, New York: Hill and Wang.

Robinson, J. (2002), *Pandora's Daughters: The Secret History of Enterprising Women*, London: Constable.

Rose, G. (2007), *Visual Methodologies: An Introduction to the Interpretation of Visual Materials*, London: Sage Publications.

Sahlins, M. (1976), *Culture and Practical Reason*, Chicago, IL: University of Chicago Press.

Scherdin, M., I. Zander and A. Wall (eds) (2011), *Art Entrepreneurship*, Cheltenham, UK and Northampton, MA, USA: Edward Elgar.

Schwartz, D. (1989), 'Visual ethnography: using photography in qualitative research', *Qualitative Sociology*, **12** (2), 119–54.

Sinclair, A. (1994), *Trials at the Top: Chief Executives Talk about Men and Women and the Australian Executive Culture*, Parkville, Vic.: The Australia Centre, University of Melbourne.

Smith, D. (1981), *Industrial Location*, New York: Wiley.

Smith, R. (2006), 'Understanding the entrepreneur as socially constructed', unpublished PhD thesis, The Robert Gordon University, Aberdeen.

Stewart, A. (1990), 'The Bigman metaphor for entrepreneurship: a "library tale" with morals on alternatives for further research', *Organization Science*, **1** (2), 143–59.

Student, M. (1989), 'The use of metaphors in studying uncertainty in entrepreneurs', doctoral thesis, University of Michigan, Ann Arbor, MI.

Suvin, D.R. (2002), 'On metaphoricity and narrativity in fiction: the chronotope as the differentia generica', in D. Tannen (ed.), *Gender and Discourse*, Princeton, NJ: Princeton University Press, pp. 51–67.

Tagg, J. (1988), *The Burden of Representation: Essays on Photographies and Histories*. Basingstoke: Macmillan Education.

Tolkien, J.R.R. (1982), *On Fairy Stories, in Poems and Stories*, London: HarperCollins.

Twine, F.W. (2006), 'Visual ethnography and racial theory: family photographs as archives of interracial intimacies', *Ethnic and Racial Studies*, **29** (3), 487–511.

Wade, G. and O. Jones (2003), 'Creating monsters: learning in the entrepreneurial process', paper presented at the 2003 International Entrepreneurship and New Venture Creation Conference, Jacksonville, FL, 17–19 September.

Wansell, G. (1998), *Tycoon: The Life of James Goldsmith*, London: Grafton Books.

Warren, L. (2003), 'A systemic approach to entrepreneurial learning: an exploration using storytelling', working paper, University of Loughborough.

Wickham, P.A. (2006), *Strategic Entrepreneurship*, Harlow: Pearson.

Wilson, D. (1998), *Dark and Light: The Story of the Guinness Family*, London: Weidenfeld and Nicolson.

Wyllie, I.G. (1966), *The Self-Made Man in America: The Myth of Rags to Riches*, New York: Free Press.

APPENDIX 5A.1 ENTREPRENEURSHIP TEXTBOOKS ANALYSED IN THE TEXT

Ács, Z.J. and L. Szerb (2010), *Global Entrepreneurship and Development Index 2011*, Cheltenham, UK and Northampton, MA, USA: Edward Elgar.

Alexander, P., A.M. Vermeulen and P.L. Curseu (2008), *Entrepreneurial Strategic Decision Making: A Cognitive Perspective*, Cheltenham, UK and Northampton, MA, USA: Edward Elgar.

Alsos, G.A., S. Carter, E. Ljunggren and F. Welter (eds) (2001), *The Handbook of Research on Entrepreneurship in Agriculture and Rural Development*, Cheltenham, UK and Northampton, MA, USA: Edward Elgar.

Audretsch, D.B., O. Falck, OS. Heblich and A. Lederer (eds) (2010), *Handbook on Research on Innovation and Entrepreneurship*, Cheltenham, UK and Northampton, MA, USA: Edward Elgar.

Barringer, B.R. and R.D. Ireland (2009), *Entrepreneurship: Successfully Launching New Ventures*, Oxford: Pearson.

Bjerke, B. and H. Ramo (2011), *Entrepreneurial Imagination: Time, Timing, Space and Place in Business Action*, Cheltenham, UK and Northampton, MA, USA: Edward Elgar.

Bygrave, B. and A. Zacharakis (2010), *Entrepreneurship*, London: Wiley.

Burns, P (2007), *Entrepreneurship and Small Business*, London: Palgrave.

Butler, J.E. (2004), *Opportunity Identification and Entrepreneurial Behavior*, Singapore: World Scientific.

Butler, J.E., A. Lockett and D. Ucbasaran (2006), *Venture Capital and the Changing World of Entrepreneurship*, Charlotte, NC: Information Age Publishing (IAP).

Casson, M., (1990), *Entrepreneurship*, Cheltenham, UK and Northampton, MA, USA: Edward Elgar.

Casson, M. and P.J. Buckley (2010), *Entrepreneurship*: Theory, Networks, History, Cheltenham, UK and Northampton, MA, USA: Edward Elgar.

Choi, D.Y. and E. Gray, (2010), *Values Centered Entrepreneurs and their Companies*, London: Routledge.

Coulter, M. (2000), *Entrepreneurship in Action*, Upper Saddle River, NJ: Prentice-Hall.

Cuervo, A.G., D. Ribeiro and S. Roig (2007), *Entrepreneurship: Concepts, Theory and Perspective*, New York: Springer.

Dana, L.P. (2006), *Entrepreneurship and SMEs in the Euro-Zone: Towards a Theory of Symbiotic Entrepreneurship*, London: Imperial College Press.

Dana, L.P. (2007), *Asian Models of Entrepreneurship – From the Indian Union and the Kingdom of Nepal to the Japanese Archipelago: Context, Policy and Practice*, Singapore: World Scientific.

Davidsson, P. (2005), *Researching Entrepreneurship*, New York: Springer.

Davidsson, P. (2008), *The Entrepreneurship Research Challenge*, Cheltenham, UK and Northampton, MA, USA: Edward Elgar.

Dibben, M. (2000), *Exploring Interpersonal Trust in the Entrepreneurial Venture*, Basingstoke: Macmillan.

Fayolle, A. (2010), *Handbook of Research in Entrepreneurship Education: International Perspectives*, Vol. 3, Cheltenham, UK and Northampton, MA, USA: Edward Elgar.

Fayolle, A. and H. Matlay (2010), *Handbook of Research on Social Entrepreneurship*, Cheltenham, UK and Northampton, MA, USA: Edward Elgar.

Grandori, A., L.G. Gaillard and J. Hayton (2011), *Organizing Entrepreneurship*, London: Routledge.

Gustafafsson, V. (2006), *Entrepreneurial Decision-Making: Individuals, Tasks and Cognitions*, Cheltenham, UK and Northampton, MA, USA: Edward Elgar.

Handscombe, R.D. and E.A. Patterson (2004), *The Entropy Vector: Connecting Science to Business*, Singapore: World Scientific.

Hindle, K. and K. Klyver (2011), *Handbook of Research on New Venture Creation*, Cheltenham, UK and Northampton, MA, USA: Edward Elgar.

Hisrich, R.D., R.D.Peters and D.A. Shepherd (2009), *Entrepreneurship*, New York: McGraw-Hill.

Kao, R.W.Y., K.R. Kao and R.W. Kao (2003), *Entrepreneurism: A Philosophy and a Sensible Alternative for the Market Economy*, London: Imperial College Press.

Kariv, D. (2009), *Entrepreneurship: An International Introduction*, London: Routledge.

Kiesner, F. (2009), *Creating Entrepreneurs: Making Miracles Happen*, Singapore: World Scientific.

Kirby, D.A (2003), *Entrepreneurship*, London: McGraw-Hill.

Landström, H. and F. Lohrke (eds) (2010), *Historical Foundations of Entrepreneurship Research*, Cheltenham, UK and Northampton, MA, USA: Edward Elgar.

Litan, R.E., (2011), *Handbook on Law, Innovation and Growth*, Cheltenham, UK and Northampton, MA, USA: Edward Elgar.

Malerba, F. and N.S. Vonortas (eds) (2009), *Innovation Networks in Industries*, Cheltenham, UK and Northampton, MA, USA: Edward Elgar.

Michellette, R.J. (2008), *Entrepreneurial Decision Making*, Bloomington, IN: Xlibris Corporation.

Mitchell, R.K. and R.N. Dino (eds) (2011), *In Search of Research Excellence: Exemplars in Entrepreneurship*, Cheltenham, UK and Northampton, MA, USA: Edward Elgar.

Mitra, J. (2011), *Entrepreneurship, Innovation and Regional Development: An Introduction*, London: Routledge.

Nyssens, M. (2006), *Social Enterprise: At the Crossroads of Market, Public Policies and Civil Society*, London: Routledge.

Nwankwo, S. and T. Gbadamosi (eds) (2010), *Entrepreneurship Marketing: Principles and Practice of SME Marketing*, London: Taylor & Francis.

Olson, D.L. and S. Kerharwani (2009), *Enterprise Information Systems: Contemporary Trends and Issues*, Singapore: World Scientific.

Parker, S.C. (ed.) (2011), *Entrepreneurship in Recession*, Cheltenham, UK and Northampton, MA, USA: Edward Elgar.

Read, S., S. Sarasvathy, N. Dew, R. Wiltbank and A. Ohlsson (2010), *Effectual Entrepreneurship*, London: Routledge.

Rickards, T., M.A. Runco and S. Moger (eds) (2011), *The Routledge Companion to Creativity*, London: Routledge.

Rosenberg, N. (2009), *Studies on Science and the Innovation Process: Selected Works by Nathan Rosenberg*, Singapore: World Scientific.

Salama, A. (2011), *Creating and Re-Creating Corporate Entrepreneurial Culture*, Abingdon: Gower.

Scherdin, M., I. Zander and A. Wall (eds) (2011), *Art Entrepreneurship*, Cheltenham, UK and Northampton, MA, USA: Edward Elgar.

Shane, S. (2003), *A General Theory of Entrepreneurship*, Cheltenham, UK and Northampton, MA, USA: Edward Elgar.

Shockley, G.L., P.M. Frank and R.R. Stough (eds) (2008), *Non-Market Entrepreneurship: Interdisciplinary Approaches*, Cheltenham, UK and Northampton, MA, USA: Edward Elgar.

Smith, A.C.T. and F.M. Sutherland (2011), *Philosophies of Organizational Change*, Cheltenham, UK and Northampton, MA, USA: Edward Elgar.

Sommer, R.A. (2006), *Public Sector Enterprise Resource Planning: Issues in Change Management*, Cheltenham, UK and Northampton, MA, USA: Edward Elgar.

Steyaert, C. and D. Hjorth (2003), *New Movements in Entrepreneurship*, Cheltenham, UK and Northampton, MA, USA: Edward Elgar.

Teng, P.S. (2008), *Bioscience: Entrepreneurship in Asia: Creating Value with Biology*, Tokyo: Asian Productivity Organization.

Ucbasaran, D., P. Westhead and M. Wright (2006), *Habitual Entrepreneurs*, Cheltenham, UK and Northampton, MA, USA: Edward Elgar.

Vedin, B. (2010), *The Design Inspired Innovation Workbook*, Singapore: World Scientific.

Windrum, P. and P. Koch (eds) (2008), *Innovation in Public Sector Services: Entrepreneurship, Creativity and Management*, Cheltenham, UK and Northampton, MA, USA: Edward Elgar.

Wüstenhagen, R. and R. Wuebker (2010), *Handbook of Research on Energy Entrepreneurship*, Cheltenham, UK and Northampton, MA, USA: Edward Elgar.

Vyakarnam, S. and N. Hartman (2011), *Unlocking the Enterpriser Inside! A Book of Why, What and How!*, Singapore: World Scientific.

6 Metaphors in communication of scholarly work

Cecilia Bjursell

THE ENTREPRENEUR – VILLAIN OR HERO?

Metaphors can be helpful in storying your research findings. Considering the amount of work that goes into collecting and analysing material in a study, it makes sense to spend some time reflecting on how to communicate effectively. Taking a pedagogical approach to communication by using metaphors can be an effective way to illustrate and contextualize what you have to say. People learn by metaphor because it allows them to apply familiar knowledge structures to new settings (Walsh 1995; Cardon et al. 2005). Metaphors facilitate understanding while they trigger new questions to be explored.

What do metaphors such as villain and hero do for our understanding of a phenomenon? How do they shape our understanding of entrepreneurship in this case? What venues for research might appear in the wake of these metaphors, and what falls outside the spotlight of a metaphor? Questions like these send chills down the spine of many researchers. They appear to go against everything we were taught about significance, generalization and precision in method classes. Yet, in the same classes, there were few discussions about academic authorship and communication of research. This chapter is an attempt to provide input for those discussions by looking at metaphors in communication of scholarly work.

The aim of this chapter is to inspire the use of metaphors in narratives to make them richer and also to better contextualize research output so that the texts will promote understanding and enhance the potential for learning. As a background to understanding the role of metaphors in communication of scholarly work, the chapter describes four ways that metaphors are used in research: (1) metaphor as artefact, (2) metaphor as inspiration, (3) metaphor as representation and (4) metaphor as expression. You will also find a discussion about the advantages and disadvantages of metaphor as style and remarks on the role of the reader.

ACADEMIC AUTHORSHIP

Social science researchers mainly produce ideas, and these ideas are often expressed as theories. Talking about academic authorship and writing as conversations (Huff 1999) is one way of moving away from the taken-for-granted way of conceptualizing research, such as might be called for when researchers are expected to move beyond their own academic communities and present their findings to students, practitioners and policy-makers. When moving between groups, it is necessary to understand different ways of communicating in order to be able to effectively get your message across: 'For it is through patterns of discourse that we form relational bonds with one another; that we create, transform, and maintain structure; and that we reinforce or challenge our beliefs. The very act of communicating is the process through which we constitute experience' (Barrett et al. 1995: 353).

Research is often described as a methodological and systematic search for answers. If we look at the practice of social science, this work is performed primarily in writing. Although there are a good number of books and articles on how to collect and analyse research material, less has been written about academic authorship and about the communication of research results. The standardized form prescribed for journal publication through author guidelines may lead academic authors to believe that there is a right and a wrong way to present research findings, but even within the formal arena of author guidelines, there is room for creativity and richness. Case study narratives approach the complexities and contradictions of real life. Cases provide context-dependent knowledge, which forms a basis for moving from a beginner's level to an expert level in the learning process (Flyvbjerg 2006). In the case of narratives, metaphors can be used to emphasize the understanding of one thing in terms of another as a way to improve the outcomes of learning.

Telling a story in order to make sense of lived experience underpins the written representation of most methodologies: interviewing, ethnography, narrative inquiry and autobiography (Lander 2000). In ethnography there is much focus on fieldwork and on the process of writing it down, but less attention has been directed to the techniques of writing it up (Van Maanen 2006). The literature on writing it up has traditionally been dominated by the unreflective, holistic style of realism, and few efforts have concerned tentative and interpretive styles (Van Maanen 1995a). One explanation of the predominance of the realist style could be that when writing up our research findings, we choose to conform to an accepted formula for how to present findings so that the text will be considered by others as 'research'. However, if the text gets too stiff, it moves away from representing the social reality studied – a world filled with contradictions and ambiguity. Czarniawska (1999) has written about organization theory as a literary genre, and Kostera (2007) describes how inspiration for writing can come from various other fields: 'Organisational ethnography is a particular kind of qualitative research. From the viewpoint of writing style it is a separate genre, drawing inspiration from numerous other genres (such as academic texts within the qualitative tradition, classic ethnography, but also several others, e.g. belles-lettres, popular novels)' (Kostera, 2007: 237).

In his classic book, *Tales of the Field*, Van Maanen (1988) discussed different forms for fieldwork representation. A major contribution of the book was its questioning of the realist approach as a standardized way of presenting studies. Another contribution was that it showed how the researcher is involved in the active construction of reality in a text. This stands in contrast to the view that the researcher is an objective observer who relies on features such as formalism and operationalism and uses a 'neutral, transparent language uncolored by any personal or partisan agendas' (Van Maanen 1995b: 688). Of special interest here is the use of metaphors as one of many *tricks* when writing up research.

NARRATING WITH METAPHORS

A focus on narratives in general, and metaphors in particular, means questioning generalizability and objectivity. This means working from the assumption that context-dependent knowledge and experience are at the very heart of expert activity and methods of learning (Flyvbjerg 2006). One of the strengths of the metaphor is that it unites reason and imagination (Lakoff and Johnson 1980).

> A metaphor provides a way of seeing or representing one thing in terms of another. It is a ubiquitous figure of speech or master trope in which a word or phrase that typically denotes one kind of object or idea is used to replace another object or idea, thus suggesting an analogy or likeness between them. A metaphor creates a figurative relationship between the two that is often unnoticed in everyday thought and speech. To say that 'organizations are machines' is to claim merely that organizations are like machines for the purpose at hand in a given communicative context (see communication). The metaphor allows speakers and listeners to consider an organization as if it were a machine. By so doing, metaphor asserts similarity in differences and, less obviously perhaps, differences in similarity. Thus, by claiming similarity, a metaphor sets something apart from other things and establishes differences from them (e.g., as a machine, an organization does not live and die but is built and dismantled); but also, by taking an object in terms of the metaphor, the object is provided with selective but distinct characteristics associated with the term of similarity

(e.g., as a machine, an organization is predictable, impersonal, functional, and occasionally in need of repair). (Van Maanen 2005)

The figurative expression of one object in terms of another sheds light on certain characteristics while others become hidden. It has been argued that making sense of something by comparing it to something else is a basic feature of human thought processes, as these are said to be essentially metaphorical (Docherty 2004). Metaphors come in different shapes: some are obvious or well-known, such as the metaphor of the organization as a machine or as a brain (Morgan 2006). Others are taken for granted expressions. Even academic theoretical models can be said to be metaphors. In addition to using metaphors straightforwardly, we can trace root metaphors through the use of certain vocabulary. A root metaphor reflects implicit beliefs that shape an individual's understanding of a situation.

Innovative approaches are called for in entrepreneurship because entrepreneurs create different models of their activities than those typically used to analyse and describe organizations (Dodd 2002). The use of metaphors as a research tool can be a means of reducing large amounts of material in order to be able to critically examine philosophies of practices and ideals in context (Wilson 2011). The use of metaphors in collaborative and process-oriented qualitative inquiries can also be a way to transform the individuals involved and enhance commitment towards engaging in a more equitable society (North 2010). The metaphor can provide a means of categorization, but it simultaneously triggers the imagination by suggesting that we should see one thing in terms of another. To achieve this effect, though, there has to be a proper balance of similarity and difference. When the appropriate metaphor is found, this helps the reader see things in a new way, but it also requires the reader to stay critical, as some insights can become distortions. To be aware of and use metaphors in organization studies is one way to express paradoxes and versatility in an organization. We will get back to advantages and disadvantages of the metaphor, but first we will explore four ways to use metaphors in research.

FOUR WAYS TO USE METAPHORS IN RESEARCH

When reading about the use of metaphors, I found four different ways to understand the roles of metaphors in research. I have called them (1) metaphor as artefact, (2) metaphor as inspiration, (3) metaphor as representation and (4) metaphor as expression (see Figure 6.1).

Metaphor as artefact refers to the fact that some metaphors have

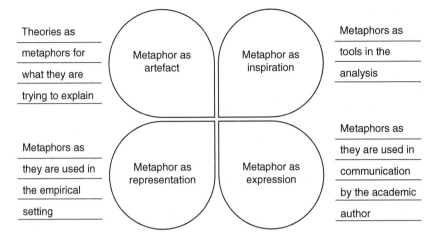

Figure 6.1   Summary of four roles of the metaphor in research

become a natural part of language and are no longer thought of as metaphors. Metaphors can be used for inspiration and creativity during the writing process; this is metaphor as inspiration. Metaphor as representation is a way to highlight and discuss metaphors encountered in the field. Finally, metaphor as expression concerns the use of metaphors in a text as a communicative device. The four roles of the metaphor are described in more detail below.

Metaphor as Artefact

Metaphor as artefact is about highlighting the taken-for-granted use of metaphors. Metaphors are often used unreflectively in scientific material (Manning 1979; Asplund 2002). One example is Adam Smith's the invisible hand, which is not literally a hand, but a metaphor for an idea about market forces. This metaphor has gained a pseudo-literal status over time (Asplund 2002). Another example from studies of organization is the use of the pyramid as a metaphor for an organization (Alvesson 2002). The pyramid is rarely used today as a device for understanding spatial or hierarchical matters; rather, it is more commonly used in everyday language as a synonym for an organization.

When concepts intended as metaphors for enhancing the pluralistic qualities of social reality achieve status as theories, this usually means that they are being used unreflectively and that the meaning transferred is being taken for granted. When a shift like this happens, the metaphor moves from being the signifier to the signified, that is, the medium becomes the message. If we are aware of a metaphor *as* metaphor, however, the metaphor might then act to extend conceptual representation to include the underlying meanings of a phenomenon. Entrepreneurship, when seen as a metaphor representing innovation, risk, proactivity and creativity, can be used by anyone who needs to explain the complex combination of the concepts that make up entrepreneurial activity (Cardow 2006).

From a methodological perspective, this means being aware of whether metaphors appear in theories as signifier (that which is used to describe something else) or signified (the intended message). Working from the premise that all theory is metaphor, we have to accept that organizational theories and perspectives are incomplete and biased, even while they are capable of creating valuable insights (Morgan 2006).

Metaphor as Inspiration

One of the basic characteristics of the metaphor is that it provides opportunities to expand ideas and challenge existing beliefs. The use of metaphors as catalysts can bring new insights to the research process. Metaphors bridge the existing elements of experience to aid our understanding of other parts of the surrounding world. The balance of differences and similarities between the subject and the metaphor for the subject is important.

> The necessary ingredient of difference has a specific cognitive function: 'it makes us stop in our tracks and examine it. It offers us a new awareness'. Metaphors are intended to be understood; 'they are category errors with a purpose, linguistic madness with a method'. Metaphors must be approached and understood as if they were true at the same time that we are aware that they are fictitious – created and artificial. (Alvesson 2002: 19)

A metaphor is true at the same time that it is artificial. A metaphor is contradictive. Some of the strengths are mirrored in some of the weaknesses. When we apply metaphors, this helps us see and think in a new way. Morgan (2006) illustrates how different metaphors expand insights and demonstrates how metaphors can be used to bring forth complementary understanding of an organization. Morgan's metaphors are used to develop and explore organizational life by combining metaphorical insights of different points of views. By using the parenthood metaphor to analyse the relational dimension of entrepreneurship, the importance of strong emotions and identification between an entrepreneur and a venture can be explored and communicated (Cardon et al. 2005).

A discussion about metaphors used can reveal our assumptions, can make us reflect on the phenomena behind the metaphor during the interpretative process and can further our knowledge about a certain area.

Table 6.1   An example of working with the villain and hero metaphors

Metaphor	Metaphor associations	Emerging questions
The entrepreneur as villain	The entrepreneur as villain suggests that the entrepreneur is someone who engages in criminal activity. With regard to business, this could mean breaking business laws or not following laws. It could also have to do with moving in grey areas of the law or finding new loopholes, new products and markets. A villain might work alone or in a group together with other villains	Questions raised by working with the entrepreneur as villain metaphor could concern the fit between entrepreneurial activities and current laws. It also points to the need for moving across and beyond boundaries and for questioning existing systems, as well as to risks connected with this. The villain could be explored as a representation of the early stages of entrepreneurial activities and the creative side of starting up new ventures
The entrepreneur as hero	The entrepreneur as hero places the entrepreneur above others, as someone who can save us and maintain order in society. The entrepreneur as hero is a lonely figure; heroes can cooperate, but they always take a leading role, that is, they are not equal to others. The hero is the good father, almost God-like. Physical strength and being just in time are other traits of the hero	The entrepreneur as hero metaphor could lead to questions about success/failure and/or performance-related issues. If a hero is viewed as more muscle than brain, what would this represent in entrepreneurship – financial strength or other assets? It could be interesting to see whether the heroic image comes from charismatic leadership or if it is a marketing result or something else

To give an example, we can revisit the title 'The entrepreneur – villain or hero' and take a closer look at the two metaphors and their consequences. In Table 6.1, the two metaphors are presented with an example of metaphor associations – connections between the metaphor and the entrepreneur and ideas that arise from this process of imagining – and questions that might emerge from the creative process involved in making such associations.

These are only suggestions for associations of the metaphor and possible questions to continue exploring. You can probably come up with many more if you sit down with some friends and engage in collaborative inter-pretation of these metaphors. To distance oneself from a suggestive meta-phor, it is relevant to remember to ask what is not in the metaphor. It is hinted that the villain could be a part of a gang, but essentially, the villain and the hero are two lonely characters. This obscures all of the networking and contacts that are part of an entrepreneur's daily activity. The villain and the hero also tend to be male characters, so we need to think about what consequences this might have for understanding women's entrepre-neurship. Both metaphors are also often portrayed as cartoons, that is, as one-dimensional characters, which might not be in line with the likely more complex business entrepreneur. Apart from fuelling interpretative action and giving rise to new questions, the metaphor can also be a vehicle for describing and prescribing relations in the research process.

Exercise

Choose an entrepreneurship magazine or select some articles about ventures and/or entrepreneurs. On your own: read the texts and make notes on the metaphors you find. In group: discuss the metaphors used – what do they highlight and what do they hide? Can you find any root metaphors (implicit beliefs that shape our understanding)? Do some metaphors appear more frequently, and if so, why?

Metaphor as Representation

Metaphor as representation has to do with how metaphors are used by people in the field. Analysing metaphors in an organizational context can provide insight into the daily life of an organization by revealing tacit information hidden in narratives (Steger 2007). As metaphors are a natural part of communication, there are bound to be metaphors in the empirical material collected during a study. When talking to people in the field or conducting interviews, metaphors recur again and again. Metaphors from the natives' points of view are part of the material collected in the research process. Quotes are used to illustrate interesting aspects of that which is being researched and are analysed to find root metaphors. In a direct representation, metaphors are used as they appear in their original context, as in the following quote of a Swedish manager using communism as a metaphor to describe Finnish management style in a cross-border merger:

> As a Swede – and I have worked in American companies as well – you're used to getting a budget for one year and then you go. 'These are the rules, go!' Now one person sits and distributes money as we go along. In Sweden we would like it to be more like 'mind your own business' but they want to be everywhere and have centralized committees and coordinate everything. We are expected to sit

in on meetings and report and get approval. More like an Eastern European state (communism). (Bjursell 2007: 88)

In this case the metaphor was intended to compare the Finnish management style with the corrupt systems and rigid bureaucracies of twentieth-century Eastern European communism. The metaphor is also value laden, portraying Finnish management style as inferior to the Swedish way of working. Another example of a metaphor in its original context can be found in the case of EuroDisney, described by Van Maanen (1992). In a newsletter to the employees, the theatre metaphor was used to explain the EuroDisney look: 'Like any theatrical presentation, the EuroDisney show is comprised of elements that create an atmosphere, an ambiance. In our case, the architecture, setting, costumes and even the look of our cast members play into this immense, three-dimensional show' (Van Maanen, 1992: 27–8). The theatre metaphor is used here to communicate rules for behaviour and appearance when working at EuroDisney. Theatre as a metaphor, as will be described in the section about metaphor as expression, can also be a device for staging a text. Apart from direct representation, and as a staging device, the theatre metaphor can emerge as a root metaphor through analysis of the vocabulary used (for example, role, actor, stage, performance). Root metaphors can reveal a deeper understanding of what is going on. When Van Maanen (1995b: 689) finds terms such as replicable, teachable, transferable concepts and methods in a text, he sees these as indicating the root metaphor of industrialization ('this is a call for the industrialization of scholarship'; ibid.). Studies of figurative language in media representations can be enlightening and they are important because newspapers describe and also define entrepreneurial phenomena (Nicholson and Anderson 2005). In a study of women's entrepreneurship, the business role and the mother role were two frequently recurring metaphors used in media articles about women and their businesses (Bjursell and Bäckvall 2011). No matter the empirical arena, it is important to understand the metaphors that entrepreneurs themselves use to understand the experience of entrepreneurship (Weick 1999).

Metaphor as Expression

The final category presented in this chapter, metaphor as expression, refers to metaphor as style. Here, the metaphor is seen as a communicative device in the process of writing up research. Alvesson (2002: 17) writes that 'in a narrow, traditional sense, a metaphor is simply an *illustrative device*' (original emphasis). When it comes to studies of organization, however, more is written on the metaphor as a theoretical tool than as an illustrative or communicative device in a text. Metaphor as expression means a shift from analysis to the design of a paper. When you know what you want to say, how should you say it? The purpose of using metaphors should be to make comparisons intended to help others understand what you want to share (Wolcott 2010). When one is aware of different forms or categories of metaphors, one can choose a style that (hopefully) will appeal to the intended reader. There are several reasons to use metaphors in a text.

First, metaphors can help bring a text to life and make it fun to read. One aspect of this is that in competition with other texts, an intriguing metaphor in the headline can be what attracts people to read the paper in the first place. However, the metaphor should indicate the content of the text in order to attract the attention of the intended audience. Kostera (2007) describes how her study, *Postmodernism in Management*, attracted readers looking for a treatise in philosophy, but as the book is a report from a field study, the actual readers felt cheated while potential intended readers missed it. Kostera also mentions that the article 'The modern crusade: missionaries of management come to Eastern Europe' got a fair number of readers and that the title might have been a main pull.

Second, metaphors can be used to create a certain mood or atmosphere in the text. The connotations of the metaphor put the reader in a certain state of mind, and a metaphor can be a way to capture the emotional side of what is going on in the field, something that can be otherwise difficult to express in plain words. Talking about an organization as a machine gives a completely different feeling than using the metaphor of a greenhouse. This is use of the metaphor as a rhetorical instrument.

Third, the metaphor can be used to sketch the illusive side of social reality that can be perceived during a study but that is hard to 'prove' or to fully understand. When Disneyland is described as 'an island of calm sanity and safety in troubled times' (Van Maanen 1992: 12), this informs the reader about the emotional difference that characterizes Disneyland compared to its surroundings in contemporary America. Most organizational theories avoid emotions, even though emotions are embedded in business practice. Through exploration of relational metaphors, for example parenting, additional insights have been made into the process of entrepreneurship by highlighting both nurturing and fear as new variables of interest (Cardon et al. 2005).

A fourth reason to use metaphors in the text is that metaphors are communicative, more efficient than literal language. In a study of entrepreneurial identity work, we emphasized two conflicting but interrelated narratives found in entrepreneurs' narratives about becoming an entrepreneur by using the 'Pippi Longstocking' and 'Alice in Wonderland' metaphors (Bjursell and Melin 2011). The use of the two stories as metaphors highlights the coexistence of a proactive and a reactive approach among entrepreneurs. However, metaphors only work if the writer and the reader share assumptions and meanings connected to the chosen metaphors. If powerful metaphors are shared by many individuals, they can contribute to shaping the social worlds in which we live (Docherty 2004). In organizational change, metaphors can be viewed as devices for promoting understanding of the need for change as well as for seeing the positive outcomes associated with change efforts (Armenakis and Bedeian 1992). Thus, metaphors are useful for connecting to the reader, possibly affecting the practical implications of a text.

Finally, an interesting way to work with metaphors is to use them to add ambiguity to a text. This goes against the ideal of exactness that is prevalent in the scientific community but, if needed, it is possible to combine precision and ambiguity in a text. One reason to add ambiguity is that it (hopefully) resonates with the reader's own experiences. Then the role of the interpreter is shared between the researcher and the reader. The choice of metaphor will hint at what the writer wanted to say, but in the end it is up to the reader to decipher the message. However carefully the metaphor is chosen, it is always up to the reader to make his or her own interpretation. Thus, a research text involves interpretation from the writer as well as the reader. Van Maanen (1995a) identifies three loosely demarked audience categories: collegial readers, general social science readers and readers in the pursuit of pleasure. Collegial readers follow specific domains, whereas general social science readers look for specific pieces that can further their own research agenda. Readers in pursuit of pleasure are attracted by storytelling and allegorical elements of ethnography. However, there is a growing distance between differing segments of ethnographic specialists, and together this makes the ethnographic community a fragmented crowd (ibid.).

While the reflective use of metaphors can be a valuable aid for thinking and can facilitate comprehension and learning, this requires that the reader and the writer have metaphorical competence (Asplund 2002). Metaphorical competence can be achieved when shifting from information oriented reading (looking at details) to reading oriented towards understanding (getting the message). Further exploration of the expectations and interpretations of the different target groups can enhance our understanding of how metaphor as style can be used in research output.

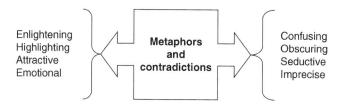

Figure 6.2   Contradictions faced in metaphor as style

ADVANTAGES AND DISADVANTAGES OF METAPHORS

To learn more about using metaphors in research, a discussion on advantages and disadvantages of using metaphors in writer-reader communication is called for. A number of contradictions are used here to illustrate the strengths and weaknesses of metaphors: enlightening/confusing, highlighting/obscuring, attractive/seductive and emotional/imprecise (see Figure 6.2).

While metaphors have the potential to enlighten the reader as figurative complements to a written text, they can also be confusing. Metaphors can enlighten the reader by pointing to specific areas that are important for understanding the discussion at hand, but if the reader takes the metaphor literally, the results can be quite absurd. The opposite can also occur: hands-on descriptions might be interpreted as metaphors. For example, the expression 'these robotic villains' could be used as a metaphor in reference to a management group, but in the case of describing Disneyland, it is merely a literal description of the Pirates of the Caribbean attraction (Van Maanen 1992: 14). Another difficulty with using metaphors is that they can be culture specific, so people from other cultures might not understand them.

A metaphor can put the spotlight on aspects one wants to bring out in the text. Morgan (2006) showed that metaphors can be used to highlight aspects of an organization, for example, but at the same time, they can conceal other aspects and overemphasize similarities. A way to deal with this can be to explicitly address the hidden aspects in order to show awareness of these; the writer can comment on what is highlighted and also on what is obscured.

The attractiveness of playing with metaphors can result in applying metaphors just for the sake of it, rather than for a specific purpose. If the metaphor is used to stimulate the creative process, there is a risk that one becomes too involved with and attached to the metaphor. In the final version of a paper, some metaphors may need to be left behind if they have played out their roles as catalysts for creativity or analytical tools in the process. The attractiveness of a metaphor can also lead to possible seduction of the reader, as metaphors can have great persuasive power.

In a text, metaphors can be a way to induce emotion and thereby present thicker descriptions. This is possible because metaphors can carry different meanings simultaneously or hint at specific aspects of interaction. The downside of this is that thick descriptions and emotional expressions can be perceived as a lack of precision and logic. Although the language of science has traditionally been literal, the use of figurative language such as metaphor can potentially yield richer descriptions and greater communicative power.

CONCLUDING REMARK

There are many reasons to consider metaphors in research and in communication of scholarly work. Metaphors are not merely decorative parts of speech, they are ways of seeing, thinking and learning and they have implications for practice (Hatch and Yanow 2008). As shown, metaphors are already part of research, although they are not always used consciously. A few reasons to use metaphors are that they:

- have great pedagogical strengths because they contextualize subjects;
- can bring together complex combinations of concepts;
- can help transfer knowledge from one area to another;
- are tools for communicating emotions;
- may lead to new insights in a familiar setting;
- might help us identify taken-for-granted assumptions; and
- are fun to use and support the creative part of research.

In this chapter, I have discussed four ways the metaphor can be used in research practice and I have directed special attention to metaphor as expression: metaphor as style in communication of research findings. To provide insight into the use of metaphors, the advantages and disadvantages of the metaphor have been presented. A picture is worth a thousand words. Using metaphors as images to stimulate imagination requires that you think carefully about what you are doing, but it also makes what you are doing fun to think about.

REFERENCES

Alvesson, M. (2002), *Understanding Organizational Culture*, London: Sage Publications.
Armenakis, A.A. and A.G. Bedeian (1992), 'The Role of Metaphors in Organizational Change', *Group & Organization Management*, **17** (3), 242–8.
Asplund, J. (2002), *Avhandlingens språkdräkt (The Language Costume of the Dissertation)*, Göteborg: Bokförlaget Korpen.
Barrett, F.J., G.F. Thomas and S.P. Hocevar (1995), 'The central role of discourse in large-scale change: a social construction perspective', *Journal of Applied Behavioral Science*, **31** (3), 352–72.
Bjursell, C. (2007), 'Integration through framing: a study of the Cloetta Fazer merger', doctoral dissertation, Linköping University, Linköping, available at: http://urn.kb.se/resolve?urn=urn:nbn:se:liu:diva-8964 (accessed 16 June 2015).
Bjursell, C. and L. Bäckvall (2011), 'Family business women in media discourse: the business role and the mother role', *Journal of Family Business Management*, **1** (2), 154–73.
Bjursell, C. and L. Melin (2011), 'Proactive and reactive plots: narratives in entrepreneurial identity construction', *International Journal of Gender and Entrepreneurship*, **3** (3), 218–35.
Cardon, M.S., C. Zietsma, P. Saparito, B.P. Matherne and C. Davis (2005), 'A tale of passion: new insights into entrepreneurship from a parenthood metaphor', *Journal of Business Venturing*, **20** (1), 23–45.
Cardow, A. (2006), 'The metaphorical rise of entrepreneurship', Department of Management and International Business Research, Working Paper Series 2006, no 8, Massey University, Auckland.
Czarniawska, B. (1999), *Writing Management: Organization Theory as a Literary Genre*, Oxford: Oxford University Press.
Docherty, J.S. (2004), 'Narratives, metaphors, and negotiation', *Marquette Law Review*, **87** (4), 847–51.
Dodd, S.D. (2002), 'Metaphors and meaning: a grounded cultural model of us entrepreneurship', *Journal of Business Venturing*, **17** (5), 519–35.
Flyvbjerg, B. (2006), 'Five misunderstandings about case-study research', *Qualitative Inquiry*, **12** (2), 219–45.
Hatch, M.J. and D. Yanow (2008), 'Methodology by metaphor: ways of seeing in painting and research', *Organization Studies*, **29** (1), 23–44.
Huff, A.S. (1999), *Writing for Scholarly Publication*, Thousand Oaks, CA: Sage.
Kostera, M. (2007), *Organisational Ethnography*. Lund: Studentlitteratur.
Lakoff, G. and M. Johnson (1980), *Metaphors We Live By*, Chicago, IL: University of Chicago Press.
Lander, D. (2000), 'Mixed metaphors for reading and writing the qualitative thesis in adult education', *Studies in the Education of Adults*, **32** (2), 148–66.
Manning, P.K. (1979), 'Metaphors of the field: varieties of organizational discourse', *Administrative Science Quarterly*, **24** (4), 660–71.
Morgan, G. (2006), *Images of Organization*, 2nd edn, Beverly Hills, CA: Sage.
Nicholson, L. and A.R. Anderson (2005), 'New and nuances of the entrepreneurial myth and metaphor: linguistic games in entrepreneurial sense-making and sense-giving', *Entrepreneurship, Theory and Practice*, **29** (2), 153–72.
North, C.E. (2010), '(De)ciphering collaborative research for social justice: reviving relationality through metaphor', *Qualitative Inquiry*, **16** (7), 531–8.
Steger, T. (2007), 'The stories metaphors tell: metaphors as a tool to decipher tacit aspects in narratives', *Field Methods*, **19** (1), 3–23.
Van Maanen, J. (1988), *Tales of the Field. On Writing Ethnography*, Chicago, IL and London: University of Chicago Press.
Van Maanen, J. (1992), 'Displacing Disney: some notes on the flow of culture', *Qualitative Sociology*, **15** (1), 5–35.
Van Maanen, J. (1995a), 'An end to innocence. The ethnography of ethnography', in J. Van Maanen (ed.), *Representation in Ethnography*, London, Sage Publications.

Van Maanen, J. (1995b), 'Fear and loathing in organization studies', *Organization Science*, **6** (6), 687–92.

Van Maanen, J. (2005), 'Metaphor', in N. Nicholson, P.G. Audia and M.M. Pillutla (eds), *Blackwell Encyclopedic Dictionary of Organizational Behavior*, 2nd edn, Oxford: Blackwell, pp. 231–2.

Van Maanen, J. (2006), 'Ethnography then and now', *Qualitative Research in Organizations and Management: An International Journal*, **1** (1), 13–21.

Walsh, J.P. (1995), 'Managerial and organizational cognition: notes from a trip down memory lane', *Organization Science*, **6** (3), 280–321.

Weick, K.E. (1999), 'That's moving: theories that matter', *Journal of Management Inquiry*, **8** (2), 134–42.

Wilson, K.B. (2011), 'Opening Pandora's box: an autoethnographic study of teaching', *Qualitative Inquiry*, **17** (5), 452–8.

Wolcott, H.F. (2010), *Ethnography Lessons. A Primer*, Walnut Creek, CA: Left Coast Press.

Metaphor methodologies in entrepreneurship research
Sarah Drakopoulou Dodd and Alice de Koning

In spite of their difference in approach, a number of common themes run through these three chapters, which, taken together, highlight the potential, the challenges, the limitations and quality assessment demands of metaphor methodologies for entrepreneurship research. In this short concluding section, we argue that metaphors act as a reminder of the necessity for scholarly self-reflection, as well as a means for carrying this out. We note that although coding schemes are presented throughout the section's chapters, there is no real substitute for engaging with one's own data directly. We argue that, complex and ambiguous though metaphors may be, their very versatility makes them uniquely ubiquitous, able to reach places other methods may not address.

First, the value of metaphors in facilitating self-reflection is evident. Indeed, these chapters have illustrated that it is imperative for we entrepreneurship scholars to engage in such self-reflection. Which images and social constructions of the entrepreneur do we ourselves enact, embrace, develop and share? Such self-reflection is imperative when doing analysis and coding, since it is all too easy to fall prey to your own personal cognitive schemata, biases and learnt tendencies. Because metaphors are such slippery, ambiguous and complex tropes, constant auto-interrogation is demanded of the scholar in an attempt to avoid 'reading into' the data being explored. This can become a rich and enriching part of the research process if shared with others, especially co-authors, allowing us a frame for re-visiting and exploring our own tacit perceptions of the entrepreneur. Robert Smith's chapter highlights the social constructions implicit within textbook images, and Cecilia Bursjell's the significance of metaphor as an expressive tool for academics. We wonder to what degree our own perceptions of the entrepreneur are conveyed metaphorically to our students, colleagues and other audiences, through the images, stories and expressions we share to give meaning. Using metaphors with greater awareness and intentionality can not only improve our communication, but also lay bear the assumptions and shared beliefs underpinning our work.

Secondly, one of the most helpful elements of these chapters is the several detailed and thorough category/coding schema for metaphors presented in the section. These, we believe, are a mixed blessing. On the one hand, after years of reviewing literature and methods, the section editors are convinced that their detailed category system is complete for almost any application of metaphor analysis. Alternative approaches are also shared by the other two authors in this section. Ready-made coding solutions are thus easily available for the would-be metaphor scholar, allowing them to shorten and tighten what can be a very long and messy process.

On the other hand, there is great value in adopting an inductive process to create categories for coding metaphors. This is because the process forces researchers to engage in all the richness of the text. Notice how the process of creation of the schemata led to richer knowledge of the data, and ultimately richer interpretation of the findings. We would therefore recommend that researchers resist the temptation to choose and implement just one of the systems so clearly presented here. At least attempt to generate your own themes inductively before reaching for an off-the-peg solution; the benefits in terms of data comprehension and immersion are substantial. Even if using one of the schema, look closely at the data and consider whether other characteristics of the metaphors-in-context provide richer insights. Examples might include looking at positive, negative and neutral enriched interpretation of one dataset, or contrasting text metaphors with visual metaphors to perhaps set up strange juxtapositions, such as those which Robert Smith found in entrepreneurship textbooks.

The metaphor is indeed slippery, yet paradoxically it is also a highly versatile and tractable research tool in the arsenal of the qualitative scholar. Within this section, examples have been shared of metaphor methodologies being used to explore the perceptions and sense-giving of individual entrepreneurs, school children, authors, national newspapers, textbook illustrators and scholarly writers. Metaphors have been sourced through interview, through questionnaires, through textual analysis and by creative writing processes. They have been themed, coded, analysed and presented in a wide range of ways, too. Metaphors can be used to carry out field research, to communicate the findings of our research, to teach our students: they are, potentially, everywhere in our work. Metaphor methodology is peculiar in its ubiquitous nature, crossing boundaries of level and topic, amenable to both qualitative and quantitative approaches, and capable of tremendous focus or great breadth. This innate versatility and wide-scale applicability of metaphor methodologies is at once a tremendous opportunity, while simultaneously representing something of a challenge. Deployed in so many ways, to research such diverse actors and structures, no clear and simple shared guidelines have emerged to aid future scholars in their study, teaching and writing. Yet it is this very diversity, flexibility and creativity which makes working with metaphor such a joy. We hope that these chapters have inspired colleagues to consider this approach, which the four of us have found not only tremendously powerful, but also enormous fun. Just remember to leave a lot of space in your diary!

PART III

CRITICAL INCIDENT
TECHNIQUE

The critical incident technique: an overview
Claire M. Leitch

BACKGROUND

It is almost 60 years since Flanagan (1954) published his seminal article on the critical incident technique (CIT), which was developed as a result of research conducted during World War II as part of the US Army's Aviation Psychology Program for selecting and training aircrews (Butterfield et al. 2005). The aim of the research was to provide solutions to practical problems. To understand the specific behaviours resulting in the success or failure of flying missions, trainee aircrew as well as expert observers recounted and/or identified specific aspects of successful and unsuccessful incidents (Kemppainen 2000). Under the categories of aptitude, proficiency and performance common threads underpinning success and failure were identified, which subsequently informed the critical requirements of each role in an aircrew.

The critical incident technique was defined as:

> A set of procedures for collecting direct observations of human behaviour in such a way as to facilitate their potential usefulness in solving practical problems and developing broad psychological principles . . . By an incident is meant any specifiable human activity that is sufficiently complete in itself to permit inferences and predictions to be made about the person performing the act. To be critical the incident must occur in a situation where the purpose or intent of the act seems fairly clear to the observer and where its consequences are sufficiently definite to leave little doubt concerning its effects. (Flanagan 1954: 327)

When the technique was developed 'the *positivist* approach to social science investigations was largely unquestioned' (Chell 2004: 45, original emphasis) and, thus, reality was assumed to be tangible. While the process of data collection through interviews and observations was essentially subjective, Flanagan (1954) held that observations were objective or factually correct when a number of independent experts arrived at the same judgement (Chell 2004; Chell and Pittaway 1998). Through analysis, which is a fundamental part of the technique, an objective set of criteria was derived, which could subsequently be applied. In the case of Flanagan's (1954) initial research, a taxonomy of the essential

Table III.1   Examples of applications of CIT in management disciplines

Discipline	Authors
Marketing	Derbaix and Vanhamme (2003); Bitner et al. (1990; 1994)
Services management and marketing	Arnold et al. (2005); Edvardsson and Roos (2001)
Customer relationship marketing	Lorenzoni and Lewis (2004); Wong and Sohal (2003)
Human resource management	Bradfield and Aquino (1999); Mitchell et al. (1997)
Industrial relations	Pilemalm et al. (2001)
Information management	Muylle et al. (2004)
Healthcare management	Mallck et al. (2003); Ölvingson et al. (2002); Kemppainen (2000)
Organization studies	Davey and Symon (2001)

requirements for effective combat leadership was developed and aptitude tests subsequently developed (Chell 2004; Kemppainen 2000).

Since its development CIT has evolved and its original focus has changed. In addition to being used to determine the job requirements necessary for success in a variety of industries it has been employed to: assess typical job performance and proficiency; design jobs and equipment; create operational procedures; establish motivation and leadership attitudes; investigate effective and ineffective ways of doing something; and determine successes and failures (Butterfield et al. 2005). Further, its influence has extended from industrial and organizational psychology to disciplines such as nursing (Kemppainen et al. 1988), education and teaching (LeMare and Sohbat 2002; Tirri and Koro-Ljungberg 2002), medicine (Humphery and Nazareth 2001), social work (Mills and Vine 1990) and management (see Table III.1).

Its application in a wide range of disciplines, Butterfield et al. (2005) attribute to its flexibility: '[CIT] should be thought of as a flexible set of principles that must be modified to meet the specific situation at hand' (Flanagan 1954: 355). However, they also observe that this might be a double-edged sword, for while potentially innovative and insightful research has resulted from its use, there has also been a proliferation of approaches and terms resulting in inconsistency and potential confusion. For instance, the technique has been variously described as critical incident analysis (Gould 1999), critical event technique (Kunak 1989), critical incident exercise (Rutman 1996), critical incident report (Kluender 1987), critical incident study technique (Cottrell et al. 2002) and critical incident reflection (Francis 1995).

In the early 1990s researchers started to employ CIT in studies conducted from an interpretive perspective, where the focus is to 'address questions concerned with developing an understanding of the meaning and experience dimensions of humans' lives and social worlds' (Fossey et al. 2002: 730). While the ontological and epistemological roots of the qualitative variant of the technique differ from the quantitative, one feature which continues to be emphasized is that 'unlike other qualitative methodologies that place emphasis on describing phenomenon in naturalistic settings critical incident studies are more highly focused on providing solutions to practical problems' (Kemppainen 2000: 1265).

Even though CIT procedures are quite precise, as the technique has evolved so too have the data collection approaches (Woolsey 1986; Ellinger and Watkins 1998; Hughes 2007). These range from conventional qualitative interviews in case study research to multi-method, large-scale data collection exercises including Likert-scale type surveys. Correspondingly, from an analytical perspective variety is also evident from the quantitative analysis of survey data to narrative-based interpretive approaches. However, despite this diversity all applications of the technique share an emphasis on both the events and dimensions of experience that are most salient and memorable and, thus, likely to be retold to others as well as the emergence, rather than the imposition, of an evaluation schema (Ruben 1993; Harrison and Mason 2004).

THE USE OF THE CRITICAL INCIDENT TECHNIQUE IN ENTREPRENEURSHIP

The technique first appeared in entrepreneurship research about 20 years ago, around the same time as the qualitative variant emerged (Table III.2). Indeed, most applications of CIT in this domain have tended to be within the interpretivist tradition where reality is not assumed to be concrete, data are subjective, knowledge is socially constructed and there is less concern about objectivity and generalization.

Arguably it has been Chell's (1998, 2004) work and her application of the qualitative technique in entrepreneurship, which has demonstrated its value to research in the field. She uses CIT (1998, 2004: 218) as a qualitative interview procedure that facilitates the investigation of significant occurrences identified by research participants. In particular, attention is paid to the way in which these events or incidents are managed as well as the outcomes in terms of perceived impacts. This, along with other studies using the qualitative variant, represents an evolution from the technique's original application from direct observations to retrospective

Table III.2   Examples of the application of CIT in entrepreneurship

Focus of research	Authors
The internal corporate venturing process	Garud and van de Ven (1992)
The networking process of entrepreneurs	Tjosvold and Weicker (1993)
Small and medium-sized enterprise (SME) networking activity	Curran et al. (1993)
The social construction of entrepreneurial behaviour	Chell and Pittaway (1998)
The relationship between entrepreneurial marketing and business development	Stokes (2000)
The conditions faced by new ventures in the early stages of their development	Kaulio (2003)
The interaction between business and household experiences	Chell (2004)
Behavourial differences, in terms of business development, between business owners in a variety of sectors	Chell (2004)
The impact of an entrepreneur's social relationships on the decision-making process.	Taylor and Thorpe (2004)
Identification of the successes and failures of entrepreneurs in different stages of the lifecycle	Nandram, S. (2008)
The process of nascent entrepreneurship and learning	Karataş-Özkan and Chell (2010)

self-reporting where participants are given the power to determine what it is they deem to be critical (Kain 2004). In addition, instead of concentrating solely on a description of the incident there has been a shift to eliciting beliefs, opinions and suggestions that formed part of it (Ellinger and Bostrom 2002). Employing the qualitative variant of CIT, which seeks context-rich, first-hand perspectives on human activities and their significance can assist in deepening understanding of dynamic processes and their outcomes.

As entrepreneurship is a multifaceted and complex social construct, knowledge production requires variety and pluralism in research perspectives and approaches. Even though the qualitative variant of CIT has been predominant in the field to date, where appropriate researchers should also consider employing the quantitative variant to address relevant problems. The three chapters in this section each provide useful pertinent insights and demonstrate how valuable both variants of the technique can be in investigating issues of concern. In Chapter 7, Chell provides a timely consideration of the differences between the quantitative and qualitative variants of CIT and using opportunity recognition compares and contrasts the value of adopting each approach. She revisits and updates her thinking on the use of CIT both in theory and practice through the application of the technique to investigate the entrepreneurial process of opportunity recognition (Chell 2008; Chiasson and Saunders 2005; Shane and Venkataraman 2000; Sarason et al. 2006). This demonstrates the power of the CIT in comparison with other qualitative techniques and how it may be used to contest extant theory and, as a consequence, aid in the building of new theory that resonates with the practitioners' perspective. To further elucidate the CIT methodologies, she compares and contrasts the two paradigmatic approaches and assesses their potential in producing theoretical and practical insights into the business development process. In the context of conducting good quality interpretivist research, in Chapter 8, Leitch and Hill present a framework that guided the design, conduct and reporting of a study which employed the qualitative variant to explore the complex interactions of between women seeking finance for business start-up and growth and those supplying it. In Chapter 9, Harrison extends the use of the qualitative variant to incorporate aspects of explication interviewing to explore the post-investment relationship between informal investors and the businesses in which they invest. This, he believes, is a more effective vehicle for uncovering the dynamics of business angel–entrepreneur dyads than previously used approaches. The observations made and lessons shared by all of the authors in these chapters should encourage junior scholars and others in the benefits of employing this technique in their own research.

REFERENCES

Arnold, M.J., K.E. Reynolds, N. Ponder and J.E. Lueg (2005), 'Customer delight in a retail context: investigating delightful and terrible shopping experiences', *Journal of Business Research Press*, **58** (8), 1132–45.

Bitner, M.J., B.H. Booms and L.A. Mohr (1994), 'Critical service encounters: the employee's viewpoint', *Journal of Marketing*, **58** (4), 95–106.

Bitner, M.J., B.H. Booms and M.S. Tetreault (1990), 'The service encounter: diagnosing favourable and unfavourable incidents', *Journal of Marketing*, **54** (1), 71–84.

Bradfield, M. and K. Aquino (1999), 'The effects of blame attributions and offender likableness on forgiveness and revenge in the workplace', *Journal of Management*, **25** (5), 607–31.

Butterfield, L.D., W.A. Borgen, N.E. Amundson and A.-S.T. Maglio (2005), 'Fifty years of the critical incident technique: 1954–2004 and beyond', *Qualitative Research*, **5** (4), 475–97.

Chell, E. (1998), 'Critical incident technique', in G. Symon and C. Cassell (eds), *Qualitative Methods and Analysis in Organizational Research: A Practical Guide*, London: Sage, pp. 51–72.

Chell, E. (2004), 'Critical incident technique', in G. Symon and C. Cassell (eds), *Essential Guide to Qualitative Methods in Organizational Research*, London: Sage, pp. 45–60.

Chell, E, (2008), *The Entrepreneurial Personality: A Social Construction*, London: The Psychology Press/Routledge.

Chell, E. and L. Pittaway (1998), 'A study of entrepreneurship in the restaurant and café industry: exploratory work using the critical incident technique as a methodology', *International Journal of Hospitality Management*, **17** (1), 23–32.

Chiasson, M. and C. Saunders (2005), 'Reconciling diverse approaches to opportunity research using structuration theory', *Journal of Business Venturing*, **20** (6), 747–67.

Cottrell, D., S. Kilminster, B. Jolly and J. Grant (2002), 'What is effective supervision and how does it happen? A critical incident study', *Medical Education*, **36** (11), 1042–9.

Curran, J., R. Jarvis, R.A. Blackburn and S. Black (1993), 'Networks and small firms: Constructs, methodological strategies and some findings', *International Small Business Journal*, **11** (2), 13–25.

Davey, K.M. and G. Symon (2001), 'Recent approaches to the qualitative analysis of organizational culture', in C.L. Cooper, S. Cartwright and C. Earley (eds), *The International Handbook of Organizational Culture and Climate*, Chichester: Wiley, pp. 123–42.

Derbaix, C. and J. Vanhamme (2003), 'Inducing word-of-mouth by eliciting surprise – a pilot investigation', *Journal of Economic Psychology*, **24** (1), 99–116.

Edvardsson, B. and I. Roos. (2001), 'Critical incident techniques: towards a framework for analysing the criticality of critical incidents', *International Journal of Service Industry Management*, **12** (3), 251–68.

Ellinger, A.D. and R.P. Bostrom (2002), 'An examination of managers' beliefs about their roles as facilitators of learning', *Management Learning*, **33** (2), 147–79.

Ellinger, A.D. and K.E. Watkins (1998), 'Updating the critical incident technique after forty-four years. Advances in qualitative research', in *Academy of Human Resource Development Conference Proceedings*, ERIC Document Reproduction Service No. ED428234.

Flanagan, J.C. (1954), 'The critical incident technique', *Psychological Bulletin*, **51** (4), 327–58.

Fossey, E., C. Harvey, F. McDermott and L. Davidson (2002), 'Understanding and evaluating qualitative research', *Australian and New Zealand Journal of Psychiatry*, **36** (6), 717–32.

Francis, D. (1995), 'The reflective journal: a window to preservice teachers' practical knowledge', *Teaching and Teacher Education*, **11** (3), 229–41.

Garud, R. and A.H. van de Ven (1992), 'An empirical evaluation of the internal corporate venturing process', *Strategic Management Journal*, **13** (S1), 93–109.

Gould, N. (1999), 'Developing a qualitative approach to the audit of inter-disciplinary child protection practice', *Child Abuse Review*, **8** (30), 193–9.

Harrison, R.T. and C. Mason (2004), 'A critical incident technique approach to entrepreneurship research: developing a methodology to analyse the value added contribution of informal investors', paper presented at the Twentieth Babson-Kauffmann Research Conference, Glasgow, 3–5 June.

Hughes, H., K. Williamson and A. Lloyd (2007), 'Critical incident technique', in S. Lipu (ed.), *Exploring Methods in Information Literacy Research*, Centre for Information Studies, Charles Sturt University, Wagga Wagga, NSW, pp. 49–66.

Humphery, S. and I. Nazareth (2001), 'GPs' views on their management of sexual dysfunction', *Family Practice*, **18** (5), 516–18.

Kain, D. (2004), 'Owing significance: the critical incident technique in research', in K. deMarrais and S.D. Lapan (eds), *Foundations for research: Methods of Inquiry in Education and the Social Sciences*, Mahwah, NJ: Lawrence Erlbaum, pp. 69–85.

Karataş-Özkan, M. and E. Chell (2010), *Nascent Entrepreneurship and Learning*, Cheltenham, UK and Northampton, MA, USA: Edward Elgar.

Kaulio, M.A. (2003), 'Initial conditions or process of development? Critical incidents in the early stages of new ventures', *R&D Management*, **33** (2), 165–75.

Kemppainen, J.K. (2000), 'The critical incident technique and nursing care quality research', *Journal of Advanced Nursing*, **32** (5), 1264–71.

Kemppainen, J.K., L. O'Brien and B. Corpuz (1988), 'The behaviours of AIDS patients toward their nurses', *International Journal of Nursing Studies*, **35** (6), 330–38.

Kluender, D.E. (1987), 'Job analysis', in H.W. More and P.C. Unsinger (eds), *The Police Assessment Center*, Springfield IL: Charles C. Thomas, pp.49–65.

Kunak, D.V. (1989), 'The critical event technique in job analysis', in K. Landau and W. Rohmert (eds), *Recent Developments in Job Analysis*, London: Taylor and Francis, pp.43–52.

Le Mare, L. and E. Sohbat (2002), 'Canadian students' perceptions of teacher characteristics that support or inhibit help seeking', *The Elementary School Journal*, **102** (3), 239–53.

Lorenzoni, N. and B.R. Lewis (2004), 'Service recovery in the airline industry: a cross-cultural comparison of the attitudes and behaviours of British and Italian front-line personnel', *Managing Service Quality*, **14** (1), 11–25.

Mallck, L.A., D.M. Lyth, S.D. Olson, S.M. Ulshafer and F.J. Sardone (2003), 'Diagnosing culture in health-care organizations using critical incidents', *International Journal of Health Care Quality Assurance*, **16** (1), 180–90.

Mills, C. and P. Vine (1990), 'Critical incident reporting: an approach to reviewing the investigation and management of child abuse', *British Journal of Social Work*, **20** (3), 215–20.

Mitchell, F., G.C. Reid and N.G. Terry (1997), 'Venture capital supply and accounting information system development', *Entrepreneurship Theory and Practice*, **21** (4), 45–62.

Muylle, S., R. Moenaert and M. Despontin (2004), 'The conceptualization and empirical validation of web site user satisfaction', *Information and Management*, **41** (5), 543–60.

Nandram, S. (2008), 'Entrepreneurship and the entrepreneur', in W. Burggraaf, R. Floren and J. Kunst (eds), *The Entrepreneur and the Entrepreneurship Cycle*, Assen: Konniklijke Van Gorcum, pp.9–26.

Ölvingson, C., N. Hallberg, T. Timpka and R.A. Greens (2002), 'Using the critical incident technique to define a minimal data set for requirements elicitation in public health', *International Journal of Medical Informatics*, **68** (1–3), 165–74.

Pilemalm, S., N. Hallberg and T. Timpka (2001), 'How do shop stewards perceive their situation and tasks? Preconditions for support of union work', *Economic and Industrial Democracy*, **22** (4), 569–99.

Ruben, B.D. (1993), 'What patients remember: a content analysis of critical incidents in health care', *Health Communications*, **5** (2), 99–112.

Rutman, D. (1996), 'Childcare as women's work: workers' experiences of powerfulness and powerlessness', *Gender and Society*, **10** (5), 629–49.

Sarason, Y., T. Dean and J.F. Dillard (2006), 'Entrepreneurship as the nexus of individual and opportunity: a structuration view', *Journal of Business Venturing*, **21** (3), 286–305.

Shane, S. and S. Venkataraman (2000), 'The promise of entrepreneurship as a field of research', *Academy of Management Review*, **25** (1), 217–26.

Stokes, D. (2000), 'Entrepreneurial marketing: a conceptualization from qualitative research', *Qualitative Market Research: An International Journal*, **3** (1), 47–54.

Taylor, D.W. and R. Thorpe (2004), 'Entrepreneurial learning: a process of co-participation', *Journal of Small Business and Enterprise Development*, **11** (2), 203–11.

Tirri, K. and M. Koro-Ljungberg (2002), 'Critical incidents in the lives of gifted female Finnish scientists', *The Journal of Secondary Gifted Education*, **13** (4), 151–63.

Tjosvold, D. and D. Weicker (1993), 'Cooperative and competitive networking by entrepreneurs: a critical incident study', *Journal of Small Business Management*, **31** (1), 11–21.

Woolsey, L.K. (1986), 'The critical incident technique: an innovative qualitative method of research', *Canadian Journal of Counselling*, **20** (4), 242–54.

Wong, A. and A. Sohal (2003), 'A critical incident approach to the examination of customer relationship management in a retail chain: an exploratory study', *Qualitative Market Research: An International Journal*, **6** (4), 248–62.

7 Researching the entrepreneurial process using the critical incident technique
Elizabeth Chell

INTRODUCTION

The critical incident technique (CIT) was first used in a scientific study over half a century ago (Flanagan 1954). The significance of this time span is that then the assumption of a functionalist or positivist approach to social science investigations was largely unquestioned. It was the dominant paradigm in the social sciences as it was in the natural sciences (Burrell and Morgan 1979; Pittaway 2000). However, in 1998 I began to consider how CIT might be utilized from a phenomenological perspective (Chell 1998, 2004). This means that there are two variants of the CIT, each to be applied to the research problematic as appropriate.

In this chapter I revisit and update my thinking on the use of CIT both in theory and practice. In my previous application of the CIT, I focused on understanding those critical issues that impacted strategic decision-making for business development at any stage of the development process. An important consideration was to understand the circumstances, context and situation that led to crystallization of the decision. This is still an important part of the research. However, in this chapter I intend to narrow the use of the CIT so that its use for theory building and testing is clarified. To achieve this objective I shall apply the technique to investigating the entrepreneurial process of opportunity recognition (Shane and Venkataraman 2000; Chiasson and Saunders 2005; Sarason et al. 2006; Chell 2008). I compare and contrast the two paradigmatic approaches and assess their potential in producing theoretical and practical insights into this much vaunted process. To this end in the next section I commence by revisiting the methodological assumptions associated with the dominant paradigm positivism and that of social constructionism whose tenets are being increasingly assumed in entrepreneurship theory development.

METHODOLOGICAL ASSUMPTIONS

Research is intended to discover new knowledge and understanding of phenomena whether physical or social. The physical sciences use the scientific method and through experimentation, inductive reasoning and sustained testing, what is known with a probability of its likely occurrence is arrived at. The physical world is assumed by the scientist to be 'out there', that is, external to the human mind, and can be observed in a detached and unbiased way. The scientist thus records clinically his or her observations and experiments by changing the conditions under which the phenomenon is observed; fresh observations are then recorded. To the scientist the phenomenon is real, not a theoretical construct, but an entity; this is its ontological status. Even in particle physics and astronomy sophisticated experiments have been constructed to demonstrate the existence (even though they are not directly observable by the human eye) of phenomena. Hence, through systematic investigation scientists reveal knowledge and demonstrate what is the case. Truth is probable not absolute and knowledge is external, public and checkable.

In the social sciences functionalism or positivism makes the assumptions of the scientist. It assumes the same ontology that social objects are tangible and that they enjoy an external existence (outside the mind of the observer). However, in the social sciences knowledge can be revealed through a systematic approach though experimental manipulation (except in the psychological sciences) may not be possible. Flanagan (1954), an occupational psychologist, made just such assumptions and adopted a scientific approach when he was tasked with discovering the reasons for pilot failure during training. The behaviours associated with flying were specifiable; the criteria of what constitutes effective or ineffective performance could be identified, and observers could be given explicit criteria for judging or evaluating observed behaviours as reaching the requisite standard. Observations were deemed to be factual and objective if a number of independent observers made the same judgement.

An example of one study reviewed by Flanagan was that of 'disorientation while flying'. The pilots were asked to describe what they 'saw, heard or felt that brought on the experience'. The study led to a number of changes in the cockpit and instrument panel design. Another study was of combat leadership. Veterans were asked to make observations of specific incidents of effective or ineffective behaviour in accomplishing a mission. This was a large-scale study and resulted in several thousand incidents describing officers' actions. The outcome of the research was a set of descriptive categories – 'critical requirements' – of effective combat leadership. By the use of expert observers whose independent judgements were compared, the essential subjective nature of this process was converted into an objective set of criteria which could be rigorously applied to further groups.

Just as the dominance of the functionalist paradigm was exposed and questioned by sociologists (Flanagan 1954), so too has it been questioned by other social scientists (Harré 1979, 1986; Shotter 1993). This alternative phenomenological approach makes totally different assumptions about the nature of reality, how we come to know and understand ourselves and the world, and what methodology is appropriate. Such theoretical perspectives point to the intangible nature of social phenomena, for example, of perceptions, ideas and mental states, the use of language, and the social construction of relationships. Knowledge and truth are relative and contextually grounded, and formulated from the integration of various perspectives and consequent interpretations. Many social constructionists assume that such phenomena are unique to individuals and based on subjective experience. As such, insights may be gleaned from sensitive analysis of individual cases but the scientific outcomes of generalization are not possible. However, other social constructionists combine phenomenological assumptions with realist methodologies. They assume that while the social phenomena identified above are ephemeral, subjective and unique to the individual, due to the fact that they are contextually embedded, articulated through language and their behavioural consequences observable, generalization to theory can be made (Yin 1984).

In the next section I take these two paradigmatic approaches and compare and contrast their adoption in the specific case of opportunity recognition theory (ORT). Why ORT? Opportunity recognition theory has become a dominant theory in entrepreneurship research, promoted particularly by positivist researchers who believe in the scientific method where convergence and consensus elevate a theory until the accumulation of new evidence overturns it. Non-positivist researchers and social constructionists in particular have begun to question the veracity of this theory on a number of grounds: lack of coherence, inoperability for empirical testing, use of language and terminology lacks a degree of validity especially with practitioners, methodological individualism, and 'alertness' being the wrong starting point (Fletcher 2006; Steyaert 2007; Parkinson and Howorth 2008; Hindle 2010; Dimov 2011). Social constructionism also brings into play the issue of how actions and behaviours are valued, depending on who, categorically speaking, is the perpetrator. This whole area is thus ripe for critical review and the use of CIT is a methodology that is able to expose deep layers of assumptions, values and context-related beliefs and actions.

Thus, the use of the CIT method and the exposure of paradigmatic assumptions will enable the researcher to better understand the theory and any practical implications that are revealed. The next section is intended to delve deeper into the underlying paradigmatic assumptions behind opportunity recognition theory.

PARADIGMATIC PERSPECTIVES ON OPPORTUNITY RECOGNITION THEORY

Opportunity recognition theory is an important theoretical perspective because it gives a basis by which we can research and understand the entrepreneurial process. As with many social science theories there is no single approach nor is there a set of assumptions that underpin ORT. Indeed, this is one of the problems with ORT from a positivist perspective. Aping the natural sciences, positivism assumes the convergence of empirical data around one theory. However, social constructionism makes no such assumption; quite the opposite in fact where, as discussed above, individual cases are assumed to be unique. In this section I discuss and contrast the positivist with the phenomenological approaches to ORT before, in the ensuing section, outlining how the CIT may be used as an investigative instrument in each case.

The basic, indeed crucial, research question is, what is the ontological status of an 'opportunity'? Does it depend, if so, on what does it depend? If not, just how do we conceptualize 'opportunity'?

First let us consider 'opportunity' from the different perspectives. For the sake of this discussion let us assume that 'opportunity recognition' is the start point of the process. Opportunities to start or develop a business may be said to be 'out there', that is, part of the external reality of an entrepreneur as framed by a positivist. In contrast, argue phenomenologists, opportunities may be said to be creations within the mind and have no tangible existence until they are externalized at a later stage in the process. These contrasting views are well articulated by Venkataraman (2003) in respect of Scott Shane's position:

> In Shane's view, every price, every invention, every bit of information already engenders within itself opportunities for the creation of new ends. However, human creativity and some idiosyncratic conditions have to exist for the *objective* opportunity to be brought to life. The reason *specific* individuals are required in the world of objective opportunities, in Shane's view, is because opportunities themselves lack agency. A human being is required to provide this agency so that when *a market can come to be, it will come to be*. This explicitly *discovery* view of entrepreneurship is in marked contrast to an alternative view emerging in the literature, namely, the *creative* view. According to the

creative view, opportunities do not exist in any objective form, but are merely a social construction. (Venkataraman, 2003: xi, original emphases)

Hence to the positivist 'opportunities' are discovered, while to the phenomenologist they are created. Clearly the positivist or functionalist would adopt Flanagan's approach were he or she to research opportunity recognition using the CIT, but if, on the other hand, the researcher sees opportunity recognition as a creation of the human mind he or she would make the assumptions associated with phenomenology.

Opportunity recognition is a process, therefore, where it would be helpful to develop further understanding of the steps in this process before considering in detail how the CIT (whichever form) might be used to explicate it further. Opportunity recognition theory is based ultimately on economic theory and the tenets of methodological individualism. It was based originally on the work of Kirzner (1982) from whose work the idea of 'alertness to opportunities' arose (Kirzner 1979: 48). Kirzner's theory is based on economic equilibrium, whereas that of Schumpeter (1934), described below, is based on economic disequilibrium. However, even given these different starting points, Shane argues that opportunities are external to the entrepreneur. However, the Schumpeterian entrepreneur is an innovator, hence the phenomenologist would argue that possible opportunities in such a context of disruption need to be constructed by the entrepreneur; as such we would disagree with Shane's position outlined below.

To Shane (2003: 12) opportunities exist and the process of discovery is linear. His argument, based on a Kirznerian view, is that opportunities exist prior to recognition; because of differential information some people recognize the opportunity for what it is, while others overlook it. In this view no new information is required, people simply use the information they possess. Those people with access to particular information recognize the opportunity – a shortage of supply of a particular good – and they obtain the resources necessary in order to meet it. Such opportunities, Shane suggests, are commonplace, equilibrating, that is, they address a market need, and as they do not require new information they are not innovative. In this view, the opportunity exists in a tangible sense independently of the entrepreneur with the information that enables him or her to recognize and exploit it.

However Shane also wants to take into account the Schumpeterian view of opportunity which, unlike that of Kirzner, disrupts the system – a process he termed 'creative destruction' – and creates conditions of economic disequilibrium. Schumpeterian opportunities require new information and conditions of change which are disruptive. Shane (2003: 23) gives examples of Schumpeterian opportunities: (1) technological change, the invention of the personal computer created the opportunity to develop and sell microchips; (2) regulatory changes in the use of seat belts and child seats created opportunities for entrepreneurs to build capacity in order to meet this new demand; (3) socio-demographic changes leading to more women entering the workforce led to a greater demand for prepared foods. Arguably, all these examples proffered by Shane suggest the existence of tangible external opportunities.

The Kirznerian view is that of passively noticing (even though 'alertness' suggests activity) through the market mechanism, while the Schumpeterian entrepreneur is portrayed as aggressive, active innovative and faithful to a 'real-world' view (Kirzner 1999: 9). Both are said to be 'alert to opportunities'. Furthermore, this concept of 'alertness' is rather important. Indeed, it could be said to pose a particular problem. Advocates of alertness suggest that this attribute of entrepreneurs distinguishes them from non-entrepreneurs or may distinguish successful from unsuccessful entrepreneurs. This resurrects the idea of a fixed trait possessed by entrepreneurs; the probability that entrepreneurs (especially successful ones) are born not made.

Gaglio and Katz (2001) elaborate on the notion of 'entrepreneurial alertness to opportunity' by suggesting that it is a cognitive skill; identifying the notion that this entrepreneurial skill includes 'veridical perception and interpretation' and the use of mental processes (specifically counterfactual thinking) to evaluate the opportunity. They suggest that an alert individual consciously processes information that provides *the context* relevant to the market opportunity (my emphasis). It is this external context of market and environmental cues to which the entrepreneur responds. Non-alert individuals discount the new information and stick with the usual way of doing business, whereas the alert individual absorbs the new information and engages in counterfactual thinking to explore new possibilities and outcomes. This leads entrepreneurial decision-makers to reconsider the 'means–ends framework' and 'radically reconsider his or her understanding of the industry, or society, or the marketplace, or more probably, all three' (Gaglio and Katz 2001: 103). This breaking of the 'means–end framework', they suggest, is a necessary step for genuine innovation and is indicative of creative thought processes at an early stage in the opportunity recognition process.

'Veridical perception and interpretation' suggests a realist view of opportunity consistent with positivist assumptions. The entrepreneur is responding to an external context of information that from his or her individual standpoint suggests an opportunity to be developed and exploited. The passive absorption of information in the case of Kirznerian incremental innovation may give way to more radical innovation (*à la* Schumpeter), is a more active thought process, and, according to Gaglio and Katz (2001), still consistent with the criteria of 'alertness', and the external status of the opportunity.

In the next two sections I explore in more detail ORT based (1) on a positivist methodology and (2) on phenomenological assumptions.

EXAMPLE OF OPPORTUNITY RECOGNITION THEORY BASED ON A POSITIVIST METHODOLOGY

Ardichvili et al. (2003) develop the theory of opportunity recognition by contrasting a set of propositions to be tested quantitatively with one to be tested by qualitative means. They focus on understanding the opportunity development phase in the recognition process. This approach, however, remains within a positivist framework and set of assumptions.

The start point of this process is entrepreneurial alertness, which is interpreted as sensitivity to product possibilities, given understanding of the market requirement. The process appears to be linear over time from opportunity recognition (the possibility) to the development of that possibility into a tangible business concept. Ardichvili et al. (2003) set out eight propositions that they derive from their exposition of ORT (see Table 7.1, left-hand column).

In the left-hand column of Table 7.1 is a set of propositions based on Ardichvili et al.'s (2003) paper. As with Gaglio and Katz (2001) these authors commence with the assumption of entrepreneurial alertness and that there is a measurable relationship between alertness and entrepreneurial success. Moreover, as proposition 2 indicates, entrepreneurs are situated in an external network of relationships, which may be identified and counted. The extent of that network can also be explored quantitatively. The existence of this network supports opportunity identification. However, following Shane (2003), prior knowledge is critical to successful opportunity identification and this may take the form of a special interest (even a hobby) and industry or sector knowledge (propositions 3 and 4). Furthermore, prior knowledge of markets is hypothesized to increase the likelihood of opportunity recognition (proposition 6). Put another way, the more sensitive entrepreneur is to product possibilities given understanding of the market need, a market solution or both, the more likely he or she will be able to develop successful business opportunities. Prior knowledge of customer problems (proposition 5) may also be a source of information that increases the likelihood of opportunity recognition. All such information is external

Table 7.1 Contrasting propositions based on (a) positivist and (b) social constructionist perspectives on opportunity recognition theory

Propositions based on a positivist approach (e.g. Ardichvili et al. 2003)	Propositions based on social constructionism (e.g. Sarason et al. 2006)
1 A high level of entrepreneurial alertness is associated with successful opportunity recognition and development	Opportunities do not exist as objective, external phenomena but are idiosyncratic to the individual
2 Successful opportunity identification is associated with the existence of an extended network	Entrepreneurial ventures are created by purposeful actions through a unique co-evolutionary interaction between the entrepreneur and the socio-economic system
3 For successful opportunity identification a convergence of special interest and industry knowledge domains is critical	The co-evolutionary processes associated with the creation and development of entrepreneurial ventures involves the reflexive, recursive processes of interpretation, action, consequence and reflection
4 Prior knowledge of markets increases the likelihood of successful entrepreneurial opportunity recognition	Because each entrepreneur is unique in his or her interpretation of, and, reaction to, the socio-economic context, entrepreneurial ventures are idiosyncratic to the individual and evolve along distinct, path-dependent trajectories
5 Prior knowledge of customer problems increases the likelihood of successful opportunity recognition	Interpretative process (signification structures) will be more salient during the discovery of entrepreneurial opportunities
6 Prior knowledge of ways to serve markets increases the likelihood of successful entrepreneurial opportunity recognition	Legitimation structures (evaluation criteria) will be more salient during the evaluation of entrepreneurial process
7 High levels of entrepreneurial alertness are related to high levels of entrepreneurial creativity and optimism	Domination structures (power to acquire and deploy resources) will be more salient during the exploitation of entrepreneurial opportunities
8 The opportunity identification process results in enriching the entrepreneur's knowledge base and increase in alertness, leading to identification of future business opportunities	The language of 'opportunity recognition' will reflect the idiosyncrasies of practising entrepreneurs

to the entrepreneur and may be collected by the researcher using quantitative survey methods.

Proposition 7 states that high levels of entrepreneurial alertness are related to high levels of creativity and optimism. Both may be measured. The underlying argument proffered by these researchers is that business concept creation is more than perception and discovery, it involves recombining resources to create something superior to what is currently available (Ardichvili et al. 2003: 111). Formal or informal consideration is then given to the evaluation of the possibility of this development; the feasibility of it is judged to result in an economic success. If the business concept (that is, potential opportunity) does not pass muster at this stage it may be aborted. The key psychological element here is judgement and the decision-making that follows. Hence it is argued that opportunities are 'made not found' and require a 'creative input' from the entrepreneur. However, the fact of business concept creation and whether it results in a successful product/service outcome may be identified and measured. The judgemental process, however, would lend itself to qualitative analysis, although it is also possible to identify and count decisions made and the nature of the information underpinning them in keeping with the researchers suggested quantitative analysis.

Ardichvili et al. (2003) suggest that proposition 8 should best be researched using qualitative methods. The proposition poses the possibility (to be tested) that the opportunity identification process enriches the entrepreneur's knowledge thus increasing his or her alertness capability and the chances of identifying future business opportunities.

How might this situation arise? Arguably prior knowledge leads to new knowledge and the development of further understanding of what the new knowledge/information pertains to. We have known for a long time that some entrepreneurs are hobbyists; they pursue a special interest for pleasure and from that develop profound knowledge. Other entrepreneurs' knowledge domain is that of their work; this gives depth of knowledge of markets, how to serve markets and resolve customer problems. The hobbyist cannot develop an entrepreneurial opportunity without knowledge of markets. Thus prior knowledge constitutes (1) profound knowledge of the topic of interest; and (2) detailed marketing and customer knowledge/ understanding. This market sector knowledge/information is cumulative thus intensifying the entrepreneur's alertness capability.

Choice of qualitative methods is not indicated by Ardichvili et al. and we should not rule out the adoption of CIT (*à la* Flanagan), on the assumption that these researchers believe that the process of knowledge accumulation can be articulated and evidenced in a systematic way; as can indicators of increased alertness and the identification of more business opportunities in the future. Social constructionists might question the total externalization of the process and they would use the alternative version of CIT in order to gain insights into just how entrepreneurs identify and develop future business opportunities.

In the next section I explore how ORT may be socially constructed and researched using this alternative methodology.

EXAMPLE OF OPPORTUNITY RECOGNITION THEORY BASED ON SOCIAL CONSTRUCTIONIST (PHENOMENOLOGICAL) METHODOLOGY

Social constructionism assumes that opportunities, indeed all social phenomena, are mediated by the observer's or agent's perceptions whether that agent is an entrepreneur, a researcher or member of the public. In ORT, from this perspective, opportunities are created in the mind; they are a social construction. Given this distinct difference in starting assumptions of the phenomenologist, the resultant propositions contrast markedly with those of positivism. Examples of such propositions from a social constructionist perspective are given in the right-hand column of Table 7.1. The research paper cited (Sarason et al. 2006) adopt Giddens' structuration theory (Giddens 1984) as the basis for elaborating the construction of the relationship between the entrepreneur and created opportunity – the structure; that is the layers of the socio-economic system with which the entrepreneur is engaged (see also Chell 2008: 58 ff.). Those layers are conceptualized as meaningful interaction, formal and informal rules and power-shaping interaction. These concepts of meaning, rules and power are the lenses through which agents or entrepreneurs in the case in point construct or construe perceived opportunity.

In focusing on the entrepreneurial process, Sarason et al. (2006) avoid investigating the entrepreneur and the opportunity as independent entities. Rather, they focus on the dynamic interaction between the two. They argue that the entrepreneur is a reflexive agent who specifies, interprets and acts on sources of opportunity in a subjective and idiosyncratic way. The individual-opportunity nexus is viewed as a duality in which entrepreneur and opportunity come together and are intertwined such that neither is independent of the other (cf. Bouchikhi 1993; Chell 2000). Hence opportunities do not exist a priori. The opportunity is viewed in a new way and due to recursive processes evolves. This contrasts with the Kirznerian view of the entrepreneur who spots an extant opportunity and develops it incrementally thereby filling market gaps. Rather, within the 'discovery, evaluation and exploitation' ORT process, structuration theory socially constructs each of the phases: discovery concerns the interpretation of a meaningful opportunity; at evaluation the process is one of legitimation, within a socially accepted system of rules and norms, focusing on assessment of the opportunity; and within the exploitation phase, power to control and transform resources is critical.

From this theoretical base we can derive a set of propositions or assumptions that reflect the above social constructionist approach to opportunity recognition. In Table 7.1 the seven propositions in the right-hand column reflect social constructionist assumptions and contrast sharply with those of the positivist (left-hand column).

The first proposition reflects the subjective nature of social constructionism; opportunities are phenomena, they are not 'out there' but are perceived by the entrepreneur as such. The opportunity as a socio-economic structure develops in the mind of the entrepreneur and on that basis; the entrepreneur makes decisions and takes action, as indicated in proposition 2. This is a 'co-evolutionary process' as indicated in the third proposition. Over time, thoughts crystallize into action, are interpreted and reflected upon, as does the development of the opportunity. Social constructionists often argue for the uniqueness of each individual case; this position is reflected in proposition 4. Further, each phase of the opportunity recognition process places differential emphasis; in the first phase initial thoughts about a potential opportunity should be meaningful and significant to the entrepreneur (proposition 5). To create successful outcomes from the perceived opportunity, proposition six indicates that entrepreneurs should test it against formal and informal rules (the legitimation structure), the criteria by which the entrepreneur and others whom he or she may be attempting to convince test the soundness of the idea so that it may be developed further. To carry out the latter step, resources are to be deployed and this step indicated in proposition 7 draws on the power of the parties involved to mobilize resources to turn the opportunity into a workable business proposal, prototype or nascent enterprise. Finally, proposition 8 suggests that adopting a social constructionist approach will reveal an idiosyncratic use of language that reflects how individual entrepreneurs perceive and develop their ideas which theoreticians label as 'opportunities' (Chalkley 2011; Chell 2013).

Given that there is duration to the opportunity recognition process, critical incidents could happen at any point during the initial interpretation where meaning and significance is being given to an opportunity, its evaluation and its exploitation. Given the highly subjective nature of this process, the case study method would appear to be the most appropriate means by which empirical investigation could proceed. In the next section I explore in considerably more detail the application of the CIT to investigation, and evaluation, of opportunity recognition theory.

METHOD

In this section, I continue making contrasts between positivist and social constructionist assumptions underpinning the research process and tease out how this affects the adoption of CIT. First it is important to be clear that there are advantages of adopting CIT as a method over other qualitative techniques. Next I revisit the positivist approach to investigating ORT. Here CIT as developed by Flanagan (1954) would be appropriately applied initially for purposes of qualitative design work to inform the content of a structured, quantitative survey instrument. I then contrast the adoption of CIT from a social constructionist perspective.

Advantages of Adopting CIT

What advantages does the CIT have over the use of other qualitative techniques?

The CIT is structured around an incident or incidents which are identified by the subject; the incidents are real to them and the process of discussion of these incidents is overt as the subject has given his or her permission to engage detailed consideration of what the incident means to him or her. This overt exploration contrasts, for example, with participant observation as an unstructured qualitative data capturing technique which is covert and raises ethical issues as a consequence. Clearly, owing to the covert nature of participant observation, information is observed in the here and now but there are likely to be problems recording that information *in situ*. Moreover the unstructured nature of participant observation means that there is an absence of focus and perspective which means that the researcher has to do much of the sense-making. Using the CIT however, the researcher can probe in such a way as to elicit sense and meaning from the subject thus avoiding imposing a sense-making frame.

Furthermore, as the incident in the CIT is critical as adjudged by the subject, recall is good, though a disadvantage is clearly that the account is always retrospective. Focus allows apt probing whereas the adoption of unstructured interview method lacks focus; it is, however, useful as an exploratory technique and may throw up unanticipated issues. The critical incident though provides a 'hook' by which the researcher can focus the interview, though there are occasions when a subject fails to identify any critical incidents. This raises the question of what the apparent absence of critical incidents implies, and places the onus back on the researcher to explore relevant situations in an unstructured way. Where critical incidents are identified, information is context-rich; it is possible to look for common themes across incidents and over time. This allows what Yin

(1984) terms 'generalization to theory'. Other qualitative techniques especially participant observation and unstructured interviews present difficulties in making connections between context and outcomes. The CIT, on the other hand, enables connections to be made between context, strategy or ways of approaching the incident and dealing with it, and outcomes (Chell 1998, 2003). This allows the researcher to build a picture of the tactics employed by the subject for managing situations, and to identify what might have gone wrong and why. This too can be explored with the subject depending on the objectives of the CIT interview. Finally, because there is specific content supplied by the subject in respect of an incident, this can be compared with the accounts of others of the same incident. In such ways rich data from multiple perspectives can be built up by the researcher.

There is a further advantage of this approach to investigating opportunity recognition using CIT and that is that it allows the researcher to draw on the language used by the entrepreneur and to test the theory from a practitioner perspective. In other words, does the entrepreneur's language resonate with opportunity theory? Or is there a case for building a new theory of the inception of entrepreneurial ideas and their subsequent development (Chalkley 2011; Dimov 2011)?

I have argued above the many advantages of adopting CIT. However, Gaglio and Katz (2001) suggest the use of 'thinking aloud protocols'; Shane (2000) used unstructured interviews, qualitative cases studies and archival records and Park (2005) used a single case study. However, the CIT allows focused, in-depth, qualitative exploration of the context, strategy or tactics and outcomes and how these elements are related. Data collected is nuanced and insightful of the processes and procedures adopted, the thinking and judgements made, and the nature of the intended outcomes.

In the next two sections I outline and contrast the adoption of CIT under, first, positivism and, second, social constructionism.

Positivism and the CIT

Adopting a positivist approach *à la* Ardichvili et al. (2003), critical incidents will take the form of information gleaned from such sources as customers, market intelligence, product development possibilities and so on. The information sources constitute information asymmetries which are more likely to be construed by the alert entrepreneur as opportunities for development and exploitation. Ardichvili et al. suggest the adoption of quantitative methods to investigate the first seven propositions outlined in Table 7.1. Attention would be needed in respect of sample framing and design. For example, a sampling frame comprising nascent entrepreneurs (say with six months' to three years' experience), controlling for sector characteristics and business size. This would help to avoid selecting on the dependent variable in this case where entrepreneurs are already successful at exploiting opportunities. The data collected would be frequency counts against a set of criteria. The authors present a causal model which comprises a set of independent variables (personality traits, social networks and prior knowledge of the entrepreneurs – the sources of idiosyncratic information), entrepreneurial alertness, which we take to be a mediating variable, and outcomes, the development of different types of opportunity. Entrepreneurs with high alertness are more likely to recognize and value new information that they believe would lead to the development of opportunity.

To address the eighth proposition set out in the left-hand column of Table 7.1 Ardichvili et al. (2003) suggest the adoption of qualitative methods. What would adoption of Flanagan's CIT reveal that an unstructured interview approach would not? The advantage of CIT over an unstructured interview approach is that it is focused in this case on process, and the underpinning accumulation of knowledge, experience and relevant information. Combining CIT within a case study method, it is possible to link contextual features, and an increase in alertness, with possible outcomes which the researchers suggest would be the increased likelihood of identifying future business opportunities.

Social Constructionism and CIT

My study in 1991 focused on business development and attempted to identify critical incidents that helped the small business owners conceive of ways and means to achieve that desired outcome (Chell et al. 1991, cited in Chell 1998: 54). The method, as developed by the author, assumes a phenomenological approach. The critical incident technique in this version is a qualitative interview procedure which facilitates the investigation of significant occurrences identified by the respondent which have a bearing on the object or focus of the research. It is intended, through the interview that is focused on critical incidents supplied by the subject, to capture the thoughts, frame of reference and feelings about an incident, event, episode or process. In the interview the respondent is required to give an account of what the incident, event, episode, issue or process means, the context and situation which makes it meaningful to the respondent, his or her life situation, present circumstances, attitude, beliefs and orientation.

Thus, in the case of ORT the 'incident' may be described as an information/opportunity recognition and development process. The data capture includes cognitive, affective, conative and behavioural aspects as the nascent entrepreneur develops an understanding of the significance, the value and means by which he or she may exploit the opportunity.

The ability of CIT to allow connections to be made between context, strategy and outcomes lends itself well to the investigation of opportunity recognition where 'opportunities' are, arguably, socially and economically embedded as phenomena in contexts that the subject has identified where others have not. Not only does the researcher want to explore these socio-economic contexts, but also how they are handled, developed and ultimately exploited, and what the outcomes are of this interaction.

I now turn to Sarason et al.'s (2006) exposition of 'opportunity' as a socio-economic phenomenon which is constructed in the mind of the agent, the entrepreneur (see Table 7.1, right-hand column).

Adopting Sarason et al.'s (2006: 294) propositions, critical incidents would take the form of perceived information-processing construed through 'the co-evolutionary interaction between entrepreneur and socio-economic system'. The critical information/opportunity becomes part of a process by which the nascent entrepreneur interprets, reflects and acts on information, which leads to a critical information pathway that is unique to the entrepreneur. The critical information/opportunity will hold significant meaning to the entrepreneur at the initial discovery phase. It will proceed through a legitimation process as the entrepreneur begins to evaluate its worth. Once evaluated, the entrepreneur will engage with the resource structure, comprising his or her power to acquire and deploy resources and thus go on to exploit the developing opportunity. Once these stages of co-evolution of the entrepreneurial information/opportunity have been successfully negotiated, a tangible outcome will emerge. From the above I suggest that we would be able to develop a detailed understanding of the opportunity recognition process at the stage of inception of an idea through its early stage formation and development. The research design would follow the case study method of Yin (1994) and use the critical incident technique as the source of primary data, supported by secondary sources of data for purposes of triangulation. While each case is unique, Yin argues that it is possible to generalize to theory, constituted in this case by those propositions indicated in the right-hand column of Table 7.1.

The propositions ensure that there are some themes that should be explored in all cases. Beyond that the method focuses on the incidents identified by each respondent, allowing the investigator to probe and explore and as such tease out information that enables insights and depth of understanding to be developed.

In the forthcoming sections I continue to make points of comparison between a positivist researcher and one pursuing a phenomenological (structuration) approach.

There are eight distinguishable aspects to the method: (1) preliminary design work and determination of the sampling frame; (2) gaining access; (3) introducing the CIT method and getting the interview underway; (4) focusing on the theme and giving an account of oneself as researcher to the respondent; (5) controlling the interview, by probing the incidents and clarifying one's understanding; (6) concluding the interview; (7) taking care of any ethical issues; (8) analysing the data (Chell, 1998: 56 ff.). These are addressed in the ensuing pages.

Preliminary Design Work and Determination of the Sample

Assuming positivism, the positivist approach of Ardichvili and colleagues (see Figure 7.1) suggests the need for some initial exploratory work with a small number of cases in order to support the design of a quantitative survey instrument. The objective of the investigation is to elucidate the opportunity identification and formation process by developing a greater understanding of 'entrepreneurial alertness'. The aims comprise:

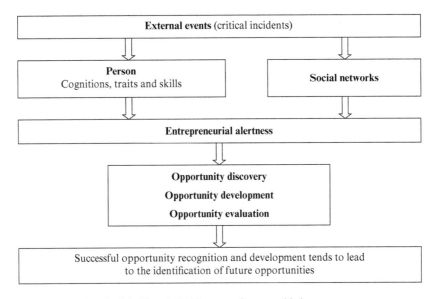

Source: Based on Ardichvili et al. (2003); external events added.

Figure 7.1   Positivist approach to opportunity recognition and the identification of external events

(1) knowing the (nascent) entrepreneur, his or her situation, orientation, motivation, differential knowledge base, abilities and experience, self-belief, creativity and optimism; (2) understanding the social embeddedness of the nascent entrepreneur, the nature and extent of his or her ties and links; (3) investigating his or her judgemental decision-making in circumstances of change, and opportunity identification; and (4) identifying the entrepreneur's intentions going forward and his or her ability and/or desire to develop future opportunities based on past success (or failed attempts).

The preliminary design work should include a pilot study of about four cases, emanating from the same industrial sector. Once the sample has been determined and access gained, the investigator should prepare a topic guide and set of preliminary questions, covering basic information about the respondent, his or her business and so forth. This would then be used to design the quantitative survey instrument.

My suggestion for the sampling frame would be to focus on nascent entrepreneurs whose experience is at a similar stage and within a comparable sector, for example, art and design, technology or whatever. It is difficult to see how a single survey at one point in time would be sufficient given that opportunity recognition and development is a process for Ardichvili and colleagues. So, in this research design stage, I suggest that a minimum of two quantitative surveys would be required. I would want to follow up with some telephone interviews but this deviates from Ardichvili et al.'s proposal. Only at proposition 8 (refer back to Table 7.1, left-hand column) do the authors suggest adopting a qualitative approach. The CIT *à la* Flanagan (1954) could be adopted here. Clearly it is being assumed that the opportunity recognition process yields positive outcomes for business development. Presumably the authors would want to identify what information is critical to the development of the entrepreneurs' knowledge and understanding that leads to the identification of future business opportunities.

Assuming social constructionism. Sarason et al.'s approach would also be enabled by preliminary design work in which the aim is to consider how to approach the co-evolution of a nascent entrepreneur's understanding of the meaningfulness and value of a perceived information/opportunity structure. This will comprise identifying the subject's idea, in what ways it is construed as an opportunity, and how it is embedded in, and emerges from, the socio-economic context (structure). Further the research should probe the nascent entrepreneur's reflections over time, actions taken, consequences reviewed and further developments – actual and intended – in respect of the perceived opportunity. The researcher should also be sensitive to the language of the respondent and aim to reflect this in the

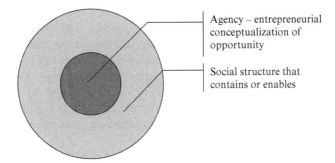

Source: Based on Sarason et al. (2006); Giddens (1984).

Figure 7.2   The co-evolution of entrepreneurial thought and opportunity based on a structure and agency view of the entrepreneurial process

questions and probes used, in order to avoid imposing a set of academic constructs on the respondent.

How might the adoption of CIT work in this instance? The object of the research is illustrated in Figure 7.2. The bubble inside the socio-economic structure represents the emergent idea – the entrepreneur's concept or construction of a possible opportunity. This idea is emerging from the socio-economic structure which is the enabling or constraining context.

In the next section I run through a suggested set of steps to be taken by the researcher investigating this process.

Detailed CIT Method in the Case of a Phenomenological Approach to Opportunity Recognition

I use the illustration in Box 7.1 – the perception of a derelict piece of land by different observers – as my reference point. This serves to illustrate the notion that there is an external physical context but also a socio-economic structure enveloping a potential opportunity that the agent may (or may not) recognize. The agent/entrepreneur is embedded in the socio-economic milieu and draws on it as he or she constructs and further develops mentally the opportunity structure.

The practical research issues are identifying and gaining access to nascent entrepreneurs, ideally in a specific industrial domain to facilitate depth of understanding, and conducting a CIT interview. One relatively easy source of nascent entrepreneurs is the student population, who may be in their final year, say, studying the built environment, and where a

---

BOX 7.1   RESEARCHING OPPORTUNITY RECOGNITION –
AN ILLUSTRATION FROM FIRST PRINCIPLES

Opportunity Recognition: Two Views

Two people stand on a broken causeway and look at a derelict piece of land. What do they see? One sees a derelict piece of land and the other an opportunity. Researchers Smith and Brown are in dispute as to how to research this 'opportunity recognition process'. Smith says that the opportunity is external to the person whilst Brown declares; 'No! The derelict piece of land is external to the person but the opportunity is inside the person's head!'

Person A, who sees the derelict piece of land, is, according to economic theory, not alert to opportunities. But Person B, who recognizes this piece of derelict land as potentially an entrepreneurial opportunity, is.

How to research the opportunity recognition process? Is the opportunity 'out there', as Shane and others have argued, or an idea in person B's head? How you answer this question as a researcher determines the assumptions you make and the method you adopt.

---

proportion is intent on pursuing the self-employment option beyond his or her studies. There are other subject domains and there are other possible populations to be drawn; the above is by way of illustration only.

Presumably a positivist researcher would view the derelict site as a building development and marketing opportunity; for example, a potential site for a sports complex, a shopping mall or a car park; something which is tangible and can be argued is 'out there'. To the phenomenologist a person may view the site as physically a derelict site, while the potential is that which he or she creatively develops initially in the mind.

The methods question is, how to elucidate any detail about possible critical incidents in the cognitive processes associated with the derelict site? In the next section I examine in more detail the procedure for conducting a CIT.

Conducting a CIT Interview

Staying with the illustration the researcher wants to elucidate both the social structure and the cognitive thought processes in which the nascent entrepreneur is engaging with regard to the opportunity recognition process.

The researcher needs to establish where the nascent entrepreneur is in the opportunity recognition process. So some introductory questions might be:

Have you had any ideas over the past six months, say, as to how you

---

BOX 7.2   CONDUCTING A CIT INTERVIEW – AN ILLUSTRATION

Researcher: 'Have you had any ideas over the past six months, say, as to how you might develop a business? What were those ideas?'

Entrepreneur: 'I saw a derelict site downtown and it occurred to me that this could be used to build a leisure complex.'

Researcher (probes): 'What was your next step?'

Entrepreneur: 'I found out who owns the site and what they plan to do with it . . .'

Researcher: 'Did you find out anything that was *critical* to your decision to develop the opportunity further?'

Entrepreneur: 'Yes, the site is covered with toxic waste – asbestos and the like; so I decided to drop the idea due to the cost of cleaning it up . . .' or,

Entrepreneur: 'Yes, the owner has gone out of business and the land's up for auction; I could get it real cheap . . .'

Researcher: 'OK so have you worked out what price you're prepared to pay? And also where the finance will come from?'

And so on as the researcher delves into each aspect of the process, probing for more detail, attempting to elicit aspects of the decision process.

---

might develop a business? What were those ideas? Why did you focus on a particular idea? How (using what criteria) did you discard other ideas? Box 7.2 contains an imagined exchange between researcher and subject.

Thus, the researcher probes each of the critical aspects of the opportunity development process: initially why is this idea meaningful? How might the idea achieve legitimacy in the eyes of significant others? So, for example, not simply the financing but also the engagement with the town planning agency; an architect, a builder and others who can aid in the development of a realistic business plan. Who has the power to block the development of this idea? Hence, the researcher also importantly identifies the constraints and facilitators in the local environment and probes how these were overcome and which (if any) continue as obstacles.

The researcher would not only want to probe the logic of the means–end framework that the nascent entrepreneur is pursuing with the intent of developing the perceived opportunity further, but also consider this from a conative and affective angle. Put simply, the researcher would seek to understand the entrepreneur's ambitions and how the perceived opportunity sits with him or her personally. Many entrepreneurs pursue hobbies and interests as business propositions, so for an entrepreneur with a sports background a leisure complex might well be something with which they feel very comfortable. On the other hand, an entrepreneur whose background is in the hospitality industry might view the opportunity to set up a hotel-restaurant business. Some prior knowledge as well as informed interests/hobbies provide the entrepreneur with both motivation and a degree of understanding to enable them to get started developing the idea.

Research suggests that entrepreneurs are socially embedded and are able to use their connections to develop further a business opportunity. Thus understanding the criticality of networks and the social milieu of the nascent entrepreneur is a further area of the critical incident interview that the researcher should address.

There are two aspects of the critical interview process that the researcher needs to control effectively: maintaining focus and direction. The interview schedule will be quite sparse and unstructured and so the researcher should have in mind which areas should be raised and probed. He or she may wish to know more about the extent of the network and which contacts proved to be the most valuable and why; he or she may also want to identify how skilfully the nascent entrepreneur went about his or her business; and how motivated the entrepreneur was in pursuing opportunity development. Thus there is a balance to be struck; being mindful of the time available, ensuring coverage of critical themes and events, and probing for desired detail. The risks are that the interview may drift and critical information is neither identified nor probed, or that the interviewee simply does not engage. In the latter case, this will occur where the respondent has not recognized or pursued an opportunity to any extent and therefore does not have the experience to draw on; the interview will thus grind to a halt. The researcher should recognize this and by, for example, discussing the interviewee's ambitions, uncover the evidence to support his or her suspicion.

Concluding the interview effectively and taking care of any ethical issues is also important. Critical incident interviews often deal with sensitive issues and confidential information so that assurances should be given; that names of various parties will not be disclosed, pseudonyms may be used and other identifiers either removed or disguised. Such assurances will probably have been made when gaining access, perhaps in the introductory letter, but it is a good idea to conclude and confirm them thus leaving the interviewee confident about the security of the information revealed.

Analysis of the CITs

The CIT can take the form of a single case study, for example, of the opportunity recognition process from inception of an idea through development and exploitation in which multiple incidents may be explored within the single case. Alternatively, this chapter has highlighted the Ardichvili et al. (2003), positivist, and the Sarason et al. (2006), phenomenologist, approaches to understanding opportunity recognition. The former would lend itself to an identification of externally-directed incidents impacting on the perceived opportunity. Ardichvili et al. state that the opportunity identification process results in enriching the entrepreneur's knowledge base and an increase in alertness, leading to the identification of future business opportunities. This implies a virtuous spiral of business development over time. However they also say that this process may only be explored by qualitative means. Further research from a positivist perspective should adopt Flanagan's (1954) approach to CIT and Yin's case study analysis techniques. The focus would be on the cognitive framing of possible future business opportunities and the external events that constrain or facilitate their emergence. The researcher might consider sampling such cases until saturation occurs and using the case study analysis to identify propositions for theory development and testing purposes.

In the phenomenological case, analysis would be of the co-evolution of opportunity and socio-economic structure. Data in the latter case would comprise, for example, an elucidation of the meaningfulness of the idea and subsequent opportunity to the entrepreneur; the rules and norms negotiated and power relationships within a multi-layered network as change and development of the opportunity and the relationships within the social structure change over time. Sarason et al. (2006) emphasize the 'path-dependency' of opportunity development, suggesting uniqueness. Deeper analysis of path-dependency should be undertaken by, for example, comparing and contrasting critical events, processes, incidents and issues as key elements of opportunity recognition in its various process phases. While each opportunity may be unique, the nature of the phases, the critical constraints and facilitators may recur within a particular industry (indeed, possibly across a number of industries), though importantly they may be dealt with differently by particular entrepreneurs. In this way the CIT enables the researcher to capture the handling strategies of the various facets of the socio-economic opportunity structure and to follow this through over time. While it may be difficult to capture linkages with outcomes, the critical nature of events being examined should facilitate a deeper understanding of the consequences of particular decisions and actions on the part of the entrepreneur. A richer analysis would be obtained by using the CIT with other key players in the opportunity recognition process. A further detailed analysis of the language used to describe the process should be undertaken as a theory testing and building exercise, that is, is 'opportunity recognition' how the entrepreneur would describe the process? If not, what terminology does he or she use and what does this mean for a new theory of entrepreneurialism?

CONCLUSION

The CIT was originated by Flanagan (1954) and thus has a long history. Since that time I have explored and developed a variant which, unlike Flanagan's, rests on the assumptions of phenomenology (Chell 1998, 2003). Using two examples from the literature, this chapter explores and contrasts the two methodologies that underpin these different approaches to CIT. It does so using the contemporary example of the opportunity recognition process. Detailed guidance is given which exposes the relationship between methodology and the particularities of method.

The CIT is often felt to be a difficult method to use. However, its advantage from a social and psychological point of view is that it exposes the subject's attitudes, feelings and orientation to situations with which they have to deal. It elicits in considerable rich detail how the subject behaves; his or her tactics; and how that situation unfolds. It depends on the research question being asked as to which method and set of assumptions should be taken, but in the illustration – opportunity recognition – the co-evolving of opportunity and socio-economic structure is revealed by the adoption of this method.

The CIT is a much more powerful technique than the interview (structured or unstructured); it exposes our assumptions, focuses on the subject's actions – behaviours, thoughts, decisions, feelings – in both positivist and social constructionist versions, and the critical events that shape those actions. It exposes theory to empirical testing. In the case of the positivist version, the theory's claim of 'veridical perception and interpretation' reveals how the subject (entrepreneur) evaluates those perceptions and by what criteria, thus getting underneath the decision-making process. Further, for the social constructionist, it enables the researcher to ask fundamental questions juxtaposing theoretical constructs against the language used by the subject; the process as revealed by the subject; and how the subject would describe the start point of the business development process for him or her. This brings into play the question of whether 'alertness to opportunity' is anything more than a theoretical construction of researchers and the actual stimulating idea may be otherwise, such as a felt need, a problem to be solved, a disease cured (Chell 2013). Thus, coupled with Yin's case study method, CIT may be used to not only build but also test theory, by as Yin puts it generalizing to propositions.

In this chapter I have developed my thinking about the use of the critical incident technique. Previously I had concentrated primarily on translating Flanagan's positivistic version into a version that could be used not only by qualitative researchers but specifically social constructionists and other phenomenologists. I was able to show how the technique could reveal rich seams of information about the thoughts, actions and feelings of subjects in respect of specific critical incidents which impacted on decisions they would take in their business lives, and how this might be difficult to separate from their personal lives (Chell 1998, 2003). In this chapter I believe that I have also demonstrated how the phenomenological version of CIT can be used to deconstruct theory, testing it and rebuilding new theory that resonates with the subjects' perspectives, language and ways of handling perceived problems, dilemmas and needs that emanate from a context that they well understand. Thus this version of CIT enables the researcher to capture the subjects' ability to make connections between embedded situations, their strategies and tactics and perceived outcomes. In the instance of opportunity recognition, potentially to turn the theory on its head; rather than 'opportunity recognition' the critical situation may be a perceived need, and the problem is to develop a business proposition that will meet that need (Chell 2013).

Finally, this chapter has explained in some detail how the CIT in both versions may be used. This it is hoped will be of value to researchers and teachers of research methodology. Also the method should be more widely adopted. By getting to the nub of issues, being embedded in the subject's perceptions, it has a great deal to offer both practitioners and those engaged in developing policy.

REFERENCES

Ardichvili, A., R. Cardozo and S. Ray (2003), 'A theory of entrepreneurial opportunity identification and development', *Journal of Business Venturing*, **18** (1), 105–23.

Bouchikhi, H. (1993), 'A constructivist framework for understanding entrepreneurial performance', *Organisation Studies*, **14** (4), 551–69.

Burrell, G. and G. Morgan (1979), *Sociological Paradigms and Organisational Analysis*, London: Heinemann.

Chalkley, L.V. (2011), *What is Entrepreneurship? A Phenomenological Enquiry into the Venture Creation Process of a Rapidly Growing Firm: The Archaeology Company*, Dublin: Dublin City University.

Chell, E. (1998), 'The critical incident technique', in C. Cassell and G. Symon (eds), *Qualitative Methods and Analysis in Organisational Research*, London: Sage, pp. 51–72.

Chell, E. (2000), 'Towards researching the 'opportunistic entrepreneur': a social constructionist approach and research agenda', *European Journal of Work and Organisational Psychology*, **9** (1), 65–82.

Chell, E. (2003), 'The critical incident technique', in M. Lewis-Beck, A. Bryman and T. Futing Liao (eds), *The Encyclopaedia of Research Methods in the Social Sciences*, Thousand Oaks, California: Sage, pp. 218–19.

Chell, E. (2004), 'The critical incident technique', in C. Cassell and G. Symon (eds), *Essential Guide to Qualitative Methods in Organizational Research*, London: Sage, pp. 45–60.

Chell, E. (2008), *The Entrepreneurial Personality: A Social Construction*, London: Psychology Press/Routledge.

Chell, E. (2013), 'Review of skill and the entrepreneurial process', *International Journal of Entrepreneurship and Business Research*, **17** (1), 6–31.

Chell, E., J.M. Haworth and S. Brearley (1991), *The Entrepreneurial Personality: Concepts, Cases and Categories*, London: Routledge.

Chiasson, M. and C. Saunders (2005), 'Reconciling diverse approaches to opportunity research using structuration theory', *Journal of Business Venturing*, **20** (6), 747–67.

Dimov, D. (2011), 'Grappling with the unbearable elusiveness of entrepreneurial opportunities', *Entrepreneurship Theory and Practice*, **35** (1), 57–81.

Flanagan, J.C. (1954), 'The critical incident technique', *Psychological Bulletin*, **51** (4), 327–58.

Fletcher, D.E. (2006), 'Entrepreneurial processes and the construction of opportunity', *Entrepreneurship and Regional Development*, **18** (5), 421–40.

Gaglio C.M. and J.A. Katz (2001), 'The psychological basis of opportunity identification: entrepreneurial alertness', *Small Business Economics*, **16** (2), 95–111.

Giddens, A. (1984), *The Constitution of Society*, Cambridge: Polity Press.

Harré, R. (1979), *Social Being: A Theory for Social Psychology*, Oxford: Blackwell.

Harré, R. (1986), 'An outline of the social constructionist viewpoint', in R. Harré (ed.), *The Social Construction of Emotions*, Oxford: Blackwell, pp. 2–14.

Hindle, K. (2010), 'How community context affects entrepreneurial process: a diagnostic framework', *Entrepreneurship and Regional Development*, **22** (7 and 8), 599–647.

Kirzner, I. (1982), 'The theory of entrepreneurship in economic growth', in C.A. Kent, D.L. Sexton and K.H. Vesper (eds), *Encyclopaedia of Entrepreneurship*, Englewood-Cliffs, NJ: Prentice-Hall, pp. 273–6.

Kirzner, I.M. (1979), *Perception, Opportunity and Profit*, Chicago, IL: Chicago University Press.

Kirzner, I.M. (1997), 'How markets work', IEA Hobart Paper, No. 133. London Institute of Economic Affairs.

Park, J.S. (2005), 'Opportunity recognition and product innovation in entrepreneurial hi-tech start-ups: a new perspective and supporting case study', *Technovation*, **25** (7), 739–52.

Parkinson, C. and C. Howorth (2008), 'The language of social entrepreneurs', *Entrepreneurship and Regional Development*, **20** (3), 285–309.

Pittaway, L. (2000), 'The social construction of entrepreneurial behaviour', PhD dissertation, University of Newcastle upon Tyne.

Sarason, Y., T. Dean and J.F. Dillard (2006), 'Entrepreneurship as the nexus of individual and opportunity: a structuration view', *Journal of Business Venturing*, **21** (3), 286–305.

Schumpeter, J.A. (1934), *The Theory of Economic Development*, Cambridge, MA: Harvard University Press.

Shane, S. (2000), 'Prior knowledge and the discovery of opportunities', *Organization Science*, **11** (4), 448–69.

Shane, S. (2003), *A General Theory of Entrepreneurship – the Individual-Opportunity Nexus*, Cheltenham, UK and Northampton, MA, USA: Edward Elgar.

Shane, S. and S. Venkataraman (2000), 'The promise of entrepreneurship as a field of research', *Academy of Management Review*, **25** (1), 217–26.

Shotter, J. (1993), *Conversational Realities: Constructing Life through Language*, London: Sage.

Steyaert, C. (2007), '"Entrepreneuring" as a conceptual attractor', *Entrepreneurship and Regional Development*, **19** (6), 453–77.

Venkataraman, S. (2003), 'Foreword', in S. Shane, *A General Theory of Entrepreneurship – the Individual-Opportunity Nexus*, Cheltenham, UK and Northampton, MA, USA: Edward Elgar, pp. x–xii.

Yin, R. (1984), *Case Study Research*, Thousand Oaks, CA: Sage.

Yin, R. (1994), *Case Study Research*, 2nd edn, Thousand Oaks, CA: Sage.

8 The efficacy of the qualitative variant of the critical incident technique (CIT) in entrepreneurship research
Claire M. Leitch and Frances M. Hill

INTRODUCTION

In this chapter we reflect on our approach to conducting good quality interpretivist research using the qualitative variant of the CIT which we employed as the sole data collection method in the third phase of a research study that focused on women seeking external finance for the businesses they owned and led in Northern Ireland (for an account of the research conducted in phase 1 and phase 2 see Hill et al. 2006). The project initially had been prompted by the findings of a prior investigation, which had revealed that the most significant difficulties for women-owned/led businesses in meeting their objectives were finance-related (O'Reilly 2005). In particular, concerns about the availability and cost of overdraft facilities and external finance for growth, that is, finance provided by banks, venture capitalists, business angels and development agencies and not provided by 'family, friends or fools' or by bootstrapping, had been reported.

Phase 1 of our research focused on the supply of finance to business owners in general, and to women business owners in particular (Hill et al. 2006). The second phase addressed a number of conceptual and methodological shortcomings of existing research into the financing of women-owned/led businesses (for example, Ahl 2004; Read 1998). In both of these phases we employed two semi-structured interview schedules to gather data. One important finding that emerged relates to Kon and Storey's (2003) concept of the 'discouraged borrower', that is, a credit-worthy individual who does not apply for finance in the belief they will be rejected. This seemed to derive from perceptions emanating from both dominant social discourses and personal experiences of seeking finance. We concluded that a reluctance to seek finance could have potentially negative consequences at several levels: first, the under-capitalization of individual businesses; second, the loss of lucrative business opportunities for funders; and third, a lack of macroeconomic business development and growth. Thus, in phase 3 we sought to explore women's perceptions of the experience of seeking finance in greater depth.

This required an interpretivist approach, a term which, elsewhere and here, we have employed to describe non-positivist research concerned with the investigation of social reality (Leitch et al. 2010; Stahl 2007). Such a perspective enables the researcher to address questions about 'how social experience is created and given meaning' (Gephart 2004: 455), to embrace the complex and dynamic quality of the social world, get close to participants, enter their realities and interpret their perceptions (Bogdan and Taylor 1975; Hoepfl 1997; Shaw 1999). It includes 'capturing the actual meanings and interpretations that actors subjectively ascribe to phenomena in order to describe and explain their behaviour' (Johnson et al. 2006: 132). In addition, we sought to give 'voice' to the experiences of women in their own right as an under-represented and under-researched group in entrepreneurship (Hill et al. 2006). In relation to the third phase of the study the specific objective was to explore, from women's perspectives, the complex interactions between those seeking finance for business start-up and growth, and those supplying it.

Since the trustworthiness of interpretivist research is determined both by how it is designed and conducted, and by the transparency of its reporting in the public domain (Thompson et al. 1989) both sets of issues are addressed in this chapter, which is structured as follows. First, an overview of the advantages and limitations of CIT in general, and its qualitative variant in particular, is provided. Second, we present the framework which guided us in the design, conduct and reporting of the research. Third, in the conclusion we reflect upon our experience of using CIT and the efficacy of the qualitative variant in the context of entrepreneurship research.

ADVANTAGES AND LIMITATIONS OF THE QUALITATIVE VARIANT OF CIT

A range of data collection methods exist under the interpretivist umbrella and, therefore, a major decision for any researcher is to decide upon the most appropriate for obtaining the data likely to fulfil the research aims and objectives. When reflecting on this issue in the context of our own study, we noted Cowling and Harding's (2005) observation that the formation and growth of businesses are dependent on the ability of their owners to access an uninterrupted supply of critical resources, including finance. Furthermore, we conjectured that the nature of interactions between suppliers of external finance and business owners will be significant, not only in terms of whether or not it is obtained, but also regarding the latter's perceptions of the quality of the experience and any potential learning that may emanate from it. These characteristics of the act of seeking finance chimed with Flanagan's (1954: 338) definition of a critical incident: 'such incidents are defined as extreme behaviour, outstandingly effective or ineffective with respect to attaining the general aims of the activity'.

Although Flanagan (1954) originally employed CIT when conducting studies within the positivist paradigm, Chell (1998, 2004, and Chapter 7 in this volume) observes that it has since been developed as an investigative tool in organizational analysis within the interpretivist paradigm. While Flanagan (1954) allowed for a wide range of data collection protocols, including interviews, case studies, archive research and ethnographic methods, qualitative CIT procedures rely extensively on interviews (Chell 1998). As Alvesson and Deetz (2000) make clear, qualitative interviews, as opposed to 'talking questionnaires' (Potter and Whetherell 1987), 'are relatively loosely structured and open to what the interviewee feels is relevant and important to talk about within the bounds of what appears to be relevant given the interest of the research project' (Alvesson and Deetz 2000: 71).

Thus, the qualitative version of CIT permits 'self-defined criticality' where the focus is on respondents' 'personal representation of salient moments' (Cope 2003: 436; Cope and Watts 2000: 112). The 'objective is to gain understanding of the incident from the perspective of the individual, taking into account cognitive, affective and behavioural elements' (Chell 1998: 56). Accordingly, CIT allows research participants to share their perceptions of issues rather than their responses to researcher-initiated questions (Gremler 2004) since they are asked to recall specific events from their personal perspective and in their own words (Stauss and Weinlich 1997), thereby giving them 'voice'. As an inductive method requiring no prior hypotheses, patterns emerge from the narratives, thereby allowing the researcher to generate concepts and theories (Olsen and Thomasson 1992). Consequently, use of the CIT enables the creation of detailed records of events (Grove and Fisk 1997) and a rich set of data (Gabbott and Hogg 1996).

Set against these advantages are a number of limitations. For example, critical incidents are generally reported from memory and are therefore subject to its vagaries. However, Flanagan (1954) took the view that this risk could be lessened by asking participants to recount recent events; moreover, he pointed out that critical incidents are to do with extreme behaviour – that which is either very effective or very ineffective with regard to the attainment of the general aims of the activity (in this case, securing external finance for a business) – and thus will probably be accurately recalled, though this is not guaranteed (Urquhart et al. 2003). Edvardsson (1992) identifies potential problems with the reporting of critical incidents owing to the interviewer filtering, misunderstanding or misrepresenting the participant, although this is more likely to be a problem when interviewers are inexperienced. Another potential concern, given the relative lack of structure, is that there is a danger the information provided will not be relevant to the research question and aims (Cope and Watts 2000). Cope (2005) has proposed that, in designing such interviews, which should allow the course of the dialogue to be largely set by the participants (Thompson et al. 1989), researchers have to find a comfortable and achievable balance between pre-understanding (structure) and unbiased openness towards the phenomenon under study. Further, Chell (Chapter 7 in this volume) cautions that 'there are two aspects of the critical interview process that the researcher needs to control effectively: maintaining focus and direction'. Thus, the researcher, as research instrument, needs to carefully judge the balance between imposing too much structure and too little.

THE PROCESS

The discussion above demonstrates the need for criticality, reflexivity and judgement when undertaking rigorous and robust interpretivist research in general and we propose that, regarding CIT, researchers should not ignore Flanagan's (1954) original principles, otherwise its potency as an investigative tool may be undermined. Moreover, Chell (1998: 51) observes 'it is critically important that the researcher examines his/her own assumptions (and predilections), considers very carefully the nature of the research problem to be investigated, and thinks through how the technique may most appropriately be applied in the particular researchable case'. Accordingly, to inform our own decision-making we reviewed and synthesized Cresswell's (1998) essential features of qualitative research, Flanagan's (1954) original principles and procedures of CIT and Chell's exposition of the qualitative variant (Chell 1998, 2004; Chell and Pittaway 1998; Pittaway and Chell 1999) (Table 8.1).

This enabled us to develop a guiding framework for the process of conducting the research and operationalizing the technique which comprised six non-discrete elements, characterized as steps in Table 8.2.

Step 1: Identification of General Aims of Study and Step 2: Choosing the Appropriate Approach

In addition to the identification of the general aims of the study (step 1) we needed to decide how best to access participants' perceptions, attitudes and meanings ensuring the inclusion of cognitive, affective

Table 8.1   Sources informing the choice and implementation of the critical incident

Features of interpretivist research (Creswell 1998)	Flanagan's (1954) five-stage procedure	Qualitative variant (Chell 2004)
Research takes place in a natural setting **(Step 4)** Researcher is the key instrument of data collection **(Step 4)** Data are collected as words through interviewing, participant observation, and/ or qualitative open-ended questions **(Step 4)** Data analysis is done inductively **(Step 5a)** *Focus is on participants' perspectives*	Ascertain general aims of the study **(Step 1)** *What is the activity under investigation?* *What is the person expected to accomplish who engages in the activity?* **(Step 3)** Making plans and specifications **(Step 3)** *Defining the types of situation; determining the situation's relevance to the general aim; understanding the extent of the effect the incident has on the general aim; deciding who will be making the observations* Collecting data **(Step 4)** *Individual interviews; group interviews; questionnaires; record forms, expert observers* Analysing the data **(Step 5a)** *Determining the frame of reference, formulating categories (induction of categories); determining the level of specificity or generality to be used* Interpretation **(Step 5b)** and reporting of results **(Step 6)** *Limitations to be discussed; nature of the judgements to be made explicit; and value of results emphasized*	Assumes a phenomenological/ interpretivist approach **(Step 2)** Aim – to gain understanding of an incident from the participant's viewpoint Inclusion of cognitive, affective and behavioural aspects **(Step 2)** Collecting data – qualitative interview procedure **(Step 4)** *Investigation of significant occurrences identified by the respondent, the way these have been managed and the outcomes* Data analysis – grounded theory; use of a conceptual framework to be tested **(Step 5a)**

Sources: Butterfield (2005); Chell (2004); Creswell (1998); Flanagan (1954).

Table 8.2   Guiding framework

Step	Descriptor
1	Identification of the general aims of the study
2	Choosing the appropriate approach
3	Determining the activity and selecting participants
4	Data collection
5	Inductive data analysis (a) and interpretation (b)
6	Presentation and discussion of findings and conclusions

and behavioural elements (Chell 1998), which required an interpretivist approach (step 2). As Cope (2005) reminds us, with this approach ontologically no assumptions are made about what is and is not real – descriptions of phenomena begin with people's experiences of them (Leitch et al. 2010). Thus, the purpose of such research is not to confirm or disconfirm prior theories, 'but to develop "bottom-up" interpretive theories that are inextricably "grounded" in the lived-world' (Cope 2005: 167). The aim of the interpretivist researcher is to capture the process of how people interpret their world (Patton 2002: 104), which requires 'carefully, and thoroughly capturing and describing how people experience some phenomenon – how they perceive it, describe it, feel about it, remember it, make sense of it, and talk about it with others'.

Step 3: Determining the Activity and Selecting Participants

To address inconsistency surrounding the terminology employed in studies using CIT (Butterfield et al. 2005: Overview) we adhered quite closely to Flanagan's own definition of a critical incident, namely: 'any observable human activity that is sufficiently complete in itself to permit inferences and predictions to be made about the person performing the act' (Flanagan 1954: 327). For the incident to be considered critical it 'must occur in a situation where the purpose or intent of the act seems fairly clear to the observer and where its consequences are sufficiently definite to leave little doubt concerning its effects' (Flanagan 1954: 327).

As Butterfield et al. (2005) emphasize, Flanagan envisaged CIT as a tool to create a functional description of an activity. Two main considerations in doing this are, first, deciding the activity's objective, and, second, establishing what the actor is expected to accomplish when engaging in it (Butterfield et al. 2005; Flanagan 1954). Researchers must, therefore, determine the aim or objective of that activity at the outset. In this case the activity, or unit of analysis, was the encounter between individual business owners/leaders and actual/potential suppliers of finance, the objective of the activity being to gain finance. While we determined the activity it was left to the participants to select the specific encounters and to define whether they were effective or ineffective ('self-defined criticality'). Therefore, in selecting participants, we required individuals who had 'directly experienced the phenomenon of interest' (Patton 1990: 104).

There are basically two strategies for the selection of participants to include in a particular investigation, which are the theory-driven approach and the data-driven approach – the choice being determined by the perspective in which the research is grounded (Gilchrist and Williams 1999). The former involves 'the use of prior theoretical knowledge in constructing a (selection) framework', where selection decision criteria are developed and implemented before commencement of the study as in most positivist research (Johnson 1990: 24). With regard to the latter approach, associated with interpretivist enquiry, new units are selected and added until theoretical saturation occurs, that is, until no new data emerge from additional cases (Glaser and Strauss 1967).

Our selection of participants was purposive in nature, so that cases rich in information concerning the issues of interest could be studied in depth (Patton 1990; Shaw 1999). This was appropriate for our study because it allowed the selection of revelatory cases which enable researchers to observe and analyse phenomena that previously have been subject to little or no investigation (Yin 1989). Since we sought to target women whose businesses potentially would be attractive to external funders, we oriented our selection towards 'gender-atypical' businesses (Blake and Hanson 2005), that is, women-owned businesses in male-dominated sectors such as construction, engineering and high technology, or with (assumed) male-pattern behaviours, such as growth-orientation and exporting (which were relatively uncommon for structural and attitudinal reasons among women business owners in Northern Ireland) (Carter and Brush 2004; O'Reilly 2005). This was achieved using a database of business owners held by Invest Northern Ireland (InvestNI), the main economic development agency in the region. Saturation was reached after nine interviews, probably because the critical incidents were so specific and the participants were relatively homogeneous owing to the selection approach employed.

Step 4: Data Collection

The integrity and rigour of interpretivist research is very heavily dependent on the quality of the researcher who is the sole data collection instrument. This includes the possession of characteristics and attributes such as ethical stance and integrity, good people skills, resilience, patience and persistence, versatility, flexibility and meticulousness (Anjen 2000), as well as intensive and personal involvement in the process (Sanjek 1990), and the ability to minimize the power distance between themselves and participants (Cresswell 1998). Interpretivist researchers gather data in natural as opposed to researcher-controlled settings, maintaining what Patton (1990: 55) calls an 'empathic neutrality', which involves developing a relationship with participants and encouraging them to be forthcoming without influencing their responses.

In this study, we, experienced interviewers, conducted the interviews ourselves and so were the only instruments of data collection. To ensure that participants were as forthcoming as possible, and in keeping with good practice, the interviews were carried out in relaxed and unthreatening surroundings, their business premises (Easterby-Smith et al. 2009). The interviews lasted between 60 and 90 minutes and all but one were audio-taped and transcribed with the permission of the participants, who were also provided with background information about the project, offered the opportunity to opt out at any time and given a guarantee of confidentiality.

The interview protocol employed was largely unstructured (see Appendix 8A.1 at the end of this chapter). Each participant was asked two main questions, namely, to reflect on and describe one effective and one ineffective encounter which she had had with an actual/potential supplier of finance. Other questions were merely prompts, attempts at preventing participants from straying too far away from the topic of interest. An advantage of employing relatively unstructured, personal interviews is being able to ask follow-up questions (probes) in order to obtain a better description and understanding of the critical incidents (Edvardsson and Roos 2001). As a participant's narrative may be considered self-disclosure, that is, 'any information exchange that refers to the self, including personal states, dispositions, events in the past and plans for the future' (Derlega and Grzelak 1979: 152), interpretivist researchers are reliant on the frankness of participants. Like Cope (2005), in this study we were surprised and stimulated by the level of candour and openness displayed by the women business owners whom we interviewed.

Step 5a: Inductive Data Analysis

Although Flanagan (1954) separated analysis of the data from interpretation (Table 8.1), in interpretivist research this is inappropriate, as interpretation is integral to inductive analysis, which is an iterative process. Nevertheless we have retained this dichotomy here for ease of explication.

The analysis of qualitative data is probably the most demanding yet least examined aspect of the interpretivist research process (Basit 2003; Gephart 2004; Gremler 2004; Hoepfl 1997; Shaw 1999) and, to demonstrate integrity, the onus is on researchers to document it thoughtfully and in detail (Leitch et al. 2010). Inductive analysis involves 'working with data, organizing it, breaking it into manageable units, synthesizing it, searching for patterns, discovering what is important and what is to be learned, and deciding what you will tell others' (Bogdan and Biklen 1982: 145). Consequently, it is an ongoing and systematic procedure, iterative but not linear in nature, which allows research findings to emerge from the dominant or significant themes teased from the raw data without the constraints of more structured methodologies (Thomas 2003). The objective of such analysis is to determine the categories, relationships and assumptions that underpin the participants' views of the world in general and of the subject matter of interest in particular (Basit 2003). Glaser and Strauss (1967: 237) observe that while the ultimate aim of the process is the generation of theory rather than theory testing or mere description, theory is not a 'perfected product' but an 'ever-developing entity'. Thus, in the context of social research, in practice this may not be the production of grand theory, but rather theory-building, that is, contributing to the existing body of knowledge, which is a cumulative and collective endeavour.

While, 'in comparison to quantitative research there are relatively few well-established and commonly accepted rules and guidelines for conducting rigorous inductive analysis' (Sekaran and Bougie 2010: 370), nevertheless, it involves a number of generic tasks:

- Close reading and re-reading of the text which can be in a number of forms including transcripts of interviews, focus group discussions and unstructured narratives.
- Coding, which is crucial to the process of analysis, and used to condense, organize and make sense of what can be extensive and varied raw data (Thomas 2003). 'The purpose of coding is to not only describe but, more importantly, to acquire new understanding of the phenomenon of interest' (Hoepfl 1997: 7). Codes are tags or categories attached to words, phrases, sentences or paragraphs and are used 'for allocating units of meaning to descriptive or inferential information compiled during a study' (Basit 2003: 144). Miles and Huberman (1994) have identified two approaches to the creation of codes: first, the grounded approach advocated by Glaser and Strauss (1967) whereby the researcher avoids pre-coding data until they are collected; and, second, the creation of a provisional 'start list' of codes deriving, for example, from the literature, the research questions and so on. Coding permits organizing and structuring data according to

the issues and topics identified by participants as being important for understanding the phenomenon of interest (Shaw 1999) which is based on the concepts and categories employed by social actors to interpret and understand their worlds (Jones 1985).

- The first task of coding, known as 'open coding' (Strauss and Corbin, 1990), involves breaking down raw data into manageable 'bits' (Dye et al. 2000) and assigning those which are apparently related to the same context to a broad category. Such categories represent a preliminary framework for analysis that fits the data, enabling the researcher to question it and to change, discard and order categories as appropriate (Basit 2003; Miles and Huberman 1994). Category identification may not be considered complete until multiple readings of the text have taken place and no sections of it, which are relevant to the research question, remain un-coded (King 2004).
- The next task is the revision and refinement of the categories and the creation of sub-categories, accompanied by attempts to determine how these relate to each other, a process known as 'axial coding' (Strauss and Corbin 1990). In addition, constant comparison of emergent codes and categories with subsequent data collected and also with concepts outlined in the literature (Glaser and Strauss 1967) is undertaken. The existence of discrepant and disconfirming cases or data that do not fit with the categories generated or existing theory, potentially can also provide important insights into the extant literature (Thomas 2003). Further, the process may also entail researchers searching for data missing from the text, that is, what participants do not mention, contrary perhaps to what the literature might suggest they would. Thus, by comparing and combining categories in new ways, the aim of coding is not merely to describe, but to develop new insights into the phenomenon of interest (Hoepfl, 1997).
- The key outcome of coding is to create a small number of summary categories which the researcher considers capture the key themes in the raw data judged to be the most important in terms of the research objectives (Thomas 2003). Although theme identification is one of the most fundamental tasks in qualitative research the process, outlined above, is rarely adequately described in the literature (Ryan and Bernard 2003).

As the dataset in this study was comparatively small we conducted the analysis manually. Where larger datasets are involved, the use of a computer-aided data analysis software (CAQDAS) package can help reduce the time and labour involved in managing the data. However, it is important to note that the researcher retains responsibility for making

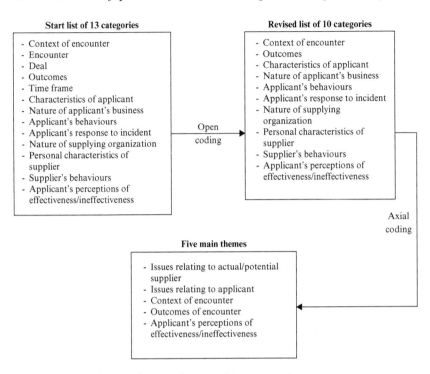

Figure 8.1   Inductive data analysis and interpretation

the major decisions about the analysis such as coding and so on (Saunders et al. 2009). All nine transcripts were read and re-read by both researchers. Based on our reading of the literature (Hill et al. 2006) and the subsequent design of the critical incident interview protocol (see Appendix 8A.1), a 'start list' of 13 preliminary codes or categories was developed (open coding – see Figure 8.1).

The benefit of employing a start list of codes and categories, instead of allowing them to emerge from the data as in grounded theory, is that prior knowledge can be built upon and/or expanded (Sekaran and Bougie 2010). We coded the texts (interview transcripts) independently on a paragraph-by-paragraph basis. Following Ryan and Bernard (2003) we 'pawed' the texts, which involved highlighting key phrases because they appeared to make some kind of sense (Sandelowski 1995). Based on a comparison of these independent codings, it became clear that there was a very high level of inter-rater agreement on the significance of text segments. Once this had been achieved, key phrases were written on individual pieces of gummed paper and then attached to a seemingly relevant preliminary category. Each section of text was coded so that it could be traced to the exact location in the relevant transcript. Since the critical incidents were specific in nature and the characteristics of the participants' businesses were similar, very little text in the transcripts remained unallocated.

After this time-consuming process had been completed, we checked all the text allotted to individual categories to ensure that the allocation of each piece appeared appropriate. If not, the text was re-allocated to a different one or, occasionally, dropped from the analysis. At this point it was clear that three of the preliminary categories were redundant, and so text was reassigned, as appropriate, to the remaining ten (Figure 8.1). For example, we were surprised that data relating to 'the deal' were missing so although this originally had been included in our start-list of categories, it was subsequently dropped. While, intuitively, one might have expected the nature of the deal struck between applicants for, and actual/potential suppliers of, finance to have influenced participants' perceptions of the effectiveness and ineffectiveness of such encounters, the findings did not support this (see below).

The induction of categories from the data is a task more subjective than objective (Flanagan 1954) and so he recommends that these are submitted to others for consideration. As Butterfield et al. (2005) observe, one of the main ways in which CIT, as originally developed by Flanagan (1954), has changed is with regard to establishing trustworthiness of the research results, which is particularly pertinent to the qualitative variant. In particular, they highlight that few standards exist regarding credibility checks to guide researchers. One of the approaches employed is to ask peers, colleagues and/or experts to examine the categories identified (Alfonso 1997; Butterfield 2001; Ellinger and Bostrom 2002; McCormick 1994). Accordingly, before axial coding and further interpretation commenced, a colleague, who is both an expert in interpretivist research and entrepreneurial finance, was asked to consider our allocation of data to categories. This required him to retrace our steps, assess the consistency of the analysis carried out at each stage, review the categories selected and, if necessary, question decisions taken. He concluded that, overall, the allocations made by us during this stage of the process were consistent and transparent.

Step 5b: Interpretation

For Miles and Huberman (1994) data analysis is a comprehensive process comprising three elements: first, data reduction (inductive data analysis – step 5a); second, data display (presenting the reduced data in a manner which helps both the researcher and the reader to understand them; this may include charts, matrices, diagrams, graphs and drawings – step 5b); third, drawing conclusions, which includes providing a coherent discussion of the findings and addressing the research question (step 6). Display facilitates this by enabling the discovery of patterns and relationships in the data (Sekaran and Bougie 2010).

In interpreting our own data we created the sub-categories related to each of the ten categories and, as suggested by Basit (2003), a series of spider diagrams were then developed (see Figure 8.2 for an illustration of three categories and their related sub-categories).

We found the creation of spider diagrams provided a useful pictorial illustration of the sub-categories underpinning the higher-level categories and enabled linkages to be made between the sub-categories, both within higher-level categories and across them (axial coding). Each category and sub-category was derived from the texts (interview transcripts) and illuminated by direct quotations from participants, including both representative and non-representative responses where the latter revealed additional insights. Tables 8A.1 to 8A.3 in Appendix 8A.2 comprise the sub-categories for three of the ten categories and a sample of related illustrative quotations in each case.

This process allowed us to reduce the ten categories to five main themes, namely: issues relating to the applicant for funding; issues relating to the actual or potential supplier; the outcome of the encounter; the context of the encounter; and applicants' perceptions of effectiveness and ineffectiveness. Each theme encompasses a number of categories and sub-categories. For example, the theme 'issues relating to actual/potential supplier' comprises three categories (namely, 'suppliers' behaviours', 'personal characteristics of supplier' and 'nature of supplying organization') and 15 sub-categories (see Tables 8A.1 to 8A.3). In most interpretivist research between three and eight themes are generally reported (Campbell et al. 2003; Jain and Ogden 1999). Owing to inexperience, some researchers present ten or more themes which potentially is indicative of not properly completing axial coding (that is combining smaller categories into more encompassing categories) or not appropriately determining those which are most important (Thomas 2003).

Step 6: Presentation and Discussion of Findings and Conclusions

A main aim of interpretivist research is to access participants' interpretations of a particular aspect of the social world, elucidate these as carefully as possible and to communicate a meaningful story to an audience, for example, other researchers, clients and policy-makers (Easterby-Smith

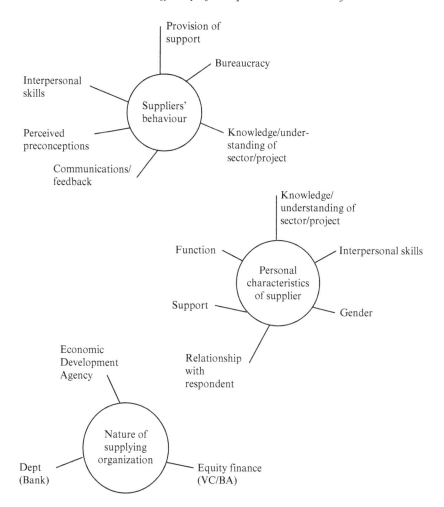

Figure 8.2   *Spider diagrams: issues relating to actual/potential supplier*

et al. 2008). However, both those conducting such research and those reading it must appreciate that the story presented is an interpretation of an interpretation and not an objective account of reality. Consequently, the researcher cannot specify the generalizability of the findings; he or she can only provide sufficient information so that the reader may determine whether or not the findings are transferable to other situations and contexts (Lincoln and Guba 1985). Thus, reports of interpretivist research should provide a detailed, compelling and powerful account of

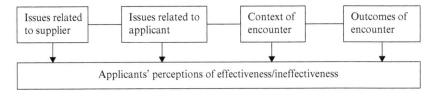

Figure 8.3   Representational model

the research process as well as convincing evidence in the findings (Leitch et al. 2010; Smith 1990; Van Manen 1990). Meeting these criteria requires a large amount of text and so, in attempting to publish such research, there is a tension between providing the requisite detail and the constraint of adhering to word limits imposed by academic journals.

In telling the story the researcher must explain what the emergent themes represent by discussing the patterns and relationships underlying them and using 'voice' in the text, that is, illustrative direct quotes from participants to reveal important insights (Hoepfl 1997). The explication of findings and the addressing of the research question(s) may be facilitated by structuring them around a conceptual or representational model/framework (Strauss and Corbin 1990) as appropriate. To illustrate, regarding our research findings, Figure 8.3 reveals that the women business owners' perceptions of the effectiveness and ineffectiveness of encounters with actual and potential funders, were shaped by several sets of variables encompassed in four themes.

In terms of the researcher's obligation to explain the emergent themes, we now employ the variables underlying one theme, 'issues relating to suppliers', to present part of the story. As was typical of Northern Ireland at the time the research was conducted, most of the women business owners were seeking finance from banks and economic development agencies rather than venture capitalists or business angels. Three main issues relating to suppliers, which had an influence on the participants' perceptions of effectiveness and ineffectiveness, emerged from the findings: first, suppliers' interpersonal skills and the support they provided; second, their knowledge and understanding of the sector, business and project; and third, the nature of the outcome of the encounter.

Although it was clear from the data that participants expected the suppliers' interpersonal skills would be good (communicative, polite and respectful) and that appropriate support would be provided both for their businesses and themselves, on occasions, such expectations were apparently not met: 'I found the client account manager on the xxx side was very good and kept me informed and so on all the time. You know it was very cordial and all of that throughout.' 'We didn't get any guiding information from them as to what they were looking for . . . they may not have been looking for technical projects at all . . . we had no idea what they were looking for . . .'

One participant, a director of a very long-established family business, reported an encounter which had greatly distressed her, especially as the firm had only used the services of one bank from the outset:

> He (the bank's business manager) came into the room and he didn't shake our hands. He sat down and started to talk immediately . . . about the problem with the overdraft. There was no lead into the conversation, there was no reference to the business plan and there was certainly no introduction or shaking of hands at the start.

In this instance the poor interpersonal skills perceived to have been displayed by the bank's business manager had actual and potential negative outcomes for both parties, as the business owner was so dismayed by his behaviour she transferred her account to another provider, a loss of business for the bank. Further, during the interview she revealed that this encounter would deter her from seeking future external finance, which may hinder the development and growth of the business.

Contrary to what might have been expected, several participants reported that some funding representatives' knowledge and understanding of both the sector and specific project were limited: 'I would say that just generally their lack of understanding and their lack of trying to get to grips with what we were about. They had their minds made up before we came through the door. You could tell that fairly quickly.'

At least two sets of implications emanate from this. First, the robustness and integrity of the funders' decision-making criteria and processes are called into question, especially as all the participants were experienced business women; and second, it suggests that business owners, particularly those in high-technology sectors, need to provide detailed contextual information about the sector, as well as specific information about the business and the project, when seeking finance. Some women had more positive experiences: 'The main thing there was asking about the business, so it really was, they understood about the business and me . . .' However, this also suggests that business owners expect funders to engage with them as individuals, which subsequently would aid the development and maintenance of a productive, longer-term relationship.

Another insight which emerged was that the outcome(s) of the encounter, as opposed to just the deal, had a more subtle and complex influence on perceptions of its effectiveness and ineffectiveness than might have been expected. For example, where an applicant failed to secure finance, the encounter was less likely to be perceived to be ineffective if they believed they had gained some potential learning from it. 'Well it's not the fact that we didn't get the outcome we wanted (finance) but the fact we didn't get any feedback.'

In terms of future attempts at seeking finance such learning may, of course, be valuable but it is also pertinent to the discouraged borrower phenomenon (Kon and Storey 2003), as lack of it may prevent business owners from seeking external finance again and, instead, opt to use retained earnings for growth irrespective of whether or not this is the right decision for the development of the business: 'We are not intending to seek other sources of finance but intend to grow the company organically.'

A further issue that emerged from the research was a mismatch between the expectations of the women seeking finance and those of the suppliers. While it is possible that some business owners' expectations were unrealistic, nevertheless there is an onus on service providers to manage applicants' expectations appropriately, in terms of explicitly articulating the type of project they are willing to support, the advance preparation required of applicants and the criteria employed in the decision-making process (Sheth and Mittal 1996). On the other hand, it is clear from the entrepreneurship literature that those seeking finance need to understand how to maximize the probability of success. For example, research by Mason and Stark (2004) revealed that business plans, rather than being generic, need to be tailored to the interests of each specific funder (Hill et al. 2006).

In this short extract we have demonstrated the multifaceted role of the researcher whose responsibilities include presenting, as accurately as possible, participants' social realities with integrity and without being judgemental. This goes beyond merely reporting the data as, in addition, it encompasses sense-making, that is, drawing insights and constructing a meaningful narrative in the context of the extant literature, as well as adding to the existing body of knowledge in order to stimulate further research and to inform both policy-makers and practitioners.

CONCLUSION

It has been observed that for unknown reasons the use of CIT in entrepreneurship research has been relatively limited (Harrison and Mason 2004). Methods are neither good nor bad but are more or less appropriate to the aims and objectives of each specific research project. Thus choice of method is a matter of aptness – different types of research question are best answered by different types of study employing appropriate methods (Leitch et al. 2010). Based on our own experiences, we offer the qualitative variant of CIT as an additional investigative and exploratory tool for consideration by entrepreneurship researchers (Chell 1998; Woolsey 1986).

In undertaking our research we found that it had a number of strengths. First, as Edvardsson and Roos (2001: 256) observe, 'the psychological literature suggests that negative incidents may have greater impact on customers than positive' and thus are more likely to be remembered, amounting to only partial recall. However, because CIT requires participants to reflect upon both the positive and negative, the researcher should obtain a more holistic account of the incident, in this case, seeking finance. Second, it permits 'self-defined criticality' whereby: participants identify personally important incidents as critical and not the researcher; the contextual significance of factors related to the incident is highlighted (Hasselkus and Dickie 1990; O'Driscoll and Cooper 1994; Wodlinger 1990); and attributed meaning is captured (Baum 1999; Morley 2003; Pellegrini and Sarbin 2002; von Post 1998). Third, it necessitates that participants are critically reflexive rather than merely critical when thinking about incidents, thereby encouraging them to confront and relate thoughts, feelings and behaviours instead of only being descriptive (Chell 1998). Cunliffe (2004) notes that critically reflexive practice involves employing subjective understandings of reality as the basis for thinking more critically about the impact of one's own assumptions, values and actions on others, a potentially valuable learning outcome. In addition, through the researcher's presentation of the findings and the telling of the story, the reader gains insights into the participants' realities which in turn may lead to beneficial learning for them.

However, to benefit from the strengths of the qualitative variant of CIT, researchers too must be thoughtful and critically reflexive. Specifically, they should be aware of the danger of a CIT interview losing its distinctiveness and potency by morphing into a generic qualitative interview. Further, the flexibility offered by its continued evolution needs to be balanced against maintaining its integrity. We found that the development of our guiding framework, rooted in Flanagan's (1954) original principles, helped us address these potential problems and enhance the robustness, rigour and integrity of the research.

REFERENCES

Ahl, H. (2004), *The Scientific Reproduction of Gender Inequality*, Stockholm: Liber.

Alfonso, V. (1997), 'Overcoming depressed moods after an HIV positive diagnosis: a critical incident analysis', unpublished doctoral dissertation, University of British Columbia, Vancouver.

Alvesson, M. and S. Deetz (2000), *Doing Critical Management Research*, London: Sage Publications.

Anjen, M.J. (2000), 'Evaluating interpretive inquiry: reviewing the validity debate and opening the dialogue', *Qualitative Health Research*, **10** (3), 378–95.

Basit T.N. (2003), 'Manual or electronic? The role of coding in qualitative data analysis', *Educational Research*, **45** (2), 143–54.

Baum, S. (1999), 'Holocaust survivors: successful lifelong coping after trauma', unpublished doctoral dissertation, University of British Columbia, Vancouver.

Blake, M.K. and S. Hanson (2005), 'Rethinking innovation: context and gender', *Environment and Planning A*, **37** (4), 681–701.

Bogdan, R.C. and S.K. Biklen (1982), *Qualitative Research for Education: An Introduction to Theory and Methods*, Boston, MA: Allyn and Bacon.

Butterfield, L.D. (2001), 'A critical incident study of individual clients' outplacement counselling experiences', unpublished Master's thesis, University of British Columbia, Vancouver.

Butterfield, L.D., W.A. Borgen, N.E. Amundson and A.-S.T. Maglio (2005), 'Fifty years of the critical incident technique: 1954–2004 and beyond', *Qualitative Research*, **5** (4), 475–97.

Campbell, R., P. Pound, C. Pope, N. Britten, R. Pill, M. Morgan et al. (2003), 'Evaluating meta-ethnography: a synthesis of qualitative research on lay experiences of diabetes and diabetes care', *Social Science and Medicine*, **56** (4), 671–84.

Carter, N.M. and C.G. Brush (2004), 'Gender', in W.B. Gartner, K.G. Shaver, N.M. Carter and P.D. Reynolds (eds), *Handbook of Entrepreneurial Dynamics: The Process of Business Creation*. Thousand Oaks, CA: Sage, pp. 12–25.

Chell, E. (1998), 'Critical incident technique', in G. Symon and C. Cassell (eds), *Qualitative Methods and Analysis in Organizational Research: A Practical Guide*, London: Sage, pp. 51–72.

Chell, E. (2004), 'Critical incident technique', in G. Symon and C. Cassell (eds), *Essential Guide to Qualitative Methods in Organizational Research*, London: Sage, pp. 45–60.

Chell, E. and Pittaway, L. (1998), 'A study of entrepreneurship in the restaurant and café industry: exploratory work using the critical incident technique as a methodology', *International Journal of Hospitality Management*, **17** (1), 23–32.

Cope, J. (2003), 'Entrepreneurial learning and critical reflection: discontinuous events as triggers for "higher-level" learning', *Management Learning*, **34** (4), 429–50.

Cope, J. (2005), 'Researching entrepreneurship through phenomenological inquiry', *International Small Business Journal*, **23** (2), 159–83.

Cope, J. and G. Watts (2000), 'Learning by doing: an exploration of experience, critical incidents and reflection in entrepreneurial learning', *International Journal of Entrepreneurial Behaviour and Research*, **6** (3), 104–24.

Cowling, M. and R. Harding (2005), 'Gender and high growth businesses in the UK', paper presented at the second Diana International Research Conference: Growth Oriented Women Entrepreneurs and their Businesses: A Global Research Perspective, Stockholm, May.

Creswell, J.W. (1998), *Qualitative Inquiry and Research Design: Choosing among the Five Traditions*, Thousand Oaks, CA: Sage.

Cunliffe, A.L. (2004), 'On becoming a critically reflexive practitioner', *Journal of Management Education*, **28** (4), 407–26.

Derlega, V.J. and Grzelak, J. (1979), 'Appropriateness of self disclosure', in G. Chelune (ed.), *Self-Disclosure: Origins, Patterns, and Implications of Openness in Interpersonal Relationships*, San Francisco, CA: Jossey-Bass.

Dye, J.F., I.M. Schatz, B.A. Rosenberg and S.T. Coleman (2000), 'Constant comparison method: a kaleidoscope of data', *The Qualitative Report*, **4** (1–2), available at: http://www.nova.edu/ssss/QR/QR4-1/dye.html (accessed 30 January 2006).

Easterby-Smith, M., K. Golden-Biddle and K. Locke (2008), 'Working with pluralism: determining quality in qualitative research', *Organizational Research Methods*, **11** (3), 419–29.
Easterby-Smith, M., R. Thorpe and P.R. Jackson (2009), *Management Research*, 3rd edn, London: Sage.
Edvardsson, B. (1992), 'Service breakdowns: a study of critical incidents in an airline', *International Journal of Service Industry Management*, **3** (4), 17–29.
Edvardsson, B. and I. Roos (2001), 'Critical incident techniques: towards a framework for analysing the criticality of critical incidents', *International Journal of Service Industry Management*, **12** (3), 251–68.
Ellinger, A.D. and R.P. Bostrom (2002), 'An examination of managers' beliefs about their roles as facilitators of learning', *Management Learning*, **33** (2), 147–79.
Flanagan, J.C. (1954), 'The critical incident technique', *Psychological Bulletin*, **51** (4), 327–58.
Gabbott, M. and G. Hogg (1996), 'The glory of stories: using critical incidents to understand service evaluation in the primary health care context', *Journal of Marketing Management*, **12** (6), 493–503.
Gephart, R. (2004), 'Qualitative research and the *Academy of Management Journal*', *Academy of Management Journal*, **47** (4), 454–62.
Gilchrist, V.J. and R.L. Williams (1999), 'Key informant interviews', in B.F. Crabtree and W.L. Miller (eds), *Doing Qualitative Research*, Newbury Park, CA: Sage, pp. 71–88.
Glaser, B. and A. Strauss (1967), *The Discovery of Grounded Theory*, Chicago, IL: Aldine.
Gremler, D.D. (2004), 'The critical incident technique in service research', *Journal of Service Research*, **7** (1), 65–89.
Grove, S.J. and R.P. Fisk (1997), 'The impact of other customers on service experiences: a critical incident examination of "getting along"', *Journal of Retailing*, **73** (1), 63–85.
Harrison, R.T. and C.M. Mason (2004), 'A critical incident technique approach to entrepreneurship research: developing a methodology to analyse the value added contribution of informal investors', paper presented to the Twenty-fourth Annual Babson Kauffmann Entrepreneurship Research Conference, University of Strathclyde, Glasgow, June.
Hasselkus, B.R. and V.A. Dickie (1990), 'Themes of meaning: occupational therapists' perspectives on practice', *Occupational Therapy Journal of Research*, **10** (4), 195–207.
Hill, F.M., C.M. Leitch and R.T. Harrison (2006), 'Desperately seeking finance? The demand for finance by women-owned and -led businesses', *Venture Capital: An International Journal of Entrepreneurial Finance*, **8** (2), 159–82.
Hoepfl, M.C. (1997), 'Choosing qualitative research: a primer for technology education researchers', *Journal of Technology Education*, **9** (1), available at: http://scholar.lib.vt.edu/ejournals/JTE/jte-v9n1/hoepfl.html (accessed 28 February 2006).
Jain, A. and J. Ogden (1999), 'General practitioners' experiences of patients' complaints: a qualitative study', *British Medical Journal*, **318** (7198), 1596–9.
Johnson, J.C. (1990), *Selecting Ethnographic Informants*, Newbury Park, CA: Sage.
Johnson, P., A. Buehring, C. Cassell and G. Symon (2006), 'Evaluating qualitative management research: towards a coherent criteriology', *International Journal of Management Reviews*, **8** (3), 131–56.
Jones, S. (1985), 'The analysis of depth interviews', in R. Walker (ed.), *Applied Qualitative Research*, Aldershot: Gower, pp. 56–70.
King, N. (2004), 'Using templates in thematic analysis of text', in C. Cassell and G. Symon (eds), *Essential Guide to Qualitative Methods in Organizational Research*, London: Sage, pp. 256–70.
Kon, Y. and D.J. Storey (2003), 'A theory of discouraged borrowers', *Small Business Economics*, **21** (1), 37–49.
Leitch, C.M., F.M. Hill and R.T. Harrison (2010), 'The philosophy and practice of interpretivist research in entrepreneurship: quality, validation and trust', *Organizational Research Methods*, **13** (1), 67–84.
Lincoln, Y.S. and E.G. Guba (1985), *Naturalistic Enquiry*, Newbury Park, CA: Sage.
Mason, C.M. and J.M. Stark (2004), 'What do investors look for in a business plan? A

comparison of investment criteria of bankers, venture capitalists and business angels', *International Small Business Journal*, **22** (3), 227–48.

McCormick, R. (1994), 'The facilitation of healing for the First Nations' People of British Columbia', unpublished doctoral dissertation, University of British Columbia, Vancouver.

Miles, M.B. and A.M. Huberman (1994), *Qualitative Data Analysis: An Expanded Sourcebook*, 2nd edn, Thousand Oaks, CA: Sage.

Morley, J.G. (2003), 'Meaningful engagement in the RCMP workplace: what helps and hinders', unpublished doctoral dissertation, University of British Columbia, Vancouver.

O'Driscoll, M.P. and C.L. Cooper (1994), 'Coping with work-related stress: a critique of existing measures and proposal for an alternative methodology', *Journal of Occupational and Organizational Psychology*, **67** (4), 343–54.

O'Reilly, M. (2005), 'Cambridge small business survey: gender analysis of Northern Ireland results', Invest Northern Ireland, Belfast, unpublished mimeo.

Olsen, M.J.S. and B. Thomasson (1992), 'Studies in service quality with the aid of critical incidents and phenomenography', in E.E. Scheuing, B. Edvardsson, D. Lascelles and C.H. Little (eds), *QUIS 3: Quality in Services Conference*, Jamaica, NY: International Service Quality Association, pp. 481–505.

Patton, M.Q. (1990), *Qualitative Evaluation and Research Methods*, 2nd edn, Newbury Park: Sage.

Patton, M.Q. (2002), *Qualitative Evaluation and Research Methods*, 3rd edn, Newbury Park, CA: Sage Publications.

Pellegrini, R.J. and T.R. Sarbin (eds) (2002), *Between Fathers and Sons: Critical Incident Narratives in the Development of Men's Lives*, New York: Hayworth Press.

Pittaway, L. and E. Chell (1999), 'Entrepreneurship in the service firm life cycle', paper presented at the Eighth Annual CHME Hospitality Research Conference. University of Surrey, April.

Potter, J. and M. Whetherell (1987), *Discourse and Social Psychology: Beyond Attitudes and Behaviour*, London: Sage.

Read, L. (1998), *The Financing of Small Business: A Comparative Study of Male and Female Business Owners*, London: Routledge.

Ryan, G.W. and H.R. Bernard (2003), 'Techniques to identify themes', *Field Methods*, **15** (1), 85–109.

Sandelowski, M. (1995), 'Qualitative analysis: what it is and how to begin', *Research in Nursing and Health*, **18** (4), 371–5.

Sanjek, R. (1990), *Field Notes: The Making of an Anthropology*, Ithaca, NY: Cornell University Press.

Saunders, M., P. Lewis and A. Thornhill (2009), *Research Methods for Business Students*, 5th edn, Harlow: Pearson Education.

Sekaran, U. and R. Bougie (2010), *Research Methods for Business: A Skill Building Approach*, 5th edn, Chichester: Wiley and Sons.

Shaw, E. (1999), 'A guide to the qualitative research process: evidence from a small firm study', *Qualitative Market Research: An International Journal*, **2** (2), 59–70.

Sheth, J.N. and B. Mittal (1996), 'A framework for managing customer expectations', *Journal of Marketing Focused Management*, **1** (2), 137–58.

Smith, J.K. (1990), 'Goodness criteria: alternative research paradigms and the problem of criteria', in E.G. Guba (ed.), *The Paradigm Dialogue*, Newbury Park, CA: Sage, pp 167–87.

Stahl, B.C. (2007), 'Positivism or non-positivism – tertium non datur: a critique of onto-logical syncretisim in IS research', in R. Kishore, R. Ramesh and R. Sharman (eds), *Ontologies: A Handbook of Principles, Concepts and Applications in Information Systems*, New York: Springer, pp. 115–42.

Stauss, B. and B. Weinlich (1997), 'Process-oriented measurement of service quality: apply-ing the sequential incident technique', *European Journal of Marketing*, **31** (1), 33–55.

Strauss, A. and J. Corbin. (1990), *Basics of Qualitative Research: Grounded Theory Procedures and Techniques*, Newbury Park, CA: Sage.

Thomas, D.R. (2003), 'A general inductive approach for qualitative data analysis', available at: http://www.fmhs.auckland.ac.nz/soph/centres/hrmas/_docs/Inductive2003.pdf (accessed 22 March 2012).

Thompson, C.J., W.B. Locander and H.R. Pollio (1989), 'Putting consumer experience back into consumer research: the philosophy and method of existential phenomenology', *Journal of Consumer Research*, **16** (September), 133–46.

Urquhart, C., A. Light, R. Thomas, A. Barker, A. Yeoman, J. Cooper et al. (2003), 'Critical incident technique and explication interviewing in studies of information behaviour', *Library and Information Science Research*, **25** (1), 63–88.

Van Manen, M. (1990), *Researching Lived Experience: Human Science for an Action Sensitive Pedagogy*, London, ON: Althouse Press.

Von Post, I. (1998), 'Perioperative nurses' encounter with value conflicts: a descriptive study', *Scandinavian Journal of Caring Sciences*, **12** (2), 81–8.

Wodlinger, M.G. (1990), 'April: A case study in the use of guided reflection', *Alberta Journal of Educational Research*, **36** (2), 115–32.

Woolsey, L.K. (1986), 'The critical incident technique: an innovative qualitative method of research', *Canadian Journal of Counselling*, **20** (4), 242–54.

Yin, R.K. (1989), *Case Study Research: Design and Methods*. Newbury Park, CA: Sage Publications.

APPENDIX 8A.1   CRITICAL INCIDENT INTERVIEW

Effective:

I would like you to tell me about an incident, as recent as possible, which exemplifies an effective encounter which you have had with an actual or potential provider of funding for your business.
Prompts:

- Please describe the encounter.
- What was the background to this?
- Explain why you feel the encounter was effective.
- Please tell me what the person did which made the encounter effective.
- Did you do anything which contributed towards the effectiveness of the encounter?
- If yes, what did you do?
- When did the incident happen?
- What kind of organization was the person concerned employed in and what was their position?
- Please describe the person in question.
- What was/were the outcome/outcomes of the encounter?

Ineffective:

I would like you to tell me about an incident, as recent as possible, which exemplifies an ineffective encounter which you have had with an actual or potential provider of funding for your business.
Prompts:

- Please describe the encounter.
- What was the background to this?
- Explain why you feel the encounter was ineffective.
- Please tell me what the person did which made the encounter ineffective.
- Did you do anything which contributed towards the ineffectiveness of the encounter?
- If yes, what did you do?
- When did the incident happen?
- What kind of organization was the person concerned employed in and what was their position?

- Please describe the person in question.
- What was/were the outcome/outcomes of the encounter?

APPENDIX 8A.2 TABLES

Table 8A.1 Suppliers' behaviours: illustrative quotes and sub-categories

Illustrative quotes (raw data)	Sub-categories
'I outlined the business to him and he has worked with me towards funding and getting funding set up for that new business'	Provision of support
'A person that managed our application, like a client executive, and they guided us through the process and the only other person . . . came out really to do due diligence'	
'The project has been hindered by the bureaucracy associated with funding, it is very time-consuming dealing with red tape. There were also delays in funding'	Bureaucracy
'*Name of Regional Development Agency* waited until X's role was officially involved'	
'The main thing there was asking about the business, so it really was, they understood about the business and me, they took time to understand and get to know me well'	Knowledge/ understanding of sector
'People reviewing the project didn't understand it – I suppose it makes it difficult to bring them up to speed. Also they don't realize with R&D project changes will take place'	
'Their staff came out and more or less gave us positive feedback'	Communication/ feedback
'The person involved started, he was unhelpful, he didn't communicate well and he started off in a poor way with us and the figures and it was evident that he hadn't prepared for the meeting in the business sense'	
'I would say, that just general, their lack of understanding, their lack of trying to get to grips with what we were about. They had their mind made up before they came through the door. You could tell that fairly quickly'	Perceived preconceptions
'They seemed to come in with preconceived ideas, they hadn't read the business plan we had prepared'	
'He came into the room and he didn't shake our hands. He sat down and started to talk immediately . . . about the problem with the overdraft. There was no lead into the conversation, there was no reference to the business plan and there was certainly no introduction or shaking of hands at the start'	Interpersonal skills
'I didn't feel he was able to give me that backing and I feel that there was no relationship and . . . he didn't offer face-to-face. All communication was taken over the phone'	

Table 8A.2   Personal characteristics of suppliers: illustrative quotes and sub-categories

Illustrative quotes (raw data)	Sub-categories
'Well, they seemed to be quite an experienced professional and they had a good understanding of the technology. And they were quite positive and supportive towards us' 'The potential investor was not familiar with software having been in manufacturing'	Knowledge/ understanding/ expertise
'He would probably have been in his early fifties and he was very abrupt, no interpersonal skills' 'I think there was a lot of goodwill there, that she would like to see us succeed in that'	Interpersonal skills
'Both were male, both in their early thirties, and both local from Northern Ireland . . . Experienced, yes, very experienced' 'She's female and she's probably late thirties, early forties . . .'	Gender
'It was this business manager who was dealing with me. I had no relationship with that person, so it was like starting from scratch . . .' 'I find the client Account Manager on the *Local Development Agency* side . . . was very good and kept me informed and so on all the time. You know it was very cordial and all of that throughout'	Relationship with respondent
'The individual wished to be involved in the running of the company which is a reasonable expectation'. 'The initial client executive (male) was very good – knowledgeable and supportive – but he left at Christmas'	Support
'Business manager role . . . so fairly senior again in charge of the small to medium-sized business in the area' 'They were both business managers in the bank looking after small to medium-sized business'	Function

249

Table 8A.3   Nature of supplying organization: illustrative quotes and sub-categories

Illustrative quotes (raw data)	Sub-categories
'... they've taken on a new structure, they're getting a new guy who's an ex-investment banker into *Local Development Agency*' '... and we approached *Local Development Agency* for details about it'	Economic development agency
'The two banks ... I was talking to are well-known, one of them is fairly new in Ireland and the other one is particularly focused on small to medium-sized businesses' 'And they centralized their business banking ... and appointed a business banking advisor ... over a number of companies that was supposed to look after us and that's where our relationship began to unravel'	Debt (bank)
'... the *Local Development Agency* who have access to Business Angels' 'the *Local Development Agency* and *Investment Fund*'	Equity finance (venture capitalist/ business angels)

9 A critical incident technique approach to entrepreneurship research using phenomenological explicative data collection

Richard T. Harrison

INTRODUCTION

Critical incident technique (CIT) is a set of procedures for collecting direct observations of human behaviour in such a way as to facilitate their potential usefulness in solving practical problems (Andersson and Nilsson 1964; Ronan and Latham 1974). In both its original application and in many of the subsequent applications in a range of contexts, CIT focuses specifically on the identification and study of specific observations of extremely good or bad performance. For Flanagan (1954), a typical CIT study should follow a five-step process (Ölvingson et al. 2002; Urquhart et al. 2003):

1. Determine the general aim of the studied activity, to be able to determine what is critical or not and whether the critical incident contributes to achieving the overall aim of the activity or not.
2. Develop plans and specifications for collecting factual incidents regarding the activity, including determining who the observers should be and how the information should be acquired.
3. Collect the data through interview, focus group or as written up by the observer, or through record forms and data sets.
4. Analyse the data, as objectively as possible (Flanagan's injunction), identifying the incidents and clustering them into categories with similar incidents.
5. Interpret and report on the findings, particularly those indicating incidents which make a significant contribution to the activity.

The CIT approach has been applied in a number of disciplines and to address a number of research issues. These include applications in management (Andersson and Nilsson 1964; White and Locke 1981), marketing (Bitner et al. 1990, 1994), services management and marketing (Jones 1999; Arnold et al. 2004), customer relationship management (Neuhaus 1996;

Wong and Sohal 2003; Lorenzoni and Lewis 2004), human resource management (Latham et al. 1980; Pursell et al. 1980; Mitchell et al. 1997; Bradfield and Aquino 1999), industrial relations (Pilemalm et al. 2001), information management (Muylle et al. 2004), health-care management (Kemppainen 2000; Ölvingson et al. 2002; Mallak et al. 2003), and organization studies (Gundry and Rousseau 1994; Davey and Symon 2001). The precise application of CIT varies considerably within these diverse studies, in terms of the data collection protocols (from conventional qualitative interviews in case study research designs to multi-method large-scale data collection exercises involving several hundred respondents and questionnaire and Likert-scale type surveys, and in one case (Muylle et al. 2004) online data collection) and analytic approaches, from the narrative-based interpretative approach at one extreme to the formal quantitative analysis of survey data at the other.

Despite this diversity, what all these applications of CIT share is a focus on the key distinguishing feature of CIT as an approach, which, in Ruben's (1993) words, allows for the emergence rather than imposition of an evaluative schema and focuses on the events and dimensions of experience that are most salient, memorable and most likely to be retold to others.

Although initially developed and applied within a positivistic framework to clearly bounded events, applications of CIT in the entrepreneurial context, though limited in comparison with other disciplines, have more often adopted a grounded theory perspective (Curran et al. 1992) or a social constructionist perspective in the context of qualitative research methods (notably case studies) as an attempt to bridge positivist and phenomenological approaches in a multi-paradigm framework (Chell and Allman 2003; Chell 2004; see also Schultz and Hatch 1996).[1] In a series of papers (summarized in Chell 2004), Chell has applied a critical incident approach to the investigation of behavioural differences, in terms of business development, between business owners across a number of business sectors, and to the interaction between business and household experiences. Curran et al. (1992) have applied a CIT methodology to the study of small and medium-sized enterprise (SME) networking activity, and have continued to call for more adventurous methodological approaches to small business and entrepreneurship research (Curran and Blackburn 2001), a call echoed in recent collections of papers on qualitative research in entrepreneurship (Gartner and Birley 2002; Neergaard and Ulhøi 2004).

Other recent applications of CIT in the entrepreneurship domain, all of them in the qualitative research tradition, include studies of the social construction of entrepreneurial behaviour (Chell and Pittaway 1998), the relationship between entrepreneurial marketing and business development (Stokes 2000), the internal corporate venturing process (Garud and

Van de Ven 1992), the networking process of entrepreneurs (Tjosvold and Weicker 1993), the management of learning, technology and innovation processes in small firms (Deakins and Freel 1998; Atherton and Hannon 1999 – although in these cases critical incidents provide the basis for organizing the presentation of the case study material without a clearly articulated CIT methodological procedure being followed), the behavioural attributes of entrepreneurial success and failure (Nandram 2002), the early stage development of new ventures (Kaulio 2003) and the nature and process of entrepreneurial learning (Cope and Watts 2000; Cope 2003).

The application of the CIT methodology varies significantly across these studies, as it does in other domains of application. In some cases, data collection is from large-scale surveys (Nandram 2002, for example, collects CIT data from 205 respondents to a postal survey, but uses descriptive rather than analytical data handling procedures to present the results). In other cases, in-depth interviews are held with around 40 respondents (Chell and Pittaway 1998; Stokes 2000), sometimes supplemented by focus groups for methodological triangulation (Stokes 2000). In yet other cases (Deakins and Freel 1998; Atherton and Hannon 1999; Kaulio 2003; Cope and Watts 2000; Cope 2003) a case study research design is adopted, with between five and eight cases included for detailed research and analysis. Often, the research design is longitudinal and multi-method (Cope and Watts 2000; Cope 2003) and identifies more than a single critical incident for each case. For example, Kaulio's (2003) study of early stage growth dynamics involves the identification of 65 critical incidents in eight case study companies, on the basis of 20 interviews with 16 different respondents, and Cope's research into entrepreneurial learning identifies multiple critical incidents – episodes – extending over time rather than bounded individual incidents as the basic unit in which entrepreneurs report their experience (Cope and Watts 2000). The potential of CIT in a single case research design, using in-depth multiple interviews around a single case, is illustrated by Chell (2004: 58), who concludes that 'CIT enables the development of case based theory grounded in actual critical events that shape future actions. The insights gleaned and the conclusions drawn . . . facilitate the development of theory'. For Chell (2004: 48) Flanagan's definition of CIT has been modified to some extent:

> The critical interview technique[2] is a qualitative interview procedure, which facilitates the investigation of significant occurrences (events, incidents, processes or issues), identified by the respondent, the way they are managed, and the outcomes in terms of perceived effects. The objective is to gain an understanding of the incident from the perspective of the individual, taking into account cognitive, affective and behavioural elements.

Given this level of interest in CIT in entrepreneurship and other domains, and its particular applicability in situations where the primary focus of attention is on uncovering behaviours and attitudes (through the direct observation of human behaviours) in situations where there is little known about the phenomena (Derbaix and Vanhamme 2003), there would appear to be scope for developing and applying this approach to the study of the value-added contribution of informal investors to the businesses in which they invest. Before doing so, however, there are a number of extensions of the 'classic' CIT approach, which go beyond the approach recommended for entrepreneurship researchers by Chell (2004), which we adopt in developing our approach, and which provide a platform for the more widespread adoption of CIT as a research approach in entrepreneurship.

ISSUES AND DEVELOPMENTS IN CIT

The range of applications of CIT, from the original positivistic studies on managerial and employee performance inspired by Flanagan (1954) to more recent interpretative applications in marketing, organization behaviour, health-care management and entrepreneurship (*inter alia*) suggests that there is no single unequivocal 'critical incident technique' which can be adopted in research. Specifically, in developing a CIT research design, and more generally in assessing the applicability of the approach as a viable and informative research methodology in entrepreneurship, there are a number of issues that need to be considered. Three in particular stand out: the nature of the incident as the focus of the research; the nature of the interview process as an increasingly common, even predominant, approach to data collection in CIT studies; and the nature of criticality itself. That is, taking a lead from a number of recent commentaries on CIT, we problematize and reformulate each aspect of the approach in developing a revised understanding of CIT as the basis for further research in entrepreneurship in general and in early stage venture capital research in particular.

THE NATURE OF THE 'INCIDENT'

First, the nature of the critical incident itself has to be re-examined. In Flanagan's (1954: 327) original treatment, the technique was developed 'for collecting observed incidents having special significance and meeting systematically defined criteria', where a critical incident should have a purpose or intent that seems fairly clear to the observer, where the consequences are sufficiently definite to leave little doubt concerning its effects (Mitchell et al. 1997: 21); that is, there is an underlying assumption that reality is tangible and discrete, and that real-world phenomena about which little is known are tapped by critical incidents (Bitner et al. 1990). In Flanagan's (1954: 327) terms, an incident is 'any observable human activity that is sufficiently complete in itself to permit inferences and predictions to be made about the person performing the act'. Many of the applications of the technique (Jackson et al. 1996; Callan 1998; Grove and Fisk 1997; Bradfield and Aquino 1999; Jones 1999; Burns et al. 2000; Mallak et al. 2003; Wong and Sohal 2003; Lorenzoni and Lewis 2004) do follow this original definition of an 'incident', and study encapsulated and clearly bounded examples of human behaviour.

However, where there is a complex interplay and interdependence between the phenomena of interest, which cannot be adequately be addressed within either the individualistic or process paradigms (Cope and Watts 2000: 104), 'the term "incident" often tends to trivialise the diversity of critical experiences faced by entrepreneurs, who often endure prolonged, difficult and highly emotional critical *periods* or *episodes*' (Cope and Watts 2000: 112, original emphasis). The 'critical incident' is a complex phenomenon that does not occur independently of the entrepreneur, and is not a discrete, isolated event. As a result, it can prove difficult in practice 'to define the chronological and perceptual boundaries of these events' (Cope and Watts 2000: 113), which do not occur 'out of the blue' but are deeply grounded in and inextricably linked to a complex set of circumstances and actions (Cope 2003: 447).

THE NATURE OF THE CIT INTERVIEW

Second, while CIT, from Flanagan on, has not been prescriptive or restrictive with respect to data collection protocols (personal interviews, telephone interviews, focus groups, group interviews, workshops, self-administered questionnaires, systematic record-keeping and direct observation, which have been subject to both quantitative and qualitative analysis – see Anderson and Wilson 1997; Kemppainen 2000; Mallak et al. 2003), there are concerns that data collection is potentially problematic. Specifically, there are disadvantages with CIT related to the twin problems of retrospection and introspection (Derbaix and Vanhamme 2003). Retrospection is associated with problems of self-censoring and recall bias, which may be mitigated when the reported incidents are recent and the 'observers' (in this case, investors and entrepreneurs) are motivated to engage in detailed observations and evaluations during the interviews.

Introspection is potentially more problematic, in part because observers may not either have engaged or be willing to engage in the analysis and reporting of private experiences, emotions and feelings. As a qualitative research method in particular, CIT may be open to potential biases arising from the nature of the resultant narratives as forms of self-disclosure (Burns et al. 2000). This problem may in part be circumvented by using other observational research methods, either as an alternative to CIT or as a supplement to the method (Grove and Fisk 1992): these approaches may include participant observation techniques (Jorgensen 1989; Brewer 2000; Waddington 2004) and the phenomenological interview (Thompson et al. 1989), which Chell (2004) argues for in an entrepreneurial context.

In part to overcome these problems, Urquhart et al. (2003) have suggested the integration of Vermersch's (1994) explication data collection technique to manage the collection and use of retrospective data. Explication is a 'thorough and specific set of guidelines . . ., which, in emphasizing how data are gathered and in providing theoretical grounding for why this should be so, also offers an interesting tool for examining purposes in gathering qualitative data' (Urquhart et al. 2003: 66). Central to explication is the encouragement of interviewees to enter a state of evocation, to relive the activity under investigation (thereby processing experience into reflection, and progressing from pre-reflected to reflected experience and from experience as it was lived to experience that is represented and verbalized – see Piaget (1977 [2000]) for the psychological and philosophical basis for this reflective abstracting approach). In a state of evocation, the kind of account given by the interviewee is more fine-grained in terms of the description of the event, and uses language which is less specifically tailored to the expectations of the audience, a common problem in retrospective accounts (Antaki 1988; Burns et al. 2000). By comparison with other retrospective methodologies, where *post hoc* rationalization is a potential problem (Ericsson and Simon 1984), evocative explication encourages interviewees to experience anew, rather than just retell, the chronology of the event. This, of course, requires a more reflective style of interviewing, in which the interviewer avoids closed or leading questions, making presuppositions or inviting the interviewee into a judgemental mode which requires interpretation rather than recall (for example, avoiding 'why?' questions) (Urquart et al. 2003:68).

THE CRITICALITY OF 'CRITICAL'

Third, just as the nature of the 'incident' in critical incident approaches can be reconsidered, to the extent that it may be more valuable in many circumstances to refer to complex episodes rather than discrete incidents (Cope and Watts 2000), so to it is necessary to reassess the criticality of 'critical' (Edvardsson and Strandvik 2000: Edvardsson and Roos 2001). To recap, for Flanagan (1954: 327) 'to be critical, an incident must occur in a situation where the purpose or intent of the act seems fairly clear to the observer and where its consequences are sufficiently definite to leave little doubt concerning its effect'. This traditional approach to CIT focuses on a limited set of issues concerning the incidents themselves, and plays down the importance of sequences or clusters of incidents embedded in relationships (Strauss and Weinlich 1997; Edvardsson and Roos 2001).

For Edvardsson and Strandvik (2000) criticality is not just something built into the act (service, experience and business contribution) but is a contextually defined phenomenon which depends on the various actors involved (customer, service provider in their analysis), the interaction and the surrounding relationship infrastructure. Building on a series of earlier studies which have begun to move towards a process-based view of critical incidents (Olsen 1996; Strauss and Weinlich 1997; Roos 1999), they argue that critical incidents are always embedded in relationships and that, accordingly, CIT analyses should be founded on a relational view of the interactions between the actors involved: 'an increased focus on relationships instead of a focus on episodes only becomes natural and necessary' (Edvardsson and Strandvik 2000: 84).

A general model of a relational approach to critical incidents is set out in Figure 9.1, which indicates the key issues and variables of interest. This identifies three sets of issues to guide CIT research. First, the identification of a relevant meta-context within which the relationship and critical incident are set. Second, the inclusion of a time dimension – the history, present and future – of the relationship, together with changes over time in the internal and external contexts of the relationship, focuses on behaviours, dynamic perceptions and future expectations: the evaluation of the criticality of an incident can be influenced by all of these. Third, there is a situational dimension to the critical incident, which relates to the internal and external context of the relationship: the external context refers to those aspects outside the focal relationship and focal actors that may influence the relationship; the internal context refers to the actors' perceptions and behaviour outside the focal relationship (Edvardsson and Strandvik 2000).

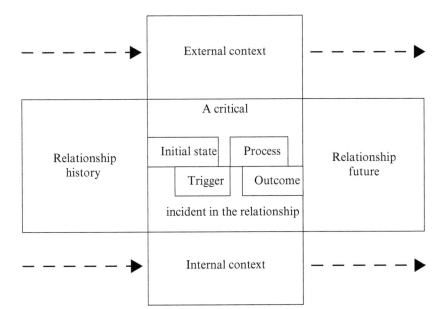

Source: Adapted from Edvardsson and Strandvik (2000: 85).

Figure 9.1   A general model of critical incidents in a relational context

RESEARCH PROCESS

An Explication Interview Approach to CIT

In this research, therefore, we aim to develop a refined and modified version of the critical incident approach which can be applied to a wide range of research contexts in entrepreneurship. We do this in the context of Churchill's (1990: 47–8) warning that 'it is possible . . . to articulate a methodology without genuinely knowing how to carry it out'. What we show in this section is the process of how to apply phenomenological explication within the context of case-study based CIT research.

The research approach is informed by Giorgi's (1985) four-step approach to phenomenological research and interpretative data analysis (Devenish 2002). First, it is important to gain a sense of the whole; that is, to gain an intuitive overview of the whole of the transcript. Second, within this the researcher focuses on the discrimination of meaning units focused on the phenomenon being researched (in this case, the value-added relationship between investor and firm). The purpose of this is to adopt a mind-set which allows for the practice of discovery rather than of verification as in conventional logical-empiricist studies. Third, having discriminated these meaning units the researcher transforms them from the subject's everyday expressions (their 'native categories' – Chapman and Buckley 2002) into entrepreneurship language with an emphasis on the phenomenon being investigated; that is, each natural meaning unit (in the subject's terminology) is interrogated for its essential meaning which is restated (or perhaps better, translated) by the researcher in terms suitable to the discipline. Finally, these translated and transformed meaning units are synthesized into a consistent statement of the structure of what has been learned from the interview; the researcher synthesizes and integrates the insights contained in the transformed meaning units into a consistent description of the entrepreneurial structure of the event (Giorgi 1985: 8–22).

In undertaking research in this vein, the researcher interviews the respondents, asks them to identify and reflect back on a critical incident in the development of the relationship (an incident which deviates significantly either positively or negatively from what is normal or expected) and relive that incident, its origins, characteristics and development. In keeping with the non-directive aspect of explication interviewing, the interviewer does not specifically prompt at the outset for the respondent to identify and summarize the nature of the content of the incident. Rather, they probe, if necessary and using non-directive questions, to identify how the incident was handled and who may have been involved in that process. This is for two reasons: first, to preserve the integrity of the research process itself and avoid leading the respondent to provide responses in line with our prior expectations (what is 'critical' to us as researchers with a prior focal interest in the topic may not be critical in practice); and second, to allow for the development of an 'emergent' understanding of the incident, as opposed to the 'prompted' approach of previous research). In other words, all data are collected, following Flanagan's protocol for CIT as amended in the light of the comments of Cope and Watts (2000), Urquhart et al. (2003) and Edvardsson and Strandvik (2000), using in-depth individual interviews.

Specifically, following Flanagan's (1954) five-stage CIT research process, and Urquhart et al.'s (2003) extension to cover explication interviewing, we recommend adopting the following research protocol:

General aims. We ask respondents to identify a 'contribution episode', which may be discrete and highly specific, or a more extended episode, in keeping with the Cope and Watts's (2001) definition. In either case, the situation is bounded, with some purpose (that is, they exclude the routine 'normal' day-to-day activity of interaction, which is, nevertheless, an important area for further study) and identified as such by the respondent. There is precedent in both the marketing (Grove and Fisk 1997) and entrepreneurship (Kaulio 2003) applications of CIT for the inclusion of multiple respondents playing different roles outside and inside (Neuhaus 1996) the organizational or service encounter context. Following the requirements of explication interviewing, where the primary interest in is encouraging the interviewee to relive the episode, we do not prompt respondents to reflect on the episodes articulated by the other, where we have multiple respondents, and we undertake to maintain the confidentiality of each interview.

Plans and specifications. In Flanagan's original methodology, the direct observation of behaviour was the responsibility of observers familiar with the activity, the groups whose behaviour was being studied should be specified and the behaviours should be categorized. The increasing use of interviews and questionnaires, rather than direct observation, has reduced the significance of this requirement, and most applications of CIT outside the health-care area involve academic social scientists rather than sector-experienced and qualified professionals. However, explication interviewing takes this a stage further; if adequate training and orientation is provided, there is no requirement that the interviewer be someone familiar with the activity described. Rather, the emphasis is on the integrity of the interview experience itself; while probing may be necessary, the emphasis in on encouraging the interviewee to relive the experience rather than fit it analytically into a framework introduced by the interviewer, either explicitly in the wording of the questions or implicitly in the nature of the interjections in the interview itself. To allow for reflection on the interview process itself, as well as to make available the responses for further analysis (for example, using content analysis, Ronan and Latham 1974, or discourse analysis, Wood and Kroger 2000), interviews are taped.

Data collection. Flanagan's original preference was for data collection through direct observation, although retrospective data collection was allowed for if the incident was relatively recent and fresh in the mind of the subject, and his account also allowed for data collection methods other than interview and direct observation. Explication interviewing is based explicitly on retrospective reflection in individual interviews, and while the respondent is usually directed to reflect on the 'most recent instance' of contribution, the focus can be wider than this. As discussed above, the explication technique is designed to aid recall and overcome the concerns about retrospective interviewing

(Ericsson and Simon 1984); the method is 'unstructured and focused but undirected' (Urquhart et al. 2003: 70) and interviewees are encouraged to talk with the minimum of intervention and direction from the interviewer. By comparison with conventional CIT studies, where sample sizes may be in the hundreds, explication-based studies are more commonly based around small samples, to ease the burden of data analysis using unstructured interview transcripts.

Data analysis. The richness of the data collected through explication interviewing makes possible a number of analysis techniques. We follow the practice of Chell (2004) in treating the data as a series of phenomenological interviews which are analysed as narratives (Burns et al. 2000), representing the accounts of the respondents. However, more detailed analysis could usefully approach analysis from the perspective of discourse analysis (Potter and Wetherell 1987; Wood and Kroger 2000; Dick 2004). Exploration of the analytical opportunities of the data sets generated from explication interviewing opens new opportunities for entrepreneurship research.

Interpreting and reporting results. As with many qualitative research approaches, it is important to acknowledge fully the limitations of the research approach (which might include potential researcher bias and the lack of representativeness in the cases selected as research sites). This points to the importance of the choice of research method and data collection technique on the definition of 'contribution' itself, and the relevance and applicability of a relatively neglected research methodology which, if more widely adopted and further refined, could significantly add to our knowledge and understanding of entrepreneurial phenomena.

Reflections on Explication Interviewing

We have already indicated that the explication technique offers a verbalization of activity, processing experience into reflection and taking subjects from pre-reflected to reflected experience and from experience as it was lived to experience that is represented and verbalized (Vermersch 1994: 80; Urquhart et al. 2003: 66). The intent is, through evocation – the reliving of an example of the activity being investigated – to help the subject recall the experience in the moment of performance of the activity and to take them deep into their recall rather than leave it at the superficial level of initial recall. What is important for the interviewer is to direct this evocation into the subject's experience only in relation to the concrete events occurring during the investor–entrepreneur interaction, or episode as we have discussed it above, and help them make their experiences explicit. This is not based on their general knowledge of or experience of such interactions but is instead based on them recalling and reliving what concrete processes related to the value-added contribution of investor–entrepreneur relations look like. This approach has a major advantage over a questionnaire-based approach commonly used in CIT studies; as Kim (2010: 255) points out, first-person reports generated from explication reveal multifaceted aspects related to the topic of research interest and are not purely subjective since these reports on first-person experience are accomplished with the help of another (the interviewer) and are therefore obtained from a second-person perspective.

For Urquhart et al. (2003: 67) the explication approach requires the following. First, the interviewer has to establish and maintain a state of evocation in the subject as it is this state that makes the detailed account and the accompanying reflection possible. Second, to do this the interviewer has to understand what an evocative state is, as something not unusual but with particular characteristics that must be understood, recognized and inspired. Third, this understanding begins with the recognition that evocation, and in particular the start of recollection about an event, frequently hinges on a specific sensory memory, for example, the colour scheme of the room in which the encounter took place or the aroma of the cologne the subject was wearing. These sensory memories may not themselves be critical or germane to the event being recalled but they are critical to the process of evocation, returning the subject to the relived experience of the event. Fourth, the interviewee, in focusing on a critical incident in this way and in answering a series of detailed questions, gives a qualitatively different account that that given in other research approaches (Vermersch 1994: 176–81). Specifically, explication interviewing makes possible a rich and fine-grained description of the incident expressed in a language which is less tailored for its audience (the researcher) than would otherwise be the case, and because the chronology of the incident is being experienced anew rather than being retold, there is less likelihood of the *post hoc* rationalization that is often found in retrospective accounts (Urquhart et al. 2003: 67).

In terms of process, explication interviewing follows a number of steps (see Urquhart et al. 2003 for more detail). First, given the in-depth rigorous nature of the method and to ensure compliance with relevant research ethics codes and approval protocols, a contract is agreed between the interviewer and the subject indicating their acceptance of being interviewed in depth about a critical incident. Second, subjects are encouraged to evoke a particular specific critical incident, and to focus in particular on a specific episode involving the activity so that it can be described in detail. As in CIT research more generally, it is important that a single occasion is chosen for the purposes of evocation, not least to encourage remembered detail rather that rationalizations and generalizations drawn from a pre-digested amalgam of memories from a series of occurrences. Third, the subject is encouraged to recollect the particular occasion/incident by sensorial questioning along the lines of 'Just put yourself back in the situation and tell me exactly what you did', 'Was it morning or afternoon?', 'Where did the incident take place?' and 'Can you describe the location?'

Fourth, the interviewer should not sit directly in front of the subject as this interferes with their ability to stare into space and dissociate from the immediate surroundings of the interview, essential for evocation to occur: in a 'normal' face-to-face encounter the subject will be encouraged to return their gaze to the interviewer and their thoughts to the present. Fifth, to maintain focus on the specific incident the subject is steered away from comments in the form of generalizations and comments of the 'Whenever I am in this situation . . .'. If opinions are expressed, the interviewer has to determine, by probing (gently and in a non-directive manner), whether these were thought at the time in the past being relived or are post-incident reflections, in which case they are dismissed as not part of the description of the incident as if the subject were conducting it again.

Sixth, the interviewer asks prompting questions to maintain the flow of the interview. Often these are of the clarifying ('You said X. Have I understood?') or echoing ('When you say you did X what did you do?') kind. Closed and leading questions are avoided, as are questions that introduce the interviewer's presuppositions into the dialogue. Specifically, Urquhart et al. (2003: 68) suggest that inaccurate assumptions about how a subject thinks tend to be more disruptive to evocation than inappropriate assumptions about what is being thought: a question of the form 'What did you see, or hear, or think or whatever?' is more helpful to the process than 'What did you see?' Seventh, evocation takes time, and the interviewer may need to engage in relevant and non-intrusive interruption and probing to elicit the fine detail of the incident in the recall process. In so doing it is important not to encourage the subject into a judgemental mode of thinking which requires interpretation rather than recall: 'Why?' questions prompt rationalizations and justifications; 'How?' and 'What?' questions carefully phrased can elicit the reasons for an answer without prompting justification (for example, 'What were you thinking at the moment when X'). Finally, within these parameters, interviewers have considerable flexibility in the approach to explication interviewing, and are free to try whatever approach that might work to encourage evocation, recognizing that what will work in one case may not work in another. In all cases, however, it remains the case that the subject's experience is paramount and that researchers 'may only explore aspects of interest

to them by probing in relevant places, giving focus, without direction'
(Urquhart et al. 2003: 69).

The interview in general, as an encounter-based data collection process,
has been described in terms of 'individuals directing their attention
towards each other with the purpose of opening up the possibility of
gaining an insight into the experiences, concerns, interests, beliefs, values,
knowledge and ways of seeing, thinking and acting of the other' (Schostak
2006: 10). Explication interviewing offers a very specific means of opening
up the subject's relived experience of an event. As such, the emphasis
on the primacy of the subject's experience over the researcher's presuppositions and prior structures and frameworks is consistent with what
Rabaté (2002) calls hystericization, the continual subjecting of author-
ized knowledge, expertise and any notion of the absolute. As Schostak
(2006: 8) puts it:

> We all ask questions, all the time. However, how we ask questions and how we
> reflect upon the answers provided will determine what we say we 'know' and
> 'believe', will influence our relations with others, the world and our actions and
> thus determine the possibility for emancipatory writing and action.

For entrepreneurship researchers, explication interviewing, discussed
here in the context of case-based critical incident analysis, offers a rich
opportunity to respond to this challenge.

CONCLUSION

There are several outcomes from this research. First, in combining
case-based research and a dyadic research design with a modified CIT
approach, we provide a guide to a methodological procedure that has
great potential in the entrepreneurship domain. Specifically, the adoption
of a relational approach to CIT, the identification of critical episodes
rather than isolated discrete critical incidents and the development of an
explication-based interviewing protocol rather than more conventional
qualitative interview techniques to collect retrospective data, can provide
a platform for an innovative approach to exploratory research in entrepreneurship and generate additional insights into the phenomenon of
interest.

NOTES

1. Note in this context that although Chell (2004) refers to social constructionist and phenomenological perspectives as one, and both schools of thought encompass a wide variety of approaches, there are differences between them as underlying philosophies of qualitative research (Burr 1995; Madill et al. 2000; Moran 2000).
2. This is itself a significant change of emphasis from both Flanagan's original specification and from most other applications of CIT, which involves shifting attention from the topic – incident – to the data collection protocol – interview. In our view, this is a potential and unnecessary implicit restriction of the domain application of CIT, and our analysis is based in part on the development of a deeper understanding of the 'incident' itself.

REFERENCES

Anderson, L. and S. Wilson (1997), 'Critical incident technique', in D.L. Whetzel and G.R. Wheaton (eds), *Applied Measurement Methods in Industrial Psychology*, Palo Alto, CA: Davies-Black, pp. 89–112.

Andersson, B.E. and Nilsson, S.G. (1964), 'Studies in the reliability and validity of the critical incident technique', *Journal of Applied Psychology*, **48** (6), 398–403.

Antaki, C. (1988), *Analysing Everyday Explanation: A Casebook of Methods*, London: Sage.

Arnold, M.J., K.E. Reynolds, N. Ponder and J.E. Lueg (2004), 'Customer delight in a retail context: investigating delightful and terrible shopping experiences', *Journal of Business Research*, **58** (8), 1132–45.

Atherton, A. and Hannon, P. (1999), 'The innovation process in the small business: an analysis of its structure, dynamics and constituent parts', paper presented at the ICSB Global Conference, available at: http://wwwsbanet.uca.edu/Research/1999/ICSB/99ics238.htm (accessed 8 January 2002).

Bitner, M.J., B.H. Booms and L.A. Mohr (1994), 'Critical service encounters: the employee's viewpoint', *Journal of Marketing*, **58** (1), 95–106.

Bitner, M.J., B.H. Booms and M.S. Tetreault (1990), 'The service encounter: diagnosing favourable and unfavourable incidents', *Journal of Marketing*, **54** (1), 71–84.

Bradfield, M. and K. Aquino (1999), 'The effects of blame attributions and offender likableness on forgiveness and revenge in the workplace', *Journal of Management*, **25** (5), 607–31.

Brewer, J.D. (2000), *Ethnography*, Buckingham: Open University Press.

Burns, A.C., L.A. Williams and J. Maxham, III (2000), 'Narrative text biases attending the critical incidents', *Qualitative Market Research: An International Journal*, **3** (4), 178–86.

Burr, V. (1995), *An Introduction to Social Constructionism*, London: Routledge.

Callan, R.J. (1998), 'The critical incident technique in hospitality research: an illustration from the UK lodge sector', *Tourism Management*, **19** (1), 93–8.

Chapman, M. and P. Buckley (2002), 'The use of native categories in management research', *British Journal of Management*, **8** (4), 283–99.

Chell, E. (2004), 'Critical incident technique', in C. Cassell and G. Symon (eds), *Essential Guide to Qualitative Methods in Organizational Research*, Thousand Oaks, CA: Sage.

Chell, E. and K. Allman (2003), 'Mapping the motivations and intentions of technology orientated entrepreneurs', *R&D Management*, **33** (2), 117–34.

Chell, E. and L. Pittaway (1998), 'A study of entrepreneurship in the restaurant and café industry: exploratory work using the critical incident technique as a methodology', *Hospitality Management*, **17** (1), 23–32.

Churchill, S.D. (1990), 'Considerations for teaching a phenomenological approach to psychological research', *Journal of Phenomenological Psychology*, **21** (1), 46–67.

Cope, J. (2003), 'Entrepreneurial learning and critical reflection', *Management Learning*, **34** (4), 429–50.

Cope, J. and Watts, G. (2000), 'Learning by doing. An exploration of experience, critical incidents and reflection in entrepreneurial learning', *International Journal of Entrepreneurial Behaviour and Research*, **6** (3), 104–24.

Curran, J. and R.A. Blackburn (2001), *Researching the Small Enterprise*, London: Sage.

Curran, J., R. Jarvis, R.A. Blackburn and S. Black (1992), 'Networks and small firms: constructs, methodological strategies and some findings', *International Small Business Journal*, **11** (2), 13–25.

Davey, K.M. and G. Symon (2001), 'Recent approaches to the qualitative analysis of organizational culture', in C.L. Cooper, S. Cartwright and C. Earley (eds), *The International Handbook of Organizational Culture and Climate*, Chichester: Wiley, pp. 123–42.

Deakins, D. and Freel, M. (1998), 'Entrepreneurial learning and the growth process in SMEs', *The Learning Organization: An International Journal*, **5** (3), 144–55.

Derbaix, C and J. Vanhamme (2003), 'Inducing word-of-mouth by eliciting surprise – a pilot investigation', *Journal of Economic Psychology*, **24** (1), 99–116.

Devenish, S. (2002), 'An applied method for undertaking phenomenological explication of interview transcripts', *The Indo-Pacific Journal of Phenomenology*, **2** (1), 1–20.

Dick, P. (2004), 'Discourse analysis', in C. Cassell and G. Symon (eds), *Essential Guide to Qualitative Methods in Organizational Research*, Thousand Oaks, CA: Sage, pp. 203–13.

Edvardsson, B. and I. Roos (2001), 'Critical incident techniques: towards a framework for analysing the criticality of critical incidents', *International Journal of Service Industry Management*, **12** (4), 251–68.

Edvardsson, B. and Strandvik, T. (2000), 'Is a critical incident critical for a customer relationship?', *Managing Service Quality*, **10** (2), 82–91.

Ericsson, K.A. and Simon, H. (1984), *Protocol Analysis: Verbal Reports as Data*, Cambridge, MA: MIT Press.

Flanagan, J.C. (1954), 'The critical incident technique', *Psychological Bulletin*, **51** (4), 327–58.

Gartner, W.B. and S. Birley (2002), 'Introduction to the special issue on qualitative methods in entrepreneurship research', *Journal of Business Venturing*, **17** (5), 387–95.

Garud, R. and A.H. Van de Ven (1992), 'An empirical evaluation of the internal corporate venturing process', *Strategic Management Journal*, **13** (1), 93–109.

Giorgi, A. (ed.) (1985), *Phenomenology and Psychological Research*, Pittsburgh, PA: Duquesne University Press.

Grove, S.J. and Fisk, R.P. (1992), 'Observational data collection methods for services marketing: an overview', *Journal of the Academy of Marketing Science*, **20** (3), 217–24.

Grove, S.J. and Fisk, R.P. (1997), 'The impact of other customers on service experiences: a critical incident examination of "getting along"', *Journal of Retailing*, **73** (1), 63–85.

Gundry, L.K. and Rousseau, D.M. (1994), 'Critical incidents in communicating culture to newcomers: the meaning is the message', *Human Relations*, **47** (9), 1063–88.

Jackson, M.S., G.N. White and C.L. Schmierer (1996), 'Tourism experiences within an attributional framework', *Annals of Tourism Research*, **23** (4), 798–810.

Jones, M.A. (1999), 'Entertaining shopping experiences: an exploratory investigation', *Journal of Retailing and Consumer Services*, **6** (3), 129–39.

Jorgensen, D.L. (1989), *Participant Observation: A Methodology for Human Studies*, Newbury Park, CA: Sage.

Kaulio, M.A. (2003), 'Initial conditions or processes of development? Critical incidents in the early stages of new ventures', *R&D Management*, **33** (2), 165–75.

Kemppainen, J.K. (2000), 'The critical incident technique and nursing care quality research', *Journal of Advanced Nursing*, **32** (3), 1264–71.

Kim, J.H. (2010), 'Towards embodiment-based research on musical expressiveness', in S. Flach, D. Marguilies and J. Söffner (eds), *Habitus in Habitat I: Emotion and Motion*, Berne: Peter Lang, pp. 245–63.

Latham, G., L.M. Saari, E.D. Pursell and M.A. Campion (1980), 'The situational interview', *Journal of Applied Psychology*, **65** (4), 422–7.

Lorenzoni, N. and B.R. Lewis (2004), 'Service recovery in the airline industry: a cross-cultural comparison of the attitudes and behaviours of British and Italian front-line personnel', *Managing Service Quality*, **14** (1), 11–25.

Madill, A., A. Jordan and C. Shirley (2000), 'Objectivity and reliability in qualitative analysis: realist, contextualist and radical constructivist epistemologies', *British Journal of Psychology*, **91** (1), 1–20.

Mallak, L.A., D.M. Lyth, S.D. Olson, S.M. Ulshafer and F.J. Sardone (2003), 'Diagnosing culture in health-care organizations using critical incidents', *International Journal of Health Care Quality Assurance*, **16** (4), 180–90.

Mitchell, K.E., G.M. Alliger and R. Morfopoulos (1997), 'Toward an ADA-appropriate job analysis', *Human Resource Management Review*, **7** (1), 5–26.

Moran, D. (2000), *Introduction to Phenomenology*, London: Routledge.

Muylle, S., R. Moenaert and M. Despontin (2004), 'The conceptualisation and empirical validation of web site user satisfaction', *Information & Management*, **41** (5), 543–60.

Nandram, S.S. (2002), 'Behavioural attributes of entrepreneurial success and failure', paper presented to Small Business and Enterprise Development Conference, Nottingham, 15–16 April.

Neergaard, H. and Ulhøi, J.P. (eds) (2004), *Handbook of Qualitative Research Methods in Entrepreneurship*, Cheltenham, UK and Northampton, MA, USA: Edward Elgar.

Neuhaus, P. (1996), 'Critical incidents in internal customer-supplier relationships: results of an empirical study', in T.A. Schwartz, D.E. Bowen and S.W. Brown (eds), *Advances in Services Marketing and Management*, vol. 5, Greenwich, CT: JAI Press, pp. 283–313.

Olsen, M.J.S. (1996), 'The critical episode model as a tool for organizational learning in service organizations', in B. Edvardsson and S. Modell (eds), *Service Management*, Stockholm: Nerenius & Santérus Förlag AB.

Ölvingson, C., N. Hallberg, T. Timpka and R.A. Greenes (2002), 'Using the critical incident technique to define a minimal data set for requirements elicitation in public health', *International Journal of Medical Informatics*, **68** (1–3), 165–74.

Piaget, J. (1977), *Recherches sur l'abstraction reflechissante*, ed. and trans. R.L. Campbell (2000), *Studies in Reflecting Abstraction*, Hove: Psychology Press.

Pilemalm, S., N. Hallberg and T. Timpka (2001), 'How do shop stewards perceive their situation and tasks? Preconditions for support of union work', *Economic and Industrial Democracy*, **22** (4), 569–99.

Potter, J. and m. Wetherall (1987), *Discourse and Social Psychology: Beyond Attitudes And Behaviour*, London: Sage.

Pursell, E.D., M.A. Campion and S.A. Gaylord (1980), 'Structured interviewing: avoiding selection problems', *Personnel Journal*, **59** (1), 907–12.

Rabaté, J.-M. (2002), *The Future of Theory*, Oxford: Blackwell.

Ronan, W.W. and G.P. Latham (1974), 'The reliability and validity of the critical incident technique: a closer look', *Studies in Personnel Psychology*, **6** (1), 53–64.

Roos, I. (1999), 'Switching processes in customer relationships', *Journal of Services Research*, **2** (1), 68–85.

Ruben, B.D. (1993), 'What patients remember: a content analysis of critical incidents in health care', *Health Communication*, **5** (2), 99–112.

Schostak, J. (2006), *Interviewing and Representation in Qualitative Research*, Maidenhead: Open University Press.

Schultz, M. and M.J. Hatch (1996), 'Living with multiple paradigms: the case of paradigm interplay in organizational culture studies', *Academy of Management Review*, **21** (2), 529–57.

Stokes, D. (2000), 'Entrepreneurial marketing: a conceptualisation from qualitative research', *Qualitative Market Research: An International Journal*, **3** (1), 47–54.

Strauss, B. and B. Weinlich (1997), 'Process-oriented measurement of service quality: applying the sequential incident method', *European Journal of Marketing*, **31** (1), 33–55.

Thompson, C.J., W.B. Locander and H.R. Pollio (1989), 'Putting consumer experience back into consumer research: the philosophy and method of existential phenomenology', *Journal of Consumer Research*, **16** (September), 133–47.

Tjosvold, D. and D. Weicker (1993), 'Cooperative and competitive networking by entrepreneurs: a critical incident study', *Journal of Small Business Management*, **31** (1), 11–21.

Urquhart, C., A. Light, R. Thomas, A. Barker, A. Yeoman, J. Coope et al. (2003), 'Critical incident technique and explication interviewing in studies of information behavior', *Library & Information Science Research*, **25** (1), 63–88.

Vermersch, P (1994), *L'entretien d'explicitation* (*The Explicitation Interview*), Paris: ESF.

Waddington, D. (2004), 'Participant observation', in C. Cassell and G. Symon (eds), *Essential Guide to Qualitative Methods in Organizational Research*, Thousand Oaks, CA: Sage, pp. 154–64.

White, F.M. and Locke, E.A. (1981), 'Perceived determinants of high and low productivity in three occupational groups: a critical incident study', *Journal of Management Studies*, **18** (4), 375–87.

Wong, A and A. Sohal (2003), 'A critical incident approach to the examination of customer relationship management in a retail chain: an exploratory study', *Qualitative Market Research: An International Journal*, **6** (4), 248–62.

Wood, L.A. and R.O. Kroger (2000), *Doing Discourse Analysis: Methods for Studying Action in Talk*, London: Sage.

Critical incident technique: some conclusions
Claire M. Leitch

Despite its relatively long history the critical incident technique has not been widely adopted in entrepreneurship. However, as all of the three chapters in this section demonstrate well, the qualitative variant of the technique can potentially bring additional insights to the complex phenomena comprising entrepreneurship. In particular, increased knowledge and appreciation of the scope of this technique can go some way to addressing many commentators' concerns with the relative paucity of good quality empirical research into entrepreneurial activity: 'the field is in desperate need of more and better empirical studies' (Deeds 2014: 10).

The technique is flexible, which can be both a strength and a limitation. Its strength lies in its ability to provide access to intangible issues and present complex textual descriptions of how people experience the research issue under consideration. As Chell emphasizes, it exposes actions, attitudes feelings and orientations to situations. This, she believes, makes it more powerful than a conventional qualitative interview in that it exposes the assumptions and critical events which have shaped behaviours and actions as well as the thoughts and decisions which underpinned them.

This perspective alleviates Leitch and Hill's concern that through incomplete understanding of the technique it may inadvertently be employed as a generic qualitative interview. Thus, they present a guiding framework to ensure that scholars remain as close as possible to Flanagan's (1954) guiding principles. It is by maintaining the integrity of the technique, they suggest, that researchers are more likely to achieve high-quality data which can be subsequently analysed and abstracted to advance understanding and knowledge.

In addition to reflexivity on the part of researchers the technique also requires it on the respondents' behalf. Through encouraging a considered response and going beyond mere description, to a particular incident context, respondents are more likely to provide thoughtful accounts of feelings and behaviours instead of simply descriptive or overly critical accounts. Specifically, by capturing insights into both positive and negative incidents a more holistic perspective of a phenomenon can be obtained. However, all interviews can be beset with the twin problems of retrospection, associated with issues of self-censoring and recall bias, and introspection, where a respondent has not engaged in the analysis of experiences and emotions. As a means of overcoming these, Harrison recommends the incorporation of the explication interview into the technique. To assist researchers he advances a five-stage research protocol and offers specific reflections on evocation, whereby respondents are asked to relive an activity at a deep rather than a superficial level.

As outlined in the overview to this section and in Harrison's chapter, critical incident technique is used to collect direct observations of human behaviours to facilitate their usefulness in solving practical problems. However, as Chell demonstrates, the phenomenological qualitative variant can also be employed to deconstruct theory, test it and rebuild new theory. Of specific importance, this is achieved through understanding actors' perspectives, language, behaviours and actions in the contexts in which they operate. In so doing, this technique has much to offer practitioners and policy-makers.

Each of the chapters in this section has highlighted the importance of accessing in a robust way an actor's re-lived experience of an entrepreneurial event or action, and each of the methodological approaches outlined has the potential to provide valuable insights for the intellectual development of the domain as well as for practice and the creation of policy.

REFERENCES

Deeds, D. (2014), 'Thoughts on the challenge of empirical research in entrepreneurship', in A. Carsrud and M. Brännback (eds), *Handbook of Research Methods and Applications in Entrepreneurship and Small Business*, Cheltenham, UK and Northampton, MA, USA: Edward Elgar, pp. 10–19.
Flanagan, J.C. (1954), 'The critical incident technique', *Psychological Bulletin*, **51** (4), 327–58.

PART IV

FOCUS GROUPS

Provenance and use of focus groups
John Watson and Rick Newby

INTRODUCTION

Blackburn and Stokes (2000: 48) suggest that focus groups have been 'relatively under used' in entrepreneurship research and that part of the reason for this might be a lack of understanding by researchers of 'what rigorously conducted focus groups can achieve'. With this in mind, the aim of this section is to provide the reader with a greater awareness of the potential for conducting focus group studies in entrepreneurship research, and specific guidance on how to organize and conduct various types of focus groups. As a qualitative research method, focus groups are particularly helpful in allowing researchers to discover not only what people think about a particular issue, but also 'why they think the way they do' (Easton et al. 2003: 719).

Nature and Purpose of Focus Groups

Led by a moderator/facilitator, focus group participants will typically be gathered around a table to discuss a particular topic of interest. Focus groups represent a qualitative method for simultaneously exploring the views and perceptions of a number of individuals about an issue, and would normally be conducted at either the beginning or end of a research project. For example, focus groups can be conducted at the beginning of a project as a precursor to a survey (Frey and Fontana 1991). Here the goal might simply be to check the wording of questions. Alternatively, the researchers may be looking to focus group discussions to stimulate their thinking and help generate hypotheses for subsequent testing. In this case the researchers would be in an exploratory phase and the focus group methodology would be employed to learn more about the phenomenon or topic under investigation (Calder 1977). Focus groups can also be used at the end (or in the latter stages) of a project to help interpret questionnaire (or other quantitative) data 'for which explanations might otherwise have to be conjectural' (Deri et al. 1948: 257), thereby contributing to a better understanding and interpretation of the material gathered.

History of Focus Groups

Although the focus group technique was discussed in 1926 by Bogardus (1926) and was mentioned occasionally in the subsequent decades, it did not become widely used until the 1950s (Basch 1987; Frey and Fontana 1991). The eventual wide-ranging adoption of the focus group technique appears to have resulted from a perceived commercial need for richer data than could be gained from market research and opinion polling (Guilford 1931; Peterson and Thurstone 1933; Lazarsfeld and Fiske 1938). Merton (1987) credits Paul Lazarfeld from the World War II (US) Office of Radio Research with re-acquainting academic researchers with the focus group method. During and after World War II, the method was used to study the social impact of mass communication, particularly the effectiveness of propaganda (Merton and Kendall 1946; Merton et al. 1956).

While opinion polling and market research originated in the US during the 1920s and 1930s, the mass-observation movement originated in the UK in 1937 (Madge and Harrisson 1939). The focus of mass-observation was those people who appeared not to have an opinion when polled about various political isues and likely election outcomes. This, often large, group in society was being ignored by the more quantitative polling techniques of the day. It was also suggested that 'public opinion could not just be mechanically measured by questionnaires' (Moran 2008: 834). Mass-observation, therefore, seems to have been a major driver for the use of focus groups in Britain (Hubble 2006; Moran 2008; Phillips 2009).

Merton and Kendall's (1946) article extolling the virtues of, and outlining the procedures involved with, the focused interview appeared to provide a clear impetus for greater use of this qualitative technique, particularly in the realm of marketing. Subsequently, Shapiro (1952) became a strong advocate of the group interview method arguing that it saved time and money, reduced bias, and allowed greater interviewer control.

Although the use of focus groups was being widely promoted in the 1950s, particularly for marketing purposes, the technique did not start to gain prominence in academic circles until the 1990s. Based on a search of EBSCOhost research databases (EBSCO Publishing 2011), Figure IV.1 tracks the number of articles published in peer-reviewed journals using the subject term 'focus groups'. As can be seen from Figure IV.1, it was not until the early 1990s that the focus group method started to gain prominence as a qualitative research method within the academic community, with its popularity showing no signs of waning. Indeed, almost three-quarters of the articles using the subject term 'focus groups' were published in the period 2006 to 2010.

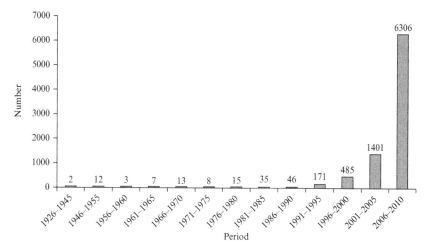

Figure IV.1 *'Focus groups' as a subject term for peer-reviewed articles in EBSCOhost*

Advantages of Focus Groups

From a review of the literature (see, for example, Goldman 1962; Fern 1982a; Basch 1987; Frey and Fontana 1991; Morgan 1996) there appear to be at least ten potential advantages associated with the use of focus groups as a qualitative research method.

- They provide a relatively easy way of learning about the opinions of sub-groups within society, for example: entrepreneurs; nascent entrepreneurs; or female entrepreneurs.
- By using audio (or audio-visual) recording equipment the researcher can obtain a permanent record of the verbal (or verbal and non-verbal) communication between group members.
- They provide a particularly flexible method of inquiry because they can be conducted with just a few individuals or a larger group (twelve or more). They can also be used in a cross-sectional design to obtain opinions at a particular point in time, or longitudinally to examine changes in opinions over time.
- Involving participants in a form of group interview will generally be less costly than conducting one-on-one personal interviews with an equivalent number of individuals.
- The turnaround time with a group interview is considerably shorter

than would be the case with in-depth interviews conducted with a similar number of individuals.

- With individual interviews the interaction is limited to the interviewer and the respondent, while in a focus group there is much more interaction between participants. This interaction can potentially provide additional explanations for, and a deeper understanding of, the views held by the group.
- In a focus group situation the moderator can probe comments as they arise to judge the reaction of the other group members, again providing potentially more depth than would be the case in an interview situation.
- It is also likely that 'group pressures may inhibit individuals from providing misleading information' (Basch 1987: 434).
- Because the focus group participants will often have similar backgrounds (and because participants may have had the opportunity to relax over some light refreshments prior to the focus group commencing) they might be more willing to voice their true feelings than would be the case in a face-to-face interview with a complete stranger.
- Consistent with a number of the previously stated advantages, proponents of the focus group method argue that the sum of the responses from a group will exceed the sum of the individual responses; that is, 'two heads are better than one'.

Disadvantages of Focus Groups

While a number of advantages associated with focus groups have been advanced, there are also some potential disadvantages that need to be recognized. Fern (1982b) notes that many of the advantages listed above have not been subjected to scientific testing, and where they have been formally tested the results suggest the stated benefits are marginal, at best. For example, Fern (1982b) found that participants interviewed in a group situation generated fewer ideas in total than an equivalent number of participants involved in one-on-one interviews; that is, there were diminishing returns (in terms of idea generation) to focus group size. However, even though the total number of ideas produced by a focus group might be less, the cost per idea generated should also be less than would be the case with individual interviews. Further, although there may be diminishing returns in terms of idea generation, the additional interaction between group members can potentially provide additional explanations for (and a deeper understanding of) the ideas and views held by the group, compared to an individual interview.

In terms of specific disadvantages associated with the focus group method, the literature (Fern 1982a; Basch 1987; Kaplowitz and Hoehn 2001) suggests eight that entrepreneurship researchers should be particularly aware of.

- Focus groups are not useful for testing hypotheses in the tradition of experimental design.
- The results from focus groups are generally not appropriate for drawing inferences about larger populations; that is, they should not be generalized.
- Only individuals who are capable and willing to verbalize their views can be studied in a focus group.
- Dominant group members may result in incomplete or biased information if other members are reluctant to speak out.
- Given the lack of anonymity, some participants might be reluctant to provide their true feelings about an issue, particularly if they believe their views to be controversial and not in keeping with those of the other group members.
- It is possible that the ideas raised and the views expressed by the group could reflect 'groupthink' rather than being representative of the diversity of views held by the wider population.
- In preparing transcripts from audio or video tapes, it is not always possible to hear all the comments, particularly if some group members are quietly spoken or if a number of participants are making points simultaneously. Further, the transcription process and subsequent analysis of the transcripts can be time consuming and can significantly delay a research project.
- There is also the issue of observer dependency, that is, the extent to which the responses provided by the group members are influenced by the researcher.

Note that, as discussed in the following chapters, many of these potential disadvantages can be minimized in a well-designed focus group run by an experienced moderator.

Types of Focus Group

While Wikipedia (2011) lists a number of different types of focus group, the following chapters will look specifically at three alternatives: the traditional face-to-face focus group; face-to-face focus groups undertaken using Group Support System (GSS) software; and online focus groups. While there have been a number of entrepreneurship studies that have used the traditional method, we felt that both the GSS and online focus group methodologies offered some potentially important advantages over the traditional method. For example, the GSS method is particularly useful for: ensuring that the discussion is not dominated by a few assertive individuals; maximizing the contribution of all members, as participants can enter comments simultaneously thus permiting each group member to have more time to contribute ideas; and overcoming a reluctance by some group members to contribute because of concerns they may be ridiculed for asking 'foolish' questions or making unpopular comments. With online focus groups there is the added advantage of being able to include individuals from remote areas (different geographical regions) who might find it difficult to attend a traditional focus group because of the travel required.

The advantages and disadvantages of using each of these focus group methodologies is further examined in the following three chapters, which also explain how to organize and conduct a focus group using each technique. Each chapter draws on past studies to highlight how the particular technique being discussed has been used in prior research.

REFERENCES

Basch, C.E. (1987), 'Focus group interview: an underutilized research technique for improving theory and practice in health education', *Health Education & Behavior*, **14** (4), 411–448.

Blackburn, R. and D. Stokes (2000), 'Breaking down the barriers: using focus groups to research small and medium-sized enterprises', *International Small Business Journal*, **19** (1), 44–67.

Bogardus, E.S. (1926), 'The group interview', *Journal of Applied Sociology*, **10** (1), 372–82.

Calder, B.J. (1977), 'Focus groups and the nature of qualitative marketing research', *Journal of Marketing Research*, **14** (3), 353–64.

Deri, S., D. Dinnerstein, J. Harding and A.D. Pepitone (1948), 'Techniques for the diagnosis and measurement of intergroup attitudes and behavior', *Psychological Bulletin*, **45** (3), 248–71.

Easton, G., A. Easton and M. Belch (2003), 'An experimental investigation of electronic focus groups', *Information & Management*, **40** (8), 717–27.

EBSCO Publishing (2011), 'EBSCOhost research databases', EBSCO Publishing, accessed 28 March 2011.

Fern, E.F. (1982a), 'Why do focus groups work: a review and integration of small group process theories', *Advances in Consumer Research*, **9** (1), 444–51.

Fern, E.F. (1982b), 'The use of focus groups for idea generation: the effects of group size, acquaintanceship, and moderator on response quantity and quality', *Journal of Marketing Research*, **19** (1), 1–13.

Frey, J.H. and A. Fontana (1991), 'The group interview in social research', *Social Science Journal*, **28** (2), 175–87.

Goldman, A.E. (1962), 'The group depth interview', *Journal of Marketing*, **26** (3), 61–8.

Guilford, J.P. (1931), 'Racial preferences of a thousand American university students', *Journal of Social Psychology*, **2** (2), 179–204.

Hubble, N. (2006), *Mass-observation and Everyday Life: Culture, History, Theory*, Houndmills: Palgrave Macmillan.

Kaplowitz, M.D. and J.P. Hoehn (2001), 'Do focus groups and individual interviews reveal the same information for natural resource valuation?', *Ecological Economics*, **36** (2), 237–47.

Lazarsfeld, P. and M. Fiske (1938), 'The "panel" as a new tool for measuring opinion', *Public Opinion Quarterly*, **2** (4), 596–612.

Madge, C. and T. Harrisson (1939), *Britain by Mass-observation*, Harmondsworth: Penguin.

Merton, R.K. (1987), 'The focussed interview and focus groups: continuities and discontinuities', *Public Opinion Quarterly*, **51** (4), 550–66.

Merton, R.K. and P.L. Kendall (1946), 'The focused interview', *American Journal of Sociology*, **51** (6), 541–57.

Merton, R.K., M. Fiske and P.L. Kendall (1956), *The Focused Interview: A Manual of Problems and Procedures*, Glencoe, IL: Free Press.

Moran, J. (2008), 'Mass-observation, market research, and the birth of the focus group, 1937–1997', *Journal of British Studies*, **47** (4), 827–51.

Morgan, D.L. (1996), 'Focus groups', *Annual Review of Sociology*, **22** (1), 129–52.

Peterson, R.C. and L.L. Thurstone (1933), *Motion Pictures and the Social Attitudes of Children*, New York: Macmillan.

Phillips, A. (2009), 'History has a lot to teach us about the future of market research', *International Journal of Market Research*, **51** (4), 556–8.

Shapiro, E.P. (1952), 'The group interview as a tool of research', *Journal of Marketing*, **16** (4), 452–4.

Wikipedia (2011), 'Focus group', 14 March.

10 Conducting a traditional focus group
John Watson, Rick Newby, Helle Neergaard and Robert Smith

INTRODUCTION

Much of the empirical research on small and medium enterprises (SMEs) has relied heavily on cross-sectional survey methodologies (mail and/or telephone). However, as closed-ended questions effectively require appropriate pre-knowledge of the area under study they are less likely (compared to more qualitative, open-ended questions) to present an exhaustive picture of a relatively unknown area of interest. Worse still, asking closed-ended questions may simply result in confirming the researcher's expectations without the researcher knowing that important detail is being missed.

One way to generate broader qualitative data is through face-to-face interviews. However, Blackburn and Stokes (2000) argue that this method may suffer from the same inherent flaw as surveys, in that business owners may try to give an 'expected' answer rather than an accurate picture of themselves or their business. Blackburn and Stokes (2000) suggest that such difficulties can potentially be overcome through the use of a focus group approach because participants may feel more comfortable about sharing their feelings and experiences within a group of peers. The psychological security derived from group membership may be particularly relevant to researching owner-managers as it is likely that such individuals will be more open about their views when interacting with other owner-managers rather than in a one-on-one interview with a researcher (particularly if there is a perceived 'culture gap'). It should also be noted that participants are more likely to be candid in a group situation because the focus is on the group and the ideas it generates rather than on the individual. A further benefit attributed to face-to-face focus groups (over other qualitative methods such as personal interviews) is the additional insights that can be gained from the interaction of group members as each speaker provides a platform upon which others can contribute, rather than only responding to a pre-determined list of questions. Given these benefits, and the fact that focus groups can be used in any situation where people's perceptions (or views) are of interest, its limited use 'as a research tool by academics studying entrepreneurs and small businesses is perhaps surprising' (Blackburn and Stokes 2000: 48).

The traditional focus group comprises a single moderator controlling/ overseeing an interactive group discussion where participants are free to talk with other group members in response to issues/questions raised. These discussions are usually captured with audio (or audio-visual) recording equipment. In the remainder of this chapter we provide some guiding principles that should be followed when conducting a traditional focus group discussion. These include decisions concerning: the number and nature of participants; the number of focus groups to be conducted; the focus group structure; selecting a suitable venue; choice of moderator; and how to run the focus group session. We then discuss, in some detail, two very different SME focus group studies to illustrate how these principles have been applied 'in practice'.

DECIDING ON THE NUMBER OF FOCUS GROUPS

Usually, several focus groups are held to ensure that a broad cross-section of views and opinions are canvassed on the topic of interest. At a minimum we would recommend holding two focus groups because it is unlikely that researchers could feel confident about achieving a satisfactory outcome on the basis of a single group discussion. This is particularly so given some of the potential difficulties that can arise when conducting focus groups, for example: the recording equipment may prove faulty; a significant number of participants may fail to show up; a very vocal/disruptive participant may stifle discussion; and, if there are too many very quiet participants, it might be hard to generate adequate discussion.

Ideally, additional focus groups should be conducted until no more new ideas are being generated (if the study is 'exploratory' in nature) or until there appears to be a reasonable consensus among the participants (if the study is 'confirmatory' in nature). In practical terms, however, focus groups take considerable planning and can be costly to run (particularly if a professional moderator is being used and participants are being provided with some recompense for giving up their time to participate) and, therefore, it would be normal practice to decide on the number of focus groups to be conducted at the outset. This would almost certainly be the case where a grant or other form of funding is being sought for the project.

In this situation three key factors need to be considered when deciding on (and justifying) the number of focus group sessions to be conducted. First is the nature of the study; 'exploratory' versus 'confirmatory'. Usually, 'exploratory' focus groups are run with fewer participants (than 'confirmatory' focus groups) and, therefore, more focus group sessions are required to achieve a reasonable outcome. Second is the number of differing participant characteristics being considered. For example, if we are examining SME owners as one homogeneous group then a minimum of two focus groups would be required. If, however, we are interested in the views of 'nascent' versus 'established' business owners then a minimum of four focus groups is likely to be required (two for each demographic group). Third, while it is clear that the greater the number of focus groups held the more confidence the researcher(s) can have in the outcomes (and the easier it is likely to be to get the findings published), it is important to note that, typically, there are diminishing returns with each additional focus group.

DECIDING ON THE NUMBER AND NATURE OF PARTICIPANTS

While there is no ideal size for a focus group, it is generally accepted that the most effective focus groups are those with between eight and 12 participants (Fern 1982). If the group is too large some participants may become frustrated because they are unable to adequately express their views, particularly where there are a number of dominant participants and there is limited time available for each question. Note that this problem is likely to be made worse if a relatively inexperienced moderator is conducting the session. Alternatively, if the group is too small there may be difficulties generating an active discussion, particularly if there are a number of very quiet participants.

As a starting point, the size of a group should first be guided by the aims of the research. For example, if the focus groups are being conducted to help generate research hypotheses (that is, they are more 'exploratory' in nature) a larger number of smaller groups, conducted in a less structured manner, is preferable to maximize the amount of information that is likely to be gathered. In contrast, if the focus groups are being conducted to interpret research findings (that is, they are more 'confirmatory' in nature) then a smaller number of larger groups, conducted in a more structured manner, is likely to be preferable.

Besides the nature of the study, there are a number of other practical considerations that need to be considered when determining the size of focus groups. First, the time available for the focus group discussion needs to be addressed. As a 'rule of thumb', allowing between 90 and 120 minutes for discussion seems reasonable (Kahan 2001). Trying to maintain the interest of the group for longer than two hours (particularly if the focus group is to be held after work, which is often the case) is likely to prove difficult. Second is the number of questions to be discussed. Third is the time that is deemed appropriate to allot to the discussion of each question. Here it is important to note that while not all participants will necessarily want to respond to every question, it is important to allow sufficient time for the moderator to try to elicit responses from the less vocal members of the group. If we assume, for example, that our focus group session is to run for 120 minutes, there are to be ten questions and allowing 1.5 minutes for each participant to provide their response, then we would ideally like to have eight participants ($8 \times 10 \times 1.5 = 120$). If there were fewer questions to be discussed, or it was felt that less time would be needed to answer each question, then it would be appropriate to invite additional participants (or reduce the time allocated for the focus group session). It is also important to note that not all invited participants who have indicated a willingness to take part in the focus group will turn up; there will be the inevitable 'no shows'. Therefore, it is generally advisable to invite one or two additional participants to ensure the size of the group is sufficient to generate a lively discussion. A final consideration in deciding on the size of the focus group is the experience of the moderator. Other things being equal, if the moderator is inexperienced it would be prudent to err on the side of smaller, rather than larger, focus groups.

Because the objective of conducting a focus group is to highlight where agreement exists among the participants, it is normal practice for the participants to be selected on the basis that they are relatively homogeneous with respect to the topic of interest. Therefore, a purposive sampling approach would usually be adopted in recruiting focus group participants. To determine how representative the views/opinions of a focus group are (and how strongly they are held) subsequent research using a probability sampling design can be undertaken. The characteristics to be considered in selecting focus group participants could include age, sex and any other factors that might influence the attitudes of the participants towards the topic of interest.

It is also suggested that, ideally, participants should be 'strangers' because having acquaintances participating in a focus group may upset the dynamics of the group and could inhibit responses (Fern 1982). While this is no doubt true for focus groups designed to investigate sensitive social issues, it is likely to be of less concern when business owners are the subject of investigation. It should also be noted that in some circumstances (for example, if female entrepreneurs in a local region form the basis of the study) it might be difficult to recruit a sufficient number of focus group participants who have never previously met.

CHOOSING A MODERATOR

The focus group discussion is led and controlled by a moderator/facilitator whose role it is to:

- create a non-threatening environment that promotes a free-flowing discussion;
- help members share their experiences by ensuring that, as far as possible, there is only one person speaking at a time;
- elicit the views of all, particularly the quieter participants;
- facilitate interaction among participants;
- ensure that all important topics and questions in the prepared outline are covered, that is, keeping group members on track;
- present questions in an unbiased way;
- use judgement to pursue alternative lines of questioning or to probe responses if this is likely to lead to a better understanding of the issue/topic being discussed; and
- ensure that the discussion is captured, usually by audio (or audio visual) equipment.

Clearly, to achieve all these outcomes requires a highly skilled moderator. Some key traits/skills that are important if a moderator is to produce a useful outcome include:

- being able to create a non-threatening environment that promotes a free-flowing discussion;
- being sensitive to the views of the participants, even if those views are not shared by the moderator;
- having an outgoing personality that helps to make the participants feel comfortable and generate discussion;
- having experience in controlling group discussions to ensure that all participants have the opportunity to have their views heard and, particularly, to ensure that a few individuals do not dominate the discussion; and
- having a good understanding of the subject matter being discussed.

Who then should be chosen to take the role of moderator? Should it be a member of the research team? Or should a professional moderator be engaged for this purpose? In choosing the most appropriate moderator there appear to be two schools of thought. The first suggests that an experienced moderator should be sought for this task (Kahan 2001). The second argues that the researcher (or one of the research team) should take the role of moderator (McLafferty 2004). Like most things in life, this is a matter of judgement and will depend on the answers to a number of questions. First, does the researcher, or a member of the research team, have any experience in moderating a discussion group? Second, are there funds available to pay a professional moderator? Third, what is the nature of the study? For example, if the study is exploratory in nature, having a deep understanding of the topic/issue might outweigh a lack of skill/experience in conduction group discussions.

Where a decision is made to use a professional moderator it is essential that sufficient time is spent with that person so the researcher (research team) can ensure the moderator has a reasonably in-depth understanding of the aims of the research project, the nature of the participants and the questions/issues to be discussed. It is also important that at least one member of the research team be present (but in the background) at all focus group sessions to observe the body language of participants, to take notes and, if necessary, to provide clarifying comments about the project.

FOCUS GROUP STRUCTURE

Depending on the purpose of the research, focus groups can be relatively structured (with specific questions asked of group members and with the moderator playing a very active/directive role) or quite unstructured (with participants being allowed/encouraged to talk more freely with each other in response to open-ended questions). For example, if researchers are simply interested in 'pilot testing' a research instrument then a fairly structured approach would be called for, with the moderator systematically progressing the discussion through each questionnaire item. Alternatively, if researchers are using a qualitative approach to generate (or select) theoretical ideas and hypotheses which they plan to verify with future quantitative research, then the focus group should be conducted in a much less structured manner (Calder 1977).

SELECTING A SUITABLE VENUE

There are a number of issues to be considered when selecting a suitable venue/room for a focus group discussion. First, it is important to try and find a suitable location that is reasonably central for the majority of the participants; the further they have to travel at the end of a hard day's work the more likely they are to be 'no-shows'. Second, the size of the venue needs to be considered. It is important that the venue is reasonably intimate to facilitate discussion, but there needs to be adequate room for all participants to feel comfortable and, ideally, there should be space at the side or rear of the room for one or more members of the research team to sit and observe proceedings. Third, the venue selected should be free from interruptions, such as phones ringing or people passing through (Basch 1987). Typically, a venue such as a boardroom (with no windows) is a good location for holding a focus group session.

CONDUCTING THE FOCUS GROUP

Having recruited the required number of appropriate participants for a focus group session and decided on both the venue and moderator, the next step is to conduct the focus group. In doing so, the following key steps should be kept in mind.

Prior to Conducting a Focus Group

First, a detailed script needs to be prepared for the session. Among other things, this script will cover the aims of the session and the questions/issues to be discussed, and is particularly important when an independent/professional moderator is to conduct the focus group. In this case the script needs to be discussed with the moderator in some detail well before the session is due to be held to ensure he or she has a thorough understanding of the aims of the research. Developing the discussion outline and, in particular, the questions/issues to be discussed requires careful thought and a considerable amount of effort. As with any questionnaire design, each item should have a specific purpose and be related to the research aims. As a general rule, items should proceed from general to specific. Ideally, it would also be useful to pre-test the script.

Second, a suitable day and time for holding the focus group has to be determined. If possible, some consultation with prospective focus group participants on this issue might be worthwhile. In our experience, conducting focus groups from about 6 p.m. onwards on a Monday to Thursday has typically worked well. A later starting time might be required if participants have to travel some distance to the venue.

Third, when obtaining confirmation from potential participants that they are willing to attend a focus group, the participants should be advised of the location and expected duration of the session. A reminder confirmation should be sent to all participants several days before the session is due to be held, again with the location and timing details provided.

Fourth, recording equipment needs to be arranged and the moderator/

researcher must ensure he or she knows how to operate the equipment. Ideally, the equipment should be installed in the venue and tested well in advance of conducting the focus group in case any problems arise, however, this might not always be practicable. Care needs to be taken with placement of the recording equipment to ensure that all comments are captured.

Fifth, given a focus group session can usually be expected to last about two hours and is likely to be held after normal working hours, it is generally a good idea to provide some light refreshments before the session starts. This will allow the participants to mingle and 'unwind' a little prior to the commencement of the session. If refreshments are to be provided, the participants should be advised of this in the confirmation letter they are sent. Depending on the size of the venue to be used for the focus group discussion, it might also be necessary to arrange a separate room in which the refreshments are provided to participants prior to the commencement of the session.

Sixth, budget permitting, a decision needs to be made concerning the reimbursement/compensation to be offered to participants for any travel costs and for giving up their time to attend the focus group session. Again, if compensation is to be provided, the participants should be advised of this in the confirmation letter they are sent.

Seventh, it is normal practice to provide participants with an information sheet and consent form prior to the focus group so that they are aware of the general aims of the project, their rights and how their anonymity will be preserved. The Appendix to this chapter provides a template for such an information sheet and consent form.

When Conducting a Focus Group

To ensure participants are reasonably close together (to maximize the quality of the audio or audio-visual recording), any surplus chairs as a result of 'no-shows' should be removed from around the table. Then, using the script provided, the moderator will typically progress through the following items.

First, the participants should be welcomed and asked if they have any questions regarding the information provided in the information sheet. If they have not already done so, they should be asked to complete and sign the consent form. If it is not obvious, the moderator might also point out to the group the location of the nearest restroom. The moderator should reiterate that all comments provided will remain confidential and that no individual will be identified in any publications that might result from the focus group discussion.

Second, the moderator should provide a brief overview of the main aim(s) of the study and how long the session is expected to last. At this stage the moderator should briefly introduce members of the research team that are present. Note, however, that members of the research team should not be seated around the table with the focus group participants; they should be seated in the background, preferably at the back of the room or at the side if there is no room at the back, but not at the front of the room.

Third, it is often useful before launching the session to ask participants to briefly introduce themselves. This tends to 'break the ice' and allows the participants to relax a little before the serious business starts.

Fourth, the moderator needs to set the ground rules; for example, there is to be only one person speaking at a time, otherwise it is very difficult to properly capture all comments.

Fifth, the moderator then works through each of the questions/issues of interest to the researcher(s). In doing so it is important that the moderator provides all participants with the opportunity to express their views. Indeed, the moderator may have to work hard to elicit the views of participants who are not particularly forthcoming. As part of this process, the moderator may have to ensure a minority within the group do not dominate the discussion. At all times it is important that the moderator remains neutral with respect to the issues being discussed and, if need be, he or she should feel free to seek clarification concerning any of the views expressed.

Sixth, at the conclusion of the session the moderator should thank all participants for their contribution. If any reimbursement/compensation is being provided to the participants, the moderator needs to facilitate this process, which will usually involve participants having to sign a document acknowledging the payment they have received.

After Conducting the Focus Group

As soon as possible after the conclusion of the focus group session it is useful if the moderator can prepare a brief summary of the main points raised during the discussion and any comments he or she might have that are relevent to the study. This should also be done by any members of the research team that observed the session.

Finally, arrangements have to be made to have the focus group discussion transcribed for subsequent analysis by the researcher(s).

TRADITIONAL FOCUS GROUP RESEARCH IN PRACTICE

The principles discussed above will now be further highlighted in an analysis of two entrepreneurship studies that adopted a traditional focus group methodology. The aim of study 1 was to enhance the researcher's understanding of how women feel about the possibilities and opportunities of them becoming entrepreneurs. In particular, the study set out to explore how images of female entrepreneurs are visually constructed and represented in television documentaries (Neergaard and Smith 2004). In study 2, focus groups were used as an alternative research methodology to attempt to reconcile the findings of two prior studies and to determine whether those studies provided an exhaustive set of dimensions (factors) into which all owner-operator objectives could be classified (Newby et al. 2003b). The study also sought to determine if there was a temporal dimension to owner-operator objectives.

Study 1: Images of Women's Entrepreneurship: Do Pictures Speak Louder than Words?

Introduction

The aim of this study was to gain a better understanding of how images of female entrepreneurs are visually constructed and presented in television documentaries, and how these images are decoded and interpreted by aspiring and practising female entrepreneurs (Neergaard and Smith 2004). This is an important issue because television is a powerful social medium of expression and, therefore, is likely to have significant influence on aspiring entrepreneurs. As noted by Danesi (2002), television influences the way in which individuals derive meaning from their daily life. The documentary the participants were shown and asked to respond to was selected from a series entitled 'Girls with power' ('Piger med power', in Danish). The aim was to analyse how aspiring and practising female entrepreneurs interpret the images and messages presented in the documentary with a view to providing a better understanding of whether such programmes are able to impact the images and attitudes women associate with entrepreneurship and, ultimately, influence the propensity of women to establish and grow new ventures.

The selected documentary depicts a female entrepreneur, Lene Mønster (LM) who founded a company called Girlsquad, going about her daily routine. The unique selling proposition of LM's company is the provision of hostesses/hosts for themed corporate events. The visual presentation of LM is that of a stereotypical 'dizzy blonde'; an appearance that LM does little to discourage. LM is filmed in six separate locations: at home, with and without her partner; at her premises, with staff and prospective employees; at the beach with a friend; at the hairdresser; at her birthday party; and holidaying/working in Saint Tropez. Regardless of the setting, the focus is on her appearance and her actions appear to be staged. This is particularly noticeable in one instance when LM picks up a book with the title *Guide to Survival for Successful Women* and sits down on her settee to read it. It is very obvious this is a rehearsed rather than spontaneous action to illustrate how she can be so busy and still remain very much a 'woman'. Interestingly, the documentary provides no information on the difficulties of starting an entrepreneurial venture; the focus is action-orientated and zooms in on the fun of doing it. LM's life seems like an endless party and the documentary highlights the fact that she is a part of the Copenhagen 'jet set'.

The focus group method was adopted for this study because it allowed participants' spontaneous reactions to the documentary to be observed (such as smiles of approval, smirks, raised eyebrows, fidgeting and so on). These non-verbal cues can provide evidence of genuine individual interpretation which might help to counterbalance any 'group effect'. The ensuing group discussion would also likely provide useful information about how participants decoded the messages embedded in the documentary.

The number of focus groups and the nature and number of participants

As a first step in trying to better understand how females might decode the messages contained in television documentaries concerning female entrepreneurs, it was decided to conduct two focus groups. Further, because it was felt that aspiring and practising female entrepreneurs could have different reactions to the documentary (and being in a mixed group might inhibit their interaction) the decision was made to run one focus group with aspiring female entrepreneurs and the second with practising female entrepreneurs. Therefore, a purposeful sampling approach was adopted with aspiring entrepreneurs being recruited from an entrepreneurship advisory centre and practising entrepreneurs from the 'Heroines of Tomorrow Network'. In both cases the organizations involved helped to recruit potential participants by promoting the study using a 'flyer' that was prepared for this purpose.

In terms of the number of focus group participants, the aim was to have about eight participants in each group. With this in mind, and noting it was likely at least one or two of the invited participants would either decline the invitation to attend a focus group or would fail to turn up, ten participants were invited to each of the two focus group sessions. All of those invited to the practising female entrepreneurs' focus group session accepted, while nine accepted for the aspiring entrepreneurs' session. Interestingly, there were two 'no-shows' for the group of practising entrepreneurs and the discussion between the eight members of this group was quite lively and, at times, rather heated. All of the participants in this group had fairly strong opinions (possibly resulting from their experiences in setting up their own businesses) and were willing to voice them.

In contrast, there were four 'no-shows' for the group of aspiring entrepreneurs and the moderator had to work considerably harder to generate discussion in this smaller group than was the case with the larger group of practising entrepreneurs. It is difficult to know what caused this high drop-out rate as only one of the 'no-shows' telephoned to advise she would be unable to attend (because of a problem with child-minding arrangements). Note that the average rate of 'no-shows' across the two groups was about 25 per cent. Had the budget available for this study allowed participants to be remunerated for their participation perhaps there would have been fewer 'no-shows'. However, this did not appear to impact on the group of practising entrepreneurs and, therefore, remunerating this group for their participation would have been a waste of scarce resources. Another reason for the high level of 'no-shows' in the group of aspiring entrepreneurs might relate to the added (particularly, time) pressures they faced in trying to establish a new venture. Interestingly, the participants in this group 'rushed off' as soon as the session had finished. In contrast, the group of practising entrepreneurs remained in the venue for some time after the formal proceedings had concluded to further reflect on the discussion that had taken place.

While Fern (1982) suggests that, in an ideal situation, it is preferable that focus group participants do not know each other (because it could limit discussion), this proved rather difficult for the group of practising entrepreneurs as they were all part of the same network organization. Interestingly, this did not appear to inhibit discussion in this group which, as noted earlier, was quite robust. This outcome supports the argument advanced by Powell et al. (1996: 198) that 'groups of friends rather than strangers are more likely to offer a supportive atmosphere conducive to frank discussions'.

Table 10.1 provides the demographic details for the participants in the two groups. Note this information was collected from potential participants (together with their contact details) when they contacted the researchers to indicate a willingness to participate in a focus group session.

The moderator
One of the research team acted as the moderator for both focus group sessions because that person: had taken a course a couple of years earlier

Table 10.1   Participant demographics

		Education	Experience	Age	Type of company	Solo/team
Aspiring entrepreneurs	1	Journalist	n/a	31	Communication consultant	Alone
	2	Literature history	n/a	28	Publishing company	Alone, but in cooperation with others
	3	Interpreter	n/a	26	Communications bureau	With the person below
	4	Interpreter	n/a	29	Communications bureau	With the person above
	5	Master of arts	n/a	28	Project development and consultancy firm	With a friend
Practising entrepreneurs	1	Journalist	n/a	32	Journalism	Alone but in close cooperation with others
	2	Technical assistant IT diploma	Technical assistant	47	Laundry and RFID technology	Alone
	3	Lawyer	Serial entrepreneur Retail and wholesale of art wares	35	Organization development consultancy to law firms	Alone but with the aid of family
	4	Journalist	n/a	27	Publishing company	With two men
	5	Fashion designer	Degree from the Fashion Institute of Technology New York	50	Dressmaking/ design	Alone, but negotiating a partnership
	6	Political science	Web-design, taxi driver	36	Transport company	Alone
	7	Architect	n/a	34	Architectural firm	With two men
	8	Grammar school teacher	Teaching Body and psyche therapist Organization development consultant	63	Institute for personal development	Alone

on conducting focus groups; had taught qualitative methods, including focus groups, to master students for some years; had participated in a number of focus groups; and, ultimately, there was no budget available to pay a professional moderator. It should be noted that because this was an exploratory study it was felt that having a deep understanding of the topic/issue was more important than having skill/experience in conducting focus group discussions.

Focus group structure

A carefully planned script was prepared well in advance of the focus group sessions (see Box 10.1). Although the script was not pre-tested it was discussed with representatives from the entrepreneurship advisory centre (from which the aspiring entrepreneurs were recruited) before conducting

---

BOX 10.1   INTERVIEW GUIDE

I.   Introduction.
a.   Purpose and practical information.
II. General discussion of female entrepreneurship in Denmark.
a.   What do you associate with the word 'entrepreneur' (*ivaerksaetter*, in Danish) – the participants are asked to write down their perceptions on paper provided – max. one sentence on each piece of paper, max. five sentences, max. seven words per sentence and written in big letters. These are then to be grouped by the participants under main headings and a discussion of the words/sentences is to follow.
b.   The participants should then be asked to discuss whether there are certain characteristics or personalities that they associate with entrepreneurs and whether these are the same for men and women.
c.   The last question in this part of the discussion concerns what expectations the participants had/have concerning life as an entrepreneur and, for practising entrepreneurs, how these expectations have been fulfilled.

SHORT BREAK

III. Documentary programme *Girlsquad*.
IV. Immediate reaction to the programme.
a.   Please spend a few minutes considering your immediate reaction to the programme – then write down the first four ideas that come to mind. Discussion.
V.   Discussion of the storyline/plot.
a.   How would you describe the personality of the main character?
b.   How do you see it in relation to the entrepreneurial role?
c.   What other roles does the main character play – are there some that you recognize and how?
d.   How does the main character balance work, family and leisure?
VI. How does a programme like this make you feel about starting your own business?

---

the focus groups. As can be seen from Box 10.1, the questions posed to the focus group participants started out fairly general and then became more specific after screening the documentary. Given the exploratory nature of this study, the moderator was mindful of the need to encourage the participants to speak freely among themselves in response to the questions raised.

The venue

The focus group sessions were held at the local university which was centrally located and, therefore, the participants did not have to travel very far to participate in the sessions. A member of the information technology (IT) department at the university assisted with setting up the video recording equipment. The meeting room had a semi-circular table which facilitated discussion between the participants. In hindsight, however, the room chosen was a little small and the video camera was unable to capture all of the proceedings. Fortunately, the video camera was able to capture all of the interaction between the participants; it was only the moderator that was missing. The room, being quite small, also warmed up very quickly and did become a little uncomfortable, particularly with the larger group of practising entrepreneurs.

Conducting the focus groups

The focus groups were held on a Tuesday and Thursday evening of the same week between 7 p.m. and 9 p.m. It was felt that by starting at 7 p.m. women with small children would have time to collect them from kindergarten/school, take them home and feed them before leaving to attend the focus group session.

As can be seen from Box 10.1, at the start of each focus group session the moderator gave a brief introduction outlining the purpose of the session and providing practical information such as: there would be a short refreshment break before viewing the documentary; only first names were to be used when addressing members of the group; only one person should speak at a time, but all participants would get a turn to speak; and the moderator's role would be to facilitate, rather than direct, the discussion. Participants were made aware of the location of the restrooms at the commencement of the short refreshment break prior to viewing the documentary.

The moderator then progressed through the script. Note that for some of the questions the participants were asked to write down their thoughts/ideas on pieces of paper that were then pinned up and discussed. This process appeared to work well as it took the focus off the individual and placed it on the comment/idea. It also served to minimize problems of group conformity as the participants had to write down their ideas before being exposed to the thoughts of the other members in the group.

As noted earlier, the moderator did have to work quite hard to stimulate an active discussion in the small group of aspiring entrepreneurs. For the group of practising entrepreneurs, the moderator's main challenge was keeping the participants focused on the questions and stopping a couple of them talking to each other rather than to the group. After viewing the documentary, the participants were asked to discuss the specific messages they gleaned from the program and the values they felt were represented by the female entrepreneur (LM). The main themes emerging from that discussion are presented in the following section.

Results
Both groups of entrepreneurs were asked about their immediate reaction to the documentary, and what values LM portrayed. They were asked to write down, in the form of key words, the first four ideas that came to mind. Table 10.2 shows that the majority of the words recorded by the participants related to LM's personal characteristics. The remaining words can be classified under three headings: the requirements to be successful in business; the place of entrepreneurship in one's life; and the factors leading to the establishment of a new venture.

During the discussion participants in both groups expressed frustration

Table 10.2   Comparing the views of aspiring and practicing entrepreneurs

	Practising entrepreneurs	Aspiring entrepreneurs
Personal characteristics	Ambitious	Autodidact
	Energetic	Cheeky
	Courageous	Creative
	Goal oriented	Cool
	Self-confident	Self-confident
	Wilful	Drive
	A 'doer'	Indomitable
	Power woman	Initiative
	Professional	
Success requirements	Focus	Networking
	Networking	Canvassing
Place of entrepreneurship in one's life	Workaholic	Leisure = work
Factors leading to a business	A good idea	Chance/accident
		Idea

concerning the lack of explanation about how LM's business was actually started. They also felt that a documentary portraying a person closer to their own world would have been preferable. Being part of the Copenhagen 'jet set' was simply unimaginable and there was too much of a picture-postcard feel to the documentary. The participants expressed the view that it was a flawed picture, with none of the hardship one usually associates with entrepreneurship but with all of the glamour. Without the glamour the participants felt it would be very easy to recognize themselves in the documentary. The aspiring entrepreneurs, who were in the process of starting their businesses, were particularly disappointed at the lack of information about how hard it was to start a business and how much work was involved. One of the participants in this group made the comment, about LM, 'I bet she has never written a business plan'.

Participants in both groups felt that to be a successful entrepreneur you had to dedicate yourself to your business, and in this sense they could relate to LM as she was clearly a workaholic. The importance of time was a pervasive theme that emanated from the discussion, particularly for the aspiring entrepreneurs. LM was seen as making good use of her time, selling herself and her society's cultural and stereotypical expectations of women; although she appeared to have fun at the same time.

There was also general agreement that in LM's line of business it was important that she looked and played the part. A lot of LM's success hinged on the harmony between who LM was and what she did. One of the practising entrepreneurs noted that 'it is important to stage yourself as a woman – men have a uniform, as women we have to stage ourselves differently for different situations or roles'. This sentiment was echoed by another participant who stated that 'it boosts the self-confidence to know you look the part'.

In seeking to articulate what values the documentary portrayed it would seem from the focus group discussion that LM portrayed the accepted (albeit accentuated and idealized) cultural values associated with women (dumb blondes) and men (hunks). She played to audience assumptions, providing her customers with a stereotypical formula that works for them. However, LM is far from the dumb blonde she portrays with the skill of an actress; she is simply playing the role expected of her. LM wants to be respected but also admired. She is a seller of dreams but the producer's message is that of selling one dream: the entrepreneurial dream. As such, both aspiring and practising entrepreneurs bought into the dream.

Given this is an ongoing research project it may be desirable to conduct further focus group sessions in the future to ensure a broad cross-section of views and opinions is obtained. For example, to counter potential variations in opinions due to the heterogeneous nature of both practising and aspiring entrepreneurs, it might be useful to conduct additional focus group sessions based on selection criteria such as age, education and the nature of the business. Further, it might be interesting to conduct focus groups with practising and aspiring *male* entrepreneurs.

Study 2: Using Focus Groups in Entrepreneurship Research: The Case of Owner-operator Objectives

Introduction

It has been argued that the economic measures routinely used for large firms may not be appropriate for assessing the performance of small owner-operated firms (Parasuraman et al. 1996). This questioning of traditional measurement techniques is based on the view that economic performance may not be valid in gauging what seem to be subjective constructs. For example, Keats and Bracker (1988: 53) note that 'performance may have a different set of meanings for small firms than for large firms', and Buttner and Moore (1997: 34) suggest that female small business owners measured success in terms of 'self-fulfilment and goal achievement. Profits and business growth, while important, were less substantial measures of their success'. It has also been found that many of the stated reasons for starting a new venture are non-financial in nature (Stanworth and Curran 1976). This suggests, therefore, that the goals and expectations of individual owner-operators will impact how they evaluate their firm's performance and the utility they derive from their ventures. Further, the lack of separation of ownership and management within SMEs allows the goals of the owners to become the goals of the firm (Naffziger et al. 1994); particularly given the significant freedom 'being your own boss' provides SME owners in the pursuit of objectives (LeCornu et al. 1996).

Prior research by Kuratko et al. (1997) and Woodliff et al. (1999) into the objectives of owner-operators report overlapping, but not identical, factor solutions. Table 10.3 lists the factors, and the items that loaded on to those factors, for these two studies. The main aim of this study, therefore, was to try and reconcile the differences between these two prior studies and to determine whether their combined findings provides an exhaustive set of owner-operator objectives. The study which was conducted by Newby et al. (2003b) also sought to determine whether there was a temporal dimension to owner-operator objectives (Cooper 1993); that is, do owner-operators substantially change their objectives over time?

As a precursor to the development of a survey instrument to (quantitatively) examine SME owner-operator objectives, four focus groups were organized to explore this issue and to 'demonstrate how a focus group methodology could be usefully employed by SME researchers'

Table 10.3   SME owner operator objectives

Woodliff et al. (1999)	Kuratko et al. (1997)
Financial return	*Extrinsic rewards*
To earn as much profit as possible now	Acquire personal wealth
To have as much disposable income as possible	To increase my personal income
To achieve financial security now	To increase my income opportunities
To build family wealth for the future	
Personal satisfaction	*Independence/autonomy*
To enjoy managing the business professionally	Maintain my personal freedom
To see things happen according to plan	Personal security
	Self-employment
	To be my own boss
	To control my own employment destiny
	Intrinsic rewards
	Gain public recognition
	Meet the challenge
	Enjoy the excitement
	Personal growth
	To prove I can do it
Family	*Family security*
Personal development opportunities for family	Secure future for family members
Employment opportunities for owner's family	To build a business to pass on
Time flexibility	
Flexibility of time for non-business activities	
Free time for non-business activity	
Staff and customer relations	
Loyalty from staff	
Security of employment for staff	
To provide high-quality products/services	

Source: Newby et al. (2003b: 240, table 1).

(Newby et al. 2003b: 238). In organizing these focus groups the decision was also made to conduct two using the traditional approach and a further two using group support system (GSS) technology (Newby et al. 2003a). While the following chapter will highlight the specific advantages/disadvantages of the GSS versus the traditional method, the focus of this chapter is on the process involved in organizing the focus groups and the key outcomes.

The number of focus groups and the nature (and number) of participants
To maximize our chances of capturing all possible dimensions (factors) associated with SME owner-operator objectives, we approached a wide cross-section of owner-operators to participate in the four focus group sessions. Potential participants were randomly selected from the following sources: a Chamber of Commerce directory (for two sessions); tenants of a business incubator (for one session); and retailers in a large shopping mall (for one session). The intention was to have about ten participants in each group and for this reason no more than 12 potential participants were approached for each session. There was some difficulty in recruiting participants from the shopping mall and in the end there were only six who agreed to participate, and one of these was a 'no-show'. A further 30 potential participants agreed to take part from the other two sources (the Chamber of Commerce and the business incubator) and six of these were 'no-shows'. However, similar to study 1, there was a considerable range in terms of the 'no-shows' across the four sessions. For example, of the 12 owner-operators from the business incubator who agreed to participate (in a focus group held at the business incubation premises) all 12 turned up. At the other extreme, of the eight Chamber of Commerce members who agreed to participate (in a session held in the Chamber of Commerce's boardroom) there were four 'no-shows'. In summary, of the 36 owner-operators who agreed to take part in a focus group discussion, there were only 29 (11 female) SME owner-operators who actually showed up to one of the four focus group sessions. This represents a drop-out rate of about 20 per cent. It should also be noted that, unlike study 1, participants in this study were given $50 as a token of appreciation for their willingness to take part in a focus group session. It would appear, however, that this payment made only a marginal difference to the rate of 'no-shows'; 20 per cent in study 2 compared with 25 per cent in study 1.

The moderator
Given neither of the researchers involved with this project had any experience in conducting focus groups, the decision was made to employ an experienced moderator known to one of the researchers. This person ran all four focus group sessions. Prior to conducting the focus groups, one member of the research team met with the moderator to go over the aims of the project and the specific questions that the study sought to address. Interestingly, even though a skilled moderator was used and there was a pre-prepared script, in one of the focus group sessions one of the questions was inadvertently skipped. Fortunately, this question was covered in each of the three other focus groups.

Focus group structure

The questions posed to the focus group participants started out at a general level (Why do people enter business?) and then became more specific (Why did you enter business?). To determine whether there was a temporal dimension to owner operator objectives, the questions were also posed under three time frames, namely: at business entry (Why did you enter business?); at present (Why do you stay in business?); and in the future (What specific business goals do you have? and What specific personal, business related, goals do you have?).

The venue

Each of the four focus groups was held in a different location. Note that the two GSS sessions required a bigger venue (than the two traditional focus groups) to accommodate the computer technology required for these sessions. The two traditional focus groups were held in boardrooms. The group comprising members of the business incubator met in the boardroom at the incubation premises and this was most likely the reason for the 100 per cent turnout for this session; it was a very convenient location that did not involve any travelling. The other traditional focus group was held in the boardroom of the local Chamber of Commerce. However, as this venue could only accommodate a maximum of ten people around the boardroom table it was not suitable for the GSS session, which required additional space for the computers. For this reason a reception room at the local City Council building was used for the second of the focus groups involving members of the Chamber of Commerce. The other GSS session was held at the nearby greyhound racing track because, again, no suitable space was available in the shopping centre from which the members of this group were recruited. All of the venues appeared to work reasonably well with no disruptions being experienced during the sessions.

Conducting the focus groups

The focus groups were held on a Tuesday and Thursday evening in two consecutive weeks. The participants were invited to attend at 5.30 p.m. for some light refreshments prior to the commencement of the focus group session at 6 p.m. The participants were informed that the session would conclude no later than 8 p.m.

At least one of the research team members attended each of the four sessions as an observer and to answer any questions about the project that might arise during the session which the moderator felt unable to answer. One of the research team also took responsibility for setting up and testing the audio recording equipment used to capture the discussion in each session. Note that for the GSS sessions much of the input from participants was captured electronically (as discussed in more detail in the following chapter).

The moderator welcomed the participants, introduced the researcher(s) present and explained the ground rules (only one person to speak at a time, and so on) prior to starting the session. The use of a professional moderator appeared to work well as the sessions ran smoothly and the moderator did an excellent job of stimulating discussion, particularly from the quieter members of the group. As noted earlier, however, there was one question that was overlooked in one of the sessions; an oversight that also escaped the notice of the researcher present.

Results

The focus group discussions supported all of the five factors identified by Woodliff et al. (1999), as depicted in Table 10.3, suggesting that this solution provides an exhaustive set of dimensions with respect to owner-operator objectives. Confidence in this outcome was enhanced by the finding that all five factors were supported for all three time frames (at business entry, at present, and for the future). Sample responses to the various questions asked of focus group participants are provided in Table 10.4.

As a rough guide to the relative importance of each of the five factors depicted in Table 10.4, a count was made of how often the focus group participants mentioned each factor (dimension). These frequencies were then converted into proportions (percentages), and are presented in Figure 10.1 under the headings: past objectives (Why do other people go into business? and Why did you go into business?); present objectives (Why do you stay in business?); and future objectives (What are the business goals of other SME owners? What are your business goals? What are the personal, business-related, goals of other SME owners? and What are your personal, business-related, goals?).

Examination of Figure 10.1 indicates that the most important dimensions concerning owner-operator objectives are personal satisfaction and financial return; with family, time flexibility and staff and customer relations appearing less significant. However, an interesting feature of Figure 10.1 is how the stated objectives of SME owner-operators change when they look ahead rather than reflect on the past or present. When focus group participants were asked about future business and/or personal goals (objectives) the personal satisfaction dimension lost its past and/or present importance; allowing the dimensions of financial return and time flexibility to dominate. Approximately 70 per cent of future (business and/or personal) goal responses related to either financial return or time flexibility; with the personal satisfaction factor more than halving from 50 per cent to 20 per cent of responses. This finding is consistent with the

Table 10.4   Sample comments by focus group participants

	Financial return; extrinsic rewards	Personal satisfaction; independence/autonomy, intrinsic rewards	Family; family security	Time flexibility	Staff and customer relations
Why do people go into business?					
Why others enter	• To maximize return for the perceived value of input • To reap the rewards of their labour	• For control of their lives • It's more challenging than working for someone else	• Flexibility, fitting work around family • They want to build a better future for their family	• To free up time for other activities • Time flexibility	• They see a need in the market and believe they could make good income by fulfilling that need
Why I entered	• To build my own income source • I was made redundant • The possibility of earning far more than I could working for someone else	• I was fed up with the working environment at that time • To be my own boss • I always wanted to own my own business (my parents were self-employed)	• To make money and to give more security to the family • I was roped in (by a family member) • To fit around my family's needs (I have school age children)	• To be able to have a week off and go fishing when it suits	• To meet with other people • I found a niche for the service I provide when working for my previous employer. His clients needed a service, which he didn't provide

303

Table 10.4 (continued)

	Financial return; extrinsic rewards	Personal satisfaction; independence/ autonomy, intrinsic rewards	Family; family security	Time flexibility	Staff and customer relations
Why do I stay in business?	• To pay off the loan, and provide a little nest egg for the future • I've no way out – my wife needs more money to keep our bills at bay	• It's great fun! • I would be frustrated working for someone with lower standards • Nobody else will have me	• The future of our son • I'm too young to give up work so this gives me time to organize my retirement	• It suits my lifestyle; I can make my own choices	• We deal with lots of other small business people and I enjoy the interaction • People/repeat customers
What specific business goals exist? Goals others have	• They want to achieve growth – to extend the firm • To make a profit – being successful	• Goals set are measured by the rewards they extract • Development with skills and motivation will prevail	• They want to survive • Plans for retirement		• To offer excellence in their particular area • To employ people

304

Goals I have	• Set growth patterns, profit requirements, debt reduction, financial stability • To make lots of money	• To be operating at the same energy levels as I do currently • To be recognized as a leader in our field	• To retire, passing the reins on to our son • To have retired	• To have more time off without lowering income	• I aim to locate and train the right people • Continual improvement of services and goods provided

What specific personal goals exist?

Goals others have	• Financial independence would be a goal, or at least improved financial standing • Larger income, car, house	• There is the promise of 'learning something new' and not having to answer to anyone	• Provide better opportunities for their families • Retirement and financial security	• Most goals relate to money, retirement, and time off • 10 weeks holiday a year	
Goals I have	• To make sure my wife has the money she needs to lead the lifestyle we would like • To retire from active participation yet still enjoy income in excess of $100k	• To be in a different business • To write a book(s) related to my field of endeavour. • To still be alive, the stresses of business take a toll on your health	• To have more time to participate in bringing up my family • To remove myself from the 'shop front' and work from home doing the admin.	• More leisure time and more money to enjoy it with • I hope to catch lots of fish!	

Source: Newby et al. (2003b: 245, appendix).

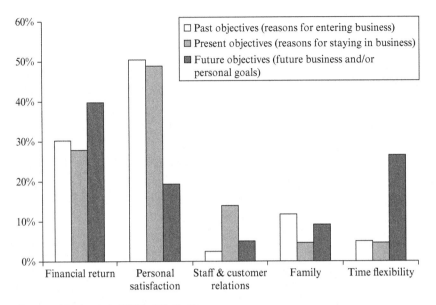

Source: Newby et al. (2003b: 241, fig.1).

Figure 10.1   *The relative importance of owner-operator objective*
dimensions

results from Cliff's (1998) investigation of entrepreneurs' (future) growth
intentions. Cliff (1998) reported that for many in her sample, and particularly for females, there appeared to be a certain size threshold beyond
which owner-operators did not intend to grow their businesses. Having
reached an acceptable size, these entrepreneurs would prefer to concentrate (in the future) on achieving a more appropriate balance between their
working life and their personal life (time flexibility).

Conclusion
The results from the four focus group discussions provided valuable
input to the subsequent development of an instrument for assessing the
relative importance male and female owner-operators attached to various
objectives (Watson and Newby 2007).

SUMMARY

The two studies discussed in this chapter clearly indicate that, as a qualitative method, traditional focus groups are an excellent vehicle for providing

researchers with an understanding of a particular phenomenon from the point of view of the participants involved (Klein et al. 2007). Although focus groups have not been widely used in entrepreneurship research in the past, we trust that the potential contribution of this method in adding to our knowledge of the motivations, rationales and experiences of small business owners has been clearly demonstrated in this chapter. In the following two chapters the role of computers and information technology in overcoming some of the potential difficulties in conducting traditional focus groups will be examined.

REFERENCES

Basch, C.E. (1987), 'Focus group interview: an underutilized research technique for improving theory and practice in health education', *Health Education & Behavior*, **14** (4), 411–48.

Blackburn, R. and D. Stokes (2000), 'Breaking down the barriers: using focus groups to research small and medium-sized enterprises', *International Small Business Journal*, **19** (1), 44–67.

Buttner, E.H. and D.P. Moore (1997), 'Women's organizational exodus to entrepreneurship: self-reported motivations and correlates with success', *Journal of Small Business Management*, **35** (1), 34–46.

Calder, B.J. (1977), 'Focus groups and the nature of qualitative marketing research', *Journal of Marketing Research*, **14** (3), 353–64.

Cliff, J.E. (1998), 'Does one size fit all? Exploring the relationship between attitudes towards growth, gender, and business size', *Journal of Business Venturing*, **13** (6), 523–42.

Cooper, A.C. (1993), 'Challenges in predicting new firm performance', *Journal of Business Venturing*, **8** (3), 241–53.

Danesi, M. (2002), *Understanding Media Semiotics*, London and New York: Arnold, Hodder Headline Group and Oxford University Press.

Fern, E.F. (1982), 'The use of focus groups for idea generation: the effects of group size, acquaintanceship, and moderator on response quantity and quality', *Journal of Marketing Research*, **19** (1), 1–13.

Kahan, J.P. (2001), 'Focus groups as a tool for policy analysis', *Analyses of Social Issues and Public Policy*, **1** (1), 129–46.

Keats, B.W. and J.S. Bracker (1988), 'Toward a theory of small firm performance: a conceptual model', *American Journal of Small Business*, **12** (4), 41–58.

Klein, E.E., T. Tellefsen and P.J. Herskovitz (2007), 'The use of group support systems in focus groups: information technology meets qualitative research', *Computers in Human Behavior*, **23** (5), 2113–32.

Kuratko, D.F., J.S. Hornsby and D.W. Naffziger (1997), 'An examination of owne's goals in sustaining entrepreneurship', *Journal of Small Business Management*, **35** (1), 24–33.

LeCornu, M.R., R.G.P. McMahon, D.M. Forsaith and A.M.J. Stanger (1996), 'The small enterprise financial objective function', *Journal of Small Business Management*, **34** (3), 1–14.

McLafferty, I. (2004), 'Focus group interviews as a data collecting strategy', *Journal of Advanced Nursing*, **48** (2), 187–94.

Naffziger, D.W., J.S. Hornsby and D.F. Kuratko (1994), 'A proposed research model of entrepreneurial motivation', *Entrepreneurship Theory and Practice*, **18** (Spring), 29–42.

Neergaard, H. and R. Smith (2004), 'Images of women's entrepreneurship: do pictures speak louder than words?', RENT XVIII, Copenhagen.

Newby, R., G. Soutar and J. Watson (2003a), 'Comparing traditional focus groups with a group support system (GSS) approach for use in SME research', *International Small Business Journal*, **21** (4), 421–33.

Newby, R., J. Watson and D. Woodliff (2003b), 'Using focus groups in SME research: the case of owner-operator objectives', *Journal of Developmental Entrepreneurship*, **8** (3), 237–46.

Parasuraman, S., Y.S. Purohit and V.M. Godshalk (1996), 'Work and family variables, entrepreneurial career success and psychological well-being', *Journal of Vocational Behavior*, **48** (3), 275–300.

Powell, R.A., H.M. Single and K.R. Lloyd (1996), 'Focus groups in mental health research: enhancing the validity of user and provider questionnaires', *International Journal of Social Psychiatry*, **42** (3), 165–80.

Stanworth, M.K.J. and J. Curran (1976), 'Growth and the small firm – an alternative view', *Journal of Management Studies*, **13** (2), 95–110.

Watson, J. and R. Newby (2007), 'Gender differences in the goals of owner-operated SMEs', in N.M. Carter, C. Henry, B. Ó Cinnéide and K. Johnston (eds), *Female Entrepreneurship – Implications for Education, Training and Policy*, London: Routledge, pp. 37–68.

Woodliff, D., J. Watson, R.R. Newby and C. McDowell (1999), 'Improving survey instrument validity and reliability: the case of SME owner objectives', *Small Enterprise Research*, **7** (2), 55–65.

APPENDIX 10.1   EXAMPLE OF INFORMATION SHEET AND CONSENT FORM

Organization Letter Head

INFORMATION SHEET

Purpose:	A discussion group to explore the perceptions of Small and Medium Enterprise (SME) owners concerning . . .
Participants:	SME owner-operators from . . .
Venue:	Conference Room at . . .
Date:	. . .
Time:	. . .
Procedures:	We will capture the group's discussion using audio-recording equipment so that we can transcribe <u>exactly</u> what is said by each participant.
Anonymity and confidentiality:	To ensure participant anonymity, transcription of the video-recording will identify each participant by a code number only (the video-recording will be destroyed upon completion of the transcription process). In addition, all material associated with the project will be kept securely under lock and key, with access limited to those directly involved in the research.
Participation:	Participants are free at any time to withdraw consent to further participation without prejudice in any way, and do not need to give any reason or justification for their withdrawal of consent.
Recompense:	To reimburse you for your time we will provide an honorarium of $100. This payment for participation, however, does not prejudice you to any subsequent right you may have to compensation under statute or common law. If you are unsure as to the meaning of any of the above, or have questions regarding the project that are not satisfactorily answered by this information sheet, please indicate this to one of the researchers observing the discussion. Otherwise, please complete the consent form overleaf.

Professor X
Professor Y
University/
   Organization

CONSENT FORM

I have read the information provided and any questions I have asked have been answered to my satisfaction. I agree to participate in this activity, realizing that I may withdraw at any time without reason and without prejudice.

I understand that all information provided will be treated as strictly confidential and will not be released by the investigators unless required to by law. I have been advised as to what data is being collected, what the purpose is, and what will be done with the data upon completion of the research.

I agree that research data gathered for the study may be published provided my name or other identifying information is not used.

Participant Name:
Participant Signature:
Date:

The Human Research Ethics Committee at the University/Organization requires that all participants are informed that, if they have any complaint regarding the manner in which a research project has been conducted they may inform the researcher or, alternatively, the Secretary, Human Research Ethics Committee, University/Organization, Address, Telephone number. All study participants will (or have been) provided with a copy of the Information Sheet and Consent Form for their personal records.

11 Conducting a focus group using group support system (GSS) software

Geoff Soutar, Rick Newby and John Watson

INTRODUCTION

Advances in information technology and computer communication networks have provided opportunities to enhance focus group research (Klein et al. 2007). In this chapter we examine the use of GSS software to help overcome some of the potential limitations associated with traditional face-to-face focus groups. In the following chapter the use of technology in conducting focus group research will be taken a step further when the advantages/disadvantages of online focus groups are examined.

While there are many advantages associated with the use of traditional focus groups as a qualitative research method, they also have a number of potential disadvantages. First, because only one person can talk at a time there is a limit to the number of thoughts participants can express in the time available. This has been referred to as 'production blocking' (Aiken et al. 1994) or 'air fragmentation' (Klein et al. 2007). As noted by Valacich et al. (1992: 51–2): 'group members who are prevented from verbalizing their ideas as they occur may forget . . . them . . . at a later time'; 'when waiting to verbalize an idea, group members focus on remembering that idea, rather than generating new ideas'; and 'listening to other members speak may preclude generating new ideas'. Second, lack of anonymity may result in some focus group participants being reluctant to express their views, particularly if they feel those views are not universally shared by other members of the group (referred to as 'evaluation apprehension' – Aiken et al. 1994). This suggests the group's views might be unduly influenced by pressures to conform, as individuals could be hesitant to express views different to those normally expected (Blackburn and Stokes 2000). Third, it is possible for a focus group session to be dominated by a few assertive individuals, thereby preventing the expression of potentially useful ideas by other members of the group; either because of a reluctance to speak out or a lack of opportunity (Newby et al. 2003). Fourth, the group might too quickly agree to the first idea presented in the discussion ('yea saying') and, again, this can result in the loss of potentially useful ideas (Newby et al. 2003). Fifth is the issue of free riding (sometimes referred to as 'loafing') whereby some group members may rely on the other participants to generate the ideas (Valacich et al. 1992). It should also be noted that, because of the potential drawbacks referred to above, the marginal productivity of a traditional focus group session tends to diminish with group size (Aiken et al. 1994). Finally, in a traditional focus group there can be a number of potential problems associated with capturing all responses from individual group members. For example, in preparing transcripts from audio tapes it is not always possible to hear all the comments, particularly if some group members are quietly spoken or if a number of participants are making points simultaneously. Further, the transcription process can be time consuming and can significantly delay a research project.

THE GSS APPROACH

It is argued that using a GSS approach can overcome (or at least minimize) many of the problems associated with traditional focus groups as responses to questions are captured electronically prior to any discussion taking place. In a typical GSS session up to ten people, each with a computer, are arranged around a table as depicted in Figure 11.1. The computers are linked to a central computer workstation that is 'driven' by a 'chauffeur' to capture responses from group members. At the appropriate time, these individual responses can be made visible to all group members via a projector screen at the front of the room (and/or the participants' computer screens).

Participants type their responses to a series of questions posed by the moderator/researcher. This allows all group members to 'talk' at once (or to 'communicate in parallel' – Aiken et al. 1994), rather than having to wait their turn. Given a similar time frame for conducting the focus group session, this parallel communication can potentially result in the generation of more ideas than would be possible in a traditional focus group. Further, the ideas generated by group members are anonymous and can only be connected to a particular participant if that person makes her/his view known in the ensuing discussion (which usually takes place after each question). This process helps to ensure that all ideas are recorded, even where participants may have reason to believe that the majority of group members do not share their beliefs, or where participants might be reluctant to speak in public. It has been suggested that this type of anonymity is one of the important advantages of the GSS technology as it: ensures that good ideas 'are allowed to dominate rather than assertive individuals' (Sweeney et al. 1997: 400); potentially reduces 'evaluation apprehension';

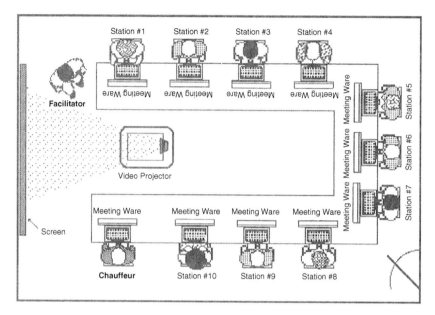

Source: Based on Lewis (1987) – GSS Meeting Works™.

Figure 11.1   A typical GSS meeting room

and promotes the 'honest, objective evaluation of contributions based solely on the merit of the idea and not the author' (Klein et al. 2007: 2115).

There are a number of other advantages associated with using GSS technology. First, it allows each group member to input 'top-of-mind' information early in the process before any individual has an opportunity to dominate the discussion. This ensures that all participants are able to have their ideas recorded and considered by the group. As a result, prior studies have suggested that using a GSS approach typically results in more ideas being captured compared with a traditional focus group. For example, Sweeney et al. (1997) found that GSS groups produced a third more ideas compared to traditional focus groups. Second, the highly structured nature of GSS groups also seems to generate more 'usable' information because unimportant sidetracks are more easily avoided and it is easier to keep participants focused on the task (Sweeney et al. 1997). Third, when using GSS technology, the 'facilitator is free to give full attention to group dynamics without having to control a queue of speakers, write ideas or take down notes' (Soutar et al. 1996: 38) and this can significantly increase the effectiveness of the process. Fourth, the GSS approach

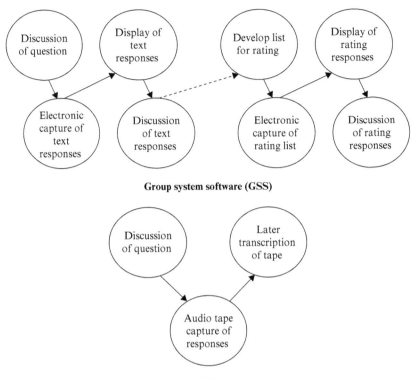

Group system software (GSS)

Traditional focus groups

Source: Newby et al. (2003: 425).

Figure 11.2   Sequence of events

allows participants to rate, or rank, the ideas generated by the group during the session. This can be useful when determining which ideas, out of a long list, should be retained for further analysis or discussion. Finally, the GSS technology permits the ideas that are generated by the group to be displayed (or printed) at important stages of the process, enabling these ideas to be used for further group discussion, and ensuring that good ideas are not 'lost'. Figure 11.2 depicts the sequence of events as they might occur in a typical GSS session compared with a traditional focus group.

One possible disadvantage of the GSS approach is that it may increase the cost of conducting a focus group session, as it requires sophisticated computer equipment (including computer hardware and software and data display facilities) and both a moderator and a chauffeur. However, there may also be some cost savings as the need to transcribe audio or video recordings is substantially reduced (or eliminated entirely); this also means that the output is available for analysis much sooner than would be the case with a traditional focus group.

Another potential disadvantage of using the GSS technology is that it may prevent a free-flowing discussion. This, in turn, may result in a less 'in-depth' understanding of the issues of interest than would otherwise have been achieved using a traditional focus group format (Sweeney et al. 1997). Whether or not this is a serious disadvantage will depend on the primary purpose of the session (that is, idea generation or in-depth understanding). In any event, significant discussion can still take place in a GSS session after participants have entered their responses. Although the purpose of this discussion is usually to simply clarify, or elaborate on, particular ideas before moving to the next question, the researcher could (as is the case with traditional focus groups) capture this interaction using audio/video recordings.

It should be noted that some participants might be reluctant to use computer technology with which they are unfamiliar. However, as the use of various forms of electronic communication becomes more wide-spread, this problem should become less of an issue (Soutar et al. 1996).

GSS FOCUS GROUP RESEARCH IN PRACTICE

The principles discussed above will now be further highlighted in an analysis of two entrepreneurship studies that adopted a GSS focus group methodology. The aim of study 1 was to specifically examine the relative benefits of traditional versus GSS focus groups. In study 2 focus groups were used to gain a better understanding of the demand side issues relating to external sources of funding for growth-oriented small and medium-sized enterprises (SMEs) and to determine if there are any notable differences between male and female owners.

Study 1: Comparing Traditional Focus Groups with a Group Support System (GSS) Approach for Use in SME Research

Introduction
We now return to the second focus group study introduced in the previous chapter (Newby et al. 2003) concerned with exploring SME owner-operator objectives. Aside from its primary purpose of investigating owner-operator objectives, the study was also concerned with comparing the effectiveness of traditional versus GSS focus groups. The purpose here is to specifically examine some of the key differences that were experienced

by the researchers in using the two focus group formats. It should be noted that the same moderator, who was experienced in running both forms of focus groups, ran the two traditional and the two GSS focus groups that were undertaken for the purposes of this study.

Conducting the focus groups

For the traditional focus groups the responses to the various questions posed (and the ensuing discussion/comments) were captured on audio tapes. These were subsequently transcribed by a person separate from the research team and the transcript was then analysed for content by one of the members of the researcher team. For the GSS sessions, all the formal responses to the focus group questions were captured electronically and these responses were then displayed (anonymously) for participants to discuss. For some questions the moderator developed a summary table of participants' responses. Participants were then asked to rate (score) the importance of each item in the summary listing. These ratings were also captured electronically for subsequent use by the researchers. The discussion/comment by participants during the GSS session was captured on audio tapes. Note, however, that the amount of material captured on audio tape (and, therefore, needing transcription) for the GSS sessions was trivial by comparison with the traditional focus group sessions.

Results from a comparison of the traditional and GSS methodologies

Table 11.1 compares the number of responses provided by the traditional and GSS focus group participants to a variety of questions about the reasons people go into business and their future goals.

It should be noted that a total of 16 participants (including four females) participated in the two traditional focus group sessions, while only 13 participants (including seven females) participated in the two GSS sessions. For this reason Table 11.1 reports both the total number of responses captured for each question as well as the responses generated per participant. Consistent with the perceived advantages of the GSS technology described earlier, the GSS groups produced more responses per participant. In particular, we experienced a significant degree of 'yea saying' by participants in the traditional groups and it seems that the mindset of the group was often driven by whoever gave the initial response to the moderator's question. For example, this effect was especially noticeable when participants were asked to identify the specific personal goals of people in small business and for themselves (last two questions in Table 11.1). The first comment made in both traditional focus groups was that business and personal goals were too intertwined to discuss separately. This comment was immediately agreed to by the other group members and, therefore, no

Table 11.1   Number of replies generated by type of focus group

	Traditional groups	GSS groups
At start-up		
Why do you think people go into business?		
Replies	17	33
Replies per participant	1.06	2.54
Why did you go into business for yourself?		
Replies	20	44
Replies per participant	1.25	3.38
At the present point in time		
What do you enjoy most about being in business for yourself?		
Replies	13	37
Replies per participant	0.81	2.85
In the future		
What are the specific business goals of people in small business?	This question was	
Replies	missed for one group	12
Replies per participant		0.92
What are your goals for the business?		
Replies	11	23
Replies per participant	0.69	1.77
What are the specific personal goals of people in small business?	Did not differentiate	
Replies	from business goals	15
Replies per participant		1.15
What are your goals for yourself in relation to the business?	Did not differentiate	
Replies	from business goals	24
Replies per participant		1.85

Source: Newby et al. (2003: 428, table 1).

meaningful replies were generated for these last two questions from the traditional focus group participants. No such problem was encountered in the two groups using the GSS technology.

Another problem that has been identified with respect to traditional focus groups is their capacity to go 'off-track', or away from the predetermined script. Our experience supports this view. Although the moderator operated from the same script in all four focus groups, an important

Table 11.2   Participants' scoring of ideas generated by the group

What do you enjoy most about being in business for yourself?

GSS group 1	Average score	GSS group 2	Average score
Control of my own destiny	2.5	Making money	2.9
Happy customers	2.0	Control of my own destiny	1.7
Being my own boss	1.2	The 'challenge'	1.5
Flexibility	1.1	Achieving	1.2
The 'challenge'	1.1	Being my own boss	1.1
Achieving	0.9	Flexibility	1.0
To be a leader	0.5	Social interaction	0.5
Recognition of our achievements	0.5	Revenge	0.1
Offering employment	0.2		

Source: Newby et al. (2003: 429, table 2).

question was missed in one of the traditional focus groups (as noted in Table 11.1 with respect to the fourth question). This could not have occurred in the GSS groups given the 'pre-programming' of questions in their expected order.

Fortunately, we did not have any particularly dominant personalities in either of the two traditional focus groups and, therefore, did not experience any of the potential difficulties discussed earlier that can arise when such personalities are present. However, there was an extremely dominant, and negative, participant in one of the GSS groups who tested the moderator's patience. The way in which the GSS technology reduced this person's impact on the group's discussion (and thinking) was noticeable, and served to demonstrate the significant advantage of using the GSS technology.

The GSS technology also made it possible for participants to be asked to rate, or rank, the importance of particular ideas (anonymously) during the session For example, once the participants had answered the question, 'What do you enjoy most about being in business for yourself', the chauffeur generated a listing of the qualitative responses produced by the group. Participants were then asked to allocate ten points across the items on the list. The average score for each item is shown in Table 11.2. This ranking of ideas, in order of perceived importance, proved helpful in subsequent efforts to develop a scale for the measurement of SME owner-operator objectives.

Finally, we found that using the GSS technology was no more

costly than running a traditional focus group. The moderator charged the same fee for each of the groups and the rental cost of the GSS software and hardware (together with the payment for the chauffeur) was less than the additional cost of transcribing the audio-tapes for the traditional focus groups. Therefore, the GSS technology provided a win-win situation; it generated more responses for a lower total cost.

Conclusion

While both approaches were useful in terms of generating ideas from the target audience, adopting the GSS technology resulted in a number of significant benefits compared with using a more traditional approach. In particular, the anonymity of responses with the GSS approach ensured that the ideas generated (or issues raised) were de-personalized in subsequent discussion. This anonymity also seemed to: increase the quantum of ideas generated; encourage participation from the more timid members of the group; and reduce the opportunity for forceful personalities to dominate the outcomes. The GSS technology also ensured that the discussion was kept 'on-track' and removed the opportunity for members to 'yea say', or agree with the first idea presented. Finally, when using the GSS technology, the moderator was able (through the chauffeur) to make findings available to the group members immediately so that clarification, correction and, in particular, some quantitative analysis of responses, could take place during the session.

Study 2: Comparing the Growth and External Funding of Male- and Female-Controlled SMEs in Australia

Introduction

'Understanding how firms grow . . ., especially small firms, is an important issue' (Carpenter and Petersen 2002: 298) because SMEs provide the 'engine of economic growth' for many countries (Berger and Udell 1998: 613). Winborg and Landstrom (2001) argue that financial problems (lack of funds) constrain the development and growth of SMEs because many SMEs are unable to access the same kinds of growth funding (particularly equity raisings) often available to large businesses. It has also been suggested that the lack of funding options is even more acute for female-owned SMEs (Riding and Swift 1990; Breen et al. 1995; Brush et al. 2001). To date, the majority of research concerned with the funding of SMEs has concentrated on supply side issues with many studies focusing on the factors that influence the investment decisions by suppliers of finance, particularly venture capitalists. Fried and Hisrich (1988) suggest that future research should also look at demand side issues where the available evidence is far more limited.

The aim of this study (conducted in 2006 by Watson, Newby and Mahuka) was, therefore, to use a focus group methodology to gain a better understanding of the demand-side issues surrounding the acquisition of growth funding for both male- and female-owned SMEs.

Background

Carpenter and Petersen (2002) examined more than 1600 US small manufacturing firms and found that the growth of these firms appeared to be constrained by a lack of internal finance. Similarly, Bruno and Tyebjee (1985) found that ventures that had received external capital achieved statistically significantly higher sales and employment growth compared to ventures without external capital. With respect to women-owned businesses, Carter and Allen (1997) noted that the availability of financial resources was the major influence on their growth. Clearly there appears to be a strong link between the availability of finance and SME growth and this has led to the notion of an 'equity (finance) gap', implying 'there may be major barriers preventing an owner-manager's access to equity' (Hutchinson 1995: 231). These barriers are generally believed to result from deficiencies in capital markets and would include instances where owners are 'discouraged' from applying for external funds because they believe their application will be rejected (Kon and Storey 2003).

However, it is possible that many SME owners might consciously decide they do not want to access external funding given the financial risks involved and/or the potential for them to lose control of their firms (Barton and Matthews 1989; Cressy 1995; Hamilton and Fox 1998). Indeed, Cressy (1995: 293) developed 'a model in which non-borrowing and non-growth are regarded as optimal . . . solutions to the problem of conflict between the productiveness of financial capital and the desire for business independence from outsiders.' Finally, it is also possible that some businesses 'are not aware of opportunities offered by alternative sources of funding' (Romano et al. 2001: 304).

Based on a large sample of New Zealand SMEs, Hamilton and Fox (1998) concluded that debt levels in small firms reflected demand-side decisions and were not just the result of supply-side deficiencies. They argued that managerial beliefs and desires played an important role in determining the capital structure of SMEs and that a deeper appreciation of these issues would lead to a better understanding of the capital structure policies of individual SMEs. Chaganti et al. (1996) also found that the major determinant of SME capital structure was owner goals, as these assisted in predicting debt versus equity and internal versus external funding.

These findings might be particularly relevant for female-controlled SMEs because, as Buttner and Moore (1997: 34) note, female entrepreneurs measure success in terms of 'self-fulfilment and goal achievement. Profits and business growth, while important, were less substantial measures of their success'.

Using structured equation modelling on a sample of Swedish SMEs, Berggren et al. (2000) sought to determine the relative impact of five factors (the size of the firm, its degree of technological development, the perceived need to grow to survive, the amount of internally generated funds and the owner-operator's aversion to losing control) on a firm's decision to apply for a bank loan. They found that the strength of the owner-operators' desire to maintain control of their firms was the principal determinant in their decision to (not to) apply for bank finance, although this was significantly moderated by the need for technological development (a proxy for industry) and the size of the firm. This finding with respect to control is consistent with the argument advanced by Cressy (1995: 292) that the '[c]hanges in management structure required by successful growth may not therefore be taken on board by owner managers who prefer to have a smaller organisation and a "finger in every pie" rather than a larger, fast-growth organisation with increasingly devolved control.' This issue might be particularly relevant for female SME owners, as Mukhtar (2002) reports that, in terms of their management styles, women had a significantly greater need (compared with men) to be in control of all aspects of their business.

Hutchinson (1995: 238) suggests that 'when the owner-manager's attitude is risk averse and is accompanied by a desire to retain control of the firm in some form, he may actively place limits on the use and growth of equity'. This could result in some SME owner-managers deliberately choosing low (no) growth options and might be particularly relevant for female-owned SMEs because:

> female entrepreneurs are more likely to establish maximum business size thresholds beyond which they would prefer not to expand, and that these thresholds are smaller than those set by their male counterparts. Female entrepreneurs also seem to be more concerned than male entrepreneurs about the risks of fast-paced growth and tend to deliberately adopt a slow and steady rate of expansion. (Cliff 1998: 523)

In summary, therefore, it would appear that existing theories on the determinants of a firm's capital structure (primarily developed from studies of listed companies) might require modification to include 'the many factors that are a part of the small firm financing decision process, among them: goals, risk aversion, and internal constraints' (Barton and Matthews 1989: 1). Based on the above literature review, the following issues/questions were identified for further investigation in this research project:

1. What are the potential obstacles SME owners face in wanting to substantially grow their businesses?
2. What external sources of funding are SME owners aware of?
3. Why might SME owners choose not to seek external funding?
4. What do SME owners see as the main disadvantages of debt funding?
5. What do SME owners believe are the main reasons for banks refusing loans?
6. How strongly do SME owners feel about maintaining control of their firms?
7. Do male and female SME owners have similar attitudes to risk?
8. What factors are likely to influence an individual SME owner's decision to access external sources of funding?

The number of focus groups and the nature and number of participants
A market research company was used to recruit a sample of 30 Western Australian metropolitan SME owner-operators who had considered (within the prior two to five years) a major expansion of their business that required significant external funding. The Appendix to this chapter contains the screening document that was provided to the market research company to help with the recruitment process. The plan was to run three separate focus groups with ten participants in each (and comprising a reasonable representation of both male and female SME owners), constituted as follows:

1. 'Discouraged' borrowers – those that had ultimately decided not to seek external funding;
2. 'Unsuccessful' borrowers – those that had been unsuccessful in their attempt(s) to seek external funding; and
3. 'Successful' borrowers – those that had been successful in their attempt(s) to seek external funding.

Unfortunately, the market research company had great difficulty recruiting participants for the second group and, therefore, this group ended up with seven successful and two unsuccessful participants (both males). Given the often-argued existence of a 'finance gap', this was somewhat surprising, but confirmed US results reported by Levenson and Willard (2000) indicating that only about 2 per cent of firms did not obtain the funding for which they had applied. It should also be noted that participants were offered a $100 incentive to attend their designated focus group session and, possibly because of this incentive, there were only four

Table 11.3 Demographics for focus group participants

Industry	Male	Female	Amount of funding required	
			<100 000	100 000–500 000
Air conditioning	1		1	
Appliance services	1		1	+
Beauty		1	1	
Bookbinder	1			1
Builder		1	1	
Carpet cleaning	1		1	
Clothing wholesaler		1	1	
Diesel engines	1		1	
Finance	1		1	
Hardware	1		1	
Health	1		1	
Landscaping supplies		1	1	
Limousine tours	1			1
Manufacturer		1		1
Manufacturer		1		1
Mechanical repairs		1		1
Mechanical services	1		1	
Motorcycle sales		1	1	
Physiotherapy	1			1
Plant hire	1		1	
Printing	1		1	
Scrap metal	1		1	
Settlement agent		1	1	
Travel	1		1	
Unknown	1		1	
Unknown	1		1	
Total	17	9	20	6

Source: Watson et al. (2006: 217, table 9.5).

'no-shows' (evenly spread such that there were between eight and nine participants in each of the three sessions). Table 11.3 provides some brief demographic information about the focus group participants. Note that the majority of participants required less than $100 000 in funding. The initial sample contained one person who required more than $500 000 but that person failed to turn up for their focus group session.

Besides the arguments advanced earlier in favour of the GSS methodology, our decision to adopt this technology in this particular study was influenced by the argument advanced by Klein et al. (2007: 2118) suggesting that when a traditional focus group 'consists of both men and women, differences in gender-related communication styles can stifle communication, and, in particular, constrain the input of women'. The other solution to this problem might have been to expand the number of focus groups from three to six to allow separate sessions for the male and female participants. However, this was not possible within the budget constraints we faced.

The venue
The facility used for the GSS focus group sessions was located in the centre of the city of Perth, ensuring participants did not have too far to travel. Given the sessions were conducted after normal business hours, parking was also not a problem for the participants.

Focus group structure
Newby et al. (2003) note that using GSS technology does not prohibit researchers from also using a traditional focus group approach for discussing those issues where a deeper understanding is desired. Consequently, a combination of both the GSS and traditional approaches was used to capture the ideas generated by the focus group participants. For example, there were a number of questions (such as, 'What sources of external funding are available to business owners wanting to substantially grow their businesses?') where the focus group participants were asked to enter their responses directly into a computer terminal. The GSS technology allowed these responses to be captured in the form of a tabular report for subsequent discussion by the group. These discussions, as well as the participants' responses to two additional questions where a more free-flowing discussion was desired, were captured on video.

The moderator
The GSS facility for the focus group sessions came with a trained moderator and chauffeur. However, two members of the research team also attended all three sessions to answer any questions the moderator may not have been in a position to answer and to help organize for the consent forms to be signed and collected, and for the payment of $100 honorarium to each participant.

Conducting the focus groups
Participants were informed that light refreshments would be provided at 6.30 p.m. prior to commencing the focus group sessions which were expected to last about two hours. The refreshments were provided in a

separate room and allowed the participants to relax and to meet with fellow participants prior to moving into the GSS meeting room.

The moderator welcomed the participants, introduced the chauffeur and the researchers present, and briefly explained to the participants how to operate the GSS technology they would be using during the session. Participants were also informed that the researchers present were available to help them should they experience any problems with the technology. Prior to commencing the discussion the moderator also ensured that all participants had read and signed a consent form and that these had been passed to one of the researchers present.

Results

Analysis of the GSS responses (and the video recording) was conducted in accordance with normal practice. Initially, two members of the research team separately coded participant responses to the various questions. These researchers then met to discuss and agree on the coding categories that would be used to group participants' responses. Inter-rater reliability was assessed by the degree to which the two researchers arrived at the same inferences (Griggs 1987) using the kappa statistic K (Siegel and Castellan 1988). For all questions and across all groups, the observed K was substantially greater than the value that would be expected by chance at a 1 per cent level of significance. Where there were any differences in the coding by the two researchers that could not be resolved, the third member of the research team was called in and the final coding decision was decided by a majority vote.

Tables 11.4 to 11.9 set out the results from the first six questions where participant responses were captured using the GSS technology. Tables 11.10 to 11.11 present a summary of participant responses (captured on video) to the final two questions where a more free-flowing discussion was sought. For the purposes of presenting the results, the responses from the second (n = 9) and third (n = 9) focus groups have been combined and this combined group has been labelled 'successful'. This combined ('successful') group included responses from two 'unsuccessful' applicants and, therefore, this is acknowledged as a limitation.[1] There were eight participants in the first focus group comprising 'discouraged' borrowers.

The first issue the focus group participants were asked to address was the major obstacles SME owners might potentially encounter if they wanted to substantially grow their business. Table 11.4 summarizes the participants' responses. The results indicate that the majority (53 per cent) of obstacles identified related to operational issues (such as lack of appropriate staff, facilities, time and expertise). Next were concerns about

Table 11.4   Potential obstacles to growth

Obstacles faced	Discouraged N = 8		Successful N = 18		Total N = 26	
	No.	(%)	No.	(%)	No.	(%)
Operational issues – lack of appropriate staff; facilities; time; supplies; and expertise/knowledge in assessing strategy, market size, competition and how to go about growing the business	18	(39)	60	(59)	78	(53)*
Funding issues – lack of internal cash flow or external funds at reasonable rate & terms	11	(24)	24	(24)	35	(24)
Government regulation – intrusion, lack of support fees and taxes	15	(33)	7	(7)	22	(15)*
Fear of failure/unsure of benefits	1	(2)	9	(9)	10	(7)
Others	1	(2)	1	(1)	2	(1)
Total	46	(100)	101	(100)	147	(100)

Note: * 'Discouraged' group significantly different to 'successful' group at 1 per cent (using chi square test).

Source: Watson et al. (2006: 218, table 9.6).

funding (24 per cent); government regulation (15 per cent); fear of failure (7 per cent); and other (1 per cent).

What was particularly interesting, were the notable differences between the group of 'discouraged' borrowers and the 'successful' borrowers. Compared with the 'successful' borrowers, the 'discouraged' borrowers were much more likely to list government regulation as a major obstacle and much less likely to acknowledge potential operational problems. There were no significant differences across the two groups in terms of the frequency with which the remaining concerns were listed, including financial issues.

When asked about potential sources of funds, most participants noted the three common sources that are grouped in Table 11.5 under the three broad headings of bank/financial institution, equity issue and leasing. However, there were a number of other potential sources of funds that many of the participants were either not aware of or had not thought of (for example: various government schemes; approaching suppliers and/or customers; and venture capital). Interestingly, the 'successful' group seemed to identify proportionately more sources of external funding than did the 'discour-

Table 11.5   Sources of external funding

Funding sources	Discouraged N = 8		Successful N = 18		Total N = 26	
	No.	(%)	No.	(%)	No.	(%)
Bank/financial institution (loans/overdraft/credit card)	6	(21)	26	(30)	32	(28)
Equity issue – new partner, employees, suppliers, listing	4	(14)	23	(26)	27	(23)
Leasing/hire – purchase/loan sharks	5	(18)	11	(13)	16	(14)
Government – grants or guaranteed loans	3	(11)	5	(6)	8	(7)
Brokers/financial advisers	3	(11)	5	(6)	8	(7)
Factoring debtors	1	(4)	4	(5)	5	(4)
Suppliers (credit)/customers (up front payments)	1	(4)	4	(5)	5	(4)
Venture capital	1	(4)	2	(2)	3	(3)
Family/friends (business angels)	1	(4)	2	(2)	3	(3)
Offshore financing	1	(4)	1	(1)	2	(2)
Franchising	1	(4)	0	0	1	(1)
Self – funded superannuation fund	1	(4)	0	0	1	(1)
Business migrants	0	0	1	(1)	1	(1)
Others/unknown	0	0	3	(3)	3	(3)
Total	28	(100)	87	(100)	115	(100)

Source: Watson et al. (2006: 219, table 9.7).

aged' group. This could possibly indicate that these owners had been more serious about expanding their firms and, therefore, had spent more time and energy researching possible sources of external funding.

Table 11.6 summarizes the responses from the participants when asked to list the reasons why SME owners might not seek external funding. As expected, consistent with 'pecking order' theory (Jensen and Meckling 1976), the most common reason given was because there were sufficient internal funds available. Other major reasons included: the risk involved; not wanting the burden of having to service additional debt; and the terms of the funding might be unacceptable. The contrast between the 'discouraged' and 'successful' groups was again of some interest. The 'discouraged' group was much more concerned about the work/hassles involved with expansion than were the members of the 'successful' group. This suggests that the members of the 'discouraged' group might have

Table 11.6   Reasons SME owners might choose not to seek external funding

Reason	Discouraged N = 8		Successful N = 18		Total N = 26	
	No.	(%)	No.	(%)	No.	(%)
Adequate internal funds	4	(15)	18	(28)	22	(24)
Risk/uncertainty about future/ potential to lose control/fear of failure	5	(19)	11	(17)	16	(17)
Burden (don't want)/can't service more debt	5	(19)	9	(14)	14	(15)
Terms unacceptable – interest rates/ security/etc	3	(11)	10	(15)	13	(14)
Expand (don't want to) can't cope/ too many hassles/lack confidence	7	(26)	1	(2)	8	(9)
Time & aggravation of trying to get a bank loan	2	(7)	6	(9)	8	(9)
Unavailable because of poor/no credit rating	1	(4)	4	(6)	5	(5)
Other	0	0	6	(9)	6	(7)
Total	27	(100)	65	(100)	92	(100)

Source: Watson et al. (2006: 220, table 9.8).

been 'discouraged' for primarily 'internal' reasons rather than because they thought their loan application would be turned down.

The groups were then asked to specifically consider the disadvantages of debt funding; their responses are presented in Table 11.7. Both groups agreed that the major issue centred on the risks involved. These risks included the obvious concern about the potential for interest rate rises, but many participants also raised a (perhaps less obvious) concern that having easy access to funds (particularly credit cards) might cause the business owner to spend unnecessarily (for example, on new equipment). For many of the participants, the additional burden and stress involved with repaying the debt was also of concern. Comparing the 'discouraged' and 'successful' group indicates that the potential for loss of control seems to be of much greater concern to the 'discouraged' group. This finding is consistent with Cressy's (1995) argument that where an owner's desire for control is strong enough, their business will be entirely self-funded. Again, this indicates the importance of 'internal' factors when SME owners consider growth options that are likely to require debt funding.

Table 11.7   Main disadvantages of debt funding

Reason	Discouraged N = 8		Successful N = 18		Total N = 26	
	No.	(%)	No.	(%)	No.	(%)
Risk – interest rate changes, can't repay debt, spend too much	12	(43)	26	(47)	38	(46)
Burden/worry/work/stress/ paperwork	4	(14)	12	(22)	16	(19)
Dislike of financial institutions/ terms/fees disclosures	4	(14)	4	(7)	8	(10)
Control may be lost – dependence on others is increased	4	(14)	2	(4)	6	(7)*
Costs	0	(0)	5	(9)	5	(6)
Other	4	(14)	6	(11)	10	(12)
Total	28	(100)	55	(100)	83	(100)

Note: * 'Discouraged' group significantly different to 'successful' group at 1 per cent (using chi square test).

Source: Watson et al. (2006: 221, table 9.9).

Table 11.8   Reasons for bank refusing a loan application

Reason	Discouraged N = 8		Successful N = 18		Total N = 26	
	No.	(%)	No.	(%)	No.	(%)
Business plan – don't have one or not convincing or bank doesn't understand	12	(31)	23	(29)	35	(29)
Track record – poor credit rating or don't have one	9	(23)	19	(24)	28	(24)
Risk – too high	8	(21)	11	(14)	19	(16)
Lack of equity/security	4	(10)	15	(19)	19	(16)
Other	6	(15)	12	(15)	18	(15)
Total	39	(100)	80	(100)	119	(100)

Source: Watson et al. (2006: 222, table 9.10).

Table 11.9   Importance of maintaining control

Rating	Discouraged N = 8		Successful N = 18		Total N = 26	
	No.	(%)	No.	(%)	No.	(%)
1	9	(100)	13	(76)	22	(85)
2			2	(12)	2	(8)
3			1	(6)	1	(4)
4						
5						
6						
7			1	(6)	1	(4)
Mean	1.00		1.67		1.38	
Std dev.	0.00		1.59		1.24	

Note: 1 = very important, 7 = unimportant.

Source: Watson et al. (2006: 223, table 9.11).

Table 11.8 sets out the participants' responses when asked to list the reasons why a bank might refuse a loan application. The majority of reasons provided by the participants can be grouped under two broad headings: perceived inadequacies in the owner's business acumen (business plan and track record), and the perceived risks (including lack of equity/ security). This suggests that business owners need to ensure they have a credible business plan that is easily understood; so that the bank manager can properly assess the risks involved. In this regard there might be an important role for external advisers; particularly for inexperienced owners and/or owners without the necessary skills to complete the task. For this question there were no significant differences between the 'discouraged' and 'successful' groups. There was also nothing in the responses to suggest that the banks routinely made 'screening errors' (Kon and Storey 2003: 37) and, therefore, the focus group results suggest that the 'discouraged' borrower syndrome, as described by Kon and Storey (2003), might be relatively trivial. This is not to say that owners are not 'discouraged' from borrowing funds for growth, but rather the causes of their discouragement might have more to do with the owners themselves (for example, their desire to maintain control and their risk aversion) rather than with deficiencies in the banking sector or the existence of a 'finance gap'.

Table 11.9 confirms just how important maintaining control was for the majority of the focus group participants. In the 'discouraged' group, all participants rated the importance of maintaining control as a '1' (very

Table 11.10   Comparing male and female SME owners' attitudes to risk*

Attitude to risk	Males	Females	Total
Women more conservative	4	3	7
Depends on personality	2	1	3
No difference	0	2	2
Men more conservative	0	1	1
Total	6	7	13

Note: * Where a participant spoke on more than one occasion, their view was only recorded once.

Source: Watson et al. (2006: 224, table 9.12).

important). In the 'successful' group there was a little more dispersion in the ratings, however, the majority of the group still attached a very high level of importance to maintaining control. The one exception was a female participant who indicated that, for her, maintaining control was unimportant.[2]

The final two tables summarize the responses from the focus group participants to the final two 'general' questions captured on video, rather than using the GSS technology. It was decided that for these questions it would be preferable for participants to have a free-ranging discussion not inhibited by the requirement to enter their thoughts into a computer terminal. This also allowed gender differences to be explored.[3] Interestingly, although more time was spent by each of the groups on these final two questions than was spent on any of the other questions, fewer ideas seemed to be generated. This was the result of the conversation being dominated by a few individuals, such that the remainder of the participants had limited opportunity to speak and to express their thoughts.

Table 11.10 reports the views of the group with respect to the risk-taking propensity of men and women. The responses for the male and female focus group participants are shown separately. Note that for Table 11.10, each person's view was recorded only once, although they may have commented on more than one occasion. Interestingly, over half the participants (mainly the males) did not express a view on this issue. The consensus of those who spoke was that women were likely to be more conservative (risk averse), although a significant number of participants believed that either there was no difference, or that it depended on the personality of the individual owner rather than their sex.

Finally, Table 11.11 sets out the key thoughts/ideas expressed by the participants concerning the factors (issues) that might influence an SME

Table 11.11   Factors likely to influence a SME owner's decision to access external funding

Key thoughts (ideas)	No. of times mentioned
Growth:	
Without profit it isn't worth it	4
Can't just decide to grow – there are competitors	2
Business conditions:	
Less likely to borrow if business is volatile and control could be lost	2
If firm is failing you might borrow to try and save the business	2
Exiting the firm:	
Additional funding isn't needed if you are planning to exit the firm	4
Unless you want to build the business up ready for sale	1
Or have someone (who you trust) willing to buy in	1
Although finding that trustworthy person isn't easy	2
I would prefer to sell the business to my staff	1
I would be prepared to offer key personnel a stake in the business	1
I am planning to hand the business over to my kids	1
Accessing debt funding:	
As you get older it is harder to get a loan (repayments)	1
As you get older it is easier to get a loan (security)	1
As you get older you may not want to borrow	1
Age makes no difference	2
Being married helps when you borrow	1
But for women the husband must often co-sign	1
Banks want security	2
Banks don't lend to businesses they don't understand	2
Bank will lend you money when you don't need/want it	1
Bigger firms find it easier to borrow	1
Bigger loans attract lower interest rates	1
More likely to borrow to modernize equipment	1
But over-capitalizing isn't helpful	1
Total	37

Source: Watson et al. (2006, Table 9.13, p. 225).

owner's decision to access external funding. Although this question overlaps a number of earlier questions, it gave the participants the opportunity to elaborate on issues they might previously have recorded using the GSS technology. Two main thoughts emerged from this discussion. First, that growth for growth's sake, without a growth in profit, was not worthwhile. Second, owners who were planning to exit the firm were unlikely to want to raise additional funding for fear of over-capitalizing the business. In terms of funding sources, it was interesting that the few negative comments made about banks (for example, banks will only lend you money when you don't need/want it; and banks won't lend to businesses they don't understand) came from members of the 'discouraged' group.

It is difficult to know on what basis they formed their views (perhaps it was from their previous experiences, or from hearing about the experiences of others) but clearly their views were not shared by the participants in the 'successful' group. However, the comment that banks don't lend to businesses they don't understand raises two important issues. First, it suggests that banks should not discount the importance of relationship (compared with transactions-based) lending for the SME sector. 'Relationship lending is generally associated with the collection of "soft" information over time through relationships with the firm, the owner, and the local community' (Berger and Udell 2002: F38). In contrast, transactions-based lending is 'generally associated with the use of "hard" information' (Berger and Udell 2002: F38), such as financial ratios, and may not be appropriate for many SMEs, particularly if the business is not routine. Second, it is important that SME owners seeking external funding ensure they have a clearly articulated business plan that makes it as easy as possible for a loan officer to understand the nature of the business and the risks involved. SME owners with limited expertise in this area should consider obtaining professional help.

Conclusion

Previous research has suggested that a lack of external funding opportunities may be inhibiting the growth of many SMEs; particularly female-owned SMEs. Because smaller firms 'are often so informationally opaque ... potential providers of external finance cannot readily verify that the firm has access to a quality project (adverse selection problem) or ensure that the funds will not be diverted to fund an alternative project (moral hazard problem)' (Berger and Udell 2002: F32). This has led to the belief there is a 'finance gap' within the SME sector. Further, Kon and Storey (2003) argue that, in some cases, owners' perceptions (beliefs) might contribute to this 'finance gap'. That is, some owners might believe that, even though they have a good project, the bank would be unlikely to lend to them and, therefore, they don't bother to apply for a loan. Kon and Storey (2003) refer to these owners as 'discouraged' borrowers.

However, the evidence from this study suggests that the significance of any 'finance gap' for Australian SMEs might be quite small, if it exists at all. This conclusion is based on two observations. First, the market research company employed to find focus group participants had great difficulty recruiting business owners who had tried unsuccessfully to raise external funding to expand their business. Second, the results from the focus group discussions did not provide any reason to believe there was a significant 'finance gap' caused by deficiencies in capital markets. Indeed, it would appear from the results that many SME owners deliberately choose not to expand their business because of the extra workload involved, rather than because of a lack of available finance.

Further, the results suggest that an SME owner's decision to access external funding depends heavily on the owner's attitude to risk and control, as these were the two key themes to emerge from the focus group sessions. It seems that the majority of participants were acutely aware of the various risks involved in business ownership and this was foremost in their minds when they considered the merits of seeking external funds to expand their business. In terms of gender differences, the majority of participants (both men and women) felt that female business owners were more risk-averse than their male counterparts. There were, however, a number of participants who felt that either there was no difference between men and women, or that it was a personality attribute not related to the sex of the owner.

The potential to lose control of their firm was the second major issue at the 'top of the mind' for the majority of the focus group participants. For many participants it seemed that this concern was a major inhibiting factor when it came to raising external funds. The one notable exception was a male who had two business partners (both male). He felt that having three partners involved in all major decision-making prevented any one of them from taking actions potentially detrimental to the viability of the business. This participant felt, therefore, that relinquishing some degree of control was beneficial for the survival prospects of the firm. Interestingly, a number of the male focus group participants who were in partnerships with their spouses expressed similar sentiments. While they believed their spouse was more conservative, they saw this as a good thing because it prevented them (the males) from taking unnecessary risks. Again, relinquishing some level of control, albeit to a spouse, was seen as beneficial for the survival prospects of the firm.

The results from these three focus group sessions should help researchers and policy-makers better understand the way SME owners view both growth and the external funding required to facilitate that growth. A better understanding of SME owners' views with regard to growing their businesses and the use of external funding for this purpose should also be helpful to business advisers who act as intermediaries between SME owners (demand side) and the providers of external funding (supply side). The results from this study formed the basis of a subsequent survey of SME owners to determine the extent, if any, of a finance gap in Australia (Watson et al. 2009).

NOTES

1. The GSS software was set up to ensure participants' responses were anonymous and, therefore, it was not possible to separate out the responses from the two 'unsuccessful' members of the group.
2. In the discussion that followed, however, it was clear that this participant was referring to control in terms of delegating responsibility to her staff rather than control in terms of having external finance providers potentially having a say in the running of the business.
3. Note that it is possible to set up the GSS sessions in a way that allows the researchers to identify the computer terminal on which each comment was recorded and, thereby, to examine gender differences in the responses from group members. However, it was felt that maintaining complete confidentiality was more important in this particular study.

REFERENCES

Aiken, M., J. Krosp, A. Shirani and J. Martin (1994), 'Electronic brainstorming in small and large groups', *Information & Management*, **27** (3), 141–9.

Barton, S.L. and C.H. Matthews (1989), 'Small firm financing: implications from a strategic management perspective', *Journal of Small Business Management*, **27** (1), 1–7.

Berger, A.N. and G.F. Udell (1998), 'The economics of small business finance: the roles of private equity and debt markets in the financial growth cycle', *Journal of Banking and Finance*, **22** (6–8), 613–673.

Berger, A.N. and G.F. Udell (2002), 'Small business credit availability and relationship lending: the importance of bank organizational structure', *The Economic Journal*, **112** (477), F32–F55.

Berggren, B., C. Olofsson and L. Silver (2000), 'Control aversion and the search for external financing in Swedish SMEs', *Small Business Economics*, **15** (3), 233–42.

Blackburn, R. and D. Stokes (2000), 'Breaking down the barriers: using focus groups to research small and medium-sized enterprises', *International Small Business Journal*, **19** (1), 44–67.

Breen, J., C. Calvert and J. Oliver (1995), 'Female entrepreneurs in Australia: an investigation of financial and family issues', *Journal of Enterprising Culture*, **3** (4), 445–61.

Bruno, A.V. and T.T. Tyebjee (1985), 'The entrepreneur's search for capital', *Journal of Business Venturing*, **1** (1), 61–74.

Brush, C.G., N. Carter, E. Gatewood, P.G. Greene and M.M. Hart (2001), 'An investigation of women-led firms and venture capital investment', a report for the U.S. Small Business Administration, Office of Advocacy, and the National Women's Business Council, CB Associates, Washington, DC.

Buttner, E.H. and D.P. Moore (1997), 'Women's organizational exodus to entrepreneurship: self-reported motivations and correlates with success', *Journal of Small Business Management*, **35** (1), 34–46.

Carpenter, R. E. and B. C. Petersen (2002), 'Is the growth of small firms constrained by internal finance?', *The Review of Economics and Statistics*, **84** (2), 298–309.

Carter, N.M. and K.R. Allen (1997), 'Size-determinants of women-owned businesses: choice or barriers to resources', *Entrepreneurship and Regional Development*, **9** (3), 211–20.

Chaganti, R., D. DeCarolis and D. Deeds (1996), 'Predictors of capital structure in small ventures', *Entrepreneurship Theory and Practice*, **20** (2), 7–18.

Cliff, J.E. (1998), 'Does one size fit all? Exploring the relationship between attitudes towards growth, gender, and business size', *Journal of Business Venturing*, **13** (6), 523–42.

Cressy, R. (1995), 'Business borrowing and control: a theory of entrepreneurial types', *Small Business Economics*, **7** (4), 291–300.

Fried, V.H. and R.D. Hisrich (1988), 'Venture capital research: past, present and future', *Entrepreneurship Theory and Practice*, **13** (1), 15–28.

Griggs, S. (1987), 'Analysing qualitative data', *Journal of the Market Research Society*, **29** (1), 15–34.

Hamilton, R T. and M A. Fox (1998), 'The financing preferences of small firm owners', *International Journal of Entrepreneurial Behaviour & Research*, **4** (3), 239–48.

Hutchinson, R.W. (1995), 'The capital structure and investment decisions of the small owner-managed firm: some exploratory issues', *Small Business Economics*, **7** (3), 231–9.

Jensen, M. and W. Meckling (1976), 'Theory of the firm: managerial behavior, agency costs and ownership structure', *Journal of Financial Economics*, **3** (October), 305–60.

Klein, E.E., T. Tellefsen and P.J. Herskovitz (2007), 'The use of group support systems in focus groups: information technology meets qualitative research', *Computers in Human Behavior*, **23** (5), 2113–32.

Kon, Y. and D.J. Storey (2003), 'A theory of discouraged borrowers', *Small Business Economics*, **21** (1), 37–49.

Levenson, A.R. and K.L. Willard (2000), 'Do firms get the financing they want? Measuring credit rationing experienced by small businesses in the U.S.', *Small Business Economics*, **14** (2), 83–94.

Lewis, L.F. (1987), 'A decision support system for face-to-face groups', *Journal of Information Science*, **13** (4), 211–19.

Mukhtar, S.-M. (2002), 'Differences in male and female management characteristics: a study of owner-manager businesses', *Small Business Economics*, **18** (4), 289–311.

Newby, R., G. Soutar and J. Watson (2003), 'Comparing traditional focus groups with a group support system (GSS) approach for use in SME research', *International Small Business Journal*, **21** (4), 421–33.

Riding, A. and C.S. Swift (1990), 'Women business owners and terms of credit: some empirical findings of the Canadian experience', *Journal of Business Venturing*, **5** (5), 327–40.

Romano, C.A., G.A. Tanewski and K.X. Smyrnios (2001), 'Capital structure decision making: a model for family business', *Journal of Business Venturing*, **16** (3), 285–310.

Siegel, S. and J.N. Castellan (1988), *Nonparametric Statistics for the Behavioral Sciences*, New York, McGraw-Hill.

Soutar, G.N., A.M. Whitely and J.L. Callan (1996), 'Group support systems: an alternative to focus groups', *Australian Journal of Market Research*, **4** (1), 35–46.

Sweeney, J.C., G.N. Soutar, D.R. Hausknecht, R.F. Dallin and L.W. Johnson (1997), 'Collecting information from groups: a comparison of two methods', *Journal of the Market Research Society*, **39** (2), 397–411.

Valacich, J.S., A.R. Dennis and J.F. Nunamaker (1992), 'Group size and anonymity effects on computer-mediated idea generation', *Small Group Research*, **23** (1), 49–73.

Watson, J., R. Newby and A. Mahuka (2006), 'Comparing the growth and external funding of male- and female-controlled SMEs in Australia', in N.M.C. Candida, G. Brush, E.J. Gatewood, P.G. Greene and M. Hart (eds), *Growth-Oriented Women Entrepreneurs and their Businesses: A Global Research Perspective*, Cheltenham, UK and Northampton, MA, USA: Edward Elgar, pp. 205–231.

Watson, J., R. Newby and A. Mahuka (2009), 'Gender and the SME "finance gap"', *International Journal of Gender and Entrepreneurship*, **1** (1), 42–56.

Winborg, J. and H. Landstrom (2001), 'Financial bootstrapping in small businesses: examining small business managers' resource acquisition behaviors', *Journal of Business Venturing*, **16** (3), 235–54.

APPENDIX 11A.1   SCREENING PROCESS

To obtain a sample of SME owner-operators for each focus group the following questions would be asked (by a representative of the market research firm) as part of the screening process:

1. Are you the owner and/or the major decision-maker (or one of the major decision-makers) for this business?
   If yes – go to Q2.
   If no – seek details of owner/major decision-maker.
2. What is the age of your firm?
   If less than 2 years – discontinue interview.
   If 2 or more years – go to Q3.
3. Have you had at some time in the last 2–5 years intentions to substantially grow your business?
   If yes – go to Q4.
   If no – discontinue interview.
4. Did this intended growth require substantial additional funding?
   If yes – go to Q5.
   If no – discontinue interview.
5. Would you be willing to participate in a focus group conducted by researchers from The University of Western Australia (UWA) for a fee of $80? It is anticipated that the focus group session will take approximately 2 hours and will most likely be held during the week between 7 and 9 p.m.
   If yes – take contact details and go to Q6.
   If no – discontinue interview.
6. Was the funding required to grow your business:
   Less than $100 000
   Between $100 000 and $500 000
   More than $500 000
7. Did you seek funding from external sources (either debt or equity)?
   By external we mean external to the business or the owners' personal resources (including close family members).
   If yes – Go to question 8.
   If no – Allocate to Focus Group 1 and terminate interview.
8. Was your application for debt and/or equity funding and was it successful?
   – Debt funding   YES/NO   SUCCESSFUL/UNSUCCESSFUL
   – Equity funding   YES/NO   SUCCESSFUL/UNSUCCESSFUL
   If successful for debt or equity – Allocate to Focus Group 2 and terminate interview.

If unsuccessful for debt or equity – Allocate to Focus Group 3 and terminate interview.

Note: It is important that the focus groups have a mixture of both males and females and ideally we would like to have a good cross-section of businesses in terms of industry, age, and type of funding obtained (debt or equity).

12 Conducting an on-line focus group
Rick Newby and John Watson

INTRODUCTION

One major disadvantage with face-to-face focus groups is the difficulty in recruiting participants from small populations and diverse geographical regions (Hughes and Lang 2004; Oringderff 2004; Brüggen and Willems 2009; Deggs et al. 2010). The rapid development and adoption of Internet technologies has, however, helped to overcome (minimize) this problem through the facilitation of on-line focus groups (Sweet 2001; O'Connor and Madge 2003; Stewart and Williams 2005; Stancanelli 2010). As noted by O'Connor and Madge (2003: 133), '[t]he attraction of cyberspace lies in its versatility as a research medium offering possibilities in an arena not restricted by geography and where researchers can interact with participants in ways which may not be possible in the real world.'

On-line focus groups can be conducted as either real-time synchronous discussions (similar to both the traditional and GSS methodologies discussed in the previous chapters) or asynchronous discussions, which might take place over many days or weeks. Each of these formats has its advantages and disadvantages. Before exploring the specific advantages and disadvantages of synchronous versus asynchronous on-line focus groups, however, it is worth summarizing the potential advantages and disadvantages of on-line versus traditional face-to-face focus groups more generally. It should also be noted that many of the advantages and disadvantages of on-line focus groups (compared to traditional focus groups) are the same as (or similar to) those associated with the GSS format discussed in the previous chapter.

ADVANTAGES ASSOCIATED WITH ON-LINE FOCUS GROUPS

Compared with the traditional focus group format, there are a number of potential advantages associated with on-line focus groups. Perhaps the most important is the ability to bring together (on-line) geographically dispersed participants who might otherwise be unable to contribute to the discussion (without substantial costs being incurred). This could be particularly important if, for example, a researcher has a relatively small number of geographically dispersed experts who are the focus of a study.

Another key advantage of the on-line format is that it enables all individuals to effectively 'talk' at the same time (referred to as 'parallel communication'), potentially leading to greater input from group members through a reduction in 'production blocking' (Aiken et al. 1994). The on-line format also minimizes the opportunity for the discussion to be dominated by particularly outspoken individuals (Sweet 2001).

It is argued that the anonymous nature of on-line focus groups can potentially lead to more ideas being generated because shy individuals (who might be reticent to speak in a face-to-face situation) are likely to feel more comfortable expressing their views in an on-line environment. Additionally, participants in an on-line environment may be more willing to say exactly what they think and to ask what might appear to be 'foolish' questions (potentially overcoming their 'evaluation apprehension' – Aiken et al. 1994).

Further, on-line focus groups should be less costly to conduct compared with traditional focus groups as there is no need to book facilities or organize refreshments and participants do not have to incur any travel costs. The use of on-line software also delivers a transcript of the discussion immediately after the focus group session, without the need to incur additional transcription costs. Finally, unlike traditional focus groups, there is little chance that issues such as the weather, traffic and transportation will affect the 'no-show' rate for on-line focus groups (Sweet 2001).

DISADVANTAGES ASSOCIATED WITH ON-LINE FOCUS GROUPS

However, there are a number of potential disadvantages with the use of on-line focus groups that should be acknowledged. Perhaps the most important is that only those individuals who are computer literate and have ready access to Internet facilities are able to participate. However, with the rapid increase in Internet use being experienced in many countries it is likely that this concern will be greatly reduced over time (although more slowly in the third world compared to the first and for the BRIC – Brazil, Russia, India and China – group of countries). Another concern is that respondents might not be fully engaged in the on-line discussion because of distractions in their home or work environment.

Aiken et al. (1994: 143) note that most people type slower than they speak and would prefer to 'talk than type' and, further, on-line discussions can be rather impersonal and '[p]articipants may miss the camaraderie and challenge of face-to-face meetings'. This, in turn, can result in reduced group dynamics leading to poorer outcomes and potentially causing participants to find on-line focus groups less enjoyable than traditional face-to-face focus groups. Adding to these concerns is the fact that the anonymous nature of on-line focus groups can increase the potential for conflict between participants with differing views, even in comparison to similarly structured GSS groups.

It has been argued that the views of the fastest typist, or the person with the highest connection speed, may dominate the discussion due to their 'primacy effect'; that is, focus group participants are likely to take these views as a starting point for their own views (Klein et al. 2007). Whether this is true, however, will depend upon how the on-line moderator releases responses to participants. For example, assuming the on-line software employed by the researcher is similar to GSS software, then the moderator can restrict the release of answers until all participants have responded at least once (thereby ameliorating the 'primacy effect').

Another concern raised by Brüggen and Willems (2009) is that while information obtained from on-line focus groups is typically spontaneous (particularly for synchronous discussions), it can also be somewhat superficial because participants typically respond with short, keyword-like answers. As a result, on-line focus group discussions can often lack the depth typically associated with traditional focus groups (and, to a lesser extent, GSS groups). This concern is compounded by the loss of non-verbal cues in on-line discussions which limits the ability of the researcher (moderator) to engage in subtle probing of participant responses.

Finally, there are five technical issues with the use of on-line focus groups that researchers should be aware of. First, technical difficulties in terms of Internet access and/or hardware/software issues can seriously disrupt an on-line focus group, particularly if it is being held in real time. Second, on-line discussions can be more demanding as a greater level of concentration is required by participants; they have to read the question being asked, then respond, then read the responses and, finally, they have to comment on the responses. Third, given that all participants can effectively 'talk' at the same time can make it difficult for group members (and the moderator) to follow the various threads that can rapidly emerge. Fourth, there is no way of being certain that on-line participants are who they say they are. Fifth, researchers using on-line focus groups need to be concerned about data security (particularly where sensitive information is concerned), although this can likely be easily resolved with the use of encryption (Stancanelli 2010).

Having outlined some of the advantages and disadvantages associated with the use of on-line, compared to face-to-face, focus groups we will now consider some of the key differences between synchronous and asynchronous on-line focus groups.

SYNCHRONOUS VERSUS ASYNCHRONOUS ON-LINE FOCUS GROUPS

There are a number of important differences between synchronous and asynchronous on-line focus groups that researchers should be aware of, and carefully consider, before deciding on the format that is likely to best suit their particular research project.

For example, with synchronous discussions:

- participants do not have time to prepare a considered response and, therefore, the views expressed are more likely to represent their initial thoughts;
- the spontaneous nature of synchronous on-line focus groups helps to create an atmosphere where discussion and interaction can flourish, similar to traditional focus groups (Stewart and Williams 2005);
- mediating synchronous on-line focus groups can often be very challenging because of the speed with which multiple conversations (threads) can emerge (Stewart and Williams 2005);
- the results of focus group discussion(s) will be available much sooner than would typically be the case using an asynchronous format because the discussion is not spread out over a period of days/weeks;
- novice internet users and those with slow typing speeds may be left behind in 'conversations' which (typically) develop very rapidly; and
- if any Internet problems arise during the discussion there may be insufficient time for these to be resolved, thus precluding those affected from participating in the discussion.

With asynchronous discussions:

- participants can respond to questions (and the comments of other group members) at a time convenient for them. This can be particularly important where participants are in different time zones;
- participants can give a more considered response as they are not under pressure to respond quickly, a factor that could be particularly important for participants with limited typing skills;
- more participants can be involved as more time is available for participants to consider and respond to the comments of others;
- the researcher(s) potentially have to be available 24 hours a day

(for a number of days/weeks) to monitor the discussion and to keep participants 'on track'; and

- maintaining the motivation of group members over an extended period of time can be difficult.

THE ON-LINE APPROACH

With on-line focus groups, researchers typically invite pre-screened, quali-fied participants to log on to conferencing software either at a pre-arranged time (synchronous on-line focus group) or at a time that is convenient for the participant (asynchronous on-line focus group). There are a variety of software options available for conducting on-line focus groups and it is important researchers ensure that the software they select has the required features (for example, the ability to show power point slides or a video) and is relatively easy for both the researchers and participants to use. The selected software should also be compatible with both Apple Macintosh and Microsoft Windows based platforms.

Well in advance of the commencement of the proposed on-line focus group discussion, participants should be provided with: instructions (including passwords if necessary) concerning when and how to log on to the session and how to use the software; contact details (including a phone number) in case they have any questions prior to the session or should they experience technical difficulties during the session; details concerning how long the discussion will last; and information concerning the group etiquette to be observed during the discussion. It is also advisable to invite participants to log on to the site a few days before the focus group session is due to take place (using the computer they will use during the group) to ensure there are no compatibility issues with the software being used (Sweet 2001).

As with traditional focus groups, a discussion guide with questions and possible probes should be developed well in advance of the planned focus group session to make it easier for the moderator to guide the on-line discussion. It is also advisable, if feasible, to conduct a mock on-line focus group discussion with volunteers prior to conducting the first focus group session (O'Connor and Madge 2003).

At the start of the on-line focus group discussion, the researchers should introduce themselves and, if considered appropriate, they could provide summary details of the participants (or the participants could be asked to briefly introduce themselves). The purpose of the discussion should also be explained to the group and they should be encouraged to be candid and honest and to feel free to agree, disagree, or ask questions of each other as this form of interaction will 'help bring the discussion to life' (Sweet 2001: 132).

O'Connor and Madge (2003) suggest it is advisable to pre-prepare as much text as possible to save time during the on-line discussion (particularly where they are being held in real time) as the moderator can cut and paste the pre-prepared material into the discussion, as required, during the session. This can substantially reduce the amount of typing needed during the session, allowing the moderator more time to concentrate on thinking about and probing responses.

At the conclusion of the session, participants should be thanked for taking part in the on-line discussion.

ON-LINE FOCUS GROUP RESEARCH IN PRACTICE

The principles discussed above will now be further highlighted in an analysis of two studies that adopted an on-line focus group methodology. Study 1 adopted a synchronous approach to examine public attitudes towards environmental taxes in Norway. In contrast, study 2 set out to examine US student experiences and expectations with respect to an online graduate degree programme, and was conducted asynchronously.

Study 1: The Demand for Earmarking: Results from a Focus Group Study

Introduction
Through this study, Kallbekken and Aasen (2010) sought to better understand the perceptions and attitudes of the general public to the introduction of environmental taxes in Norway. The authors note that any plan for a new tax is typically met with fierce public resistance and, therefore, a better understanding of this issue might help policy-makers design an environmental tax system that is both efficient and, perhaps more importantly from a political standpoint, acceptable to the public. Given the qualitative nature of their research objective, the authors decided to adopt a qualitative research methodology; namely, focus groups. Kallbekken and Aasen (2010: 2185) argued that '[t]he open-ended nature of a focus group study makes it well suited to exploring the breadth and depth of public opinion' on the issue of environmental taxes, with the outcomes from such a study then providing a platform for conducting a subsequent larger scale quantitative study.

Kallbekken and Aasen (2010) were interested in soliciting a wide range of views, including those from rural communities, and the difficulty associated with bringing a diverse group together in one location no doubt

Table 12.1   Focus group demographics

Group	Age	N	Location	Children	Residence	Transport
1	25–40	9	Inner Oslo	No	Apartment	Public
2	33–45	9	Suburban Oslo	Yes	Detached/terraced house	Car and public
3	31–48	7	Small rural town	Yes	Detached house or apartment near the town	Car
4	50–64	10	Rural area	Yes	Remote detached house	Car

Source: Kallbekken and Aasen (2010: 2186).

motivated their use of the on-line focus group format. They also opted for synchronous rather than asynchronous discussions, presumably because all potential participants were located within the same time zone.

The number of focus groups and the nature and number of participants
Because they felt that different groups in society (for example, car owners versus users of public transport) would have different opinions about various environmental policy instruments, Kallbekken and Aasen (2010) recruited their subjects strategically to ensure they had a heterogeneous mix in terms of: age; type of residence; car ownership; household status (children or no children); and location (urban or rural).

However, to ensure participants felt as comfortable as possible in sharing their views, Kallbekken and Aasen (2010) also believed it would be advantageous if there was a relatively homogeneous mix of participants within each of the four focus group sessions they planned to conduct. Table 12.1 provides a summary of the demographic details for the 35 participants in the four *on-line* synchronous focus group sessions that were undertaken by Kallbekken and Aasen (2010) between 24 March and 16 April 2009.

Conducting the focus groups
The on-line focus group discussions were directed by an interview guide comprising six sections (see the Appendix to this chapter). First, the researchers welcomed the participants and provided a brief introduction. Second, the researchers opened the discussion with a number of fairly general questions about environmental problems and possible solutions (for example, 'Are there any environmental problems which you are particularly concerned about?' and 'What makes policy instruments work?'). Third, the researchers moved to the issue of environmental

taxes with questions such as 'Which environmental taxes do you know about?' and 'Can environmental taxes have any negative effects?' Fourth, the participants were asked for their views about how the revenue raised from environmental taxes should be used (with questions such as: 'Environmental taxes produce revenues. What do you believe these revenues should be used for?'). The final set of questions revolved around distributional effects with questions, such as:

> Some environmental taxes have to be paid by all who use a service or a product, like the fuel tax or the tax on electricity consumption. Some would claim that this is unfair as the tax does not depend on whether you have any alternatives nor on the level of income. What do you think about this?

The researchers then made some closing remarks, thanked the participants for their input, and provided the participants with information concerning the gift card (valued at approximately US$100) they would receive in recognition of the time they had devoted to participating in the project.

Kallbekken and Aasen (2010) note that throughout the on-line discussions they were careful not to infuse the discussion with any of their own personal beliefs. They also note that, in all four focus group sessions, the discussion moved to the issue of environmental taxes before they had reached any of the direct questions on this subject.

It is also worth noting that while the implementation of the synchronous *on-line* focus groups conducted by Kallbekken and Aasen (2010: 2186) were 'relatively problem free', they did have some technical problems, which forced them 'to cancel one group and recruit new people for another discussion.'

Results

> *Attitudes towards policy instruments in general*: The discussion in all groups suggests that economic incentives do work and are an important motivating factor to promote environmentally friendly behaviour. In this regard, participants felt that rewards worked better than punishment. Three of the groups also noted that a lack of information often prevented policy instruments from working as well as might otherwise be the case if the public were provided with more (understandable) information.
>
> *Attitudes towards environmental taxes*: Kallbekken and Aasen (2010: 2186) report that the majority of participants commenting on the issue believed 'that the main purpose of environmental taxes is to stimulate behavioural change', that is, to direct consumers towards more environmentally friendly alternatives and away from less environmentally

friendly alternatives. However, the participants raised concerns about the effectiveness of such measures where there are few (or no) environmentally friendly alternatives available, or where the cost of such alternatives is extremely high (that is, where the price elasticity is fairly low; for example, if there is limited public transport available in a rural area).

A further concern raised by the participants related to how revenues generated from environmental taxes are spent. All but two of the participants commenting on this issue believed that the revenues generated by environmental taxes should be earmarked for environmental projects designed to mitigate environmental damage caused by the activity being taxed, or to provide incentives for the development and use of environmentally friendly alternatives. However, some participants did comment that earmarking may have a downside in that it could become very inflexible and might, therefore, lead to sub-optimal spending policies.

Differences between the four groups: Kallbekken and Aasen (2010) found that the most significant differences in attitude towards environmental taxes occurred between the participants in groups 1 and 2. In general, the participants in group 1 appeared favourably disposed towards the need for environmental taxes and had faith in the government. By way of contrast, the participants in group 2 generally had little faith in the government and expressed serious concerns about the effectiveness of environmental taxes (particularly fuel taxes). It is worth noting that the participants in group 1 were typically younger, lived in the inner city of Oslo, had no children, and used public transport. In contrast, the participants in group 2 were typically a little older, lived in suburban Oslo and used a mixture of private and public transport. These demographic differences are the likely reason for the significantly different views expressed by these two groups and highlights the need to include a broad cross-section of participants when conducting exploratory qualitative research.

Conclusion

Kallbekken and Aasen (2010) note that their findings are generally consistent with the prior literature surrounding environmental taxes. In particular, Kallbekken and Aasen (2010: 2188) report that their on-line focus group participants: had a 'very strong preference for earmarking the revenues from environmental taxes for environmental measures'; did 'not comprehend the idea of using revenues from environmental taxes to reduce other taxes, like income taxes'; 'would generally like more information about the taxes'; and took 'a more favourable view of subsidies than taxes'.

Study 2: Using Message Boards to Conduct On-line Focus Groups

Introduction

The primary purpose of this on-line focus group study undertaken by Deggs et al. (2010) was to explore the experiences and expectations of working adults with respect to an online master of education degree at a US research university in the mid-south. The students selected to participate in this project had to be at least halfway through their degree course and must have maintained a fulltime job while continuously enrolled in the programme.

Deggs et al. (2010) felt that participant anonymity was crucial to the success of this project because if students felt there was a possibility that the views they expressed might jeopardize their course completion chances they could be reluctant to engage in an open and frank discussion about their university experiences. Given the need for anonymity, together with the fact that the students were geographically dispersed and rarely came to campus, an on-line approach was deemed the most appropriate.

Further, because the students were all working fulltime, and some were likely to have family commitments, Deggs et al. (2010) felt that an asynchronous approach would be their best option so as to give the participants plenty of opportunity to join in the discussion at times that were most suitable to them. Given the reasonably homogeneous nature of the population under investigation the decision was made to only recruit sufficient participants for one on-line focus group.

Conducting the focus group

Deggs et al. (2010) examined a number of platforms before selecting an on-line message board system that allowed the selected students to participate in the on-line focus group by directing them to a registration page that was not accessible to all web users. This process ensured student anonymity and complete confidentiality of all comments made during the focus group discussions. Students who matched the selection criteria were contacted via email and invited to participate in the on-line discussion. They were notified that their participation was voluntary and that they could withdraw at any time without affecting their standing in the degree programme in any way. The students were further assured that their responses would remain confidential. Nine of the 11 students invited to participate took part in the on-line discussions, which involved three rounds of questions posed over a six-week period. The students were advised to log on to the system at least weekly to respond to the questions posed and comments made by their peers. The students were also informed about the dates when each of the three rounds of questions would commence.

The focus group discussion was carefully monitored throughout the six-week period with follow-up questions being interjected, when appropriate, to seek clarification or to expand upon issues raised. The researchers were keen not to steer, or control, the discussion in any particular direction, apart from ensuring that the discussion was related to student experiences in an online degree programme.

Deggs et al. (2010: 1031) began their on-line focus group with a 'grand tour question' which asked the students to 'discuss their overall experience with the online graduate degree program'. Based on the students' responses to this first question, they were probed to try and obtain further details concerning the ways in which 'they had been able to apply the content that they learned in the program' and 'if there was something that they would like to learn that they had not learned in the program'. The second round of questions posed by Deggs et al. (2010: 1032) again commenced with a fairly general question asking 'students to discuss meaningful assignments that they completed in coursework during their enrollment in the online graduate degree program'. The third, and final, primary question asked the students 'to explain what keeps them enrolled in the online graduate degree program'.

Results

An interesting outcome from this example of an asynchronous on-line focus group was the response (participation) rates by the nine participants over the six-week discussion period. As can be seen from Table 12.2, the highest response rate, particularly for the students, was during round 1 (the first two-week period). During this period the nine students provided a total of 16 responses to the researchers and a further 14 responses to comments by other students. By the last two-week period (round 3) these numbers had fallen to seven and three, respectively. Deggs et al. (2010: 1034) note that, despite the significant drop-off in responses over the period of the discussions, they were still able to reach a reasonable level of consensus among the on-line focus group participants primarily because they took an active role in terms of monitoring the discussion and interjected 'follow up questions to elicit more information and greater detail from the participants.'

Conclusion

In conclusion, this study demonstrates that asynchronous on-line focus groups can work well with participants that are both geographically dispersed and where it might be difficult to arrange a common time for all to be involved. Owing to their study and full-time work commitments, the students involved in this study were encouraged to log on to the

Table 12.2   Response frequencies

Participant	Round 1		Round 2		Round 3	
	Response to researchers	Response to other participants	Response to researchers	Response to other participants	Response to researchers	Response to other participants
A	1	3	1		1	
B	2	3	2	1	1	1
C	1	2	1		1	
D	1	1	2		1	
E	2	1		1		
F	2		1		1	1
G	2		3	1	1	1
H	2	1	2			
I	3	3			1	
Totals	16	14	12	3	7	3

Source: Deggs et al. (2010: 1033, table 1).

on-line focus group discussion at a time that was convenient for them. The researchers involved in this study believe that their careful monitoring of the on-line discussion (particularly during the first two weeks) helped to deliver substantial insights from the participants about online education programmes for students working full time.

REFERENCES

Aiken, M., J. Krosp, A. Shirani and J. Martin (1994), 'Electronic brainstorming in small and large groups', *Information & Management*, **27** (3), 141–9.

Brüggen, E. and P. Willems (2009), 'A critical comparison of offline focus groups, online focus groups and e-Delphi', *International Journal of Market Research*, **51** (3), 363–81.

Deggs, D., K. Grover and K. Kacirek (2010), 'Using message boards to conduct online focus groups', *The Qualitative Report*, **15** (4), 1027–36.

Hughes, J. and K.R. Lang (2004), 'Issues in online focus groups: lessons learned from an empirical study of peer-to-peer filesharing system users', *Electronic Journal of Business Research Methods*, **2** (2), 95–110.

Kallbekken, S. and M. Aasen (2010), 'The demand for earmarking: results from a focus group study', *Ecological Economics*, **69** (11), 2183–190.

Klein, E.E., T. Tellefsen and P.J. Herskovitz (2007), 'The use of group support systems in focus groups: information technology meets qualitative research', *Computers in Human Behavior*, **23** (5), 2113–32.

O'Connor, H. and C. Madge (2003), '"Focus groups in cyberspace": using the internet for qualitative research', *Qualitative Market Research*, **6** (2), 133–43.

Oringderff, J. (2004), '"My Way": piloting an online focus group', *International Journal of Qualitative Methods*, **3** (3), 1–10.

Stancanelli, J. (2010), 'Conducting an online focus group', *The Qualitative Report*, **15** (3), 761–5.
Stewart, K. and M. Williams (2005), 'Researching online populations: the use of online focus groups for social research', *Qualitative Research*, **5** (4), 395–416.
Sweet, C. (2001), 'Designing and conducting virtual focus groups', *Qualitative Market Research*, **4** (3), 130–35.

APPENDIX 12A.1   INTERVIEW GUIDE

A.1. Introduction

General introduction/welcome.

A.2. General discussion on environmental problems and solutions (policy instruments)

1: The topic for tonight is challenges related to the environment. Are there any environmental problems which you are particularly concerned about?
2: Who is responsible for finding solutions to the problems?
3: What do you believe are good approaches for the authorities to handle environmental problems?
   Information: Measures are physical acts which reduce polluting emissions (e.g. replacing an oil furnace with electricity). Policy instruments are political tools or framework conditions which can trigger the physical measures (a tax on fuel oil).
4: There are many ways to make people behave more environmentally friendly in their everyday lives. What motives you to act (be) environmentally friendly?
5: What makes policy instruments work?
6: What prevents policy instruments from working?
7: What about subsidizing environmentally friendly goods and services?
8: If there is to be a subsidy — where is the money to come from?
9: What about banning goods and services which are not environmentally friendly?
10: Have you noticed any information campaigns on environmental issues?
11: Have any of these had any effect on you [your behaviour]?

A.3. Environmental taxes

12: Which environmental taxes do you know about?
13: How do you believe they are intended to work?
14: In which situations can environmental taxes be a good thing?
15: In which situation do you think that environmental taxes do not work?
16: Are there any environmental taxes which do not have an effect on you?
17: Can environmental taxes have any negative effects?

A.4. Use of the revenue from environmental taxes

18:    Environmental taxes produce revenues. What do you believe these revenues should be used for?

19:    The revenues from environmental taxes can be used to reduce other taxes. What do you think about this solution?

20:    [This question was in the interview guide, but was never asked because the issue had already been raised by all groups before we got to the question] When authorities introduce an environmental tax they can choose whether or not to spend the revenues in one specific area or on one specific measure — often called earmarking. Should the revenues be earmarked? Why? Why not?

21:    Is there anything about earmarking which is not good?

22:    In some countries they have used the revenues from environmental taxes to reduce payroll taxes. What do you think about this?

23:    Do you trust that the authorities use the revenue from [environmental] taxes in a good way?

A.5. Distributional effects

24:    Some environmental taxes have to be paid by all who use a service or a product, like the fuel tax or the tax on electricity consumption. Some would claim that this is unfair as the tax does not depend on whether you have any alternatives nor on the level of income. What do you think about this?

25:    What about compensatory measures? The revenues can be used to increase the basic (tax-free) allowance, or alternatively to provide direct transfers to [vulnerable/exposed] groups.

A.6. Closing remarks

Thank you and information about gift cards.

Source: Kallbekken and Aasen (2010: 2189, app. A).

Focus groups: what have we learned?
John Watson and Rick Newby

What have we learned from the preceding three chapters about how focus groups (in their various forms) can be used to advance our understanding of entrepreneurship issues? In particular, is it reasonable to conclude that focus groups are a useful qualitative technique for helping researchers better understand the world of the entrepreneur? Based on personal experience and the limited studies to date that have used this qualitative method in entrepreneurship research, our view is an unequivocal YES! In its various forms (traditional, GSS and on-line) the focus group technique has been shown to deliver useful outcomes for researchers in a variety of contexts; thereby serving to demonstrate the potential contribution of this method as a vehicle for 'adding to our picture of the motivations, rationales and experiences of small business owners' (Blackburn and Stokes 2000: 61). As noted by Klein et al. (2007: 2117) 'focus groups build on the potential for individuals to think synergistically in a group setting. As participants interact, they feed off each other's ideas, potentially creating a snowballing effect and enabling them to develop new insights that they might not have been able to develop independently'. The outcome of this process is far richer results than would be possible from one-on-one interviews. It is also important to note the critical role played by the moderator in helping to draw out ideas from the group by probing individual responses and encouraging robust discussion.

WHICH FOCUS GROUP FORMAT SHOULD I CHOOSE (TRADITIONAL, GSS OR ON-LINE)?

The answer to this question is not straightforward and will depend on a number of factors. Perhaps the most important of these is the depth to which researchers look to explore the ideas of interest. The more depth required (and the fewer questions) the more likely a traditional face-to-face focus group will provide the best outcome. At the other extreme, if there are many questions and the researchers are primarily interested in quick responses, a synchronous on-line (or GSS) format might be the best alternative. That is, on-line focus groups are likely to work best where the researchers are looking to generate ideas (or test survey questions) rather than looking to gain an in-depth understanding of an issue from an interactive discussion between participants.

A second major issue that needs to be considered is how easy (or otherwise) it is likely to be to arrange for the appropriate target group to meet in the same place and time. For geographically dispersed groups this is likely to prove very difficult and, even if it could be done, it is likely to be very costly. In this case the researcher might have no option other than to adopt an on-line format. We would suggest that where depth is needed an asynchronous group would be best, as it provides more opportunity for the conversation to develop.

Of course, there is nothing preventing the researcher from adopting a mix of methods. That is, face-to-face focus groups might be conducted for those participants where attending such a session would not be too burdensome, while on-line sessions are conducted for geographically dispersed participants (Sweet 2001).

CHALLENGES AND LIMITATIONS ASSOCIATED WITH THE USE OF FOCUS GROUPS

While focus groups can be used to generate richer data than might otherwise be possible using surveys or one-on-one interviews, using focus groups to help researchers better understand the world of the entrepreneur is not without its challenges. For example, attempting to bring together, in one place and at one time, a group of very busy individuals (as entrepreneurs typically are) can be very challenging and will require the researcher to be in regular contact with the potential participants in the period leading up to the focus group session. While this issue may be particularly problematic for traditional and GSS sessions, it is likely to also be an issue for on-line focus groups, even if they are held asynchronously.

The outgoing (outspoken) nature of many entrepreneurs can also pose problems for the moderator, in terms of ensuring that all members of the focus group are afforded the opportunity to express their views. This is where making use of GSS technology can be particularly helpful in ensuring that ideas are not lost because of one (or a few) dominant individual(s) making it difficult for other participants to have their ideas heard and discussed.

As non-probability, purposive sampling is typically used to form focus groups, the major limitation with this methodology is that it is not useful for traditional hypothesis testing or drawing inferences from a large population (Basch 1987). As noted by Kahan (2001: 132):

focus groups in contemporary research are both an art and a science. They are an art to the extent that science is identified as precision and replicability of data collection. But they are a science to the extent that the protocol guides the session and that rules specify how the session will be conducted.

CONCLUSION

In conclusion we would agree with Blackburn and Stokes (2000: 62) that an 'analysis of the data emerging from group interaction can provide a rich understanding of process issues . . . as well as the rationales of business owners' and, therefore, we would recommend that 'focus groups should be used more widely by those seeking to understand the world of the business owner'. Further, we suggest that while reading about 'best practice' in conducting focus groups can be extremely helpful, the skills needed for planning, conducting, and analysing focus groups are 'gained best through practice and experience' (Basch 1987: 414).

REFERENCES

Basch, C.E. (1987), 'Focus group interview: an underutilized research technique for improving theory and practice in health education', *Health Education & Behavior*, **14** (4), 411–48.
Blackburn, R. and D. Stokes (2000), 'Breaking down the barriers: using focus groups to research small and medium-sized enterprises', *International Small Business Journal*, **19** (1), 44–67.
Kahan, J.P. (2001), 'Focus groups as a tool for policy analysis', *Analyses of Social Issues and Public Policy*, **1** (1), 129–46.
Klein, E.E., T. Tellefsen and P.J. Herskovitz (2007), 'The use of group support systems in focus groups: information technology meets qualitative research', *Computers in Human Behavior*, **23** (5), 2113–32.
Sweet, C. (2001), 'Designing and conducting virtual focus groups', *Qualitative Market Research*, **4** (3), 130–35.

PART V

REPERTORY GRID
TECHNIQUE

Repertory grids in entrepreneurship: practical examples from research
Rita G. Klapper

INTRODUCTION

This section introduces repertory grids, the methodological tool of personal construct theory (PCT), as a research tool. Repertory grids have been used in different contexts such as customer relationship management (Lemke et al. 2011), change management (Fransella et al. 2003), in personal construct psychotherapy (Neimeyer and Baldwin 2003), child development (Mancuso 2003; Ravenette 2003) and teacher education (Pope 2003). In management research Dima and Jackowicz (2013) used this method to understand the constructs behind proactive/reactive environmental behaviour in Ontario's (Canada) wine industry, Oppenheim et al. (2003) investigated decision-making and information use among managers using the grids, and Stewart and Stewart (1982) suggested it as a technique that appears to offer a highly relevant framework and methodology for mapping the decisions investors have made in the past and how these would, consciously or unconsciously, affect their perceptions and judgements in the future. Hisrich and Jankowicz (1990) used the repertory grid technique to study intuition in venture capital decisions and found that some aspects of the investment decisions used by venture capitalists, in particular the nature and extent of decisions involving intuition and methodology for mapping the decisions, had received less attention in the literature.

Repertory grid application in entrepreneurship has been scant so far: for an exception see Klapper (2008, 2014) as well as Klapper and Tegtmeier (2010) and Shaw et al. (2006). This section provides an overview of George Kelly's personal construct theory (PCT) as the theory underpinning repertory grids, followed by three practical research applications illustrating the operationalization of repertory grids in different entrepreneurial contexts. The section closes with some comments about the advantages and disadvantages of repertory grids.

359

KELLY'S PERSONAL CONSTRUCT THEORY

Personal construct theory was developed by the psychologist George Kelly (1955) and aims to elicit concepts defined in the participants' own words in a systematic way, enabling comparison between different construct systems. Personal construct theory is a theory of individual and group psychological and social processes that takes a constructivist position in modelling cognition (Aranda and Finch 2003; Fransella 1988; Klapper 2011a, 2011b). Following Fransella (1988), Kelly's key question was 'How does a person, consciously or unconsciously, construe the world?'

As Chell (2000) outlines, the social construction of reality is both subjective and objective, a phenomenon Burrell and Morgan (1979) have referred to as 'ontological oscillation'. Applied to an organizational setting that is continually transforming, progressing and adjusting to the environment, this implies that its members are constantly producing and reproducing social structure through communication (Shotter 1993). Edley (2001) summarized the problematic succinctly: reality 'is the *product of* discourse, both the subject and the result of what talk is all about' (Edley 2001: 437, original emphasis). Reality is thus treated as subjective in the way that the individual in the situation deals with it according to their perception and interpretation of the different factors, and objective in so far as people use a common language to interpret and express the meaning of situations. People provide evidence to support a particular interpretation which then becomes accepted as reality, a shared and understood reality (Chell 2000).

Kelly's (1955) work was pioneering and revolutionary, as his demand for the individual to be actively involved in anticipating events from the inside out (Fransella 1988). The emphasis is on 'real-life' problems, with the primary purpose of enhancing the understanding of individual human action and the personal context from which experience originates. Kelly preferred this approach to testing theory for its own sake (Adams-Webber and Mancuso 1983; Klapper 2011a, 2011b), and as Jahoda (1988) emphasizes, Kelly sought and developed an approach that would make it possible to quantify individual uniqueness. His key postulate was that a person perceived the world in terms of whatever meanings this person applied to it. Human beings are assumed to be free agents who make meaning of their realities; this implies that perception depends not only on the presented stimulus, but also on internal hypotheses, expectations and stored knowledge. This is in line with Rudes and Guterman (2007: 388) who argue that 'knowledge is not a reflection of objective reality but, rather, the result of an individual's own, subjective cognitive processes', that is, the individual constructs his or her own subjective realities. The aim of PCT is to understand each person's unique view of the world by means of exploring their thoughts, feelings and beliefs (Cooper 1998). These are the basic, but important elements of Kelly's theory.

THE INDIVIDUAL AS SCIENTIST

Elaborating on the above, a central idea of PCT is that human beings are like scientists, each having their own personal ideas, philosophies and theories about the world. On the basis of their personal theories human beings develop hypotheses, which are tested, revised and then developed into theories, with the underlying aim of making sense of these experiences (Adams-Webber and Mancuso 1983, Beail 1985, Cooper 1998, Jahoda 1988, Klapper 2011a, 2011b). Human beings understand the world in which they live by constructing a 'personally organised system of interpretation or constructs of experienced events' (Beail 1985: 1). Given that interactions with other beings are an important part of our lives, Cooper (1998: 11) likewise concludes that we spend considerable time 'trying to evaluate (or construe) other individuals in order to predict their likely behaviour'. As Kelly (1955: 591) concluded: 'it is the future which tantalises man, not the past. Always he reaches out to the future through window of the present'.

CONSTRUCTIVE ALTERNATIVISM

As Kelly (1955) suggests, different people construe differently and as a result there are differences between the models individuals build of how others will behave. The latter was called by Kelly 'constructive alternativism', which suggests that ideas are not 'institutionalized' (Adams-Webber and Mancuso 1983; Klapper 2011a, 2011b), but subject to revision and change. This allows any two individuals to construe the same event differently, yet the same person could also construe the situation differently in the future when the context has changed (Adams-Webber and Mancuso 1983; Klapper 2011a, 2011b).

THREE BASIC STEPS

Accordingly PCT proposes three basic steps: (1) observing behaviour, (2) trying to understand what is going on and (3) testing whether this 'mental model' actually works, that is, whether it can really predict other individuals' behaviour in other situations (Cooper 1998; Klapper 2011a, 2011b). Clearly the success of this process is subject to recognizing that different individuals perceive different features in others and that even though two people may use the same words, this does not necessarily mean that they refer to the same thing. In addition, an individual's background and values may impact the way he or she construes behaviours.

THE ROLE OF THE RESEARCHER/EXPERIMENTER

Very different from most psychological experiments, where the subject is guessing what the experimenter is looking for, Kelly wanted the experimenter to guess what the subjects were thinking (Jahoda 1988). This suggests reversed roles between the two parties. This requires the experimenter to respect the individual and not impose any artificial frames of reference on the person (Fransella 1988, Klapper 2011a, 2011b). In fact, Kelly encouraged his research students to treat the individuals involved in their experiments as active collaborators in the scientific enterprise (Adams-Webber and Mancuso 1983).

THE REPERTORY GRID

As Lemke et al. (2011) explain, the repertory grid technique originally derived from psychology and anthropology. It is a method for investigating personal construct systems, where the respondent knows the answer indirectly and it is difficult to convey tacit knowledge directly (Goffin 2002). Lemke et al. (2011) and Szwejczewski et al. (2001) emphasize the greater depth of construct elicitation through repertory grids than through semi-structured interviewing alone. Repertory grids aim to provide information about the make-up of an individual's system of personal constructs, how this evolves over time as well as its limitations and potential (Beail 1985).

CONSTRUCTS

The fundamental concept of PCT is the construct. For Aranda and Finch (2003), constructs are concepts defined in the participants' own words and groups of constructs form individual repertory grids, which can be presented in a matrix form. Constructs represent qualitative properties and the ratings are treated as non-parametric values (that is, it is not necessary to know the numerical values that the wider population would assign). As Beail (1985: 1) comments, a construct 'is our way of distinguishing similarity from difference – thus a construct is essentially a discrimination which a person can make'. Kelly preferred to see constructs as bipolar, which underlines the fact that we both affirm and negate something simultaneously (Beail 1985) (for example, when something is black it is as a consequence not white, blue or another colour; if it is one particular mix of colours, then it is not another mix of colours, and so on). Beail pointed out, however, that these constructs are organized into a system, in fact: 'they are linked, related and integrated into a complex hierarchical structure or system containing many sub-systems' (ibid.: 1). The repertory grid technique relies on semi-structured interviews where participants discuss specific stimuli such as objects, people and places. By comparing and contrasting these elements it is possible to map personal constructs (Aranda and Finch 2003). Kelly (1955) concluded that the development of a person's construct system is vital to the person's mental health and he recommended a relatively small, but well-chosen and structured construct system in order to gain the best possibilities for predicting the behaviour of others. Construct systems are, however, not rigid, as the individual endeavours to refine them constantly. One important group of constructs are those related to one's self, the so-called core constructs (Cooper 1998).

EXAMPLES IN PRACTICE

The following section of the book provides practical illustrations of the operationalization of Kelly's repertory grids, in research conducted in the Canadian and German entrepreneurial contexts.

Anja Hagedorn's research contributes to the extant literature with an explorative research study that has investigated personal factors that motivate founders to use different business support agents (BSAs) during the venture creation process in Germany. The focus is on the personal experience of founders with these different agents, and George Kelly's repertory grid technique (Kelly 1955) is used to investigate patterns, similarities and commonalities in the relationships with different support agents. The author uses Cohn's (1997) four categorization criteria, namely, the factual level, the individual level, the interaction level and the framework conditions, to analyse the qualitative data emerging from semi-structured interviews that accompanied the application of repertory grids.

The second application of repertory grids in an entrepreneurial context comes from Enrique Díaz de León and Paul Guild who apply the repertory grid technique to assist early-stage investors who are seeking to manage new product portfolios of start-up ventures. The study explores the possibility of using the grid technique to enhance the traditional assessment of business plans by including estimates of venture viability which have greater predictive validity. The assessment of investment opportunities seems limited by the ability to communicate those aspects that are intangible. The authors investigate the perspective of both (1) expert investors and (2) expert entrepreneurs. The former included a group of venture capitalists investing in technology-based ventures in Canada. This study on venture capital and entrepreneurship has important implications for both practitioners and researchers; in particular, its major finding, which highlighted the high relevance of intangibles in the assessment of business plans from technology-based ventures.

Carmen Dima's work with repertory grids draws on the author's experience of conducting studies related to environmental entrepreneurship in Ontario's (Canada) wine industry. This chapter places PCT in the context of the constructivist paradigm, introduces repertory grids as a procedure derived from PCT, and presents details related to its components and procedures. This contribution adds particular value as it demonstrates the ideographic and nomothetic approach to knowledge specific to repertory grids. From an idiographic perspective, the individual grids reveal personal underlying insights that are central to cognition and less influenced by time and context. By using cognitive categorization and grouping, which produces insights based on similarities and differences, repertory grids facilitate a nomothetic approach to knowledge. As Carmen Dima concludes, we are able to expand from individual to group to understand common traits and behaviours.

REFERENCES

Adams-Webber, J. and J.C. Mancuso (1983), *Applications of Personal Construct Theory*, Toronto: Academic Press.
Aranda, G. and E. Finch (2003), 'Using repertory grids to measure changes in risk-taking behaviour', *Journal of Construction Research*, **4** (1), 101–14.
Beail, N. (1985), *Repertory Grid Technique and Personal Constructs: Applications in Clinical and Educational Settings*, Beckenham: Croom Helm.
Burrell, G. and G. Morgan (1979), *Sociological Paradigms and Organisational Analysis*, London: Heinemann Educational Books.
Chell, E. (2000), 'Towards researching "the opportunistic entrepreneur": a social constructionist approach and research agenda', *European Journal of Work and Organisational Psychology*, **9** (1), 63–80.
Cohn, R.C. (1997), *Von der Psychoanalyse zur themenzentrierten Interaktion* (*From Psychoanalysis to Theme-Centered Interaction*), 13th edn, Stuttgart: Klett-Cotta.
Cooper, C. (1998), *Individual Differences*, London: Arnold.

Dima, C. and D. Jankowicz (2013), 'Environmental entrepreneurship in Ontario (Canada) wine industry', *Advances in Economics and Business*, **1** (2), 187–98.

Edley, N. (2001), 'Unravelling social constructionism', *Theory & Psychology*, **11** (3), 433–41.

Fransella, F. (1988), 'PCT: still radical thirty years on', in F. Fransella and L. Thomas (eds), *Experimenting with Personal Construct Psychology*, London: Routledge & Kegan Paul, pp. 26–35.

Fransella, F., R. Bell and D. Bannister (2003), *A Manual for Repertory Grid Technique*, 2nd edn, Chichester: John Wiley & Sons.

Goffin, K. (2002), 'Repertory grid technique', in D. Partington (ed.), *Essential Skills for Management Research*, London: Sage, pp. 199–225.

Hisrich, R.D. and A.D. Jankowicz (1990), 'Intuition in venture capital decisions: an exploratory study using a new technique', *Journal of Business Venturing*, **5** (1), 49–62.

Jahoda, M. (1988), 'The range of convenience of personal construct psychology – an outsider's view', in F. Fransella and L. Thomas (eds), *Experimenting with Personal Construct Psychology*, London: Routledge & Kegan Paul, pp. 69–79.

Kelly, G.A. (1955), *The Psychology of Personal Constructs*, vol. 1, Norton: New York.

Klapper, R. (2008), 'The role of social capital in French entrepreneurial networks', unpublished PhD thesis, Leeds University.

Klapper, R. (2011a), 'Innovations in entrepreneurship teaching: the use of repertory grids within the French Grande Ecole context', *International Journal of Euro-Mediterranean Studies*, **3** (1), online publication available at: http://www.emuni.si/press/ISSN/1855-3362/3_113-133.pdf (accessed 12 June 2015).

Klapper, R. (2011b), *The Role of Social Capital in French Entrepreneurial Networks: Using Contacts for Successful Start-ups*, Saarbrücken: Lambert Academic.

Klapper, R. (2014), 'A role for George Kelly's repertory grids in entrepreneurship education? Evidence from the French and Polish context', *The International Journal of Management Education*, special issue, available at: http://www.journals.elsevier.com/the-international-journal-of-management-education/recent-articles/ (accessed November 2014).

Klapper, R. and S. Tegtmeier (2010), 'Innovating entrepreneurial pedagogy: examples from France and Germany', *Journal of Small Business and Entrepreneurship Development*, **17** (4), 552–68.

Lemke, F., M. Clark and H. Wilson (2011), 'Customer experience quality: an exploration in business and consumer contexts using repertory grid technique', *Journal of the Academy of Market Science*, **39** (1), 846–69.

Mancuso, J. (2003), 'Children's development of personal constructs', in F. Fransella (ed.), *International Handbook of Personal Construct Psychology*, Chichester: John Wiley & Sons, pp. 275–83.

Neimeyer, R.A. and S. Baldwin (2003), 'Personal construct psychotherapy and the constructivist horizon', in F. Fransella (ed.), *International Handbook of Personal Construct Psychology*, Chichester: John Wiley & Sons, pp. 247–55.

Oppenheim, C., J. Stenson and R.M.S. Wilson (2003), 'Studies on information as an asset II: repertory grid', *Journal of Information Science*, **29** (5), 419–32.

Pope, M. (2003), 'Construing teaching and teacher education worldwide', in F. Fransella (ed.), *International Handbook of Personal Construct Psychology*, Chichester: John Wiley & Sons, pp. 303–10.

Ravenette, T. (2003), 'Constructive intervention when children are presented as problems', in F. Fransella (ed.), *International Handbook of Personal Construct Psychology*, Chichester: John Wiley & Sons, pp. 283–93.

Rudes, J. and J.T. Guterman (2007), 'The value of social constructionism for the counselling profession: a reply to Hansen', *Journal of Counseling & Development*, **85** (Fall), 387–92.

Shaw, E., L. Wing, S. Carter and F. Wilson (2006), 'Theory, practice and policy: an integrated view on gender, networks and social capital', paper presented at the International Council for Small Business World Conference, Melbourne, 18–21 June.

Shotter, J. (1993), *Conversational Realities: Constructing Life through Language*, London: Sage Publications.

Stewart, V. and A. Stewart (1982), *Business Applications of Repertory Grid*, London: McGraw-Hill.

Szwejczewski, M., K. Goffin, F. Lemke, R. Pfeiffer and B. Lohmüller (2001), 'Supplier management in German manufacturing companies: an empirical investigation', *International Journal of Physical Distribution & Logistics Management*, **31** (5), 354–73.

13 Using repertory grid technique to explore the relationship between business founders and support agents
Anja Hagedorn

INTRODUCTION: THE IMPORTANCE OF SUPPORT AGENTS FOR BUSINESS FOUNDERS

Research findings reveal that business founders have an essential impact on the implementation of routines and processes, at least in the early stages of their venture, which foster competitiveness and the ability to survive. It appears that there is a direct positive correlation between the abilities, the knowledge, and the experience of founders, defined as 'entrepreneurial competencies', and the survival of the firm (Kollmann 2008). Hence the more developed the competencies of founders are, *ceteris paribus*, the higher is the possibility of their firm's survival. Because of this, the acquisition of individual entrepreneurial competencies is a key success factor for young entrepreneurs in setting up and maintaining a start-up.

At the same time research by, for instance, Gries et al. (1997) suggests that founders have a high need of external support due to their activities, tasks as managers and founders, particularly in view of the responsibilities they assume for management and for the development of the founded enterprise. Moreover, nascent entrepreneurs know about and use various forms of external expertise, such as consultants, tax advisors, venture capitalists or business angels (Gries et al. 1997; Müller and Diensberg 2011; Tegtmeier et al. 2010; Stubner et al. 2007; Schefczyk and Gerpott 2001). For instance, a recent study shows that founders see the supporting and coaching activities of business angels as the most important benefits of using external agents, after financial support (Holi et al. 2013). Furthermore, we know from venture capital research that the support of founders in their management activities and business decisions is an important success factor (cf. Stubner et al. 2007; Schefczyk and Gerpott 2001). Through this, founders seek feedback, gain orientation, reduce the complexity of the founding process, and receive practical and strategic support for their creation as well as develop their entrepreneurial competencies.

Most research in this area concentrates on very innovative and fast growing business ideas that are very likely to obtain venture capital, although they represent only a minority of founded companies. The majority of business creations are small and medium-sized ventures, whose founders do not necessarily intend to grow fast but prefer develop on a smaller scale (Kreditanstalt für Wiederaufbau 2012; Bretz et al. 2013). Hence, venture capital companies or business angels often do not support these founders, although their founders have a similar need for supporting activities as they lack personal capacities, experience, or knowledge (see, for instance, Gries et al. 1997; Schefczyk and Gerpott 2001; Lueger et al. 2007). At the same time little is known about how these ventures develop supportive relationships or which qualitative characteristics of supporting activities are useful and effective to promote a positive business performance.

In this chapter I contribute to current research on management support with an explorative research study that has investigated personal factors that motivate founders to use different business support agents (BSAs) during the venture creation process. I concentrate in particular on the personal experience of founders with these different agents and I use George Kelly's repertory grid technique (Kelly 1955) to investigate patterns, similarities and commonalities in the relationships with different support agents.

RESEARCH FOCUS

Arguably a founder needs sufficent management support during the founding process in order to avoid fundamental problems that may have irreversible consequences for the young company (Gries et al. 1997). Stubner et al. (2007) and Schefczyk and Gerpott (2001) show that support regarding the management of young ventures can have a significant impact on the performance of the start-up. What we do not know so far is, which qualities and properties a relationship between a founder and a BSA must display in order to increase or positively impact the venture's performance. This study aims to investigate the individual experiences of founders with different BSAs during the founding process. The main research questions are:

1. How do founders perceive their relationship with BSAs?
2. What factors are important to them when evaluating the quality of the relationship?

The overall objective is to measure the way individual founders assess their relationships with others in the context of support during the venture creation process (see also Smith and Ashton 1975). I successfully reached the goal of interviewing ten respondents who have founded one or more companies.

For the research the founders were questioned using George Kelly's repertory grid (1991) (cf. also Fransella 2003). The focus was on the forms of support available for founders and the latter's experiences with that support. Within the context of management support for founders, the repertory grid technique can be used for two different purposes: for practical research and for fundamental research. While it can be applied in the former way to evaluate the meanings of the supporting activities and by this directly help improve the quality of the learning outcomes of the founders, in the latter way it can be used on a meta-dimension to examine how founders perceive situations, processes and actors. In this article repertory grids are used for practical research, to elicit the individual perspectives of founders regarding their relationships with BSAs.

REPERTORY GRID TECHNIQUE

The repertory grid technique (RGT) is a method with which individual attitudes, emotions, and perceptions can be elicited and quantified. Hence, it provides an approach to discovering personal ideas and values in arguably a more profound way than other psychological methods. The RGT was developed by George Kelly, a psychologist, and first published in 1955 (cf. also Kelly 1991) based on the personal construct theory (Kelly 2003).

The Personal Construct Theory

The basic assumption of the personal construct theory (PCT) is that people do not only respond to stimuli but build cognitive images of their surroundings that are structured within a systematic framework, which Kelly called 'personal construct systems'. Kelly also proposed that the personal construct systems differ among individuals, which results in varying perceptions of the world, the self, others and events (Kelly 2003).

A personal construct system is built through experiences, education and socialization. It permanently changes as experiences and knowledge evolve (Yorke 1978; Riemann 1983). As a result, a situation or event cannot be perceived in exactly the same way by two individuals but can at least be perceived as being similar (Easterby-Smith et al. 1996). People distinguish themselves in how they construct events, which Kelly described as individuality corollary (Kelly 2003; Easterby-Smith et al. 1996). This is the reason why knowledge cannot objectively be evaluated as 'right' or 'wrong', it can only be evaluated as being meaningful to a person and has to be evaluated in the context of its creation (Easterby-Smith et al. 1996).

A personal construct system consists of a finite hierarchical system of bipolar constructs with a finite scope (cf. Bannister and Fransella 1977; Yorke 1978; Riemann 1983). Those opposing poles determine the meaning of the construct (Bannister and Fransella 1977). Every construct is built by the individual linkage of similarities and differences that define the two construct poles. Similarities and differences are derived from so-called 'elements', which induce a comparison process and by this define the construct poles regarding a certain topic. Elements are the nominating focus of a person's thoughts with which values and concepts are linked and can be events, people or non-living things (Thomas and Harri-Augstein 1984; Richter and Derry 2012). At least three elements are needed to establish a construct; elements from which the opposing poles are derived (Riemann 1983). This is due to the fact that one pole is built by the similarity between two elements and the other one by the difference regarding the third. Several of those constructs create the construct system for a specific question, situation or reference area (Bannister and Fransella 1977).

The Process of Inquiry

The goal of the RGT is to describe the individual construct system (Easterby-Smith et al. 1996). The method can be used, for instance, to understand roles and relationships of interviewees and of their network (Smith and Ashton 1975). Thus, the interviewer is verbally reconstructing a respondent's personal construct system, but he or she is doing this in conversation with the interviewee. As a result, information about a respondent's perceptual framework as well as direct expressions of the individual operating constructs can be gained (Smith and Ashton 1975).

There are several different ways to conduct a repertory grid interview and to extract the contrasting poles. Usually, three elements are chosen randomly and the constructs are verbalized by asking the respondent to find similarities between two of the elements and a difference regarding the third (Yorke 1978). Those build the above-mentioned construct poles. Elements can be selected by asking the respondent or they can be provided by the interviewer (Riemann 1983). At the same time, the RGT gives information about how the constructs are used. This is done through comparison of the elements, which are ranked on a scale that is defined by the previous derived poles. Those poles are elicited by triads (Riemann 1983) or dyads system (Easterby-Smith et al. 1996). Usually, eight to ten elements are enough for the interview in order to elicit a sufficient number of constructs (Richter and Derry 2012).

Advantages and Disadvantages of this Method

Almost all researchers who have used the repertory grid technique and who have valued the underlying philosophical paradigm emphasize the advantages of the method. The most obvious advantage is that one can access the personal perceptions of the respondent regarding a certain aspect (especially relationships) in an easy and structured way (Easterby-Smith et al. 1996) without forcing the interviewee along a preconceived survey (Smith and Ashton 1975). Through this method, it is possible to gain new insights about certain aspects of any respondent including self-assessments, which would not have been possible when using a regular interview technique (for instance, semi-structured interviews). In addition, a development of the respondent's perceptions can be elicited post hoc (Smith and Ashton 1975), which is why this method is often used in training programmes. Furthermore, it is possible to compare the individual perceptions of respondents, provided the same amount of elements and constructs have been derived. Moreover, the instrument is very flexible which allows different results (Smith and Ashton 1975; Watson et al. 1995; Richter and Derry 2012). The grid can be analysed in a qualitative and as well in a quantitative way, which means that the strategy of analysis is not limited by the research technique (Millward et al. 2010). A further benefit is the potential to reuse the elicited constructs for other purposes subsequently, such as quantitative surveys.

Despite many significant advantages, however, the method also has its pitfalls or disadvantages. On the practical side the influence of the interviewer should not be underestimated. The RGT is, like all interview-based data-sampling techniques, a reflective and very sensitive method that requires good interviewing skills of the researcher. Therefore, the researcher must permanently reflect on his or her own role and the interviewing process while conducting the interview. For instance, it is important that the interviewer properly explains what has to be done without influencing the respondent. This involves explaining the process without giving examples or commenting on it, which can be frustrating or difficult for the respondent initially (Yorke 1978). Another pitfall is the support of the interviewer in the verbalization of constructs. It is important that the respondents take their time to think about their answers. Hence, the process can be very time consuming (Yorke 1978); external disturbances, stress and time pressure must be avoided in order to produce useful results. The method can be hard to adapt to the respondent, which can lead to discomfort and, in extreme cases, to demotivation, if the interview fails to uncover the answers sought. Overall, the process of inquiry can be exhausting for respondents (Yorke 1978). Owing to the sensitivity of the data, a confidential atmosphere must be established by full non-disclosure or confidentiality agreements (Yorke 1978). Finally, since the personal construct system is highly individual, the elicitation of the construct system provides unique information about the characteristics of a respondent (Bannister and Fransella 1977). This can pose a contradiction for more quantitatively minded users, who may wish to draw generalizable conclusions from the results.

DATA SAMPLING

Selection of Respondents

For this study respondents, who had used a minimum number of different supporters during the founding of their business, were selected and are presented in Table 13.1.

Ten respondents were interviewed who have founded one or more companies, to meet the quality criteria of explorative analysis. All respondents were located in the region of Leipzig, Saxony. As shown in Table 13.1, they came from very heterogeneous branches. Eight of the business owners were male and two were female. Five of the interviewees are single founders and the remaining five founders had one or more partners committed in their venture. Two interview partners worked together in at least one of the mentioned businesses (Nos 1 and 8). Also,

Table 13.1   Characterization of respondents of the conducted repertory grid interviews

Respondent			Branch of start-up	Founding Phase	Founding Year
No.	Gender	Age			
1	M	30–40	Gastronomy & quality management	Growth	2012
2	F	20–30	Education	Planning	–
3	M	30–40	E-commerce	Growth	2013
4	M	30–40	Gastronomy	Growth	2012
5	M	30–40	Data analysing services and education	–	2011
6	M	30–40	Healthcare services	Growth	2013
7	M	20–30	Education	Growth	2011
8	M	40–50	Quality management	Growth	2012
9	F	30–40	Interior design	Growth	2011
10	M	30–40	Beauty and health services	Implementation	2014

the start-ups were founded not more than three years ago. Thus, eight of the founders said that they are currently at the expansion or growth stage, while two of the founders see their ventures in the conceptualization phase or have recently approached the market (Nos 2 and 10).

To avoid language barriers that would lower the quality of the findings, all interviews were held in German. The resulting repertory grids were translated into English. An independent professional German–English translator supervised this translation process. Furthermore, supporting information came from additional questions before and after the interview, which the interviewer had recorded during the meeting with the respondents.

Interview Strategy

The focus of the research project is on the exploration of the relationship between a founder and his or her individual network partners that function as BSAs during the founding process. This is achieved by collecting data from the different constructs the founder uses when interacting with the BSAs. The software Gridsuite 4 was used to manage the inquiry; it also enabled the preparation and control of the process.

Interview Preparation

For the process of verbalization of constructs, I provided the respondents with two triggers that aimed to support their reflections. First, I showed each of the participants a growth model using a combination of the models by Klandt (1999) and Gries et al. (1997) and asked them to position themselves and their venture in one of the phases of the model. For this, I used a combination of schemes, presented in Figure 13.1.

I then offered a set of elements, which consisted of common BSAs in the founding process. The set of elements had been prepared by using earlier research done by Gries et al. (1997) and Tödt (2001). Gries et al. (1997) examined in their study the types of support different groups of founders have used during the venture creation process. Table 13.2 provides a breakdown of actors from the different business support organizations and institutions. Following Gries et al. (1997) I have standardized the elicitation process and presented the seven most commonly used institutions/organizations for start-ups to the interviewees to explore the relationship between the latter and those organizations in the start-up.

In order to avoid undue influence on the part of the researcher, the interviewee was asked to think of other BSAs that he or she had experience with, after providing some standardized elements (Millward et al. 2010).

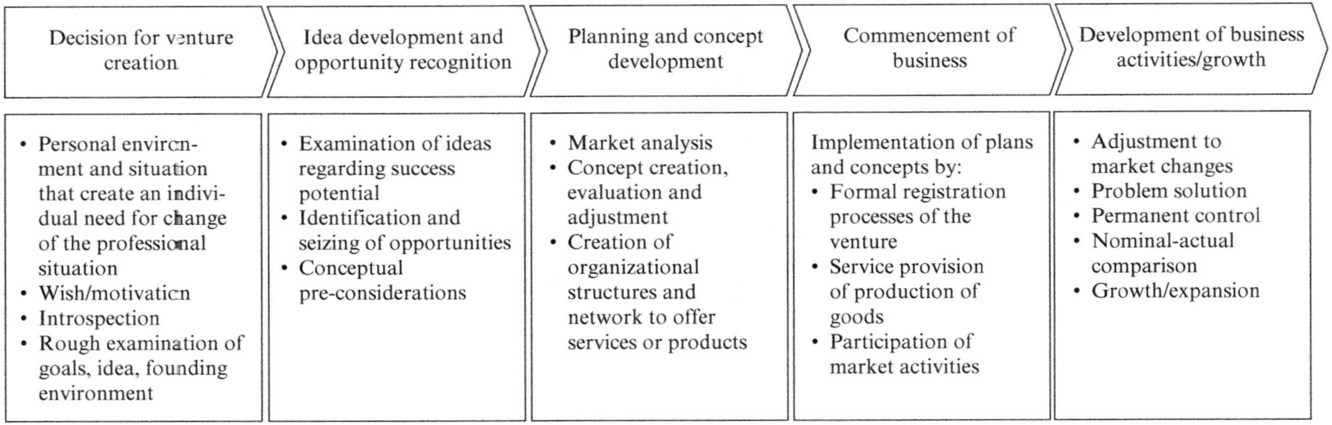

Decision for venture creation	Idea development and opportunity recognition	Planning and concept development	Commencement of business	Development of business activities/growth
• Personal environment and situation that create an individual need for change of the professional situation • Wish/motivation • Introspection • Rough examination of goals, idea, founding environment	• Examination of ideas regarding success potential • Identification and seizing of opportunities • Conceptual pre-considerations	• Market analysis • Concept creation, evaluation and adjustment • Creation of organizational structures and network to offer services or products	Implementation of plans and concepts by: • Formal registration processes of the venture • Service provision of production of goods • Participation of market activities	• Adjustment to market changes • Problem solution • Permanent control • Nominal-actual comparison • Growth/expansion

Figure 13.1   Employed scheme of business development according to Gries et al. (1997) and Klandt (1999)

*Table 13.2   Awareness and evaluation of support institutions of founders,
extracted from the study of Gries et al. (1997)*

Support institution	Awareness of founders (%)	Evaluation of usefulness (%)	Recommendation to other founders (%)
Consultant Chamber of Commerce	82.6	79.4	42.5
Consultant Chamber of Handicrafts	59.9	73.7	30.7
Banker	78.2	56.3	16.4
Employment officer	68.9	32.3	4.0
Tax adviser	66.9	86.1	16.0
Business consultant	37.4	66.0	9.4
Acquaintance, who is also a founder	58.2	86.0	7.0

Here I also considered prerequisites regarding quality criteria (homogeneity, representativeness and non-equivocalness) of the elements, as proposed by Easterby-Smith et al. (1996) and Fromm and Paschelke (2010).

Thus the interviewee had to identify one person from these BSAs that he or she was familiar with (Millward et al. 2010). Smith and Ashton (1975) recommend writing the names on the element-proposing cards. However, since the respondents of this inquiry were known well to the interviewer, being part of the interviewer's network, confidentiality and an atmosphere of trust were considered very important. Hence, the respondents were asked to hide the names rather than recording these openly (Smith and Ashton 1975).

Elicitation of Constructs

For the actual elicitation process, I followed the recommendations of Smith and Ashton (1975), Easterby-Smith et al. (1996) and Fromm and Paschelke (2010):

1. Three cards were selected that contain three different BSAs (triad method; see, for instance, Easterby-Smith et al. 1996). The interviewee had to describe which two agents were similar to the opposite third one. Through probing questions, queries and clearing questions respondents were motivated to describe the similarities and differences before supporting the interviewer in summarizing the descriptions in a compact phrase that fulfilled the prerequisites of the construct poles (Fromm and Paschelke 2010).

2. The dialogue of question and answer was reduced in the course of the interview as the respondents learned how the method worked.
3. Every element was ranked on a Likert-scale (for example, 1–5, 1–7 or 1–9) containing the contrasting poles. The interviewer supported the respondent in establishing a link between the elements and the construct poles.
4. The process was repeated starting with step 1 and randomly selecting three cards each until no further actors needed discussing and no further constructs were produced.

In this study every respondent produced a different number of constructs which ranged from six to 13 constructs, depending on the number of previous selected elements, which influenced both the number of combinations in order to acquire useful constructs, external factors (available time and lack of a relaxing atmosphere) as well as internal factors (respondent's ability to concentrate and motivate).

ANALYSIS AND FINDINGS

Both qualitative and quantitative measures are available to investigate the relationships between constructs (Fromm and Paschelke 2010). However, the quantitative analysis proved to be difficult for several reasons. Even though a standardized set of elements was employed by providing the most common BSAs, following Gries et al. (1997), in order to foster comparability, the founding processes were not comparable since not all start-ups used the same agents. Furthermore, not all companies of the interviewees had been in the same development phase. As a result, a quantitative analysis would be difficult given that the sample size of this study was too small. Consequently, a qualitative content analysis following Mayring (2000) was favoured to describe the constructs (see 'Constructs' section) and those BSAs (see 'Elements' section) which were used by the vast majority of the respondents in order to match generalizability criteria. A typologizing structuring content analysis was used, following Mayring (2000), which seeks to filter relevant distinctive information from the data by the means of using a category system (cf. Flick et al. 2004; Kohlbacher 2006). Hence, the material was reduced and relevant characteristics of the interviews were extracted and compared. The category system that was used is based on the theme-centred interaction model of Ruth Cohn (1997).

Constructs

Ruth Cohn's model explains the interaction dynamics of people applying four analysing categories (Cohn 1997; Langmaack 2011): framework conditions of the relationship, interaction level, factual level and individual level. These categories were applied here as follows: framework conditions of the relationship are the external conditions based on which the BSA and the founder interact; for instance, the circumstances under which a service is paid for by the government, and therefore, other interests besides the founder's interest become relevant. The interaction level refers to aspects or factors that build and influence the quality of interaction between BSAs and founder, such as the degree of independence of the latter from the former. The factual level contains all constructs which describe or create aspects of objectively performed services, such as the transfer of knowledge and experience; for example, the 'internal finance perspective versus the finance-related perspective from the outside'. Finally, all constructs describing personal factors that were brought into the relationship by founder or agent and are based on psychological characteristics, such as 'scepticism', were covered by the category 'individual level'. The overall classification of the constructs and the elements employed by each respondent are represented in Table 13.3.

Table 13.3 shows how interviewees construct the different relationships with BSAs. One can see that, among others, emotional aspects such as 'sympathy', 'trust' or 'credibility', but also objective factors like the level of experience and knowledge of the agent, matter for the relationship quality with the interviewees. In addition, emotional factors and personal characteristics, which are given by the interviewee or the BSA, can become relevant on an individual level. The latter may also influence the quality of the interaction, depending on the founder's attitudes towards an agent and vice versa. In conclusion, the four categories, as shown in Table 13.3, are characterized by a complex interplay that impacts the founder's perception of his relationship with different BSAs.

Elements

This study aimed to explore the experience of founders with different support agents during the different stages of the company's development process. Cohn's (1997) four categories, as discussed earlier, were applied to structure the content analysis and its related findings. Furthermore, Mayring (2000) suggests the use of the following filter criteria in the typologizing structured content analysis: extreme characteristics in the data, varieties of particular interest or characteristics that occur relatively often

Table 13.3 Repertory grid interviews and their elements and constructs

No.	Elements: supporters in the founding process	Constructs: quality criteria that matter for the relationship
1	Business consultant, self-employed acquaintance, coach, tax adviser, employment officer, advisor from a chamber/association, designer, insurance adviser, a well-known start-up, family member, book keeper, IT adviser	*Factual level*: objective evaluation – subjective vision, objective experience – subjective experience, acting on the level of a company's strategy – acting on an operative level; internal finance perspective – finance-related perspective from the outside; caring for conceptual issues – caring for financial issues *Individual level*: emotionally involved – left out *Framework conditions*: public authority – free trade and industry *Interaction level*: consulting – coaching
2	Business consultant, self-employed acquaintance, coach, tax adviser, employment officer, advisor from a chamber/association, designer, insurance adviser, a well-known start-up, family member, book keeper, IT adviser	*Factual level*: individual advice – standardized advice, strategic consultancy – operative process *Individual level*: profit-oriented – interest in me as a person, acting analytically – acting creatively, replaceable – indispensable *Framework conditions*: monetary perspective – agency perspective, is free – is constrained *Interaction level*: network dependent – network independent, emotional support – functional support, service provider – performance enhancing, I am independent – I am dependent
3	Business consultant, self-employed acquaintance, coach, tax adviser, employment officer, adviser from a chamber/association, designer, insurance adviser, a well-known start-up, family member, book keeper, IT adviser	*Factual level*: quantitatively oriented (on hard facts) – qualitatively oriented (on soft facts), interesting topics – duties; fit in online sector – fit in offline sector *Individual level*: – *Framework conditions*: cost-intensive services – free services, private background – governed by public law, consulting with external specifications – unconstrained consulting *Interaction level*: high credibility – low credibility in the area of venture creation, reliability in task fulfillment – sloppiness in task completion

4	Business consultant, self-employed acquaintance, employment officer, adviser from a chamber/association, designer, insurance adviser, a well-known start-up, family member, book keeper	*Factual level*: general knowledge – specific knowledge, acting based on profound knowledge – acting based on gut instincts *Individual level*: trust – healthy suspicion, solid/enduring – wild/creative, young and fresh – conservative/traditional, dispensable – inevitable, biased – neutral *Framework conditions*: changing (regarding political interests) – lasting *Interaction level*: I am independent – I am dependent, work-related feeling of security – private feeling of security
5	Business consultant, self-employed acquaintance, co-founder, employment officer, a well-known start-up, venture creation manager	*Factual level*: experience with founding a business – lack of experience with founding a business *Individual level*: – *Framework conditions*: voluntary/unpaid – full-time/professional *Interaction level*: sympathy – unpleasant person, unstructured/creative conversations – structured/uncreative conversation, intense communication – sporadic communication, peers/private relationship – business relationship, autonomy – involvement (when founding)
6	Business consultant, self-employed acquaintance, tax adviser, employment officer, designer, insurance adviser, a well-known start-up, family member, IT adviser	*Factual level*: sound and applicable advice – useless advice, unfunded/unspecific knowledge – validated/transparent facts, sound concept – unclear/unstructured concept *Individual level*: trust/feeling of security – sceptical/insecurity, familiar/intimate person – unfamiliar person, stressing the risks/creation of fear – motivating/convincing/reaffirming, own experiences through founding – naive/unrealistic expectations/euphoric *Framework conditions*: – *Interaction level*: productive and efficient advisers – wasting time and ineffective, uncomplicated/not time-consuming – complex/costly/time-consuming, existing sympathy – antipathy (because of attitudes)

Table 13.3 (continued)

No.	Elements: supporters in the founding process	Constructs: quality criteria that matter for the relationship
7	Business consultant, self-employed acquaintance, tax adviser, designer, a well-known start-up, family member, mentor from a scholarship	*Factual level*: high-life experience – low-life experience, highly relevant experience – slightly relevant experience *Individual level*: high trust in judgement – low trust in judgement *Framework conditions*: cost-intensive services – free services *Interaction level*: Formal conversation – informal conversation, concrete objective of the support – general communication, one-sided conversation – dialogical conversation, openness in conversation – reserved conversation, rare interaction – frequent interaction
8	Business consultant, self-employed acquaintance, employment officer, adviser from a chamber/association, insurance advisor, family member, book keeper, IT adviser	*Factual level*: objective/emphasis on facts/actual state – creative/emotional/visionary, objective regarding recommendations – subjective regarding recommendations *Individual level*: – *Framework conditions*: specific service – continuous service *Interaction level*: sceptical/distant – familiarity, impersonal service agent – face-to-face service agent, use of services upon request – dependence regarding services

| 9 | Business consultant, self-employed acquaintance, coach, tax adviser, employment officer, advisor from a chamber/association, designer, insurance adviser, well-known start-up, family member, book keeper, IT adviser | *Factual level*: specific topic – general advice, a lot of experience in dealing with being self-employed – little experience in dealing with being self-employed, broad operational area – constrained operational area
Individual level: emotional distance – emotional closeness
Framework conditions: neutral consulting services as an external actor – biased consulting service
Interaction level: personal relationship – unemotional relationship, common experiences – no common ground, similar life situation – different life situation, settled/ready/predetermined – everything is open/unfinished/flexible |
| 10 | Business consultant, self-employed acquaintance, tax adviser, advisor from a chamber/association, insurance adviser, family member, IT adviser | *Factual level*: experience regarding autonomous work process – order processing/service agent, detailed/helpful background information – operational/organizational support, extensive/ competent consulting – well-meant advice, consulting based on facts – consulting based on emotional support, facile consulting – profound remarks
Individual level: –
Framework conditions: support until founding process begins – support starting from the founding
Interaction level: private/professionally independent – demand-driven/ professionally-targeted support |

in the data. In this case I focus on the extremes and on the characteristics that occur relatively often in the data. Since not all actors had been used by all interviewees, the analysis focused on the business consultant, founder's coach, employment officer, tax adviser, self-employed acquaintance as well as the consultant, who is employed by a chamber or association. For the description of the elements interview findings were grouped by elements and re-categorized according to the already classified constructs of each element. The detailed analysis of selected elements was carried out by analysing the rating behavior of each respondent in the context of the respective construct categories.

Business Consultant

Factual level. At this level, respondents stressed the aspects of experience (No. 10) and specialization (respondent Nos 4 and 7) as well as conceptual (No. 6), strategic (No. 2), financial (No. 3) and marketing (No. 3) foci in the consulting process. Furthermore, quality criteria like helpfulness and well-founded knowledge (Nos 4, 6 and 7) as well as the attention to detail (No. 10) and objectivity (No. 8) of the advice were mentioned as highly important. Respondent No. 2 appreciated the individual advice given by the business consultant. Conversely, one respondent (No. 9) stated that she became aware that the BSA had little experience in founding a business, while providing unspecific and general support in combination with a wide operating range. This impression was partly confirmed by interviewee No. 5.

Individual level. In this category one respondent (No. 9) described an existing emotional distance to this BSA, which she scored higher as compared to other BSAs. The same interviewee as well as interviewees No. 4 and No. 7 attributed only little trustworthiness to the business consultant, while respondent No. 6 perceived this agent as highly trustworthy. On the contrary, respondent No. 4 showed both, positive and negative attiudes, towards this BSA; he mentioned aspects such as providing stability, but also attributed conservativeness, pointlessness and giving biased advice.

Framework conditions. What was appreciated by six respondents (Nos 2, 3, 4, 5, 8 and 9) was the fact that the business consultant was acting more independently compared with other agents, for instance the consultant of a chamber, while providing cost-intensive advice (Nos 3 and 7). The appreciation was expressed by positive scores of the BSA on constructs, such as 'constrained service', 'neutral advice' and 'independency'.

Interaction level. Depending on the individual context of the respondent the linkages between the element 'Business consultant' and the respective constructs differed widely. One respondent (No. 6) mentioned his high sympathy for the BSA, which was a result of the factors such as time-efficient and uncomplicated working style as well as the motivating effect the agent had on the founder. In contrast, respondents mentioned the sporadic (Nos 5 and 9), punctual (No. 8), one-sided interaction (respondent No. 7) as well the highly informal relationship and exchangeability of individual actors. In addition, non-personal communication was mentioned once by respondents Nos 7, 2 and 8. Furthermore, one respondent (No. 9) stated critically that there was no common ground in the relationship between him and the consultant and that both found themselves in different life situations.

Founder's Coach

The founder's coach is a BSA who is supposed to not only concentrate on the factual side when supporting founders but also on the individual-emotional side and was chosen by four respondents (for more information on founder's coaching, see Gries et al. (1997); Müller and Diensberg (2011)). Respondents who had mentioned this person were either using a coach from the university-network 'SMILE' (three times) or a coach from the federal programme 'Gründercoaching Deutschland' (once).

Factual level. At this level interviewee No. 1 described the agent as focused on venture issues, caring for the conceptual establishment of the venture and working on strategy matters in a holistic manner. At the same time, the respondent stressed the individual advice to be a special benefit when working with a founder's coach compared with the standardized advice of other BSAs. This includes not only venture matters but also personal issues such as soft skill development or the development of personal coping strategies with stress or challenging situations. One respondent (No. 9) valued the neutral advice and broad experience of the BSA in founding businesses and providing extensive support for founders very highly. On the other hand, this respondent mentioned that the agent was particularly constrained in his or her area of operation, compared with other agents, when it came to specific and detailed advice on venture development. The reason was that the BSA was not familiar with the branch the respondent was operating in.

Individual level. As for the reciprocal aspects of coaching, one respondent

(No. 3) found the coach more credible and reliable than the business consultant, while interviewee No. 2 saw him acting more analytically than other BSAs.

Framework conditions. The coach was perceived by respondents No. 2 and No. 9 as acting more freely and independently from her or his own personal network in comparison to other actors. This could be helpful for founders, since an outsider's view could lead to more objective and independent advice. To the contrary, respondent No. 3 had troubles choosing the right founder's coach owing to missing objective quality signals in the market. She also criticized the cost-intensiveness of the service for those founders, who get no financial support.

Interaction level. Respondent No. 1 saw the coach as more emotionally involved than other actors. Respondents No. 1 and No. 2 mentioned that the coach is more interested in the individual aspects of a person and that the supporting process is more personal than with any other BSA. This, together with the high level of independence, can be considered as one great advantage of a founder's coach compared to other BSAs.

Employment Officer

Overall, the employment officer was mostly rated very poorly as seven of the ten respondents had negative experiences with that actor regarding the fulfilment of their needs.

Factual level. Respondent No. 6 described the relationship as a 'waste of time' and 'useless' (No. 4), owing to the unfunded and unsubstantial character of the advice given and the lack of founding experience (Nos 5 and 6). Moreover respondent (No. 9) perceived the BSA as having had little experience in founding a business and therefore offered general support in a wide operating range, which resulted in unspecific and advice useless to the interviewee. Hence, this respondent saw no common basis for working together.

Individual level. The description of emotional aspects was characterized by negative feelings such as: sceptical sensation (Nos 4 and 6) and uncertainty as well as unfamiliarity (Nos 6 and 10), dislike and low credibility (No. 3). However, there were also positive statements: founder (No. 8) described the employment officer as reasonable, fact-orientated but more subjective. The BSA was also perceived as uncreative but very structured (No. 5). A feeling of familiarity was attributed to him (No. 5).

Framework conditions. The former two levels reflect framework conditions relating to the employment officer. For instance, respondents Nos 2, 4, 6 and 9 mentioned having a feeling that their BSA would rather have an interest in providing them a position as an employed person rather than supporting them during the founding process. Clearly the employment officers have to excute current agency policies that are a main driver of framework conditions. One explanation could be that the placement of qualified personnel in already existing companies is preferred owing to the shortage of skilled workers in Germany. Hence, the service is without charge but not free in terms of time-costs, and the consulting service is provided on the basis of legal specifications (No. 3) and therefore highly dependent (Nos 1, 3 and 9) on political and legal control. Respondents who took this actor into account mostly interacted because of the lack of capital and need for general advice.

Interaction level. One respondent (No. 9) stated that the advice given by the employment officer was highly biased in favour of the agency, that there was no common ground in the relationship, which resulted in high emotional distance. Respondent No. 5 stressed the infrequent exchange and dependency on an agent's personal decision regarding the worthiness of supporting the venture creation process as well as the lack of involvement in founding a business. This may be explained simply by the fact that this BSA is not an expert in entrepreneurship but rather a general adviser, in particular for future career aspirations. Hence, interview partner No. 10 saw the relationship as complicated and time-consuming.

Tax Adviser

Factual level. Some respondents saw this BSA as more operational than other BSAs and expected the agent to be focused on financing issues (Nos 1, 2 and 3). Moreover, half of the respondents (Nos 4, 6, 7 and 10) perceived the tax adviser as highly specialized and competent with profound knowledge in his area as well in the area of business venturing. Respondent No. 9 stated that the tax adviser only had little experience with venture creation and his operating range was broad. It was also mentioned that his support was unspecific, and therefore less useful for the respondent's individual needs.

Furthermore, respondent No. 2 perceived the tax advisor as highly analytical, and operative. She also had the impression that the actor was providing standardized services, which was similar to respondent No 9. Here it has to be mentioned that this respondent had little experience with this BSA since her venture was in its planning phase and the interaction with the tax adviser was less intense at this time, which may lead to insufficient or biased statements.

Individual level. In this category, the perception of the tax adviser varied greatly. Respondent No. 3 valued the fact that the tax adviser took care of tasks in a very reliable manner. The security provided by the BSA, who looked after the financial well-being of the company, was another positively rated aspect by respondent No. 1. On the contrary, interviewee No. 9 felt more emotionally distanced from this actor compared with the coach, for instance, which fitted with other statements made by this person about the BSA.

Framework conditions. Since the tax adviser is working in a private business environment, it is no surprise that respondent No. 7 stressed the cost-intensiveness of the service. Moreover respondent No. 2 perceived the tax adviser as independent but also as exchangeable and profit oriented, while interviewee No. 9 valued the high independency and neutrality of the BSA.

Interaction level. Here it is worth mentioning, that respondent No. 6 stated that he trusted this actor very much and that he felt secure in working with the BSA. The tax adviser supported the respondent also by motivating him in stressful times and troubles. This might have been an exceptional behaviour of the BSA since the tax adviser was a member of the family. Moreover, interview partner No. 7 valued relational aspects in this element and valued trust in his judgement and openness in the conversation very positively, but also the rare one-sided exchange with the agent.

Consultant of Chambers or Associations

Factual level. This agent was attributed with the element of little experience in founding a business, biased recommendations and support. In contrast to this, however, interview partners valued the objectivity of the recommendations and the factual orientation of the consultant, such as his ability to give advice on strategic matters (No. 8 and No. 2). Respondent No. 1 thought that his consultant had an experienced view of the company regarding quantitative issues such as financial aspects. Others perceived the support as very useful in terms of providing objective, detailed, profound and helpful background information which were also based on facts and figures and therefore seen as professional knowledge (interviewees No. 1 and No. 10).

Individual level. Although, seen as very reliable in solving tasks, one respondent (No. 3) attested his consultant low credibility. Respondent No. 9 mentioned a high emotional distance owing to former experiences with the BSA. In contrast, interviewee No. 4 perceived the agent as consistent and trustworthy, but also as conservative and 'useless'. Interviewee No. 2 perceived the agent as profit oriented in his service for founders and as acting in an analytical manner.

Framework conditions. It has to be mentioned that founders normally have to register at a chamber or association and pay a fee in relation to the annual profit. Thus, it is not surprising that some respondents may have higher expectations regarding the service quality of the BSA. This service quality seems to be reduced by further constraining framework conditions. Respondent No. 1 viewed the framework conditions the consultant was acting within as very bureaucratic and inflexible, while interviewee (No. 4) mentioned the frequent replacement of consultants which created an impression of unsteadiness.

Interaction level. This type of consultant was viewed as very ambivalent. Some respondents (No. 9) mentioned that they had no common ground and that the relationship was less emotional or more distant and impersonal (No. 8) which resulted in scepticism regarding the respective BSA. Others saw the relationship as highly reliable in solving tasks (No. 5), factual autonomy (No. 10) and very service oriented (No. 2).

Self-employed Acquaintance

Factual level. At the factual level one respondent (No. 1) valued the objective evaluation and venture-oriented financing view of this BSA. Clearly, for him, the actor was more than an acquaintance; he was directly involved in the operational processes of the company as the interviewee later confirmed. Moreover, half of the respondents (Nos 1, 5, 6, 9 and 10), who used this BSA, valued his or her high level of experience in founding a business while this actor was highly involved in their own founding process (No. 5).

One respondent (No. 10) answered in an inconsistent way. On the one hand, he viewed the support as detailed and helpful regarding the provision of background information. On the other hand, he described the support as superficial. This can possibly be explained by taking into account that the founder was working with two self-employed acquaintances from different branches: with the first he discussed general information relating to the founding process, with the second branch-specific support. Another possibility would be that the respondent simply thought of two different persons or situations.

Individual level. Respondents Nos 4, 6 and 7 attributed the highest level of confidence to the agent compared to other BSAs, while respondent No. 2 viewed the BSA as highly emotionally involved in the founding process. This is explainable in so far as the relationship between the BSA and the founder can be assumed to be more like a friendship rather than based on a professional working basis. In addition, respondent No. 4 saw the agent as highly inevitable and progressive (construct 'young and fresh'), but in contrast also as biased in terms of providing professional and objective advice. The agent might have given advice in favour of the founder because of the type of relationship.

Framework conditions. Here, respondent No. 2 viewed the framework conditions as very unstructured, flexible and spontaneous compared, for instance, with the employment officer or consultant of chambers or associations. Interviewees No. 3 and No. 5 mentioned that the BSA works free of charge, which might be due to the very personal and friendship-like relationship between founder and agent. Respondents No. 5 and No. 7 valued the free of charge personal advice very highly. The support of this agent was considered as useful until the business was acutally operating in the market.

Interaction level. At this level, the BSA can be distinguished from others regarding the establishment of a private, and therefore, more informal (Nos 5, 6, 9 and 10), bilateral (No. 7) and non-exchangeable (No. 2) relationship. Respondent No. 2 viewed the interaction more as a coaching than as a consulting service. Furthermore, this relationship is characterized, among others, by a high level of trust (Nos 4 and 7) and credibility as well as openness and frequent interactions (No. 7).

However, one respondent (No. 6) had a negative perception of this BSA since the agent pointed out the risks of founding a business which created doubts and fear in the founder. In fact, the BSA advised against founding the business. Furthermore, the acquaintance was providing unfunded knowledge to the founder. Here, the criterion 'subjectivity' was stressed which was also mentioned as a possible criterion by respondent No. 8.

CONCLUSIONS

In this chapter I examined the relationship founders have with their management BSAs using the repertory grid technique. Following Cohn's (1997) four categorization criteria, namely, the factual level, the individual level, the interaction level and the framework conditions, the individual experience of ten respondents was clustered in a qualitative contents analysis. Certain patterns became apparent among the respondents and were discussed in this text. Commonalities in the findings became obvious owing to similar framework conditions under which BSAs and founders operate and factual aspects that founders and BSAs share. At the individual level and in connection to relational aspects it is more difficult to identify those patterns. Here, the individual personalities of founders and supporters were of great importance.

Although highly individual, the repertory grid technique enhanced insights into qualitative aspects of the relationship between founders and BSAs, which can be used to develop recommendations for improving the quality of start-up support and, ultimately, the performance of the company. For instance, changing framework conditions in terms of fostering independence, availability, flexibility and specialization of institutional supporters, such as employment officers, potentially has a positive effect on the quality of the relationship. The professionalization of the relationship level (expressed in terms of credibility, sympathy and trust) had a similar effect on private BSAs such as consultants and coaches. It can be concluded that BSAs come from many different professions and environments with widespread experiences and backgrounds. Hence, personal attitudes and intentions as well as personal values are important factors for the successful support of founders. This involves, for instance, identification with the personal role, discovering individual capabilities and raising awareness for own preferences which are preconditions for positively influencing the professional business support. This means that the emotional and individual factors should be taken into account by BSAs. In doing so, the relationship is built on solid ground.

LIMITATIONS OF RESEARCH

Some limitations of the study relate to the use of the RGT such as (1) limited generalizability and (2) limited reliability of the findings (Kelly 1991). The former issue occurs owing to the fact that only ten interviews were conducted. Here a study with a higher sample size could increase the quality of the findings and thus the generalizability. The latter issue relates to the fact that personal constructs are not stable over time, since personal constructs evolve (cf. 'The personal construct theory' section). However, according to Anderberg (1973) the findings of a qualitative analysis applied to RGT should be compared with other data in order to validate them. This was, to some extent, achieved by using the interview transcriptions in the triangulation.

Furthermore, even though all efforts have been made to foster a comfortable atmosphere of trust, it is difficult to eliminate the possibility that respondents were influenced in their choice of answers, for instance by social desirability bias, stress or disturbing situations. However, the RGT is a time-consuming and demanding method. The interviewees had been observed during the interview and feedback about the technique had been sought by the interviewer in order to avoid useless data sampling (Easterby-Smith et al. 1996). Finally, no follow-up research has been conducted regarding the relationships of the founders with the BSAs. The collection of longitudinal data would be promising to analyse the development of constructs and thus relationships between founders and business support staff.

REFERENCES

Anderberg, M.R. (1973), *Cluster Analysis for Applications*, New York: Academic Press.
Bannister, D. and F. Fransella (1977), *Inquiring Man*, Harmondsworth: Penguin Books.
Bretz, M. et al. (2013), 'KFW-ZEW Gründungspanel. Junge Hightech-Unternehmen trumpfen auf' ('KFW-ZWE Founding Panel. Young high-tech companies boast'), available at: http://ftp.zew.de/pub/zewdocs/gruendungspanel/KfW_ZEW_Gruendungspanel_122013.pdf (accessed 20 March 2014).
Cohn, R.C. (1997), *Von der Psychoanalyse zur themenzentrierten Interaktion* (*From Psychoanalysis to Theme-Centred Interaction*), 13th edn, Stuttgart: Klett-Cotta.
Easterby-Smith, M., R. Thorpe and D. Holman (1996), 'Using repertory grids in management', *Journal of European Industrial Training*, **20** (3), 3–30.
Flick, U., E. v. Kardorff and I. Steinke (2004), *A Companion to Qualitative Research*, London and Thousand Oaks, CA: Sage Publications.
Fransella, F. (2003), *International Handbook of Personal Construct Psychology*, Chichester and Hoboken, NJ: John Wiley & Sons.
Fromm, M. and S. Paschelke (2010), *GridPractice*, Norderstedt: Books on Demand.
Gries, C.-I., E. May-Strobl and M. Paulini (1997), *Die Bedeutung der Beratung für die Gründung von Unternehmen* (*The Importance of Consulting for Founding Businesses*), Bonn: IfM.
Holi, M., S. Golla and H. Klandt (2013), 'Unterstützungsleistungen durch Business Angels – eine empirische Analyse der Unterstützungsleistungen durch Business Angels aus Perspektive der Beteiligungsunternehmen' ('Support services from business angels – an empirical analysis of the support services from business angels from the perspective of holding companies'), paper presented at the Seventeenth Annual Interdisciplinary Entrepreneurship Conference, 7–8 November 2013, Koblenz.
Kelly, G. (1991), *The Psychology of Personal Constructs*, London and New York: Routledge in association with the Centre for Personal Construct Psychology.

Kelly, G. (2003), 'A brief introduction to personal construct theory', in F. Fransella (ed.), *International Handbook of Personal Construct Psychology*, Hoboken, NJ: John Wiley & Sons, pp. 3–39.

Kelly, G.A. (1955), *The Psychology of Personal Constructs*, New York: Norton.

Klandt, H. (1999), *Gründungsmanagement*, Munich: Oldenbourg.

Kohlbacher, F. (2006), 'The use of qualitative content analysis in case study research', *Forum Qualitative Sozialforschung/Forum: Qualitative Social Research*, **7** (1) (available at: http://www.qualitative-research.net/index.php/fqs/article/%20view/75/153January%20 2006 (accessed 18. April 2014).

Kollmann, T. (2008), *E-Entrepreneurship*, 3rd edn, Wiesbaden: Betriebswirtschaftlicher Verlag Gabler.

Kreditanstalt für Wiederaufbau (2012), 'KfW/ZEW-Start-up Panel 2012', available at: https://www.kfw.de/Download-Center/Konzernthemen/Research/Research-englisch/PDF-Dateien-KfW-ZEW-Gr%C3%BCndungspanel/Gruendungspanel-2012-KF.pdf (accessed 23 March 2014).

Langmaack, B. (2011), *Einführung in die themenzentrierte Interaktion (TZI)*, 5th edn, Weinheim: Beltz.

Lueger, M., H. Frank, A. Kessler and C. Korunka (2007), 'Zur Dynamik der Mobilisierung von Resourcen im Gründungsprozess: Kreditverhandlungen' ('On the dynamics of the mobilization of resources in the start-up process: loan negotiations'), in M. Fink (ed.), *Sozialwissenschaftliche Aspekte des Gründungsmanagements: Die Entstehung und Entwicklung junger Unternehmen im gesellschaftlichen Kontext* (*Sociological Aspects of Foundation Management: The Formation and Development of Young Companies in the Social Context*), Stuttgart: Ibidem-Verl., pp. 88–114.

Mayring, P. (2000), 'Qualitative content analysis', *Forum Qualitative Sozialforschung/Forum: Qualitative Social Research*, **1** (2), available at: http://www.qualitative-research.net/index. php/fqs/article/view/1089 (accessed 18 April 2014).

Millward, L.J., M. Asumeng and A. McDowall (2010), 'Catch me if you can?', *Journal of Managerial Psychology*, **25** (3/4), 384–407.

Müller, K.-D. and C. Diensberg (eds) (2011), *Methoden und Qualität in Gründungslehre, Gründungscoaching und Gründungsberatung: Interventionen und Innovationen* (*Methods and Quality in Establishing Doctrine, Establishing Coaching and Start-up Advice: Interventions and Innovations*), Cologne: Eul, Lohmar.

Richter, K. and B. Derry (2012), 'Repertory grid interviews: new ESL uses for an old research instrument', available at: http://www.anupi.org.mx/PDF/12007_RichterDerry. pdf (accessed 19 March 2014).

Riemann, R. (1983), 'Die Erfassung individueller Einstellungen mit Hilfe der Gridtechnik' ('Understanding individual attitudes by using the grid-technique'), *Zeitschrift für Sozialpsychologie*, **14**, 139–151.

Schefczyk, M. and T.J. Gerpott (2001), 'Management support for portfolio companies of venture capital firms: an empirical study of german venture capital investments', *British Journal of Management*, **12** (3), 201–16.

Smith, M. and D. Ashton (1975), 'Using repertory grid technique to evaluate management training', *Personnel Review*, **4** (4), 15–21.

Stubner, S., T. Wulf and H. Hungenberg (2007), 'Management support and the performance of entrepreneurial start-ups', *Schmalenbach Business Review: SBR*, **59** (2), 138–59.

Thomas, L.F. and E.S. Harri-Augstein (1984), *Self-organised Learning*, London and Boston: Routledge & Kegan Paul.

Tegtmeier, S., R. Schulte and C. Wille (2010), 'Experiences, competencies, attitudes on the market for start-up counseling – evidence from Germany', Inter-ICSB online publication, **3**, 44–64, available at: icsb.org/InterICSB.asp, 2010.

Tödt, A. (2001), *Wirkung und Gestaltung von Beratung und Weiterbildung im Prozess der Existenzgründung* (*Impact and Organisation of Consulting and Further Education during the Business Start-Up Process*), Munich: Mering: Hampp.

Watson, W., L. Ponthieu and J. Doster (1995), 'Business owner-managers' descriptions of entrepreneurship: a content analysis', *Journal of Constructivist Psychology*, **8** (1), 33–51.

Yorke, D.M. (1978), 'Repertory grids in educational research: some methodological considerations', *British Educational Research Journal*, **4** (2), 63–74.

14 Using repertory grid to assess intangibles: uncertainty reduction for lean start-ups in entrepreneurship
Enrique Díaz de León and Paul Guild

INTRODUCTION

As defined by Guild and Bachher (1996: 788), technology-based ventures are 'those companies intending to commercialize a technology for the first time and thereby expecting to derive a significant source of sustainable competitive advantage from the technology'. What is considered an intangible aspect of such a venture is one that cannot be readily perceived or is not capable of being appraised at an actual or approximate value. Examples of intangible aspects are knowledge, intellectual capital, skills, abilities, and beliefs and ideas (Bachher et al. 1999).

Several authors have argued that traditional approaches to financial assessment based on concrete aspects are perceived as less reliable and relevant (Stewart 1997; Shepherd and Douglas 1999; Smart 1999; Sullivan 1999). Correspondingly, there is an increasing interest in the proper assessment and communication of intangible aspects. This occurs largely because of the evolution towards a knowledge-based economy in which intangible factors play an increasing role. Stewart (1997), for example, highlights the importance of intellectual capital. He argues that 'knowledge has become the primary ingredient of what we make, do, buy, and sell' (Stewart 1997: 9). As a result, he points out, 'managing it – finding and growing intellectual capital, storing it, selling it, sharing it – has become the most important economic task of individuals, businesses, and nations' (Stewart 1997: 9). Beyond a national perspective, Pope John Paul II affirmed the increasing significance of 'know-how, technology, and skill' in his 1991 encyclical Centesimus Annus, writing, 'whereas at one time the decisive factor of production was the land, and later capital . . . today the decisive factor is increasingly man himself, that is, his knowledge' (John Paul II, Centesimus Annus, para. 32).

When potential investors assess a business plan, they usually focus on such concrete attributes as the proposed balance sheet and predicted cash flows. However, these financial indicators do not accurately reflect all the possibilities for success offered by technology-based ventures. The results of such traditional assessments therefore often lead to the rejection of potentially viable technology-based ventures. However, when evaluating these investment opportunities, expert analysts frequently face approximate or soft data, often presented linguistically. In this case, subjective qualitative evaluations, presented by the entrepreneur through a business plan, lie at the heart of the decision to be made. This is particularly the case for new technology-based ventures in their early stages. In many such ventures, the investment opportunity consists of an idea presented by a team of energetic innovators, who are convinced of its value. There is no convincing balance sheet or predicted cash flow.

Assessing intangibles is thus a challenging task for investors. Although no prior research exists to suggest venture capital 'accuracy rates' when assessing intangibles, anecdotal evidence confirms that this is a most troublesome factor to assess accurately (Dubini 1989; Harvey and Lusch 1995). Kozmetsky et al. (1985: 5) described this problem succinctly: 'The talent criteria [intangibles], perhaps the most important quality a venture capitalist looks for in a portfolio company, is also one of the most difficult areas to assess'. Gladstone (1988: 30), when president of a public venture capital firm, reported: 'The problem with the venture capital business is that when we analyse people, our perceptions of others are usually wrong'. Smart (1999) corroborated this finding with the results of his study. He found that venture capitalists fail to achieve an accurate human capital valuation in 57 per cent of the deals. That is, investors experience significant surprises in their assessment of intangibles over half of the time. Hence, there is definitely a need for an accurate method to elicit and measure some of the intangibles in business plans.

A review of the literature suggests that the repertory grid might be a valuable tool for eliciting intuitions and personal experience (Ford et al. 1990; Hisrich and Jankowicz 1990). Stewart and Stewart (1982) allude to it as a technique that appears to offer a highly relevant framework and methodology for mapping the decisions investors have made in the past – decisions that, consciously or unconsciously, will affect their perceptions and judgements in the future.

Hisrich and Jankowicz (1990) used repertory grid technique to study the effect of intuition in venture capital decisions. Their study was not particularly focused on technology-based ventures. However, they found that some aspects of the investment decision used by venture capitalists have been less researched, in particular the nature and extent of decisions involving intuition, 'personal chemistry' or 'gut feeling'. They emphasize not only the content of venture capitalists' constructs – what they actually say about the proposals used – but also the way in which investors concretize their intuitions about a typical proposal.

Repertory grid is a technique developed by Kelly (1955) based on the rationale that people assign significance to all phenomena utilizing their own construct system. Kelly wanted to develop an investigative technique that would remove the influence of the observer's frame of reference on what was observed. In addition, he was interested in a method that would enable him to make precise statements – and confident predictions – about the behaviour of individual people.

With these concerns in mind, Kelly developed his theory of personal constructs over the years. Kelly's theory rests on the assumption that people are actively engaged in making sense of, and extending, their experience: he expressed this most succinctly in the definition 'man is a scientist'. According to Kelly, the degree to which we understand other people – or ourselves – is measured by the extent to which we understand how they make sense of their experience. The term 'personal construct' in Kelly's theory refers to the set of models, hypotheses or representations that each person has made about his or her world. Kelly invented repertory grid interviewing as a way of getting people to reveal their own personal models.

Essentially, in a grid procedure a number of objects or elements are compared by judging these on several attributes or constructs. Kelly's own application of personal construct theory was restricted to the technical setting and was but loosely tied to the implementation of the repertory grid technique. Subsequent clinical applications have emphasized the grid technique itself as both a diagnostic instrument and a therapeutic tool (Adams-Webber 1979; Bannister and Fransella 1986). Later applications, in the field of education, have stressed the individual nature of personal construct systems and their abstraction from the grid (Bell 1990). In the field of expert systems design, the grid has been explored as a tool for knowledge acquisition and inference structure derivation (Boose 1988). Additionally, the technique has been a rather popular method for automated knowledge acquisition (Shaw and Gaines 1987). However, it has been most appropriately applied as a tool for the development of knowledge-based systems, when the solutions to the problem at issue can be enumerated and judged on their degree of similarity. This makes it a suitable technique for the present investigation.

Moreover, as described by Ford et al. (1990), genuine expertise is more than the successful accumulation of 'book knowledge'. This seems to be the case in most interesting domains, for example, in the assessment or communication of investment proposals. In fact, much of an expert's unique collection of knowledge and skills are of his or her own construction. In other words, human experts acquire their expertise not only from explicit knowledge such as that found in textbooks (that is, widely shared consensual beliefs), but also from personal experience. Consequently, they construct a repertory of working hypotheses, or 'rules of thumb', which, combined with their fund of book knowledge, make them expert practitioners (Agnew and Brown 1989). Several studies have reported that when domain experts are asked to explain how they have reached a given conclusion, they often construct plausible lines of reasoning that have little or no relevance to their actual problem-solving methods (Johnson 1983; Ford et al. 1990). As described by Waterman (1986), the more competent domain experts become, the less able they are to describe the knowledge they use to solve problems. Thus, the greater their expertise, the more the experts' schemata or construct systems can deviate from those of typical practitioners, and the greater the importance of personally constructed knowledge. Consequently, experts may not be able to verbalize the incremental knowledge responsible for their evolution. One possible explanation of this problem is the lack of a shared method for expressing it. So, each expert has developed a unique collection of functional, but fallible hypotheses (that is, a personal construct system). In some important respects, these hypotheses do not coincide with publicly available domain knowledge, making it difficult to state explicitly. However, perhaps herein lies the most significant facet of expertise. From this perspective, repertory grid seems to be a tool able to bring the experts' self-constructed knowledge to the surface – making explicit the valuable heuristic knowledge that experts possess but are frequently unable to articulate (Díaz de León 2001).

The following study thus explores the possibility of using the repertory grid technique to enhance the traditional assessment of business plans by including estimates of venture viability, which have greater predictive validity. The assessment of investment opportunities seems limited by the ability to communicate those aspects that are intangible. We assume that in order to enhance our understanding of this process, we should observe not only the investor perspective but also the expertise of those who have been successful in transmitting the value of a new idea. Thus, we consider two kinds of experts: (1) expert investors and (2) expert entrepreneurs.

Venture capitalists are considered experts in new venturing financing (Zacharakis and Meyer 1998). In our study, we selected these experts from a group of venture capitalists investing in technology-based ventures in Canada. Professional venture capital is defined as the funding provided by firms of such full-time professionals. One of their objectives is to invest alongside management in new, rapidly growing or changing ventures that have the potential to develop into significant competitors in global markets.

As discussed by Timmons and Sapienza (1992), the successful development of a business can be critically impacted by the interaction of the involved venture capitalists with the management team. Interestingly, venture-capital backed ventures have been found to achieve a higher survival rate than non-venture capital backed businesses (Zacharakis and Meyer 1998). The expertise of venture capitalists derives from the number of business plans and proposals they usually assess, sometimes 100 or more a month, from which they typically invest in only one to three (Timmons 1994).

The second group of experts represents successful 'high-technology' entrepreneurs in Canada. Their expertise is based on their experience of successfully launching a technology-based venture. The importance of such experts comes from the complementary knowledge that they incorporate into understanding some of the current demands placed on business plans for new technology-based ventures.

Reliability, Signability, and Validity of Repertory Grids

Considering the broad application of different forms of repertory grids to different domains of human expertise, it is obvious that the question regarding the validity and reliability of repertory grids cannot be answered (Bannister and Fransella 1986). As mentioned by Smith and Stewart (1977), from a methodological viewpoint, it is doubtful if concepts of reliability and validity can be applied to ideographic uses of the grid. Kelly himself referred to 'reliability' (specifically test–retest) of the grid as a measure of how much the person has failed to develop since the last time (Ryle 1975). Slater (1976: 92) illustrates this concept with a convincing argument: 'the reliability and significance of a grid cannot be investigated by the methods used for a battery of tests given to a group of subjects'. Then, he elaborates:

> [T]he reason is that the theory from which psychometric methods for measuring reliability and significance are derived assumes that samples can be drawn at random from an objectively defined population. The assumption can be satisfied by the nomothetic [actual] data in a table of test scores but not by the ideographic data of a grid. (Slater 1976: 69)

Slater further argues that to assess the significance of a grid, one should test the null hypothesis by asking this question: 'What is the probability that I would obtain these results by chance alone?' As a step towards answering this question, he produced the program GRANNY, which generates random numbers for grids of any specified size. For example, one hundred 10 6 10 random grids had a first component accounting for an average of 30 per cent of the variance (standard deviation 0.0635). Thus, a 10 6 10 experimental grid, in which the first component accounts for more than twice this percentage of the variation is almost certainly not random and almost certainly has some additional significance. Such is the case with all our experiment results (see Table 14.2). Notwithstanding these very persuasive arguments, some researchers have attempted to assess reliability and validity of the grid in conventional terms. For example, Epting (1975) obtained test–retest reliabilities of grids in three areas of 0.65, 0.62 and 0.64.

Fransella and Bannister (1977) also provide a detailed consideration of reliability. They argue, 'If we consider forms of grid to be attempts to enquire into a person's construct system then under what circumstances would we expect stability or change?' (Fransella and Bannister 1977: 82). They conclude this way: 'We should look to the grid not to repeat the same result but to see, when it shows change, what it is signifying. In short, reliability is perhaps best seen as merely one aspect of validity' (Fransella and Bannister 1977: 83).

The validity of the grid itself is also complex to assess. With respect to construct validity, however, there is considerable evidence in the literature that the results obtained from repertory grid studies are consistent with the assumptions underlying personal construct theory (Adams-Weber 1979). Perhaps more relevant to the topic of this study is the research related to measuring predictive validity of grids in management studies. Bender (1976) reports a study in which grids were used to predict the behaviour of certain men towards other people. These predictions were then validated against their wives' reports of actual behaviour towards the same people. The results were highly significant ($p = 0.00006$). Fransella and Bannister (1967) attempted to forecast voting preferences from the results of a grid with 10 people known to the subjects as elements. Five hypotheses were tested, and the authors concluded, 'The repertory grid has both concurrent and predictive validity when used as a measure of political construing' (Fransella and Bannister 1977: 104).

METHOD

Constructing a repertory grid involves the selection of a topic, which in our study is intangibles in business plans, and the generation of a list of items, called elements, relating to that topic. The elements help to define the kind of conversation to have with the expert. There are several themes related to intangibles in business plans. However, we are particularly interested in obtaining a better understanding of how experts assess such intangibles. Therefore, it makes sense to use actual business plans of various kinds as elements in the interview.

Perhaps the best analogy when thinking about choice of elements is to consider what surveyors do when mapping out a new piece of ground. They start by selecting a series of key points on that piece of ground: salient features, such as church spires, hilltops or ponds. Then, when they have the salient features identified they take a series of measurements between the features, which give them more and more data about the territory until they are ready to draw the complete map. It is rather as if when eliciting constructs you are looking at the relationships between features on the map, and the elements themselves can be thought of as the features from which the surveyor starts when mapping the territory. From this analogy, you might infer that the number of elements in an interview session is not as relevant as the precision with which each element is defined and the range selected over the elements' area (Adams-Webber 1979; Stewart and Stewart 1982; Shaw and Gaines 1987).

The elicitation session proceeded with an open interview as follows. Each interviewee was asked to recall six business plans. Such investment proposals, from early stage technology-based ventures, had to have been assessed or created during the previous 18 months. It is important to note that specific details about the ventures remained completely confidential since each interviewee was asked only to recall such investments. The six business plans became the elements under examination and were distributed as follows:

- two business plans considered 'big hits';
- two business plans considered 'average or marginal'; and
- two business plans that were 'rejected or where the investment had been lost'.

During the interview, we randomly selected three business plans from the six and presented them to the expert who had originally remembered them. We then asked the expert to distinguish between these plans so that two of them shared an intangible element not possessed by the third. This property we call a construct. Each expert categorized such constructs as bipolar attributes in such terms as 'good management skills/poor management skills', 'experienced entrepreneur/inexperienced entrepreneur' and so forth. In other words, this method involves selecting groups of three elements (triads) from the list of elements (business plans), and the expert is then invited to say in what way two of the plans are alike and in what way the third plan is different from the other two in terms of its intangible aspects. This procedure is intended to produce two contrasting poles for the construct, although it is sometimes suggested that the poles should be opposites. However, the difficulty with requesting 'opposites' is that it tends to produce logical opposites rather than opposites in meaning. For example, the logical opposite of ambitious is 'not ambitious'; but the expert may think of the real opposite of ambitious as being 'does not trample on colleagues'. Clearly, the latter, contrasting, approach indicates far more about the meaning of the construct.

Next, we provided the expert with a simple five-point rating scale. Once a construct had been elicited, the expert assigned each of the six plans a value from 1 to 5. For example, a value of one could be assigned to a plan in one pole of the construct, say 'experienced entrepreneur'. Correspondingly, a value of five would be assigned to another element on the other pole of the construct, in this case 'inexperienced entrepreneur'.

The technique proceeded to elicit all further constructs from the expert by presenting successive fresh triads of plans. The expert could then add important constructs that may not have been possible with the random combination of plans being presented. All the ratings elicited from the expert were structured in the form of a matrix known as a repertory grid.

Figure 14.1 shows an example of a completed repertory grid: how one of the respondents construed the six business plans. The text describes the results of four kinds of analysis: a content analysis, which classifies the constructs

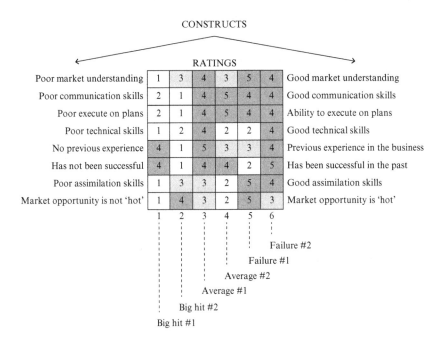

Figure 14.1   Example of a completed repertory grid

Table 14.1   The content categories of the respondents' constructs

Category	No. of constructs	
	Entrepreneurs	Venture capitalists
Skills of the management team	23	41
Personality of the entrepreneur	14	24
Background of the management team	11	8
General attributes of the management team	13	6
Business plan (business model)	4	4
Investor – entrepreneur relationship	1	
Total	66	83

provided by the respondents (see Table 14.1); a cluster analysis, which shows the ways in which each respondent grouped his constructs together, indiating the patterns of meaning he perceived (Figures 14.2–14.11); a principal components analysis, which shows the main concerns underlying his thinking (Figures 14.12 and 14.13) and an extremity analysis, identifying each person's most meaningful constructs (Table 14.4).

FINDINGS

We elicited 149 constructs from the ten interviewees. Out of those, a total of 83 constructs were obtained from the five investors. Correspondingly, the five entrepreneurs provided 66 constructs. The constructs were content-analysed following a standard procedure proposed by Honey (1977). Table 14.1 summarizes the content of the constructs classified in six main category headings.

Honey (1977), suggests a two-stage process in order to check the reliability of the classification scheme. Following this procedure, first, we grouped similar constructs together. Once we were satisfied with the classification of all the constructs, they were randomized, and two independent researchers were asked to reassign the constructs to the six categories. Their respective success rates were 84 per cent and 73 per cent, supporting our original ratings. We then discussed and amended the category scheme based on the inaccurate assignments. For example, we renamed two of the categories to better reflect the theme of the constructs they were grouping. The last step consisted of randomizing and assigning the constructs to the new set of categories; on this occasion, the constructs were successfully reassigned in 89 per cent and 86 per cent of the cases by two other researchers.

One interesting finding of this study is the similarity between investors and entrepreneurs in terms of their assessments of importance. A quick look at the number of constructs from each group shows that both investors and entrepreneurs regard the management skills of the founder (or management team) to be critical. This category includes not only the skills of the management team but also their core competencies, abilities and business acumen. The category thus includes constructs related to the personality of the entrepreneur. Examples of these include honesty, integrity, passion and business etiquette.

The results presented here represent constructs in the exact way they were communicated by the experts in this study. This is important to note, since, for example, considering the complete list of constructs, one could misinterpret a false suggestion that skills, abilities and competencies have the same connotation. The relevance of this matter resides somewhat in recent debates aimed at understanding differences between abilities and attitudes (Douglas and Shepherd 2000).

However, one characteristic of the repertory grid technique is to avoid 'contaminating' the constructs and focus its analysis on understanding a personal meaning to the expert. In other words, perhaps the abilities and attitudes of an entrepreneur are construed with the same meaning in an expert's mind, or perhaps not. What is important, however, is our understanding of the meaning to the expert of such construct when evaluating a business proposal.

The results shown in this study replicate some of the findings of Hisrich and Jankowicz (1990) in which management was identified as the most important category. They provided scientific proof of otherwise anecdotal evidence with regard to intangibles in investment of technology-based ventures. In our study, investors mentioned several times the importance they usually place in honesty on the part of the entrepreneur. Also, having 'good business etiquette' seemed to be decisive for some investors. When asked for elaboration, one investor stated: 'if they don't show any courtesy with us as partners, how could we expect that they will respect and anticipate their customers' needs?'

GRID ANALYSIS

Once the summary of the general results was complete, we analysed each grid following three separate procedures. First, we cluster-analysed the data in order to identify ways in which the individual respondents structured their thinking about investment applications. As a second test, we completed a principal component analysis on each grid to gain an idea of the cognitive complexity of each respondent. This analysis was performed using commercial software. There are several options of software available in the market, however, we have been very comfortable with Repgrid®.[1] Afterwards, we also calculated the rating extremity, a measure frequently interpreted as an indication of the importance or 'meaningfulness' of the subject of a given construct or element (Bonarius 1977).

Cluster Analysis

Using software based on the FOCUS technique (Jankowicz and Thomas 1982, 1983), the grids were cluster-analysed. This technique uses a nearest-neighbour distance metric. That is, the algorithm depends on a two-way cluster analysis based on pattern recognition, grouping items (elements and constructs) by their interrelationship.

The FOCUS algorithm computes the summed differences between pairs of ratings in each grid, calculating first by columns and then by rows. A cluster-analysed grid (see Figure 14.2) repositions the most similarly rated constructs to appear side by side. As mentioned by Shaw (1980), the result is a graphic representation of patterns of groupings of elements on constructs and constructs on elements. This technique provides a personal theory from each respondent employed either when making a funding decision (venture capitalist) or when presenting a funding proposal (entrepreneurs) (Hisrich and Jankowicz 1990).

Cluster Analysis for Venture Capitalists

Figure 14.2 shows the corresponding cluster analysis for venture capitalist 1. The 'tree-diagram' at the right shows a link in the respondent's rationale. Constructs connected along neighbouring 'branches' are closer together in the respondent's mind than those connected along non-adjacent branches. The scale shows the percentage similarity of constructs, calculated from the respondent's original ratings: follow any pair of adjacent branches to the right until they meet, then, read up from that point onto the scale. For example, there is a 95 per cent match between 'honesty and integrity' and 'character in general' in this respondent's thinking. Whenever he says 'honesty and integrity', he also says 'character in general', and vice versa.

Respondent 1 shows three principal clusters. That is, one sub-cluster associates the importance of having a competitive strategy with the ability to 'make things happen' or 'bias for action'. A second sub-cluster consists of the entrepreneur's honesty, integrity and character in general as opposed to not having a 'reality orientation'. A third sub-cluster groups

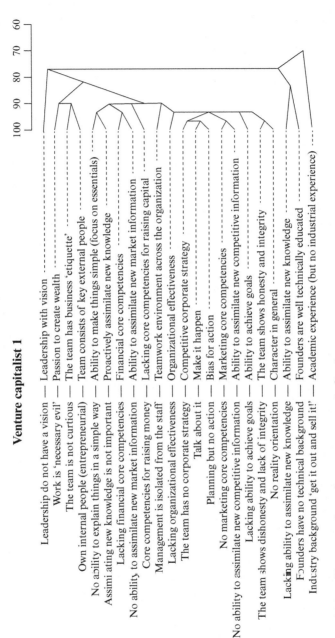

Figure 14.2 Cluster analysis from venture capitalist 1

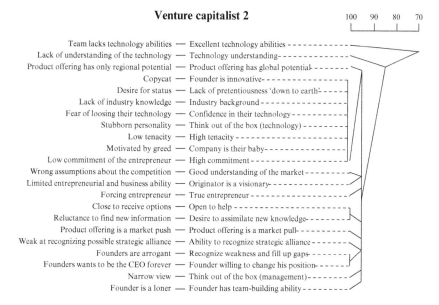

Figure 14.3   Cluster analysis from venture capitalist 2

the entrepreneur's ability to assimilate new competitive information as well as marketing core competencies.

Respondent 2 shows three highly matched (100 per cent) clusters. As shown in Figure 14.3, the first is a cluster grouping eight constructs; it reflects the importance that this investor places on the entrepreneur's ability to 'think out of the box'. Constructs in this cluster range from tenacity, commitment, innovativeness and confidence to lack of pretentiousness of the entrepreneur. A second cluster reflects the importance the investor places on the desire of the entrepreneur to assimilate new knowledge as well as the entrepreneur's openness to opinions and help. A third cluster includes two constructs dealing with the entrepreneur's ability to recognize weaknesses and fill gaps in the team as well as the entrepreneur's lack of arrogance when recognizing the need to change his position in the future.

Respondent 3 shows a looser structure (Figure 14.4). In other words, the different constructs are utilized as rather independent ways of assessing a proposal. One sub-cluster associates the ability for understanding the market opportunity with the importance of assimilating new market information as well as the market perceived as a 'hot' market or as a niche. The entrepreneur's business experience and past successes are somewhat less closely related to other constructs and represent factors to which this investor gives separate and distinct consideration.

Figure 14.4   Cluster analysis from venture capitalist 3

Respondent 4 also shows a somewhat loose structure (Figure 14.5). One cluster associates three highly matching constructs (96 per cent). These constructs relate to the responsibility of the entrepreneur as well as to openness to listening and accountability to the board by way of corporate governance. There are two constructs slightly related to this sub-cluster dealing with realistic expectations of the entrepreneur and consistency in management decisions. Qualified entrepreneurs with good operating procedures constitute independent aspects of this investor's decisions.

Respondent 5 shows two tight clusters (Figure 14.6), one of which groups two highly matched (100 per cent) constructs related to the ability of the team to overcome difficult situations. 'Surviving when something goes wrong' and having a 'full team in place' characterize these constructs; in contrast, ventures with an incomplete team are more vulnerable to 'falling apart' when things do not happen as planned. This investor seems to relate surviving with the corporate culture of the new venture as well as the 'team's ability to make good decisions and learn from [mistakes]', also the ability to 'reinvent their business model overnight'. A second cluster includes another highly matched pair of constructs. These constructs are characterized by the desire of a founder to succeed and his motivation to make money, as opposed to the determination of founders unwilling to relinquish the leadership of a new venture due to a feeling of the venture being 'their baby'. This cluster includes two somewhat looser constructs related to the experience and know-how of the founder.

Cluster Analysis for Entrepreneurs

Respondent 1 shows a loose structure (Figure 14.7). This entrepreneur considers as an important factor of success the wisdom of the founder to trust the management of the new venture to a more qualified manager. In other words, this is the opposite of a founder who wants to control his venture indefinitely. The contrast is interesting, for the construct corresponds to what several investors considered a very problematic situation.

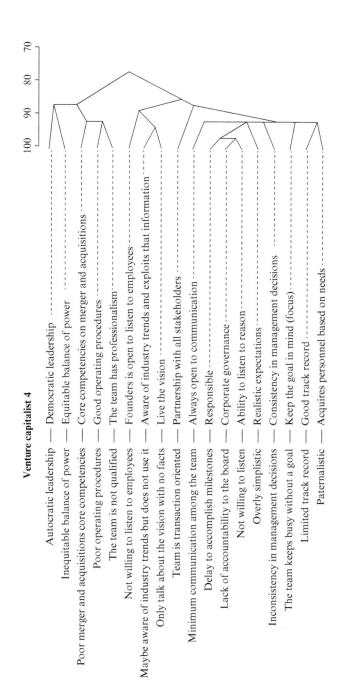

Venture capitalist 4

Autocratic leadership — Democratic leadership

Inequitable balance of power — Equitable balance of power

Poor merger and acquisitions core competencies — Core competencies on merger and acquisitions

Poor operating procedures — Good operating procedures

The team is not qualified — The team has professionalism

Not willing to listen to employees — Founders is open to listen to employees

Maybe aware of industry trends but does not use it — Aware of industry trends and exploits that information

Only talk about the vision with no facts — Live the vision

Team is transaction oriented — Partnership with all stakeholders

Minimum communication among the team — Always open to communication

Delay to accomplish milestones — Responsible

Lack of accountability to the board — Corporate governance

Not willing to listen — Ability to listen to reason

Overly simplistic — Realistic expectations

Inconsistency in management decisions — Consistency in management decisions

The team keeps busy without a goal — Keep the goal in mind (focus)

Limited track record — Good track record

Paternalistic — Acquires personnel based on needs

Figure 14.5   Cluster analysis from venture capitalist 4

407

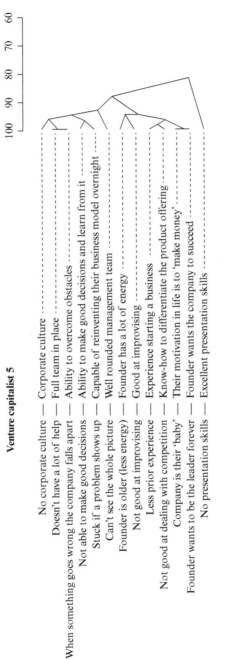

Venture capitalist 5

| | 100 | 90 | 80 | 70 | 60 |

No corporate culture — Corporate culture

Doesn't have a lot of help — Full team in place

When something goes wrong the company falls apart — Ability to overcome obstacles

Not able to make good decisions — Ability to make good decisions and learn from it

Stuck if a problem shows up — Capable of reinventing their business model overnight

Can't see the whole picture — Well rounded management team

Founder is older (less energy) — Founder has a lot of energy

Not good at improvising — Good at improvising

Less prior experience — Experience starting a business

Not good at dealing with competition — Know-how to differentiate the product offering

Company is their 'baby' — Their motivation in life is to 'make money'

Founder wants to be the leader forever — Founder wants the company to succeed

No presentation skills — Excellent presentation skills

Figure 14.6   Cluster analysis from venture capitalist 5

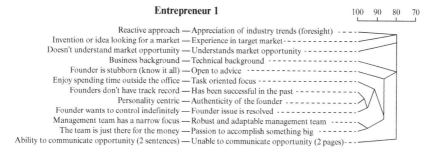

Figure 14.7 Cluster analysis from entrepreneur 1

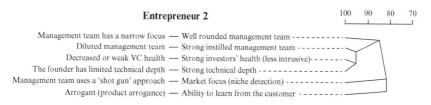

Figure 14.8 Cluster analysis from entrepreneur 2

One could argue that these constructs are part of the respondent's personal theory with respect to success of a new venture. In this case, he is associating this issue with two highly related constructs: 'founder has been successful in the past' and 'founder is genuine'. Having a 'robust and adaptable management team' and 'passion' are two additional constructs that belong to this sub-cluster.

Respondent 2 shows a sub-cluster with three constructs (Figure 14.8). One deals with the 'health' of the investor. When asked to elaborate, the entrepreneur explained this in terms of 'being more intrusive/being less intrusive', where an investor with financial difficulties would be considered more intrusive, therefore putting unnecessary pressure on the management team. This interesting finding would not have surfaced had we considered only investors in the study. It would seem to have important implications for those entrepreneurs looking for financing.

The construct dealing with 'health' of the investors is associated with the strong technical grounding of the founder as well as a 'strong instilled' management team. On the other hand, 'niche detection' and the ability to learn from customers constitute issues that indicate separate concern.

Respondent 3 shows one main cluster (Figure 14.9). A group of six

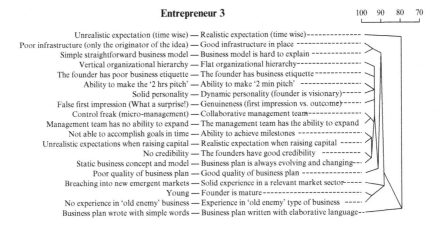

Figure 14.9   Cluster analysis from entrepreneur 3

constructs form a tight (96 per cent) sub-cluster: a dynamic business plan 'constantly evolving and changing' and good credibility are related to the ability to achieve milestones to 'keep the money happy' as well as to have realistic expectations of 'how much capital to raise' and 'when'. Moreover, the team's 'ability to expand' seems to be influenced it's having a collaborative management team. A group of five constructs dealing mainly with the personality of the founder complements this cluster. Issues associated with 'business etiquette' and 'dynamic personality' as well as 'genuineness' belong to this group of constructs.

Respondent 4 shows one tight cluster (Figure 14.10). Integrity and honesty are highly related to his concept of 'being an entrepreneur', also linked to a 'potential to succeed'. Similarly, a 'reasonable' rather than an 'incompetent' management team is one with an ability to make 'quick' and

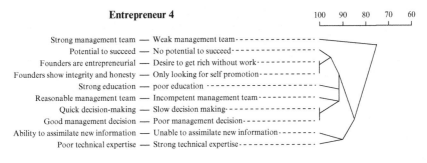

Figure 14.10   Cluster analysis from entrepreneur 4

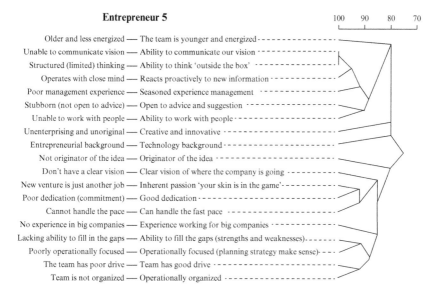

Figure 14.11   Cluster analysis from entrepreneur 5

'good' management decisions. 'Education of the founders' is explained as 'having professional degrees' and belongs to this cluster as well. 'Strong technical expertise' and the 'ability to assimilate new knowledge' are constructs to which this participant gives different consideration.

Respondent 5 provided a total of 19 constructs (Figure 14.11) clustered in two main groups. An ability to communicate the founder's vision is associated with an ability to 'think outside the box'. Similarly, 'being open to advice and suggestions' is linked not only to experience but also to proactive reaction to new information as opposed to operating with 'a closed mind', which is closely related to the ability to 'work with people'. A second group includes constructs associated with 'inherent passion', 'dedication', 'clear vision' and 'handling a fast pace'. Linked to this cluster are abilities to 'fill in the gaps in terms of weaknesses or strengths', 'be operationally focused', 'have good drive' and 'be operationally organized'. Interestingly, team characteristics such as 'being creative and innovative' as well as 'being originators of the idea' are issues of separate concern to this entrepreneur. In general, these descriptions are diverse with several distinct constructs in each case. That is, while investors and entrepreneurs draw on a fairly common set of constructs, they associate them in different ways and form their impressions of a venture proposal by focusing on different aspects.

Some constructs were represented as independent of the main clusters and are worthy of separate analysis. A possible explanation of this circumstance is the fact that some of the constructs are unique to each venture and therefore should be assessed on an individual basis. One could hypothesize that when assessing a new venture proposal, all investors and entrepreneurs look for the presence of certain characteristics (the founder's experience and background, for example). At the same time, there are idiosyncrasies particular to each venture. The conclusion might be that, initially, investors are matching a venture proposal's characteristics against somewhat standard criteria.

After an evaluation of certain fundamentals, investors focus on the particularities of such a venture. One implication is that, in assessing a new venture, a simple verification of a list of criteria would probably result in unrealistic understandings of its value. In other words, only a comprehensive assessment process can produce a more realistic value for a new venture proposal.

PRINCIPAL COMPONENT ANALYSIS

A principal component analysis provides a description of the connections between elements and constructs in a grid. It reveals how a large number of individual judgements made by the subject in rating all the elements on all the constructs are manifestations of a relatively more simple underlying structure. It also shows contrasts between the different elements (business plans, in this case). These contrasts are indicated in terms of which constructs are of major importance in the subject's system.

The principal component analysis extracts successive components: the first being able to account for the most variation, the second accounting for the most residual variation and so on. In most grids, the first principal component accounts for between 30 per cent and 50 per cent of total variance, the second for 10 per cent to 25 per cent and subsequent components for diminishing proportions (Ryle 1975). For most practical purposes, the first two or three components provide an adequate picture of the subject's system (Bell 1990).

Our interest in analysing principal components is to obtain an indication of the cognitive complexity that investors and entrepreneurs use when assessing proposals. Cognitive complexity can be summarized in terms of the differences in which subjects construe the same issues independently of each other (Adams-Webber 1996). For example, a highly complex individual will take into account markedly different aspects of an issue when thinking about it, as opposed to viewing it in terms of the one or two

Table 14.2   Summary of the results of separate principal component analyses for each individual grid

	Principle component no.					
	1	2	3	4	5	1 + 2
Venture capitalists						
1	75.70	12.29	6.42	3.90	1.69	**87.99**
2	89.80	7.47	2.14	0.54	0.05	**97.27**
3	47.87	39.01	8.21	3.27	1.65	**86.88**
4	73.95	14.49	4.63	3.82	3.11	**88.44**
5	79.60	10.59	5.75	3.10	1.40	**89.75**
Entrepreneur	1	2	3	4	5	1 + 2
1	57.91	17.79	10.90	7.50	5.89	**75.7**
2	69.98	15.70	9.52	2.86	1.92	**85.68**
3	64.32	21.49	7.43	4.38	2.38	**85.81**
4	78.35	11.85	6.12	2.64	0.64	**90.6**
5	53.15	27.71	9.76	6.52	2.85	**80.86**

themes dominating his thinking. As described by Adams-Webber (1970), the proportion of total variance accounted for by the largest factor or first principal component provides an index of the cognitive complexity. A useful rule of thumb in repertory grid work is to regard a situation in which 60 per cent or more of variance is accounted for by the first principal component as an indication of low cognitive complexity (Smith and Stewart 1977, Smith 1980).

Table 14.2 provides a summary of separate principal component analyses of each individual grid. The results of these analyses indicate that all respondents show a relatively low complexity with just one or two themes representing their thinking. After analysing each grid, we labeled the themes corresponding to each participant. Those labels were taken from the nearest two constructs to the first principal component axis. Table 14.3 shows a summary of these labels for the first principal components.

A perusal of Table 14.3 shows that the predominant themes (from both investors and entrepreneurs) relate to the adequacy of the management team with the business proposal. Associating the two main constructs from each first component with their groups (described in Table 14.1) corroborated this result. We found that most of the two main constructs belong to groups two and five (personality of the entrepreneur and business proposal respectively). In this area, our results correspond to those reported by Hisrich and Jankowicz (1990).

Figure 14.12 shows an example of a loose construct structure, which is

Table 14.3   Themes underlying the respondent's thinking

	Label	Theme
Venture capitalist		
1	Organizational effectiveness Character in general	Effective of management team Honesty and integrity
2	Entrepreneurial abilities Market understanding	Tenacity, high commitment, innovativeness Knowledge of market potential
3	Hot market Successful entrepreneur	Attractive product offering Solid experience and background
4	Goal oriented Awareness of trends	Keep goal ill mind Open to communication
5	Corporate culture Full team in place	Persistent management team Well rounded management team
Entrepreneur		
1	Team has focus Authentic management team	Task oriented management Trustworthy management
2	Technical background Investor's health	Founder has strong technical depth Less intrusive venture capitalist
3	Collaborative management Dynamic business plan	Synergetic management Always evolving and changing
4	Entrepreneurial team Personal quality	Desire to succeed Founder's integrity and honesty
5	Fill gaps (weakness/ strength) Motivated team	Effective management team Team has drive

characteristic of high cognitive complexity. In this particular case, the first two principal components account for 76 per cent of the variance. This example of a relatively loose construct structure corresponds to venture capitalists 3. A perusal of Table 14.2 shows how for this expert, the first component (horizontal axis in Figure 12) explains only 47.87 per cent of the variance and the second component (vertical axis in Figure 14.12) accounts for only 39.01 per cent of the variance. The sum of both principal components corresponds to 76 per cent of the variance. When evaluating business proposals of high-technology new ventures, this expert has several constructs in mind, which seem to be independent from each other. Hence the high cognitive complexity of the expert represented in Figure 14.12.

Figure 14.13 shows most constructs sketched together neighbouring the first (horizontal) principal component: a tight structure, characteristic of low cognitive complexity. This is a case where 'everything relates

A loose construct structure

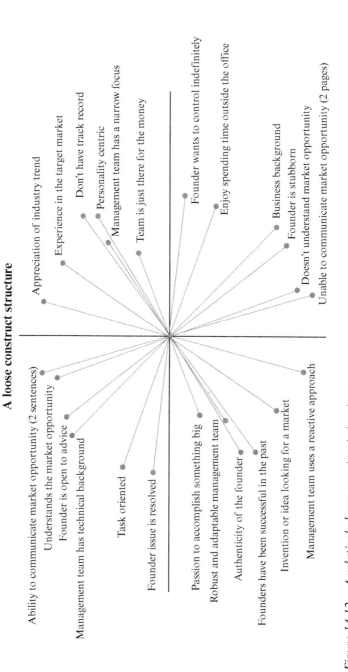

Figure 14.12   A relatively loose construct structure

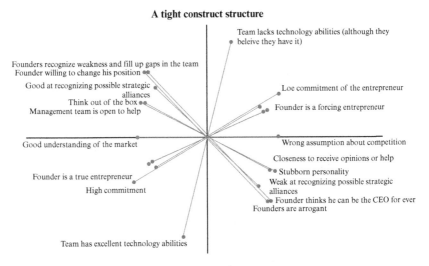

Figure 14.13   A relatively tight construct structure

to everything else'. In this example, the first two principal components account for 97 per cent of the variance. This is venture capitalist 2. From Table 14.2, the sum of 97 per cent comes from adding the variance accounted with the first component (89.80 per cent) and the variance explained by the second component (7.47 per cent). When evaluating business opportunities, this expert considers only a couple of constructs to validate a decision.

ANALYSIS OF EXTREMITY

Several studies have defined rating extremity as an indication of personal meaningfulness (Shepherd 1999). For instance, Bonarius (1970) has shown that subjects rate their close associates (for example, best friend) more extremely than remote acquaintances (for example, my doctor). This means that the value of an extremity evaluation is of higher value. There is general agreement that the higher the extremity scores, the more meaningful the statement is for the respondent. In other words, an extremity score indicates how far a respondent rated the elements from the midpoint of a scale. There is also considerable evidence, reviewed by Adams-Webber (1979), that subjects tend to rate themselves and others more extremely on elicited constructs than on supplied ones. Moreover, as discussed by Adams-Webber and Benjafield (1973), rating extremity also correlates with personal judgements of the relative meaningfulness of supplied constructs. Rating extremity is then calculated by the absolute value of subtracting the midpoint of a scale from each assigned rating. In our case we used a scale of 1 to 5 to evaluate each of the constructs within a grid. In other words, after an expert provided a bipolar construct following the repertory grid technique, we asked to rate each of the elements using a scale from 1 to 5 (Figure 14.1). In a scale of numbers between 1 and 5, the midpoint is 3. For example, a rating of 1 on a scale from 1 to 5 would have an extremity score of $|1 - 3| = 2$. The resulting extremity scores for each element (business plans in our study) are added up and divided by the number of plans rated (in this study, there were six). Table 14.4 provides a summary of the two higher extremity scores for each participant. The last column shows a checkmark (✓) indicating those constructs that not only have the most extreme values but also correspond to the top two highest weights from the principal component. These constructs contribute two characteristics. First, they are meaningful to the participant. Second, by knowing their loading, we can predict the participant's ratings more accurately (please refer back to Table 14.2 to confirm the variance accounted for by the first component of each grid).

CONCLUSION

This study on decision-making, where the assessment of intangible aspects is paramount for a suitable answer, has important implications for both practitioners and researchers. A major finding is the high relevance of intangibles in the assessment of business plans from technology-based ventures. There is extant literature that shows the important role played by intangibles and intuition during an investor's due diligence process. However, a lack of tools to evaluate intangibles is a major challenge. Apparently, repertory grid is a method that may fill such a gap. The results of this study not only provide evidence of the effectiveness of using repertory grids to elicit intangibles but also increase our knowledge of the venture capital decision process. We used an innovative approach considering two perspectives – the investor's and the entrepreneur's – in this decision-making problem. Thus, we gained new appreciation of the elements in a subjective evaluation of early stage technology based ventures.

Furthermore, the outcome of the FOCUS-based cluster analysis provides additional evidence of individual differences among venture capitalists with respect to their cognitive complexity in terms of their evaluations of entrepreneurs, which supplements that derived from the principal component analysis. Moreover, while investors and entrepre-

Table 14.4　Summary of the two higher extremity scores for each participant and the correspondent loading weight in the principal component

Participant	Description	Extremity score	Loading in first component	Within two heaviest weights?
Venture capitalist				
1	Organizational effectiveness	1.67	4.364	✓
	Character in general	1.67	4.078	✓
2	Confidence in technology	1.83	4.328	✓
	Thinking 'out of the box'	1.83	4.328	✓
	Industry background	1.83	4.328	✓
	High tenacity	1.83	4.328	✓
	'Down to earth'	1.83	4.328	✓
	Not motivated by greed	1.83	4.328	✓
	Innovative founder	1.83	4.328	✓
	High commitment	1.83	4.328	✓
3	Ability to execute on plans	1.33	2.171	
	Successful in the past	1.33	0.039	
4	Founder has realistic expectations	1.50	3.823	✓
	Merger and acquisitions core competencies	1.50	3.103	
5	Know-how to differentiate product offering	1.67	3.517	
	Excellent presentation skills	1.67	2.845	
Entrepreneurs				
1	Invention or idea looking for a market	1.50	1.887	
	Founder has been successful in the past	1.33	2.956	
2	Strong technical depth	1.50	3.298	✓
	Less intrusive investor	1.33	3.276	✓
3	Business plan evolving and changing	1.67	3.871	✓
	Experience in 'old economy'	1.50	2.545	
	Collaborative management team	1.50	4.001	✓
4	Founders are entrepreneurial	1.67	4.134	✓
	Integrity and honesty	1.67	4.134	✓
5	Team is originator of idea	2.00	1.737	
	Operationally organized	1.67	4.098	✓

Note:　✓ Indicates a construct that is within the two largest weights in the principal component.

neurs draw on a fairly large set of constructs, they associate them in different ways and form their impressions of a venture proposal by focusing on a variety of aspects. This is a result of major significance. In other words, it very effectively illustrates the fundamental importance of personally constructed knowledge in the development of high-level expertise.

The results of this study show a similarity in the way investors and entrepreneurs construe investment proposals. For example, an analysis of the constructs from each group reveals that both place high importance on the perceived qualifications of the management team. This category considers not only the skills of the management team but also their core competencies, abilities, and business acumen. Constructs related to the personality of the entrepreneur – honesty, integrity, passion and business etiquette, for example – are also included.

Some of our results replicate the findings of Hisrich and Jankowicz (1990) in which management was regarded as the most important category. Furthermore, using this rather new technique, we provide a scientific proof of otherwise anecdotal evidence with regard to intangibles in investment of technology-based ventures. For example, the investors' frequent mention of honesty confirms how important this intangible is, just as 'good business etiquette' seemed to be decisive for some investors. When asked for an elaboration of such construct, one investor stated, 'if the entrepreneur doesn't show any courtesy with us as partners, how could we expect that they will respect and anticipate their customers' needs?'

The findings of this study are not fully consistent with research by Hall and Hofer (1993). Their main point was that venture capitalists are not concerned with the assessment of human capital when screening new investment proposals. Perhaps their findings were due to the design of their study, which determined only the earliest phase of deal screening. This is where venture capitalists are sifting through hundreds of proposals by target company managers. One possible assessment method used by investors at this time is to screen opportunities by comparing the new proposal's characteristics against general working guidelines, such as area of investment, geographic location, and stage of the venture. By the time the investors move to the in-depth due diligence research phase, it is very clear from the results of this study that venture capitalists are concerned with an effective assessment of some of the intangibles involved in the proposal.

Another interesting finding of this study, although mentioned only once by an entrepreneur, is the construct related to the 'health of the venture capitalist'. We think this is worth mentioning since this study, different from others, includes a consideration of the point of view of the entrepreneur. A further explanation of this construct detailed how a 'healthy' investor is one without financial troubles. According to this entrepreneur, a venture capitalist struggling with financial difficulties is 'more intrusive' and puts 'unnecessary pressure' on the management team.

Finally, these findings cause us to reconsider our earlier efforts to locate a set of fully generalized 'intangibles' and the use of Repertory Grid technique as a means of investigating them. We better understand the contextual idiosyncratic and dynamic nature of these important attributes. The repertory grid is thus a useful approach to assist early-stage investors who are seeking to manage new product portfolios of start-up ventures and demonstrate an efficient approach to uncertainty reduction and generation of evidence to guide so-called lean start-ups.

FUTURE RESEARCH

Future studies could make a contribution by focusing a microscope on early stages of new technology-based ventures at various points. In other words, a longitudinal study could provide evidence of the dynamism as well as the idiosyncratic characteristics of a new venture. That is, technology-based ventures not only experience constant change but also need to overcome this change in order to survive. This situation is even more critical for new ventures. Therefore, having a list of criteria to appraise the value of these ventures at only one point in time would probably result in an unrealistic assessment. Thus, our results show that an assessment process is probably more appropriate than a one-time assessment. We need a method to assess a new venture over different points in time.

Our investigation suggests that a longitudinal study should consist of eliciting impressions and significance of a new venture from a group of entrepreneurs, incubators and venture capitalists at three points. The first occurs when an idea is initially presented to an investor and, curiously, interest is piqued. The second comes when the entrepreneur presents the idea in the form of a business plan to an incubator. The third takes place when the new venture is ready for its first round of financing, usually from a venture capitalist. The longitudinal study allows us to consider three angles of the same problem: (1) the ideas, which usually come from an entrepreneur; (2) the management, which is usually provided by incubators; and (3) the capital, which usually comes from a venture capitalist.

NOTE

1. Repgrid® is a software developed by Mildred Shaw and Brian Gaines. More information is available on www.repgrid.com.

REFERENCES

Adams-Webber, J.R. (1970), 'An analysis of the discriminant validity of several repertory grid indices', *British Journal of Psychology*, **61** (1), 83–90.

Adams-Webber, J.R. (1979), *Personal Construct Theory: Concepts and Applications*, New York: John Wiley and Sons.

Adams-Webber, J. R. (1996), 'Cognitive complexity', in R. Corsini, and A.J. Auerbach (eds), *Encyclopedia of Psychology*, New York: John Wiley and Sons, pp. 154–65.

Adams-Webber, J.R. and J. Benjafield (1973), 'The relation between lexical marking and rating extremity in interpersonal judgement', *Canadian Journal of Behavioural Science*, **5** (3), 234–241.

Agnew, N.M. and J.L. Brown (1989), 'Foundations for a theory of knowing: II. Fallible but functional knowledge', *Canadian Psychology*, **30** (2), 168–83.

Bachher, J.S., E. Díaz de León and P. Guild (1999), 'Decision criteria used by investors to screen technology-based ventures', in D.F. Kocaoglu and T.R. Anderson (eds), *Technology and Innovation Management*, Portland, OR: Portland International Conference on Management of Engineering and Technology, pp. 269–73.

Bannister, D. and F. Fransella (1986), *Inquiring Man: The Psychology of Personal Constructs*, 3rd edn, Dover, NH: Croom Helm.

Bell, R.C. (1990), 'Analytic issues in the use of repertory grid technique', in G.J. Neimeyer and R.A. Neimeyer (eds), *Advances on Personal Construct Psychology*, vol. 1, Greenwich, Connecticut: JAI Press, pp. 25–48.

Bender, M.P. (1976), 'Does construing people as similar involve similar behavior towards them? A subjective and objective replication', *British Journal of Social and Clinical Psychology*, **15** (1), 93–5.

Bonarius, J.C.J. (1970), *Personal Construct Psychology and Extreme Response Style. An Integration of Meaningfulness, Maladjustment, and Communication*, Amsterdam: Swets and Zeitlinger.

Bonarius, J.C.J. (1977), 'The interaction model of communication: through experimental research toward existential relevance', in J.K. Cole and A.W. Landfield (eds), *Nebraska Symposium on Motivation*, Lincoln, NE: University of Nebraska Press, pp. 291–343.

Boose, J.H. (1988), 'Uses of repertory grid-centered knowledge-acquisition tools for knowledge-based systems', *International Journal of Man-Machine Studies*, **29** (3), 287–310.

Díaz de León, E. (2001), 'Toward an expert assessment of intangibles in technology-based ventures', doctoral dissertation, University of Waterloo.

Douglas, E.J. and D.A. Shepherd (2000), 'Entrepreneurship as a utility maximizing response', *Journal of Business Venturing*, **15** (3), 231–52.

Dubini, P. (1989), 'Which venture capital backed entrepreneurs have the best chances of succeeding?', *Journal of Business Venturing*, **4** (2), 123–32.

Epting, F.R. (1975), 'Order of presentation of construct poles. What are the factors to be considered? A reply', *British Journal of Social and Clinical Psychology*, **14** (4), 427–8.

Ford, K.M., J.R. Adams-Webber, H.A. Stahl and M.W. Bringmann (1990), 'Constructivist approaches to automated knowledge acquisition', in K.L. McGraw, and C.R. Westphal (eds), *Readings in Knowledge Acquisition: Current Trends and Practices*, New York: Horwood, pp. 34–54.

Fransella, F. and D. Bannister (1967), 'A validation of repertory grid technique as a measure of political construing', *Acta Psychologica*, **26**, 97–106.

Fransella, F. and D. Bannister (1977), *A Manual for Repertory Grid Technique*, London: Academic Press.

Gladstone, D. (1988), *Venture Capital Investing*, Englewood Cliffs, NJ: Prentice Hall.

Guild, P.D. and Bachher, J.S. (1996), 'Equity investment decisions for technology-based ventures', *International Journal of Technology Management*, **12** (7), 787–95.

Hall, R. and C.W. Hofer (1993), 'Venture capitalists' decision criteria in new venture evaluation', *Journal of Business Venturing*, **8** (1), 25–42.

Harvey, M.G. and R.F. Lusch (1995), 'Expanding the nature and scope of due diligence', *Journal of Business Venturing*, **10** (1), 5–21.

Hisrich, R.D. and A.D. Jankowicz (1990), 'Intuition in venture capital decisions: an exploratory study using a new technique', *Journal of Business Venturing*, **5** (1), 49–62.

Honey, P. (1977), 'The repertory grid in action', *Industrial and Commercial Training*, **11** (6), 452–9.

Jankowicz, A.D. and L.D. Thomas (1982), 'An algorithm for the hand-cluster-analysis of repertory grids', *Personnel Review*, **11** (4), 15–22.

Jankowicz, A.D. and L.D. Thomas (1983), 'An algorithm for the hand-cluster-analysis of repertory grids', *Personnel Review*, **12** (1), 22–30.

Johnson, P.E. (1983), 'What kind of expert should a system be?', *Journal of Medicine and Philosophy*, **8** (1), 77–97.

Kelly, G.A. (1955), *The Psychology of Personal Constructs*, 2 vols, New York: Norton.

Kozmetsky, G., M.D. Gill Jr and R.W. Smilor (eds) (1985), *Financing and Managing Fast-growth Companies: The Venture Capital Process*, Lexington, MA: Lexington Books.

Ryle, A. (1975), *Frames and Cages: The Repertory Grid Approach to Human Understanding*, London: University of Sussex Press.

Shaw, M.L.G. (1980), *On Becoming a Personal Scientist. Interactive Computer Elicitation of Personal Models of the World*, London: Academic Press.

Shaw, M.L.G. and B.R. Gaines (1987), 'An interactive knowledge-elicitation technique using personal construct technology', in A.L. Kidd (ed.), *Knowledge Acquisition for Expert Systems*, New York: Plenum Press, pp. 109–136.

Shepherd, D.A. (1999), 'Venture capitalists' assessment of new venture survival', *Management Science*, **45** (5), 621–32.

Shepherd, D.A. and Douglas, E.J. (1999), *Attracting Equity Investors: Positioning, Preparing, and Presenting the Business Plan*, Thousand Oaks, CA: Sage.

Slater, P. (1976), *Explorations of Intrapersonal Space*, London: Wiley.

Smart, G.H. (1999), 'Management assessment methods in venture capital: an empirical analysis of human capital valuation', *Venture Capital*, **1** (1), 59–82.

Smith, M. (1980), 'Applications and uses of repertory grid in management education', in J. Beck and C. Cox (eds), *Advances in Management Education*, London: Wiley, pp. 197–213.

Smith, M. and Stewart, B.J.M. (1977), 'Repertory grids: a flexible tool for establishing the content and structure of a manager's thoughts', in D. Ashton (ed.), *Management Bibliographies and Reviews*, vol. 3, Bradford: MCB Press, pp. 209–30.

Stewart, T.A. (1997), *Intellectual Capital*, New York: Doubleday.

Stewart, V. and A. Stewart (1982), *Business Applications of Repertory Grid*, London: McGraw-Hill.

Sullivan, P.H. (1999), 'Profiting from intellectual capital', *Journal of Knowledge Management*, **3** (2), 132–42.

Timmons, J.A. (1994), *New Venture Creation: Entrepreneurship for the 21st Century*, Homewood, IL: Irwin.

Timmons, J.A. and H.J. Sapienza (1992), 'Venture capital: the decade ahead', in D.L. Sexton and J.D. Kasarda (eds), *The State of the Art of Entrepreneurship*, Boston, MA: PWS-Kent, pp. 402–37.

Waterman, D.A. (1986), *A Guide to Expert Systems*, Reading, MA: Addison-Wesley.

Zacharakis, A.L. and Meyer, G.D. (1998), 'A lack of insight: do venture capitalists really understand their own decision process?', *Journal of Business Venturing*, **13** (1), 57–76.

15 Repertory grid technique: an ideographic and nomothetic approach to knowledge
Carmen Dima

INTRODUCTION

This chapter introduces the personal construct theory (PCP) and its derived technique: repertory grid as an intricate data collection technique applicable to entrepreneurial studies. It draws from the author's experience conducting studies related to environmental entrepreneurship in Ontario's (Canada) wine industry. This chapter starts by placing PCP in the context of the constructivism paradigm; subsequently, repertory grids are introduced as a procedure derived from PCT and details related to its components and procedures are presented. Finally, the ideographic and nomothetic approach to knowledge specific to repertory grids is demonstrated thorough typical analysis and reflections at both individual and collective levels.

CONSTRUCTIVISM

The constructivist approach considers meaning as constructed, not discovered. As Crotty (1998) mentioned, this approach invites a 'radical spirit of openness' to be employed, which accommodates multiple meanings and a variety of individual experiences. The different meanings of the same phenomena are due to different constructs derived from a variety of experiences. The constructivist psychology investigates how humans create meanings about their world and experiences.

Constructivism's flexibility in combining both pragmatism and phenomenology bestowed its broad uses in entrepreneurial behaviour (Woods 2006; Dima and Jankowicz 2014) and intentional group development (Akrivou and Boyatzis 2006), in social science and business (Díaz de León and Guild 2003; Butt 2008), tourism (Pike 2007), in education (Foster 1992; Macsinga and Maricutoiu 2008), counselling and clinical practice (White 1996; Fransella et al. 2004), organizational behaviour (Jankowicz 1995), marketing research (Pike 2007), and strategic issue diagnosis (Dutton et al. 1989), to name just a few.

Personal construct theory, founded on constructive alternativism, was introduced by George Kelly as a major psychological theory erected at the intersection between conventional philosophy and psychology. In Kelly's words: 'As a philosophy it is rooted in the psychological observation of men. As a psychology it is concerned with the philosophical outlooks of individual men' (Kelly 1963: 16). Kelly (1963) views the individual as an incipient scientist ('man-the-scientist') that creates his or her own ways/ constructs of seeing the world and events. 'As a scientist, a man seeks to predict and control the course of events. The constructs which he formulates are intended to aid him in his predictive efforts' (Kelly 1963: 12). In other words, understanding the meanings that individuals create as a result of personal experiences will trigger anticipation and a predictive behaviour. In Kelly's (1963: 5) words: 'the scientist's ultimate aim is to predict and control'.

At the individual level, PCT recognizes the uniqueness of each person in their construction and organization of events (individuality corollary, organization and dichotomy corollary) yet, the same individual will form relationships and construe on each other's constructions in order to be able to understand one another better (commonality corollary). Kelly's (1963) experience corollary notes that experience is created through successive replications of events, and as such, events could be anticipated and an elaborative choice made (choice corollary): 'Man gradually discovered that he could lay a sight on the future through the experience of the past' (Kelly 1963: 75). His construction corollary specifies that the anticipation of events is based on construing replications of past events within a range of convenience and limited by the constructs' permeability (range and modulation corollary). In his words: 'What is predicted is not that tomorrow will be a duplicate of today, but that there are replicative aspects to tomorrow's events that may be safely predicted' (Kelly 1963: 53). The sociality corollary is defined as the pattern of behaviour that an individual will follow and/or modify based on his or her understanding and prediction on his or her social environment. The individual's free choice to constructive alternativism postulates that people conceptualize events in many different ways and new dimensions of meaning are continuously created as a result of re-evaluation of existing constructs (fragmentation corollary – Kelly 1963). Thus, personal constructivism recognizes individuality but also makes room for further abstracting of these individual constructs to generate understanding about common and general human conceptualizations.

REPERTORY GRID AS AN IDEOGRAPHIC AND NOMOTHETIC APPROACH

Consistent with the ontology and epistemology derived from PCT, the repertory grid data collection procedure features a qualitative research focus based on the interpretation of meaning yet also allows statistical analysis to be conducted (Jankowicz 2004). In Jankowicz's words: 'meaning is captured by a technique that uses both numbers and words and the qualitative/quantitative distinction is unhelpful' (2004: 71–2).

Most recently this technique was used in entrepreneurial studies related to entrepreneurial networks (Klapper 2008) and entrepreneurial pedagogy (Klapper and Tegtmeier 2010), while in management research Dima and Jackowicz (2013) used this method to understand the constructs behind an entrepreneurial proactive/reactive environmental behaviour in Ontario's (Canada) wine industry. The authors used the theory of planned behaviour (TPB) and PCT as the frameworks of analysis. Through a constructivist approach using multiple case study design, their research explored the determinants of intention with a particular emphasis on identifying the reasoning and sense-making of organizations that took an entrepreneurial stance towards environmental practices. Repertory grids were used as the chosen data collection technique to extract individual constructs and through a combination of qualitative and quantitative analysis aggregate them to reveal group perceptions and meanings.

Tanner (1999) used repertory grid to elicit behavioural constraints related to environmental behaviour while Oppenheim et al. (2003) investigated decision-making and information use among managers.

In other research fields, repertory grids were used to elicit consumer perceptions of products (Meilgaard et al. 2001), while Klapper (2008) uses it successfully in his entrepreneurship studies. Ginsberg (2007) used repertory grids to elicit and quantify the top managers' mindset in strategic selection and mix of businesses. Furthermore, in 1990, Hisrich and Jankowicz used this technique to study intuition in venture capital decisions, perceptions and judgements and how investors materialize them in relation to a proposal. Without being exhaustive, the variety of research studies employing this technique suggests that repertory grid is a useful instrument in eliciting personal beliefs and meanings.

In other words, developed as an investigative technique, repertory grid has the potential to, first, remove the observer's error on what was observed and, second, allow individuals to reveal their own personal meanings. The method's ability to draw from the participant's experiences and reveal individual perspectives is what I would define as an idiographic approach to knowledge; that is, investigating individuals to understand their unique perceptions. This, in turn, enables confident predictions about an individual's behaviour, increases in data accuracy and reduction in social desirability of answers (or 'faking good') (Jankowicz 2004; Macsinga and Maricutoiu 2008).

Repertory grid's ability to extract individual cognitions is established through the interplay of its four components: main theme (subject of the grid and focus of exploration), elements (events and objects), constructs and linking systems. In one of my studies (Dima 2010), the main theme was to identify the determinants of the intent to implement environmental practices at the operational level.

The elements are related to the subject and the context of interest. They could be elicited or provided by the researcher (Jankowicz 2004; Pike 2007) ranging anywhere from nine (Pike 2007) to 37 (Foster 1992). The elements that I have selected in my study were pulled from a government published source of recommended environmental practices for sustainable operations. A total of 12 practices were analysed (see Figure 15.1 later in this chapter).

The constructs could be supplied by the researcher (Jankowicz 2004) or elicited through a conversation between interviewer and interviewee. Capturing the most accurate picture of personal meaning and prediction of behaviour is done through direct construct elicitation from the respondent (Kelly 1963). For each of the environmental practices analysed, I have selected to elicit the individual constructs from the participants. A triadic method was used, laddering up and down to ensure accuracy and clarity.

The construct elicitation process is quite complex and could alter the individual sense-making. The original procedure for eliciting constructs (defined as a complex image or idea) is the triadic difference method (Kelly 1963). Groups of three elements (triads) are selected and the respondent is asked to identify and label two elements that are alike from the third different element (forming the emergent pole) and elaborate upon why the third element is found to be different (forming the implicit pole) (Kelly 1963). Other methods of elicitations have been developed since: triadic opposite method, dyadic method and contrast/opposite method (Neimeyer et al. 2002), yet Caputi and Reddy (1999) found that the triadic method produced constructs that are less functionally independent of other constructs, are more discriminating as a set of elements and are of higher cognitive complexity. In addition, from a qualitative perspective, participants tended to focus first on the positive attributes of the elements and formed a greater number of antonym pairs.

Another common technique for construct generation or for construct clarification of meaning is laddering up and laddering down (pyramiding or drilling down). Laddering is simply drilling down or looking for more specific ways of expressing constructs, while pyramiding is elaborating the superordinate–subordinate relationship in expanding detail, by expanding and examining each pole separately (Jankowicz 2004). The technique incorporates a series of 'how' questions, which results in enunciated detail about the construct and increases the understanding of what the research participant means. The question 'why' produces constructs of greater generality, while the question 'what/how' produces more specific constructs (Easterby-Smith 1980). This method should be used in conjunction with the triadic approach in order to ensure that the constructs generated are not vague, highly situational, permeable (general) or impermeable (applicable to a small scale only) (Kelly 1963).

Caution needs be exercised during the initial instructional process. The type of examples used by the researcher could influence the nature of bipolarity of contrasts and the contrasting nature of constructs. To understand it, a distinction between the difference method and opposite method needs to be noted. The difference method asks for the differences between elements, the opposite method solicits for opposites. With other words, the bipolarity could have a different nature, such as negation (happy–not happy), negation/opposition (happy–unhappy), opposition (happy–sad) and non-contiguous opposition (happy–business-like) (Yorke 2001: 176). Therefore, in order to capture the individual sense, Easterby-Smith (1980) recommends that contrasting poles and not opposition poles must be elicited, as opposites are mostly logical opposites rather than opposites in meaning.

From a research participant's perspective, repertory grid is challenging and borderline annoying owing to the triadic process during the elicitation phase. Time limits might present a concern, with each interview lasting more than one hour, and thus accessibility to executives might be impeded (Jankowicz 2004). My participants considered the method quite difficult and demanding yet, as Eden (2004) mentioned, the process allowed them to develop new insights and articulate these in ways that would influence their present and future cognition.

As an open method, repertory grids proves to be extremely useful as a diagnosis instrument for 'in-depth analysis and self-analysis' (for example, Easterby-Smith 1980). From this perspective this techniques permits access to personal dimensions that are otherwise lost through the use of surveys or closed-ended interviews (Daniels et al. 2002). Cassell et al. (2000) accentuates another two major benefits derived from this technique: first, the ability to access information embedded in an individual's personal construct that gives the participants the opportunity to reflect on their own constructs and, second, it allows the researchers to challenge and clarify their own understanding of the situation.

Linking the elements and the constructs could be done by any of the three methods below, (1) dichotomizing, (2) ranking, (3) and rating:

1. Dichotomizing requires that the elements are sorted into two categories for each dimension (the 'two poles' or 'ticks and crosses' technique) (Easterby-Smith et al. 1996): if closest to the left pole, a tick is placed in the grid, otherwise a cross.
2. When ranking, all elements must be placed in order (1 to n) along each construct, while rating uses Likert scales, since it is assumed that points on the scale indicate equal gradations (Easterby-Smith 1980). Element-by-element ratings require the individual to consider one element at a time, and rate that element down each of the constructs in succession, while construct-by-construct or row-wise ratings (recommended by Kelly 1955) require a respondent to consider one construct at a time and rate all elements along.
3. Rating scales allow the research participants to reflect again and to check if the elements are really in the range of convenience of all the constructs. Minor alterations to the grid could be made; however, a multitude of these corrections could indicate a faulty grid design (Easterby-Smith 1980).

Owing to the level of freedom that the respondent has in making judgements (Pike 2007) during the elicitation and rating process, repertory grid technique offers strong face validity. As an idiographic approach, it grounds the data within the culture of the participant by revealing personal patterns and relationships and reduces the evaluator's subjective framework (Macsinga and Maricutoiu 2008). Yet, through a nomothetic approach all these individuals could be also brought together and common themes, traits and collective meanings for specific groups could be generated and used for further investigations.

Versatility in Data Analysis

The data that results from a repertory grid interview is organized in matrix format, providing a graphic representation of an individual's perceptual framework. Each respondent's matrix of constructs and comparison measurements is idiosyncratic, as it is inductively constructed from that individual's experiences and observations and is used by that individual to model what they would expect to occur, given an encounter with similar personalities, events, or situations in the future. These perceptual frameworks provide rich data regarding both retrospective and futuristic individual views.

As previously mentioned, repertory grids allow both qualitative and quantitative analysis. The combination of quantitative and qualitative measures provides a rich, detailed, and measurable description of identity frameworks that traditional hermeneutic and ethnographic analyses cannot replicate.

Qualitative Analysis

From an idiographic perspective, the individual grids delve into personal underlying insights that are central to cognition and less influenced by time and context. By using cognitive categorization and grouping the insights based on similarities and differences, we move into a nomothetic approach to knowledge. That is, we are able to expand from individual to group to understand common traits and behaviours.

Each individual grid can be analysed by starting with a description of the basic grid: eyeball analysis and construct characterization. The categorization could be performed based on a bootstrapping technique, theory based, or a combination of both. The problem with the categorization, however, is the reliability of the process. Reliability is a necessary criterion for validity in any study, and without it all results and conclusions in the research project may be put in doubt or even considered meaningless. To avoid this, Jankowicz (2004) suggests the use of multiple researchers, discussion of individual classifications, and recording and reconciliation of convergence success rates. Jankowicz (2004) also suggests another content analysis method: Honey's procedure (1979). This method assesses the relative importance of constructs by supplying an 'overall construct and converting the ratings obtained on this construct into similarity scores' (Honey 1979; Jankowicz 2004: 169–77). The advantage of this method is that it aggregates the sets of constructs for the sample but also allows the preservation of individual views (Jankowicz 2004).

Quantitative Analysis

Individually, each grid could be analysed using cluster analysis. Cluster analyses are based on a mathematical algorithm that calculates sum differences between ratings in each grid (calculating it by both columns and rows) and generates similarity codes (Díaz de León and Guild 2003).

Principal component analysis, commonly used for grid analysis, better known as singular-value decomposition or Eckart–Young decomposition, consists of an iterative process that approximates a grid by the product of two matrices: a matrix of columns (elements) and a matrix of rows (constructs) component loadings. The process identifies patterns of variability (components) in a descending order. Once the largest amount of variability is removed, the next is identified (Jankowicz 2004: 128); the more components extracted, the better the approximation of the original data (Fransella et al. 2004). That is, the process identifies a weighted composite for as much variance as possible and continues the process for the remaining variance.

The component loadings are based on decomposing the grid into eigenvalues and eigenvectors for both columns (elements) and rows (constructs). Therefore using single decomposition we obtain two sets of eigenvectors and a single set of singular value that form a product that approximates to the data grid. The loadings are transformed by using a 'symmetrical normalization process' (multiply each element and construct eigenvector by the square root of the singular values). In addition, the loadings are not unique, and the process rotates the factor loadings (varimax rotation) so that the approximated solution has a structure reflecting components with high loadings and others near zero (Fransella and Bannister 2004: 112).

The largest variation in the first component could account for up to 50 per cent of total variance and is used as an indicator of cognitive complexity (Fransella et al. 2004). According to Adams-Webber (1996), a low cognitive complexity would be attributed in a situation in which the variance in the first component is higher than 60 per cent. Cognitive complexity reflects the individual associations of different issue aspects: a higher cognitive complexity suggests a variety of aspects being considered as opposed to only one or two dominating themes (Adams-Webber 1996: 154). This approach is recommended by Fransella et al. (2004: 119) as 'an approach able to distinguish between different patterns of construct relationships' and was also one of my main analyses to understand differences in cognitive complexity within and between groups of participants.

From a sample size perspective, if the unit of analysis is the constructs elicited, it is anticipated that an average number of constructs would be around 10–30 per grid. Some academics consider that this number is inadequate for a principal component analysis (Sapnas and Zeller 2002).

While the singular-value decomposition analysis as well as factor analysis traditionally requires a larger (N = 50) sample size, De Winter et al. (2009) conducted an exploratory factor analysis (EFA) on a psychological dataset and investigated factor recovery when deviating from a simple structure. They used six combinations of sample sizes to analyse the interaction between the determinants when N = 25 small, N = 100 medium and N = 1000 high, and level of loadings at low = 0.4 and high = 0.9, and concluded that when data are well conditioned (high loadings, commonalities and low number of factors) with factors well defined and limited in number, EFA can yield reliable solutions for sample sizes below 50 (De Winter et al. 2009). They also found that even a very small sample size (10–17) was adequate for satisfactory factor recovery. The authors mention: 'considering that models are useful unless grossly wrong and a small sample size factor analytical model is not per definition grossly wrong, applying factor analysis in an exploratory phase is better than rejecting EFA a priori (citing MacCallum 2003)' (De Winter et al. 2009: 171).

Other possible analyses related to cognitive structures are number of constructs and elements generated (Tan et al. 2002), the intensity score which reflects the strength of correlations (Fransella et al. 2004), the ordination score of Lanfield which relates to the flexibility and discriminative power of elements or constructs (Lanfield 1971), extreme ratings reflecting the subjective meaningfulness of specific constructs and elements (Feixas et al. 2004).

From a grid content perspective a variety of indices could be calculated, such as: construct centrality (sometimes termed construct significance – Ginsberg 2007), element distance as perceived similarity between elements (Kelly 1963) and element preference as perceived desirability to the interviewee of each element to all other elements.

On an aggregated basis, indices of similarity could be calculated or cluster analysis conducted based on multidimensional scaling of inter-element distance that maps the structure of collective meanings among members of a group. This method creates a map of the relative positions of elements to one another that account for differences among individual perceptual structures (Ginsberg 2007). This societal 'cognitive map' may then be used as a starting point from which to test assumptions that are often made about the perceptions a particular group or society.

Once identified, groups of individuals with similar levels of cognitive structure can be examined using multi-variant techniques such as analysis of variance, regression analysis and discriminant analysis in order to understand the pooled results of individual repertory grids structures (Ginsberg 2007).

The list of statistical tests is not exhaustive, however, Yorke (2001) remind us of the importance of using both quantitative and qualitative approaches when analysing repertory grids and avoiding a strong emphasis on statistical analysis only.

Validity and Reliability of Repertory Grids

Validity and reliability of repertory grid is a complex subject. According to Jankowicz (2004: 150, citing Hill 1995), reliability includes three elements: stability, reproducibility and accuracy. The stability looks for a lack of variability over time; reproducibility looks after the ability to replicate the data while accuracy looks after consistency in applying established definitions. Following Jankowicz (2004) and Fransella et al.'s (2004) recommendations, the stability criteria is accomplished by recognizing similarities in meaning between participants' constructs (as opposed to focusing on the constructs themselves) which are time resilient. Kelly (1963: 80) replaces the term stability with permeability: 'permeable constructs, because they possess resiliency under the impact of new experience, do tend to be stable'. The reproducibility and accuracy condition is accomplished by involving an independent researcher to analyse and categorize the data according to the established definitions and recommended (Jankowicz 2004: 163) reliability coefficients are calculated to confirm agreement. Smith (2000) analysed repertory grids' reliability and validity by using a test–retest format on 20 primary school teachers over a one-year period. The results reflected a coefficient of convergence of 0.77. The main procedures and statistical analysis that I employed as part of my project to address the reliability issue are presented in the next section. Fransella et al. (2004: 150) confirmed the predictive validity of the repertory grid in an analysis of voting behaviour in 74 people. They included the main political parties; a total of ten elements and nine supplied constructs (including 'Self' and 'Ideal Self') and found the 'Ideal Self' as the best predictor of voting behaviour. The prediction that 'the political parties would agree about the relationship between them was validated'. The results aligned with the assumptions underlying PCT: 'A central tenet of PCT is that it is a psychology of the whole person. Thinking, feeling and behaviour do not function separately' (Fransella et al. 2004: 150). Many other studies confirmed the usefulness of Kelly's (1963) concept of validity of repertory grids and Fransella et al. (2004) dedicate a whole chapter (chapter 8) to a detailed listing and brief description of relevant studies in various fields, such as: business, clinical psychology, politics, market research.

EXAMPLE OF A REPERTORY GRID TECHNIQUE APPLICATION

This part of the chapter presents and discusses the critical issues related to the application of the repertory grid technique. The research project focused on identifying the main constructs and drivers that underlie decision-makers' thinking regarding the adoption of environmental practices at the operational level. The project employed two distinct approaches as the analytic frameworks to understand both the drivers, and the adoption process: the TPB (Fishbein and Aizen 1975), as helpful in predicting action, and Kelly's (1955) PCT, for understanding individual and organizational sense-making. The former is predicated upon individuals being rational and informed, particularly with regard to consequences, and deliberately choosing behaviour that is volitional (Bonnes et al. 2003: 176–97); the latter offers an understanding of how this rationality emerges from an individual's past experience to be used as a guide to future action (Chiari and Nuzzo 2003).

RESEARCH DESIGN

A multiple-case design was selected as being more robust than a single-case study, permitting both literal (predictive of similar results) and theoretical (predictive of contrasting results for predictable reasons) replication as a basis of reliability (Yin 2003: 47). Contrast formed the basis of the research design (King 2000). A total of 20 wineries were identified and selected using purposive sampling design (ten proactive in their adoption of environmental practices and ten reactive) and one person from each organization (someone with immediate responsibility for implementing and maintaining operational level environmental policy, in most cases, the winemaker) was interviewed and data collected using repertory grid technique. According to Yin (2003: 34), using a replication logic strengthens the data generalization and increases the design's external validity. The replication logic is similar to multiple experiments logic and requires a careful selection of cases that would predict either similar or contrasting results (Yin 2003).

The Technique

The interviewee was presented with a set of elements (issues to which he or she pays attention when addressing any situation) and is requested to compare and contrast them to identify the constructs he or she uses to make sense of that situation. The elements used in the present study were a set of environmental practices (appropriately enough given that our focus on process came from TPB) selected from the Wine Council of Ontario's *Environmental Charter* list of recommended environmental practices for sustainable winery operations. Once the interviewee's constructs have been elicited, each element is rated on each of the constructs using a five-point scale to identify the extent to which one pole or the other of the construct applies. The result is a grid in which the interviewee's own meanings have been carefully identified, and a set numeric rating, open to statistical analysis, obtained.

A basic triadic technique (Fransella et al. 2004, Jankowicz 2004) was followed in each interview. That is, the interviewee was presented with three elements at a time, and a construct elicited by being asked in what way he or she felt that two of the elements are alike while being different from the third, discussion continuing until a non-trivial and precise bipolar construct was obtained. Each interview process took more than one hour and required several reminders and reflections from the participants in order to ensure that the constructs were clear and well defined in the individual perception.

The elements were then rated on a five-point scale in which each pole of the construct serves as anchor to the '1' or the '5' end of the scale. Further triads of elements were offered, constructs elicited, and elements rated, until no fresh constructs were obtained. A total of 315 constructs were elicited from the 20 interviewees. See Figure 15.1 for an example of a repertory grid matrix generated.

DATA ANALYSIS

WebGrid 5 software package and Microsoft Office Excel 2007 were used for analysis. The repertory grids generated by using WebGrid5 software were grouped into proactive and reactive types and analysed as follows: cluster analysis to understand how the respondents organize their thinking, principal component analysis to assess the cognitive complexity and main cognitive themes, content analysis as outlined by Jankowicz (2004) to assess the strength of the categories and the TPB application, and content analysis using Honey's technique (Honey 1979, Jankowicz 2004: 169–77) to identify and evaluate the constructs that participants relate to the need to implement environmental practices at the operational level.

The analysis targeted two aspects: the individual grid analysis and the aggregate grid analysis by group (proactive and reactive). Each individual grid was analysed in two steps: description of basic grid (eyeball analysis and construct characterization) (Jankowicz 2004: 72) and description of structure in the grid (cluster analysis and principal component analysis) (Jankowicz 2004: 95–144). The unit of analysis in this repertory grid work was the construct rather than the interviewee.

Cluster analyses are based on a mathematical algorithm that calculates sum differences between ratings in each grid (calculating it by both columns and rows) and generates similarity codes (Díaz de León and Guild 2003). The most similar related constructs are presented side by side in a graphic, with the constructs that are connected by 'branch' sharing a comparable percentage of similarity and reflecting the individual rational-

435

Display P1
'Environmental implementation'

Left pole	E1	E2	E3	E4	E5	E6	E7	E8	E9	E10	E11	E12	Right pole
Financial investment required	2	2	1	2	1	1	2	1	2	2	3	3	Carrying on with what we have
Creates extra work and effort	2	2	4	1	2	2	5	5	3	3	3	3	No extra work or effort necessary
Increased operating costs (labour, gas)	3	2	2	1	2	2	3	1	2	2	2	2	More cost efficient using the existing practices
Increased manpower	2	2	3	1	2	3	3	3	3	3	3	3	Less manpower required
Requires more administration	5	1	4	3	2	1	3	3	5	5	5	4	No administration required
Justify ROI	2	2	2	1	3	4	5	5	3	3	4	3	Increased operating costs
Giving a marketing advantage	5	5	1	2	3	3	3	3	3	2	3	3	Being left behind the industry
Reduces pollution	3	3	2	5	1	1	1	2	3	2	1	1	Not environmentally sustainable
No modification required to existing equipment	2	2	3	2	2	2	3	4	4	4	4	3	Modification required to existing equipment
Obtain better results	1	1	3	3	3	2	4	2	2	2	2	2	More time consumed with no better results
Affects profitability positively	3	3	4	4	4	3	5	3	4	4	4	4	Reduces profitability
Need to implement	3	3	1	3	5	5	3	5	1	2	1	3	No need to implement

Elements (E1–E12):

- E1: Install mechanisms to prevent backflow
- E2: Install shut-off valves, flow restrictors
- E3: Install alternative fuel sources and equipment
- E4: Store pesticides on impermeable floors
- E5: Incorporate solar/geothermal energy
- E6: Use pallets made from recycled plastic
- E7: Introduce cleaning procedures: ozone systems
- E8: Introduce product technology without DE earth
- E9: Triple rinse, pressure rinse containers
- E10: Install low-energy tank agitators, lighting
- E11: Distillation of mark, leaks and development of products
- E12: Use cleaner approach for barrel testing

Figure 15.1   Basic triadic technique

ization. This type of analysis allowed us to determine patterns of meaning by identifying, for each proactive and reactive group, individual construct groupings.

Thorough principal component analysis maps were generated for each participant to reflect how constructs and elements are positioned along each component. The distance (angle) between any two constructs accounts for the level of correlation between these constructs: the smaller the angle, the higher the correlation. Indicators of cognitive complexity were calculated for each participant group and comparisons conducted. Differences in cognitive complexity between the groups could be marginal, therefore additional information should be pulled from the individual loadings and the cluster analysis to support your conclusions.

The content analysis complexities related to issues of reliability and validity, which are specific to qualitative analysis, were addressed through specific procedures and statistical analysis.

The employed content analysis combined a bootstrapping and theory-based approach as exemplified by Jankowicz (2004: 173–6).

Categories were derived in two stages. First, all the constructs were assigned to one or other of a set of (sub-)categories determined from the content of the constructs themselves (constructs with similar meanings were grouped into sub-categories as determined by the researcher). Second, these sub-categories were assigned to a set of five main categories (derived from Ajzen's theory of planned behaviour), plus two more categories established by the researcher. While defined so as to be mutually exclusive, the five categories were not completely exhaustive and additional sub-categories were created.

A reliability check was conducted by recording the allocation of each construct, randomizing them, and asking a co-researcher to repeat the content analysis independently using sub-categories devised by him, within the overall framework of the five main, TPB-derived main categories. These were discussed by both researchers, resulting in 22 agreed sub-categories giving a Cohen's kappa of $k1 = 0.66$ and a Perrault–Leigh Index of 0.81. (Perrault–Leigh has the advantage of being less sensitive to the number of categories than Cohen's kappa, while permitting the derivation of a confidence interval, here, the $p = 0.05$ interval being 0.79–0.84.) The main categories were reliable at a Cohen's kappa of 0.97 and a Perrault–Leigh Index of 0.99, the $p = 0.05$ confidence interval being 0.96–1.00.

The differences between the two researchers were discussed and reconciled. As a result, some of the sub-categories were either expanded or renamed to suit the topic described by the constructs.

Ultimately, 32 sub-categories were identified with a calculated final Cohen's kappa of 0.98 and a Perrault–Leigh Index of 0.99 ($p = 0.05$

confidence interval being 0.96–1.0). After all of the adjustments, the main categories resulted in a final calculated Cohen's kappa of 0.98 and a Perrault–Leigh Index of 0.99 (p = 0.05 confidence interval 0.97–1.0). Since the content analysis is based on data collected from two different independent groups with the same number of respondents with two response sets, a bivariate analysis without interactions using nominal dichotomous scale of measurement was conducted for each sub-category. A 95 per cent confidence level was selected as typical for social and marketing studies (De Vaus 2002: 134–6) and z-test for two proportions was calculated using Excel spreadsheets.

In order to assess the relative importance of constructs, a specific analysis procedure was conducted for a researcher-supplied construct: 'need to implement'. The procedure follows Honey's technique (Honey 1979; Jankowicz 2004: 169–77) in which the ratings obtained on this supplied 'overall' construct ('need to implement' in this study) only are converted into similarity scores.

These similarity codes are separated into three indexes: high, intermediate and low (H, I, L) and allocated to the predetermined categories from TPB. The results are tabulated to reflect the relative importance of constructs within each category. This method aggregates the sets of constructs for the sample but also allows the preservation of individual views (Jankowicz 2004). That is, a participant could score, for example, a 75 per cent on a construct which would be an Intermediate (I) score for him (all his or her constructs score between 60 and 90 per cent), while another participant would have a High (H) score assigned for the same percentage (all his or her constructs score between 50 and 80 per cent). This is owing to the fact that the second participant's scores are overall lower in comparison to the first participant's scores. As such, the method preserves the individual scores while aggregating them into categories.

The construct differentiation between proactive and reactive organizations was obtained through the cross-case analysis. Common constructs between cases (based on proactive–reactive organization classification) and their frequency were investigated.

A concurrent embedded strategy of triangulation was used. Following Creswell's (2009: 214) recommendations, in this method of triangulation, both quantitative and qualitative data were collected simultaneously, with one providing a supporting role and being nested within the predominant method.

Using the repertory grid technique allowed the identification of perception commonality within a specific group as well as understanding of similarities and differences in perceptions between groups. A modified entrepreneurship model was derived to reflect specific characteristics for the groups and the region being studied. While previous studies in environmental entrepreneurship literature and business strategy used this technique for descriptive purposes only (Dutton et al.1989; Tanner 1999), this study employed a variety of analysis methods to answer the research questions. The analysis included both quantitative and qualitative elements and provided a valuable description of individual and group frameworks that culminated with direct practical application in the industry's regional policies.

The example presented shows a specific use of PCT and repertory grids to identify the drivers of environmental entrepreneurship in a specific industry and should be use as a guideline. It is my hope that this example will ignite new interest for further research of entrepreneurial concepts in other areas that require identification of individual perceptual frameworks and group-construing similarities within a given set of stimuli.

CONCLUSION

This chapter introduces the concept of constructivism, the PCT and the repertory grid as an intricate data collection technique. Highlights of an actual research project were presented to demonstrate that through PCT the individual is considered from a holistic perspective able to conceptualize events in many ways and create new meanings. Employing the repertory grids allows us to access an ideographic and nomothetic approach to knowledge through which a personal perceptual framework is revealed, in a relatively unbiased manner, and contributes to the understanding of commonality of perceptions within a specific social, ethnic or any other group.

By supporting both qualitative and quantitative analysis of individual and collective frameworks, repertory grids offers rich and detailed data superior to the traditional hermeneutic and ethnographic analysis. Whether in entrepreneurship, marketing, organization behaviour or environmental studies, researchers are recognizing this method's merits and continue to recommend it for further research. Fields such as management cognition, education, investments and behavioural economics could only be enriched by studies employing repertory grids and ultimately contribute new insights and superior models to the existing knowledge.

REFERENCES

Adams-Webber, J.R. (1996), 'Cognitive complexity', in R. Corsini and A.J. Auerbach (eds), *Encylopedia of Psychology*, New York, John Wiley and Sons, p.154.

Akrivou, K., E. Boyatzis and P. McLeod (2006), 'The evolving group: towards a prescriptive theory of intentional group development', *Journal of Management Development*, **25** (7), 689–706.

Bonnes M., T. Lee and B. Marinno (2003), *Psychological Theories for Environmental Issues*, Aldershot: Ashgate.

Butt, T. (2008), 'Kelly's legacy in personality theory: reasons to be cheerful', *Personal Construct and Practice*, **5**, 51–9.

Caputi, P. and P. Reddy (1999), 'A comparison of triadic and dyadic methods of personal construct elicitation', *Journal of Constructivist Psychology*, **12** (3), 253–64.

Cassell C., P. Close, J. Buberley and P. Johnson (2000), 'Surfacing embedded assumptions: using repertory grid methodology to facilitate organizational change', *European Journal of Work and Organizational Psychology*, **9** (4), 561–73.

Chiari, G. and M.L. Nuzzo (2003), 'Kelly's philosophy of constructive alternativism', in F. Fransella (ed.), *International Handbook of Personal Construct Psychology*, Chichester: John Wiley & Sons, pp. 41–9.

Creswell, J. (2009), *Research Design*, 3rd edn, Thousand Oaks, CA: Sage Publications.

Crotty, M. (1998), *The Foundations of Social Research: Meaning and Perspective in the Research Process*, Upper Saddle River, NJ: Pearson Education.

Daniels, K., G. Johnson and L. de Chernatony (2002), 'Task and institutional influences on managers' mental models of competition', *Organization Studies*, **23** (1), 31–62.

De Vaus, D.A. (2002), *Survey Research*, 5th edn, Abingdon: Routledge.

De Winter, J.C.F., D. Dodou and P.A. Wieringa (2009), 'Exploratory factor analysis with small sample sizes', *Multivariante Behavioural Research*, **44** (2), 144–81.

Díaz de León, E. and P. Guild (2003), 'Using repertory grid to identify intangibles in business plans', *Venture Capital*, **5** (2), 135–60.

Dima, C. (2010), 'Implementation of operational environmental practices in Ontario (Canada) wine industry: perceptions, constructs, intent', DBA dissertation, Heriot Watt University, Edinburgh.

Dima, C. and D. Jankowicz (2013), 'Environmental entrepreneurship in Ontario (Canada) wine industry', *Advances in Economics and Business*, **1** (2), 187–98.

Dutton, J.E., E.J. Walton and E. Abrahamson (1989), 'Important dimensions of strategic issue, separating the wheat from the chaff', *Journal of Management Studies*, **26** (4), 379–96.

Easterby-Smith, M. (1980), 'The design, analysis and interpretation of repertory grids', *International Journal of Man-Machine Studies*, **13** (1), 3–24.

Easterby-Smith, M., R. Thorpe and D. Holman (1996), 'Using repertory grids in management', *Journal of European Industrial Training*, **20** (3), 3–30.

Eden, C. (2004), 'Analyzing cognitive maps to help structure issues or problems', *European Journal of Operational Research*, **159** (3), 673–86.

Feixas, G., L. Bach and E. Laso (2004), 'Factors affecting interpersonal construct differentiation when measured using the repertory grid', *Journal of Constructivist Psychology*, **17** (4), 297–311.

Fishbein, M. and I. Ajzen (1975), *Belief, Attitude, Intention, and Behavior: An Introduction to Theory and Research*, Reading, MA: Addison-Wesley.

Forster, J. (1992), 'Eliciting personal constructs and articulating goals', *Journal of Career Development*, **18** (3), 175–85.

Fransella, F., R. Bell and D. Bannister (2004), *A Manual for Repertory Grid Techniques*, 2nd edn, Chichester: John Wiley & Sons.

Ginsberg, A. (2007), 'Construing the business portfolio: a cognitive model of diversification', Journal of Management Studies, **26** (6), 417–38 (first published July 1989).

Hill, R.A. (1995), 'Content analysis for creating and depicting aggregated personal construct derived cognitive maps', in R.A. Neimeyer and G.J. Neimeyer (eds), *Advances in Personal Construct Psychology*, Greenwich, CN: JAI Press, pp. 101–32.

Hisrich, A.D. and A.D. Janckowicz (1990), 'Intuition in venture capital decisions: an exploratory study using a new technique', *Journal of Business Venturing*, **5** (1), 49–62.

Honey, P. (1979), 'The repertory grid in action: how to use it to conduct an attitude survey', *Industrial and Commercial Training*, **11** (11), 452–9.

Jankowicz, A.D. (1995), *Business Research Projects*, London: International Thompson Business Press.

Jankowicz, A.D. (2004), *The Easy Guide to Repertory Grids*, Chichester: John Wiley & Sons.

Kelly, G.A. (1955), *The Psychology of Personal Constructs*, New York: Norton.

Kelly, G. (1963), *A Theory of Personality*, New York: W.W. Norton.

King, A. (2000), 'Organizational response to environmental regulation: punctuated change or autogenesis?', *Business Strategy and the Environment*, **9** (4), 224–38.

Klapper, R. (2008), 'The role of social capital in French entrepreneurial networks', unpublished PhD thesis, Leeds University.

Klapper, R. and S. Tegtmeier (2010), 'Innovating entrepreneurial pedagogy: examples from France and Germany', *Journal of Small Business and Enterprise Development*, **17** (4), 552–68.

Lanfield, A.W. (1971), *Personal Construct Systems in Psychotherapy*, Chicago, IL: Rand McNally.

MacCallum, R.C. (2003), '2001 presidential address: working with imperfect models', *Multivariate Behavioral Research*, **38** (1), 113–39.

Macsinga, I. and L. Maricutoiu (2008), 'The applicative potential of repertory grid concerning exploratory research studies in educational environment', *Cognition, Brain and Behaviour*, **12** (1), 45–56.

Meilgaard, M., S. Bennett and J. Murray (2001), 'Sensory technology – its strategic application to brand management', *Technical Quarterly*, **38** (4), 219–25.

Neimeyer, C.J., R.A. Neimeyer, C.L. Hagans and D.L. Van Brunt (2002), 'Is there madness in our method? The effects of repertory grid variations on measures of construct systems structure', in R.A. Neimeyer and C.J. Neimeyer (eds), *Advances in Personal Construct Psychology: New Directions and Perspectives*, Westport, CT: Praeger.

Oppenheim, C., J. Stenson and R.M.S. Wilson (2003), 'Studies on information as an asset II: Repertory grid', *Journal of Information Science*, **29** (5), 419–32.

Pike, S. (2007), 'Repertory grid analysis in group settings to elicit salient destination image attributes', *Current Issues in Tourism*, **19** (4), 378–92.

Sapnas, K.G. and R.A. Zeller (2002), 'Minimizing sample size when using exploratory factor analysis for measurement', *Journal of Nursing Measurement*, **10** (2), 135–54.

Smith, H.J. (2000), 'The reliability and validity of structural measures derived from repertory grids', *Journal of Constructivist Psychology*, **13** (3), 221–30.

Tan, S. and G.M. Hunter (2002), 'The repertory grid technique: a method for the study of cognition in information systems', *MIS Quarterly*, **26** (1), 39–57.

Tanner, C. (1999), 'Constraints on environmental behaviour', *Journal of Environmental Psychology*, **19** (2), 145–57.

White, A. (1996), 'A theoretical framework created from a repertory grid analysis of graduate nurses in relation to the feelings they experience in clinical practice', *Journal of Advanced Nursing*, **24** (1), 144–50.

Wine Council of Ontario (2007), 'Sustainable winemaking Ontario, an environmental charter for the wine industry', available at: http://winecountryontario.ca/sites/default/files/A%20NEWCOMERS%20PRIMER%20-%20The%20Environment%20and%20the%20Wine%20Industry%20in%20Ontario.pdf (accessed 17 June 2015).

Woods, C. (2006), 'Asking the entrepreneur: an enquiry into entrepreneurial behaviour', *Personal Construct Theory and Practice*, **3** (1), 1–11.

Yin, R. (2003), *Case Study Research: Design and Methods*, 3rd edn, Thousand Oaks, CA: Sage Publications.

Yorke, M. (2001), 'Bipolarity or not? Some conceptual problems relating to bipolar rating scales', *British Educational Research Journal*, **27** (2), 171–86.

Concluding thoughts on repertory grids
Rita G. Klapper

The contributions to this section made by Carmen Dima, Anja Hagedorn and Enrique Díaz de León and Paul Guild have illustrated the use of repertory grids in different entrepreneurial research contexts in Canada and Germany. These studies have demonstrated the benefits researchers can derive from working with repertory grids: first, in terms of the ability to access information embedded in an individual's personal construct system which gives the interview partners the opportunity to reflect on their own constructs. Secondly, working with repertory grids allows the researchers to challenge and clarify their own understanding of the situation. Thirdly, the combination of quantitative and qualitative measures provides a rich, detailed and measurable description of identity frameworks that traditional hermeneutic and ethnographic analyses cannot replicate.

However, the repertory grid method is not without criticism, though these generally apply to qualitative work in general, which usually explores in depth at the expense of particular types of generalizability. Carmen Dima, for instance, commented on the time that is necessary to work effectively with repertory grids to elicit the required information. Other authors, among them Anja Hagedorn, pointed out the limited generalizability and limited reliability of the findings that were established through repertory grids (Kelly 1991). Anja Hagedorn, for instance, conducted ten interviews with business support agents and concluded that a study with a higher sample size could increase the quality of the findings and thus the generalizability. Authors such as Anderberg (1973) have suggested triangulating the repertory grid data with other available data. An important limitation is also that repertory grids are time-specific: people change and hence their constructs change. As a result, we see that personal constructs are not stable over time, since personal constructs evolve. This is, of course, a feature of all but longitudinal work.

The contributions to this section have shown that repertory grids still have value as a research tool for investigating deeper cognitive aspects in entrepreneurial contexts. Moreover, George Kelly's personal construct theory (PCT) and constructivism continue to serve as a guiding theoretical framework. The foregoing chapters document the utility of the tool in a variety of contexts, implying that repertory grids continue to have the potential to play a significant role in entrepreneurial research.

REFERENCES

Anderberg, M.R. (1973), *Cluster Analysis for Applications*, New York: Academic Press.
Kelly, G. (1991), *The Psychology of Personal Constructs*, London and New York: Routledge in association with the Centre for Personal Construct Psychology.

Index